The Magazines Handbook

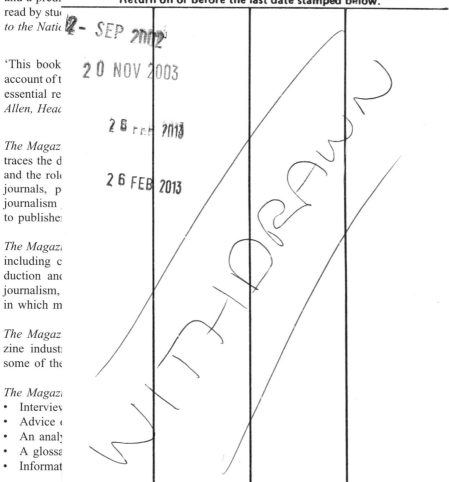
'The Maga
and a predi
read by stu
to the Natic

'This book
account of t
essential re
Allen, Head

The Magaz
traces the d
and the rol
journals, p
journalism
to publishe

The Magaz
including c
duction and
journalism,
in which m

The Magaz
zine industi
some of the

The Magaz
- Interviev
- Advice
- An analy
- A glossa
- Informat

Jenny McKay has worked as a journalist in television, newspapers and magazines as well as international aid agencies. She has taught at City University and Strathclyde University and is currently Senior Lecturer in Journalism at Napier University. She is Secretary of the UK-wide Association for Journalism Education.

Media Practice

edited by James Curran, Goldsmiths College, University of London

The *Media Practice* handbooks are comprehensive resource books for students of media and journalism, and for anyone planning a career as a media professional. Each handbook combines a clear introduction to understanding how the media work with practical information about the structure, processes and skills involved in working in today's media industries, providing not only a guide on 'how to do it' but also a critical reflection on contemporary media practice.

Also in this series:

The Radio Handbook

Peter Wilby and Andy Conroy

The Newspapers Handbook 2nd edition

Richard Keeble

The Advertising Handbook

Sean Brierley

The Photography Handbook

Terence Wright

The Television Handbook 2nd edition

Patricia Holland

The Magazines Handbook

Jenny McKay

London and New York

First published 2000 by Routledge
11 New Fetter Lane, London EC4P 4EE

Simultaneously published in the USA and Canada
by Routledge
29 West 35th Street, New York, NY 10001

Routledge is an imprint of the Taylor & Francis Group

© 2000 Jenny McKay © The contributors, individual chapters

Typeset in Times by Florence Production Ltd, Stoodleigh, Devon
Printed and bound in Great Britain by St Edmundsbury Press,
Bury St Edmunds, Suffolk

British Library Cataloguing in Publication Data
A catalogue record for this book is available from the British Library.

Library of Congress Cataloging in Publication Data
McKay, Jenny, 1953–
    The magazines handbook / Jenny McKay.
        p.   cm. – (Media practice)
    Includes bibliographical references and index.
    1. English periodicals. 2. Periodicals, Publishing–Great Britain.
    3. Journalism–Vocational guidance.
    I. Title. II. Series.

PN5124.P4 M39 2000
052–dc21   00-028186

ISBN–0–415–17034–6 (hbk)
ISBN–0–415–17035–4 (pbk)

This book is for my mother,
Eileen McKay,
who bought me my first magazines

Gladly wolde he lerne and gladly teche
Geoffrey Chaucer

Contents

Notes on contributors

Tom Ang is Senior Lecturer in Photographic Practice at the University of Westminster and a freelance photographer. He has been Editor of *Photography Magazine* and Picture Editor of the *Sunday Correspondent*.

The day **Tim Holmes** started his first magazine job the management decided to close the magazine down. Undeterred, he moved on to EMAP Nationals, where he was fortunate enough to work with talented people who taught him all he needed to know to start his own publishing company. After nine years he sold up and now teaches and researches magazine journalism at the Centre for Journalism Studies, Cardiff University.

Anthony Richards LL B (Hons), B.Ed., MA, Barrister-at-Law (non-practising) is Lecturer in Journalism and Law at Lambeth College, London. He is a former Press Association Law Service reporter.

Dawn Kofie, **Anna Levin** and **Mark Robertson** are freelance journalists based in Scotland.

Acknowledgements

....

I could not have progressed far in writing this book without the help of The Periodicals Training Council, the Periodical Publishers Association, the Audit Bureau of Circulations, the National Union of Journalists and the National Readership Surveys.

Those people who have helped may not agree with my conclusions but I hope they will recognise the picture of the magazine world that I have tried to draw. I am grateful to Christopher Cudmore at Routledge and to the following people for helping me with questions or discussion: Rod Allen, Chris Atton, Alastair Balfour, Stuart Barr, Alison Barratt, Joanne Butcher, Ruth Chatto, Susan Crane, Robert Dawson Scott, David Finkelstein, Louise Hayman, Amanda Holloway, Micheál Jacob, Christine Jardine, Myra Macdonald, John McKie, Jessany Marsden, Mark Meredith, Karen Newman, Jan Patience, Angela Phillips, Lee Randall, Jean Rafferty, Lesley Riddoch, Barbara Rowlands, Chris Small, Simon Stuart, Noel Young, Susan Young. I am grateful, too, to the journalists who agreed to be interviewed and to those writers who contributed chapters or interviews. The many students I have taught and been challenged by also deserve my thanks, especially those who keep me in touch with their careers as they progress.

For secretarial assistance I owe thanks most of all to Gordon Smith, but also to Margaret Philips, Betty Ritchie, Myra Tait and Cath Wales. My thanks to William Duff for help with temperamental computers.

I am pleased to acknowledge an award by the Association of Senior Members of St Hilda's College, Oxford, which enabled me to make use of the Bodleian Library.

No parent could write a book without feeling secure about the well-being of her children and so thanks are due to Susan Clark for her devoted care of my family, Jack, Alfred, Barnaby and Cressida. My husband, Simon Frith, deserves thanks for his unfailing support in every way.

1 Introduction

If a sermon be ill grounded, if the Preacher imposes on us, he trespasses
on a few; but if a Book Printed obtrudes a Falshood, if a Man tells a
Lye in Print, he abuses Mankind, and imposes upon the whole World, he
causes our Children to tell Lyes after us, and their Children after them, to
the End of the World.

Daniel Defoe

Magazines have been an essential part of my life since I bought my first
pocket-money copy of *Robin* to read the latest adventures of Andy Pandy.
From Andy I moved on to *Bunty* with her cut-out paper dresses and I
remember my first disappointment with cover-mounts when a magazine called *Princess*
was launched with TV adverts promising a princess outfit to wear. This, as it turned
out, was only for a competition winner and not something you could pick up at the
newsagent.

Illustrations in another girls' magazine for a story called 'Judy swims to Fame' left
me thinking for months that men with chiselled features and blonde hair were apt to
be called 'fame', a word I hadn't hitherto encountered. A magazine called *Petticoat*
left me with the conviction that every girl in the world but me had a collection of
twenty pairs of identical court shoes in different psychedelic colours. With further
dismay I learnt from grown-up magazines that one of the world's ten best-dressed
women spent at least ten minutes every day plucking the individual hairs on her legs.
Fortunately, I'd already discovered *OZ* and *New Society* by this time so I was able to
change magazines.

At school I worked on the staid annual magazine. The editorial dilemma we faced
was whether to abandon the old-fashioned printer and move to a new printing company
which could do exotic things with photographic reproduction. A school cruise to the
Caribbean saw my contributions appear in a magazine called *Aqueous Humour*, devised
as a way to keep us amused for the ten days' uninterrupted sailing at the end of the
trip. This magazine was reproduced on an antiquated Gestetner machine. From there
to university where I regularly read *Spare Rib*, obscure journals about medieval literature, *Vogue* if I could borrow a copy, the Survival Society newsletter and the student
magazine I eventually edited, *Isis*.

Anyone who has worked in student journalism will know what it is to go without
sleep for three nights in a row, to beg multinational companies for money, to encounter
the joys and limitations of PR at first hand, and to argue about who spilled the Cow

Gum over the typewriter or, the modern equivalent, beer over the keyboard. Student journalism convinced me I wanted to work in magazines and left me with that inability to walk past a news-stand without stopping that will be familiar to readers of this book. If it's not, then maybe you're reading the wrong book.

I now find myself living in a house filled with magazines of all sorts. Seven people with completely varied interests in music, fashion, entertainment and sport live here. The ages span fifty years. A five-minute survey revealed the following recently bought titles in a list which does not include any that are here for research purposes alone, nor does it include newspaper supplements: *Adbusters*, *Ms*, *Brill's Content*, *Time*, *The New Yorker* from the United States; *The Big Issue Scotland*, *Dirt*, *Later*, *Vibe*, *Muzik*, *M8*, *MBUK*, *The List*, *Radio Times*, *Melody Maker*, *NME*, *Flipside*, *Shoot*, *Young Scientist*, *Bird Life*, *The Jam*, *FBX*, *Reportage*, *Granta*, *Playdays*, *Pingu*, *Toybox*, *High Life*, *Total Film*, *The Spectator*, *Music Week*, *Music and Copyright*, *European Journal of Cultural Studies*, *Screen*, *Popular Music*, *British Journalism Review*, *Product*, *Parallax*, *Hello!*, *Condé Nast Traveller*, *The Beano*, *London Review of Books*, *Critical Quarterly*, *The Wire*, *Press Gazette*, *Trouble and Strife*, *Red Herring*, *Cover*, *New Statesman*, *Prospect*, *Mslexia*, *Birds*, *Private Eye*.

Maybe such a range is not typical but I can think of homes which come close. Nor is it that surprising when you consider the average newsagent stocks about 450 titles and even that's only a small fraction of the total number of titles published in the UK. So what is it about magazines that there are so many and that they are being bought in increasing numbers?

Why are magazines so popular?

The most immediate answer is that people like to read them for information and entertainment. The popular illustrated general magazines such as *Picture Post* may have gone (although *Reader's Digest* still sells 1.5 million in the UK alone, 27 million worldwide) but in Europe there is still life in the general weekly magazine formula as the continued success of *Paris Match* and *Stern* shows. Nowadays what magazine publishers claim as one of their strengths is their ability to identify niche markets. They can profitably produce publications for quite small groups of people whose shared interest may be as obscure as smoking cigars (*Cigar Afficionado*) or keeping carp (*Koi Carp*). More popularly they can produce magazines such as *FHM* which within a few years of its launch reached a circulation of three-quarters of a million.

Information may be anything from how to maintain your mountain bike (*MBUK*), the best place to go to learn windsurfing (*Windsurfer*) or an explanation of the options for Nato in the Balkans war (*Time*). Nor is the information all in the editorial. Many magazines provide a wealth of information through their adverts, particularly the classified ones. Sports magazines list dealers specialising in arcane equipment; interior decoration magazines are good places to look for suppliers of furniture or flooring; wildlife magazines provide useful addresses for ecotourist travel and suppliers of birdseed.

The magazines which cater for special interests or hobbies act as a substitute or extension of the reader's own social circle of like-minded people: if you're the sole 14-year-old fan of dance music in your village, then you catch up on the general gossip with your *Source*. This function is also part of the appeal of the Internet, and chat rooms in particular, where there is the added advantage of a more direct contact with other people. The business or trade press equally circulate information to those who share an interest in a particular field.

What constitutes entertainment is even more varied. It might be joky pictures of celebrities (*More!*), pin-ups of bare-breasted girls (*Front, Loaded, GQ*) or of red-breasted mergansers (*Birds, BBC Wildlife*), profile articles about politicians (*New Statesman*) or sportsmen (*Shoot*), romantic fiction (*The People's Friend*), quizzes, horoscopes, personal columns or real-life stories of the 'My best friend stole my husband so I bedded hers' variety (*That's Life!*). Sometimes reading magazines even becomes a group activity when friends choose to chat together about what they've read.

Another appeal of magazines is that they act as a badge of the reader's allegiance to certain values or interests. Just as a rap fan wouldn't be seen dead with a copy of *Smash Hits* under his arm, so a reader of the feminist magazine *Ms* would know she had wandered into alien territory if she found *Playboy* on the coffee table next to *Penthouse*. This aspect of magazines is not confined to readers with minority interests. Jane Reed, who was editor of *Woman* in the 1970s, put it this way: 'A magazine is like a club. Its first function is to provide readers with a comfortable sense of community and pride in their identity' (Winship 1987: 7). There's a lot of truth in this idea that magazine readership can create a sense of belonging to a wider group although what she says is not quite right in that the first function of most commercial magazines is to make money for the publishers: a loyal readership is essential for this and what Reed describes is just one strategy editors have as they struggle to create and maintain that readership. There are, of course, also magazines whose publishers don't have any interest in making money. Fanzines in music and sport, for example, are usually put together by fans for other fans, simply to share the love of a particular sound or club. But even these have a connection with the commercial world of magazine publishing: James Brown, who has been editor of *Loaded* and *GQ*, began his career by publishing his own fanzine and in 1999 set up his own publishing company.

Who should read this book

This book is for people who want to work as magazine journalists. It's also for people who don't yet know which branch of journalism they want to work in. The uncertainty doesn't matter. As the chapters on careers and training make clear, career paths are now far more flexible than a generation ago and there is a lot of movement between the various media. This means there may also be people who have been working as journalists in one of the other media who find themselves joining a magazine or looking for work on one. The book should be useful for them too. While writing it I have tried to keep the requirements of these different kinds of readers in mind, while aiming to write a book which university tutors in journalism will find useful both for the information it provides and for the issues it raises.

Where information is concerned one problem is that some of the detail changes very fast, as with any twenty-first-century industry which is subject to market forces. I'm thinking here of things like who edits or owns which magazine and which sectors of the consumer market are flourishing or wilting, rather than what constitutes a good piece of feature writing. For this reason, where I have given examples from specific magazines or companies I have tried to place them in a general context and also tried to make clear where the kind of information I am discussing comes from so that students can trace the most up-to-date figures for themselves.

Where issues are concerned it is important to make clear that this is not something that always forms part of a journalist's training. Increasingly it does, since university courses in journalism got underway in the UK in the early 1970s. But there is still suspicion in some editorial offices that training, even for graduates, is about teaching people how things are done (and have always been done) rather than allowing any discussion about why they are done that way and whether there might be other ways of working. Academics are criticised for asking too many questions about the practice of what I would call a craft or trade but some like to call a profession. I wouldn't deny that some theoretical academic debate can miss the point either through being too earnest or through a lack of common sense. However, my own experience as one who trained and worked as a journalist, who has taught journalism skills for several years and has also read much of the recent academic work on journalism, is that some of it can be of great help to trainee journalists, even if that's not its purpose. If someone had offered me Galtung and Ruge's article on the structuring and selecting of news while I was training as a reporter, I would have understood much more quickly what the news editor was trying to say about news values. (See Chapter 7 and Galtung and Ruge 1973.) Besides, the media are influential both in determining what issues get a public airing and in the way they comment on and shape the discussion of those issues. It is important, therefore, that the choices they make about what is significant, the agenda they help to set for the rest of society, should be open to question from both those who want to work as journalists and those who, as media commentators or as academics, study what journalists do.

Magazine or newspaper journalism?

One curious thing about magazine journalism is how much less academic attention it has attracted than newspaper journalism. (This holds true for all aspects of magazines that academics might study: history, ethical issues, influence of regulatory bodies, language, sociology and so on.) Even attention from the general public is comparatively limited unless there is the spectacular firing of an editor or a fashion spread which causes offence. This neglect is reflected in the relative numbers of university training courses devoted to newspaper and periodical journalism. Never has journalism been so popular as a career choice for graduates but for most of them, and their careers advisers, journalism still means chasing fire-engines to daily deadlines or following politicians on the campaign trail.

There are understandable reasons for this. Hard news is seen as exciting, frontline and edgy, largely about war or crime or affairs of state. Magazines, with their less frequent deadlines, are thought to be light, less important and soft, largely about things that don't matter quite so much. Countless films and television shows, from *The Front Page* to *Drop the Dead Donkey*, feature wise-cracking, cynical, hard-nosed newshounds. But the magazine offices portrayed by popular culture are filled mainly with the fragrant folly of the sitcom *Absolutely Fabulous*.

Part of the problem may be that the word 'magazine' implies 'women's magazine' to many people, even though that must surely be changing now that there are so many lifestyle magazines aimed at men. Anything produced specifically for women has traditionally been accorded less value than that which is otherwise regarded as the mainstream. But the consumer magazine market includes a majority of publications not targeted at women and is too important to dismiss. Consumer magazines, according to the Periodical Publishers Association (PPA), are those which provide leisure-time information and entertainment. In the UK there are, according to PPA figures, 3,174 publications which fall into this category and almost double that number of magazines fall into what's known as the business-to-business sector and used to be called the trade press. That's another 5,713 titles. Clearly this is a thriving market but it is much less visible than the consumer market because so many trade publications are sold by subscription: people see only the ones related to their own fields of interest.

Taken together, then, these two sectors (consumer and business-to-business), with a total turnover approaching £6bn, form a strong magazine industry. And it's not just in the UK but in many other countries where new markets are opening up (see Chapter 16). According to government figures the periodicals and journals sector of the UK publishing industry provided employment for more than 53,400 people at the end of 1996 compared with the newspaper industry which employed around 47,000. The trend here is significant too: for magazines the 1996 figure is a rise of more than 9,000 in three years; for newspapers it represents a fall of 6,000 (Department of Culture, Media and Sport 1998: 086).

Another under-reported statistic is that more than half of all journalists in the UK are employed in magazines rather than newspapers (Delano and Henningham 1997). In his book *News and Journalism in the UK* Brian McNair looks as if he is about to redress the balance of significance as between newspapers and periodicals: 'No overview of the British print media would be complete without some reference to the periodical sector: those weekly, fortnightly, and monthly publications which straddle the boundaries between journalism, leisure, entertainment, and business.' Yet there is something dismissive in that phrase 'some reference', given that the periodicals industry is considerably bigger than the newspaper industry however you measure it (Department of Culture, Media and Sport 1998: 086). McNair notes the journalistic emphasis of both *Private Eye* and *The Economist* but again with the idea that these are journalistic because they are about the common hard news preoccupations of economics and politics. This implies that much of the written material that finds its way into the more than 3,000 consumer titles and the 5,700 plus trade titles is not journalistic. I wouldn't challenge that view by citing the frothier lifestyle magazines but I would argue that there is a lot of excellent journalism being pursued in periodicals, even if some of them are little-known trade publications such as *The Engineer* or what could almost be called 'alternative' magazines such as *New Internationalist* and *The Big Issue*. There are plenty of magazines which deal with serious subjects and demand of their writers the highest standards in writing and research.

In the USA, too, the magazine industry is not only healthy but flourishing. More than a thousand titles were launched there in 1998, a statistic that leads Peter Preston, former editor of *The Guardian*, to conclude that the future of newspapers, as they compete with electronic news, lies 'in targeting, in niche markets, in an extension of newspapers' attitude towards features' (Preston 1999). These are precisely the things at which the best magazines already excel.

Even if you use McNair's own criteria to define news, there are stories with economic and political implications being broken or followed through in the trade press with more expertise or thoroughness than some newspapers can manage. (*Computer Weekly*'s tracking of the evidence surrounding the Chinook helicopter crash on the Mull of Kintyre is a good example.) Furthermore, journalists who work for specialist publications are constantly asked by reporters who work for general newspapers to give quotes or background briefings or even write articles when a story breaks in their field of expertise.

What exactly is a magazine?

There are other reasons, too, for suggesting that newspaper and magazine journalism should be accorded more equal status. Journalists now move freely between the two media (see Chapter 2) and almost all daily and weekly national newspapers now bring along in their wake a selection of what can only be described as magazines. *The Sunday Times*'s colour magazine, launched in the early 1960s, was the first UK example and was soon copied by most of the other Sunday newspapers. These colour supplements contained a miscellany of articles including, typically, some hard-hitting coverage of social problems or of wars. But their stories were not tied to the same daily or weekly deadlines as the news sections and so gave their writers and photographers the chance to produce a more considered kind of work. The supplements were also printed on better quality paper. This, along with the coloured inks and the different size, meant that readers of the colour supplements, in the early days, would always have known that what they held in their hands was a magazine.

How much more confusing the situation is now. Many papers publish subsidiary sections which aren't glossy, which may be daily, which are a different size from the main paper and which, by virtue of not being tied to the hard news agenda, have a magazine 'feel' to them. Take *The Guardian*'s 'Weekend' or the *Mail on Sunday*'s 'Night and Day' sections: are they magazines? If not why not? The *M* section launched by *The Mirror* in October 1999 has all the characteristics of a weekly women's magazine but at a bargain price, given that it comes free with the newspaper. All these publications look like magazines.

For a definition of a magazine or periodical we could look to the industry body for help but it doesn't provide a full answer. The members of the Periodical Publishers Association are companies which know they produce magazines. But those newspaper publishers who produce publications such as the *The Times Saturday Magazine* (a weekly with heavy, glossy paper, full-colour photographs and illustrations, and a miscellany of stories) do not belong to it. So membership of the PPA can't help much with definitions. Whereas everyone knows more or less how to define a newspaper, the definition of magazinehood is much less distinct – so many kinds of journalism are published in magazines, so many kinds of journalists are employed on them.

If there can't be an exact and limiting definition of what goes into a magazine it is perhaps because the word was first used to imply something miscellaneous. Edward Cave, a printer and publisher, is usually credited with being the first to use the word magazine in the title of a periodical when he launched his *Gentleman's Magazine* in 1731. There were publications that we now would describe as magazines before that date, notably Defoe's *Review* and the first women's magazine, launched in 1693, called *The Ladies' Mercury*. But these were not, as far as we can tell, referred to as magazines. Gradually, after Cave's venture became well-enough known, the word magazine, which is related to the French word for shop, *magasin* (which in turn derived from the Arabic for emporium or warehouse of goods), acquired its modern meaning. Not only that, it has come to be used in other media, such as television and radio, to refer to programmes which provide a miscellany of stories within a limited field: *In Touch* was a 'magazine' programme for the blind on radio; *Tomorrow's World* is a television magazine programme about science and technology. Perhaps the description given by Ruari McLean in his book about magazine design is as helpful as any: 'A magazine is, usually, less ephemeral than a newspaper, less permanent than a book' (McLean 1969: 1). No one could quarrel with that as the 'usually' allows for exceptions to the rule.

Looking ahead

As we have seen, the magazine industry at the start of the twenty-first century appears to be in fine form. The introduction of computer technology to print publishing during the 1980s breathed new life into magazines, allowing them to experiment with design, to cut costs and, in theory at least, to shorten lead times. As so often with technological innovation, some predictions did not come true. It was assumed that as desk-top publishing became a financial possibility then there would be a burgeoning of cheap, alternative magazines produced by anyone who had something to say and the hope that someone would want to read it. This hasn't really happened and you could certainly argue that the development of the photocopier actually made more difference to the publication and distribution of alternative publications than did computerised setting (Atton 1999).

In the 1990s the great change was the arrival of the World Wide Web and the Internet. Forecasts about the possible effects of this on magazine publishers have been at wild variance. Some heralded it as the start of the collapse of magazines and even newspapers: who would need them once they could have a tailored digest of news and features stories ('The weekly/monthly Me') sent directly to their desks in electronic form? The funny thing about how wrong this prediction has so far turned out to be is that digests of the contents of magazines are increasingly popular (*The Week*, *The Editor*) but provided in hard-copy form as yet more magazines.

Publishers were then worried that they ought to keep up with everyone else by getting into web publishing but without really knowing what to do with a website or whether they could make money with one. As Tim Holmes shows in Chapter 12, publishers do now seem to have come to terms with the digital communication revolution. Some are generating extra business or building up databases, and the word from the USA is that there is money to be made in electronic publishing, especially in the business information field, either through advertising or through the direct selling of knowledge or products. Some publishers are merely providing an extra service to readers through their websites but by doing so are learning more about their readers' interests and improving public recognition of their brands.

The mood in the industry at the turn of the new century was, then, rather upbeat, as witnessed at the 1999 annual conference of the Periodical Publishers Association which represents 80 per cent of the UK market. The huge expansion of the business-to-business sector was much talked about and fields of activity such as brand extension, exhibition organisation and masthead programming were all thought to offer strong grounds for optimism. Many publishers are going global in their operations and many more are working across the different communications media with success. The frequency of launches was mentioned: in the first three months of 1999 *Heat*, *Later*, *New Eden*, *Chocolate Magazine*, *FBX* and *The Jam* were just a few and in 2000 there are set to be at least five new monthly glossies for women. Understandably there was less discussion of the closures such as *Options*, *Eat Soup* and *Cover*.

Magazine publishers boast that there is a magazine for every taste. In fact that's not true. There is certainly a magazine for many hobbies (reptile keeping in *The Reptilian*, embroidery in *Cross-Stitch*), and for many kinds of weird sexual obsessions as in, for example, *Leg Sex*. These publications represent niche marketing in the extreme yet some mainstream subject areas are hardly touched by magazines because their potential target audiences are not sought by advertisers. One obvious gap in the current marketplace is for magazines which deal intelligently and wittily with a much broader range of subjects for women and for girls than any of the current British ones do. Given that there are more than eighty magazines for women on the news-stands, it is surprising how similar groups of them are. The competition in all sectors of the consumer market is fierce (there are at least twenty UK magazines devoted to home decoration for example) but for publishers the remedy seems to lie in further fragmentation of the market, rather than in consolidation of their products.

Scope of this book

Business and industry perspectives are dealt with in Chapters 15 and 16. For some reason these aspects of publishing life are largely ignored in the training of newspaper journalists but thought by many to be essential for magazine journalists. I think it is useful for workers in any industry to have some idea about how it is financed and what problems are currently worrying the owners and managers. For magazine publishers at the turn of the new century, as I've already mentioned, the impact and potential of the Internet is one concern. So too is the effect that changes in the pattern of retailing in the UK may have on magazine distribution. Will supermarkets drive local CTNs (the industry's name for confectioner, tobacconist, newsagent shops) out of business? Will they be willing to stock such a wide range of magazines as the CTNs? Another, raised by Felix Dennis of Dennis Publishing, is the functional illiteracy of a quarter of the nation's teenagers: 'How many magazines will they be reading in ten years' time?' he asks. A further worry, voiced by Dennis, is the environmental impact of destroying so many trees to produce magazines. Even if publishers don't worry too much about that, he implies, the environmental lobby will and this could eventually have an impact on sales especially now that an electronic alternative is available (*Press Gazette* 21 May 1999).

From outside the industry concern is regularly expressed about the content of magazines. There has long been discussion about the limitations of the material published specifically for women. Criticisms include worries about the possible bad effect on women (especially young women) of a literary diet of little but beauty, fashion and titbits of gossip, whether about celebrities or 'ordinary' people. This kind of argument can be patronising to women, assuming as it sometimes does that they read little else or that they need more protection and education than men.

There is, too, a strong strand of feminist criticism which argues that by their very nature magazines aimed at women do acquire a role as shapers and definers of what women are and how they are perceived (Ferguson 1983; Greer 1999; Macdonald 1995 and many others). If that's so then it does matter what images of women are provided by these publications and what social roles women and girls are seen to play in them. Some commentators have also analysed why the subject matter of commercial women's magazines is, on the whole, so limited and have looked at what this means in terms of what is left out of magazines (Steinem 1994).

There are also commentators who have decided that consumer magazines are not influential because their readers don't take them seriously, using them merely as light relief from busy lives (Hermes 1995). These points will be discussed further at appropriate points in the following chapters although I'll now declare my own position. First, I believe magazines do wield a strong influence over their readers. I base this on common sense, my own experience and, much more convincingly, on the research undertaken by publishers and advertisers. Second, I am firmly on the side of Cynthia White who argued in her Royal Commission report that magazines should cover a much wider range of subjects the better to prepare girls and women for life in a real world instead of one bounded by agonising over how they look and how to cope with domestic drudgery. She was writing in the mid-1970s but her conclusions are, regrettably, still valid (White 1977).

Third, I take what might be called a traditional feminist position in that I find the picture of women's lives to be gleaned from reading many women's magazines disheartening as well as unrealistic even allowing for a bit of fantasy and plenty of light-hearted fun. The underlying assumption of so many publications is that women are obsessed by their appearance and with good reason as that is what will define them in the eyes of the world. The argument here is also commercial as American feminist editor Gloria Steinem described in 'Sex, lies, and advertising' (Steinem 1994): lack of confidence about looks leads to expenditure on clothes and cosmetics, without which consumer magazines would not exist. (It will be interesting to see whether men's lifestyle magazines will convince men to spend as much time, energy and money on their appearance as women are now expected by editors to do.) Romance and marriage have been pushed aside since White was writing it is true, but they have been more than replaced by sex dressed up in various guises on the problem pages, the fashion pages, the general features and the health pages. Nothing wrong with that if people want to read about it but it is the fact that there is so little in the way of debate about anything vaguely contentious (as opposed to prurient) that gives rise to criticism.

Added to that now is the well-publicised concern over how explicit sexual material is being used, with great success in the case of the newish men's lifestyle titles (and mixed success in the case of magazines for teenage girls), as a means to boost circulation. A regulatory framework had to be set up by the PPA in 1996 following questions in Parliament about the material being sold to young teenage girls (McKay 1999). The issue of the sexualisation of lifestyle magazines is covered in Chapter 17.

In one book it is not possible to discuss every aspect of writing, editing and publishing that might interest journalists who want to work in magazines. This is because the range of titles is so varied that there are not many general points that cover every case. Consequently it is not really possible either to give representative examples of texts. Instead I have referred to a wide variety of periodicals on the assumption that where this book is being used as part of a course, tutors and students will want to find their own examples to illustrate (or, indeed, challenge) the points made here. What I have tried to do is to concentrate on the areas that are most important for a beginner to know about.

One of the differences between newspaper and magazine journalism is that there are certain agreed things that news reporters need to know how to do and among these, apart from newswriting, are included some features writing and some subbing. Even within newspaper offices, though, a basic reporter's training will not now make provision for all the kinds of writing and editing that the magazine sections of newspapers require. Yet most journalism training is taken up with the inculcation of news values and the skills required to write hard, or hardish, news stories. This book doesn't, therefore, seek to cover the same ground as newspaper journalism training books for the simple reason that there are several of these and there is much less available to the magazine journalist.

An elementary knowledge of government is an essential part of a news journalist's training. While it may well be useful knowledge for magazine journalists, no one could argue that they all need it and indeed most editors and publishers I've spoken to said if there has to be a choice they think it is more important for all their staff to know something about the magazine publishing industry than about the mechanics of government. Again, the ground is covered in most newspaper training books as well as in the books by Ron Fenney and others recommended at the end of Chapter 5.

There is, however, no doubt at all among editors about how important it is for all their staff to have a knowledge of the law as it affects journalists. For this reason Chapter 18, written by Anthony Richards, is devoted to the subject. Although many magazine journalists will pass an entire career without attending a criminal court or an inquest there are nevertheless aspects of the law about which everyone who ventures into print ought to know.

This book is written primarily for journalists who work in magazines, so it doesn't attempt to explain how advertising sales executives do their job or indeed what magazine designers or photographers or stylists need to know. It does, though, include chapters on magazine design (by Tim Holmes) and on picture editing and illustration (by photographer Tom Ang). These chapters provide an introduction to how the experts in the visual aspects of magazines approach their task so that the writers and subeditors who work with them will have an informed understanding of how certain decisions are made. Many magazines have small staffs, and writers and subs on magazines are therefore more likely to be involved in decisions about the look of their publications than they would be on many newspapers.

Chapter 11, which looks at subediting and production, concentrates on aspects of writing and presentation. It does not venture into the realms of computer software. It's true that many subs these days will need to know how to use QuarkXpress but it would be impractical for a general book such as this to attempt to teach it in one chapter. The practicalities of an individual system are best taught by computer specialists, so the aspects of subediting in Chapter 11 are, broadly speaking, the ones that apply whatever software (or indeed whatever technology) is being used to produce a magazine.

Because there is so much variety in magazine content readers will find plentiful references to further sources of information and an extensive bibliography to help them explore the areas that interest them most. At the end of each chapter is a list of books which are recommended to supplement the points made in the text. Full bibliographical references for these are made in the Bibliography. I have included wherever possible references to examples of good journalism in the hope that these will act as a kind of inspiration about what it is possible to achieve as a journalist. One thing that puzzled me as a trainee journalist on a hotly competed for graduate training scheme was that there was no discussion of the best journalistic writing or of the literary value of journalism. In my own teaching I have always tried to go against this tradition by urging journalism graduate students to read good journalistic writing whether from among what is current or from anthologies. So I make no apology for including in these pages references to writers who with courage, grace or skill open windows on the world, which is the most important thing a writer can do for me.

I would like to be able to recommend a comprehensive history of periodical journalism, but it doesn't yet exist. Those who are interested to know what has gone before, once they have exhausted Cynthia White on women's magazines (1969) and David Reed on popular magazines from 1880 to 1960 (1997), will have to browse in general press history journals and books, some of which are listed at the end of this chapter. For current coverage of the magazine world students should look regularly at *Press Gazette, Private Eye*, and *The Guardian*'s 'Media' section on Mondays as well as its supplement, 'The Editor', on Fridays. The American monthly *Brill's Content* is not too hard to find in the UK and provides information and comment about what is going on across the Atlantic. At the back of the book there is a glossary of technical terms, a list of addresses and a bibliography, divided into three sections.

The only other thing it remains to do is to explain how I came by the information and opinions that are set out on the following pages. The reason this is necessary is that there is, as I have already hinted, a lingering suspicion among some journalists that anyone who doesn't make a living as a journalist has nothing useful to teach about journalism. I would counter that argument, in my own case at least, by saying that I was a journalist for ten years and part of me still is. More important than that almost is the fact that I have taught a lot of journalists. They keep me informed about current practice. So too do the journalists who kindly accept invitations to speak to my students and the editors I talk to on a regular basis. So, in addition to the sources in published material (books, magazines, industry documentation, websites), my most important sources are journalists, the men and women whose job is an important and a fascinating one if not in every circumstance an enviable one.

Recommended reading

Books

Armstrong, L. (1998) *Front Row*.

Braithwaite, B. (1998) 'Magazines',

Coleridge, N. (1999) *Streetsmart*.

Griffiths, D. (ed.) (1992) *The Encyclopaedia of the British Press 1422–1992*.

Peak, S. and Fisher, P. (eds) *The Media Guide*, updated annually.

Reed, D. (1999) *The Popular Magazine in Britain and the United States 1880–1960*.

Smith, A. (1979) *The Newspaper: An International History*.

Stokes, J. and Reading, A. (eds) (1999) *The Media in Britain*.

White, C. (1969) *Women's Magazines 1693–1968*.

Periodicals

Adbusters, *Brill's Content*, *Campaign*, *The Editor*, *Granta*, *Guardian* 'Media' section, *Media Week*, *Press Gazette*, *Private Eye*.

2 Training for magazine journalism

....

I did it by *not* going to journalism school, *not* getting an education and *not* training in the provinces as the NUJ demand. Feet first into the legend, that's the only way to go.

Julie Burchill, *Sex and Sensibility*

Aspiring journalists will find a degree in any subject is more or less mandatory. After that the ways into employment are many and vague, usually mundane, and always badly paid.

The Media Guide 1999

For many careers the route to a job is clear. Even if competition for jobs is fierce there is often a recognised qualification you must have before you apply for a first post. After that the contacts, the determination, the luck, the job market all play their part, but that vital first step is to get the basic training.

The position in journalism is different and confusing not only to outsiders hoping to get in but also to many of those who already work as journalists and are in the position of hiring recruits. In this chapter I will concentrate on entry into magazine journalism but much of what I cover applies to other aspects of journalistic work in the media.

Qualifications

....

There are no minimum qualifications for journalists so in theory you could get a job without a GCSE or an A level or a Scottish Higher Still. And however many training courses there are available there will always be some magazine editorial staff who get in by informal means: by talking their way into a job as an editorial assistant perhaps, by going to an office for work experience and contriving to become indispensable, by bombarding an editor with such good cuttings or story ideas that in the end a job has to be offered. This is anathema to those who believe that journalism is a profession but it is a fact of journalistic life. If you write well enough and are able to convince an editor of your worth, the lack of a paper qualification in anything, let alone in journalism, is no barrier to success. Except, of course, for the fact that so many people, including some of the best graduates, want to be journalists too, many of them in magazines. They will be competing fiercely for jobs and so editors can look for flair in addition to educational achievement, not instead of it.

In practice, then, almost all entrants to journalism nowadays have been to university or college and often that includes a postgraduate vocational qualification after a first degree in some other subject. Of those currently working in magazine journalism about 90 per cent are graduates and for all journalists, including newspapers, the figure is about 80 per cent. This change has come about in the course of a single working generation and the obvious reason is the huge growth in the proportion of the population which goes to university.

If you're unlucky as a new journalist you'll come up against the older hand whose advice can be summed up as: 'Training, what training? I never had any training. No need for it. Journalists are born not made.' For this kind of hack there is only one thing worse than training and that is training that takes place in a university. Luckily this approach is not as common as it was even twenty years ago but if you find yourself in an editorial office where the view prevails you are likely to find your life made miserable if you ever make the slightest mistake or ask a simple question about practice. Luckily, too, for readers of this book at least, this attitude is less prevalent in magazine offices than it is, or at least was, in newspapers, particularly the regional dailies and weeklies.

If you do come up against it you'll need to find your own way to deal with it. Being astoundingly competent at your job is usually a good way to silence critics (even if it irritates them) but if you're a beginner there will be things you still need to learn even if you've completed a course of training. For many people the puzzle is that if wizened hacks really believe that journalism can only be taught on the job, why do they create an atmosphere where asking questions or discussing how things should be done are respectively treated as an admission of incompetence and a demonstration of arrogance?

One answer may be insecurity. Journalism is madly competitive, staff jobs are on the way out and – the clincher this – if training really isn't needed for journalism and anyone can do it, why shouldn't editors hire those who are younger and cheaper? Another answer is history. From the 1960s to the 1980s it was virtually impossible, thanks to agreements between unions and managements, to get a job on a national newspaper without first serving an apprenticeship on a regional daily or weekly paper. Whatever else recruits had done before, those indentured years helped them to learn under the guidance, in the best offices, of experienced reporters and subeditors.

Of course in-house, on-the-job training was, and still is, a lottery, since it was usually fairly unsystematic and depended on the editor allocating good members of the editorial team to the job, rather than the less good, whose time could be spared from more important duties. During this period and beyond there were pre-entry courses that school-leavers or graduates could take at colleges or universities, some lasting just a few weeks, others up to an academic year and leading to the award of a diploma or even a master's degree. The pioneering courses in the UK were at Cardiff University and City University in London. Not only did they train graduates for newspaper journalism, they realised that there was scope for training graduates in other kinds of journalism too, periodicals as well as broadcasting. The graduates who did postgraduate journalism courses at university were still expected, if they wanted to work in news, to sign indentures with newspapers but for a shorter period.

What many entrants to the trade of journalism had in common was that at some point they would sit examinations organised by the National Council for the Training of Journalists (NCTJ). These gave newspaper editors (and other employers) guidance about whether certain skills and knowledge had been acquired but they were never an absolute requirement for entry into journalism, however much the NCTJ and some editors would have liked them to be.

Journalism in universities

Until the early 1970s, there was no formal route into magazine journalism at all. (This may be partly why careers advisers in both schools and universities often assumed that journalism as a career meant newspaper journalism because there was at least some kind of pattern to training for this.) Journalists who wanted to join magazines from newspapers would sometimes find their qualifications helpful but equally could encounter magazine editors who had never heard of the NCTJ. A similar problem arose as the various further education and higher education courses in journalism got under way. They don't all teach exactly the same things or at least don't emphasise the same skills. The qualifications are at differing levels (from certificate, through HND to graduate diploma and MA or M.Litt or even M.Sc.) and there is no consistency in the level at which applicants join. Some universities cater only for graduates, some teach undergraduate journalism degrees, some FE colleges cater for school-leavers on block-release courses. You can see why this is confusing already, before we even get to the vexed subject of media studies.

To digress for a moment. There is a great deal of contempt shown by senior journalists (who really should be better informed) about media studies. The distinction is clear to university staff but perhaps they have not made enough effort to explain it to those outside the academy. Put simply media studies is the analysis of what journalists and others who work in the media produce. A media studies course may or may not contain some elements of journalism practice but in essence it is an academic study in the same way that English literature is the study of what novelists and poets produce, not a training in how to write novels or poems. Journalism studies by contrast is mainly a vocational training for those who want to be journalists. In universities this will certainly involve academic analysis of what journalists produce but the point of journalism courses in universities is to train journalists not to train academics, even if those journalists are able to reflect critically on what they do for a living.

Much of the prejudice about media studies courses comes from those who are ignorant of this distinction and their comments about media studies being a bad preparation for a media career are therefore not worth listening to. Those who graduate in journalism studies are, if they are any good, very successful indeed at finding jobs as journalists, sometimes more successful than their talent merits. There are a tiny number who decide during a course that they don't want to be journalists after all but the skills they acquire on university journalism courses should prove valuable in many other careers.

However, even those critics who can see the distinction between media studies and vocational journalism training are wrong when they argue that students who take degrees in media or communications are misled into expecting to work in the media afterwards. First, no one deliberately misleads them and, second, lots of them do, in fact, go on to be very successful in the media. Michael Jackson, with a glittering career in television, went on to head BBC2, then Channel 4: he studied communications. So too did Colin Cameron, head of production at BBC Scotland as I write, and eminent television documentary journalist. Just two examples but there are many more. Media studies courses do not (or not necessarily) provide much training in practical skills but for many students that suits well. If you're passionate about television, or radio or the printed mass media what is wrong with devoting a period of academic study to their critical analysis? They are worthy fields of study in their own right and if by the end of a degree the student decides to try to work in the media then what's wrong with knowing how to write a feminist critique of women's magazines or how to deconstruct a television documentary in the manner of Raymond Williams or John Fiske. As an intellectual training at undergraduate level (always assuming the course is a good one) study of the communications media is as good an intellectual training as any other more traditional degree. Why should it be that a degree in Greek is not frowned on as a preparation for an aspiring journalist but one in media studies is? So long as there is no confusion for students or teachers about what a practical, vocational training is then there shouldn't be a problem.

Confusion does nevertheless seem to reign even in the minds of government ministers which makes it difficult for anyone who teaches anything to do with the media to get it right. Brian Wilson, former journalist and then Scottish Office minister for education, said in 1998 that the problem with media education was not that it did not train people in practical skills but rather it did too much of that. This is exactly the opposite criticism from that usually levelled at university courses in media studies (Peak and Fisher 1998: 23).

For those who want to do journalism studies courses at undergraduate or graduate level that are vocational and therefore a direct preparation for work in journalism, there are certain indicators to look out for that the right kind of work will be done and assessed on the course.

Accreditation

What might seem to be the simplest check is to look for accreditation by an industry body. Accreditation ideally follows an examination by industry and training professionals of the way that a course is run. For magazines the situation is fairly straightforward, in that any courses which are accredited by the Periodicals Training Council (PTC) are likely to be worthwhile. However, this doesn't mean that all those which are not accredited are not good, as newer courses will not yet have arranged for the expensive and time-consuming visits and assessments to take place. Nor, if they are very new, will they have been able to provide the accrediting body with a list of graduates and their employment records. Perhaps the thing to do is to check whether an application for accreditation has ever been turned down. For newspapers the position is, at the time of writing, much more complicated because the traditional accrediting body, the National Council for the Training of Journalists (which in spite of its title was only ever involved in the training of local newspaper journalists), has lost the confidence of many employers and journalists as well as of most institutions of further and higher education which were training reporters. One among many reasons for this is that as well as assessing college courses it was also in direct competition with them as an organisation which provided its own training and set its own examinations, which students were obliged to take at their own expense in addition to their university qualifications. The PTC does not set exams or train. It merely monitors, on behalf of magazine publishers, the efforts of those who do and there is therefore no conflict of interest.

One indicator for the future is the decision in 1998 of two key organisations with an interest in this field, the trade bodies for magazines and regional newspapers, the Periodical Publishers Association and the Newspaper Society, to form an alliance to lobby on several issues, including the establishment of a National Training Organisation (NTO in the jargon). What this will mean and how it will relate to the national newspaper trade body, the Newspaper Publishers Association (and the equivalent newspaper bodies in Scotland), and whether there will be any formal link with that for training purposes, remains to be seen.

So if accreditation is a useful but not an infallible guide what else can you look for? Check in the course literature whether those who teach the practical journalism aspects of the course have worked as journalists. It's also worth checking how much experience they have of teaching as it's not every former journalist who can teach well without some practice. Check the timetables to see what proportion of time is devoted to developing practical skills. Ask to see the facilities that will be available to you as a student and for how much time. (A computer-filled newsroom with five phones and a fax-machine is only as useful as the amount of access to it students have.) Ask to see samples of student work, ideally ones that have been marked by tutors. At the least ask to see a list of assignments set in any given year. Most importantly, ask to see a list of the career paths of graduates. You could even phone one or two recent graduates to ask what they think about the course.

For some candidates there won't be much choice as they will be offered only one place. Competition for the good journalism courses in universities is fierce, certainly, but number of applicants alone is not always a reliable guide as most serious candidates will apply to several courses. Universities, too, are in competition for the really good candidates who will therefore be likely to have a choice about where to go. There may be overriding personal reasons which point a student in one direction or another, but if there aren't then the considerations I have listed above should influence the decision. Financially a graduate course is a big investment so you have a right to make sure you will get value for money. There doesn't seem to be much conformity about the costs of courses at graduate level largely because they are all funded in different ways by their host universities. It's a point to watch out for. The cheapest course might just be less good. On the other hand it may offer less in the way of computers and telephones but for the difference in fees you could equip yourself with what is needed (laptop computer and mobile phone perhaps) and still have them to use at the end of your year's study.

Students aiming at careers in magazines will probably try to choose the periodicals courses in universities but a newspaper training will almost certainly contain many of the same elements (with perhaps less emphasis on production). Career paths are not tightly fenced into one medium and so if money dictates that you study at the nearest college and that offers only newspaper journalism, if you take up a place there it does not mean you can't expect to work in magazines. Apart from anything else it could depend on what kind of magazine job you aspire to. If you want to be South-east Asia correspondent of *The Economist* then a solid news training would be the most useful thing.

The point about career paths is important. It is rare for journalists today to make a career entirely in one medium. They move jobs from television to newspapers to magazines or the other way round, or while having a job in one they do freelance work for another. This means that throughout your training and your career you should be aware of the developments in other media and how they might affect your own work.

On-the-job training

One development which can be seen as an attempt to clarify the muddle over qualifications for many occupations in industry and commerce, including journalists, is the move by the government to encourage the establishment of a system of NVQs or National Vocational Qualifications (SVQs in Scotland). These are designed to establish a coherent national framework for vocational qualifications. Each NVQ comprises a number of units or job-related tasks and when the NVQ is awarded it is proof that the candidate is competent to work in a particular area such as newswriting or subediting. Preparation for the NVQ is carried out on the job and in most cases assessed in-house by a trained assessor. Small companies can get help with this from the PTC. The standards for these NVQs were established by the PTC and the examinations are controlled by the Royal Society of Arts. The aim is that this harmonised set of qualifications could be acquired by anyone working in magazines, whatever their previous educational background, to show that they had reached nationally agreed standards of competence. The advantages are obvious both for recruiters and for hard-pressed journalists who sometimes have to fight for any kind of training from their employers. However, there are disadvantages in the amount of monitoring and assistance senior staff need to provide for the benefit of juniors. This may be one reason why so far not many employers of journalists are involved in the NVQ or SVQ system.

A further disadvantage with any on-the-job training for beginners is that it means employers are having to pay people who are not yet fully competent. They may not pay them much but any salary is a drain on resources, especially if the postholder is completely untrained and untried. One reason that many publishers of newspapers gradually defrosted their attitude to university graduate journalism diplomas was that they realised the cost of initial training was being shifted to the pockets of students. Publishers used to have to pay while trainees learnt the elementary skills as well as paying fees for the block-release courses – now they start to pay the graduates, at least, when these have a good knowledge of all the basics, plenty of practice as reporters and probably some worthwhile cuttings to prove they have what it takes to get published. (As far as NVQs are concerned, universities are not part of the system although a university-trained journalist ought to be able to acquire the appropriate NVQs almost immediately if an employer wants to standardise the qualifications of its staff.)

One of the best options for an aspiring magazine journalist, especially one on a limited budget or one who is simply tired of classrooms, is to be taken on by a magazine publisher as a trainee. There will be a salary, formal training, the chance to practise immediately and under guidance what has been learned in training, and the immediate opportunity to start building up a portfolio of cuttings and a list of contacts. Unfortunately the days when many big companies took on trainees on these terms have gone.

One way to find out about courses run by universities, colleges or private companies is to write to the PTC which will send you a list of those it accredits. A fuller list of courses, whether or not accredited, is to be found in *The Media Guide* for the current year published by *The Guardian*. This also lists the names and addresses of most magazine publishers and so could save you a lot of time if you are writing speculative letters. On the rare occasions when publishers have traineeships to advertise they are likely to use *The Guardian*'s media pages on a Monday (reprinted in Saturday's 'Jobs and Money' section), or advertise in *Press Gazette*. Traineeships are more likely to be found in the trade or business press, the publications that are not so easy to come across in newsagents but which can be an excellent way into the world of magazine publishing, provided, of course, you have no objection to becoming, for a year or two at least, an expert in cement mixing or print buying, in the timber trade or in dentistry or insurance. (See Chapter 3 on careers.)

Costs

If you do decide to train at your own expense there is an enormous range in how much you might have to spend. This partly reflects a lack of agreement over what you need to know to work as a journalist on any magazine compared with what you need to know to work on a specific one. My own list would run like this. For any magazine: the skills of touch-typing, shorthand, computer operation including QuarkXpress, written English, subediting, research skills (online, paper-based and interpersonal such as interviewing face to face and by telephone), basic knowledge in the fields of business, government and media law. Beyond those (and I recognise how arguable this list is) it would be desirable for most if not all magazine journalists to have some knowledge of the history, business and design of magazines as well as an understanding of the media studies approach and a developed interest in the field they hope to write about whether it is fashion or economics. In practice this last point is almost the least important, as many journalists find themselves writing about subjects in which they have no expertise.

The courses run by colleges, universities and private organisations vary wildly in the prices they charge as I have noted. To give some examples from the guide published by the PTC, 'A career in magazines' 1998/9 edition. For £3,700 you could do a nine month graduate diploma at Cardiff University. For £557 you could do a thirteen-week certificate course at The London College of Printing, while Highbury College in Portsmouth charged £1,142 for a one-year training.

For some aspiring magazine journalists these sums sound impossibly high, especially when you take into account the modest salary levels which are paid for first jobs and out of which you might be expected to pay off a student loan or a career development loan. Note, though, that first pay at the junior level in magazines is likely to be considerably higher than in local weekly newspapers.

For a few students there is help in the way of scholarships to study at certain universities. The Association of British Science Writers makes four substantial awards each year to science graduates, and ethnic minority students can win funded places at the University of Westminster.

Preparation for finding work

Some graduates decide to break into magazine journalism as freelances. This kind of work is discussed fully in Chapter 4 but here it is worth outlining the pitfalls for the beginner. To be a successful freelance you have to be sure that the work you produce is of professional standard and is properly presented and you also need contacts who have responsibility for commissioning copy. A new freelance can build up the contacts by pitching exciting ideas and producing good copy. But if you have never worked as a staff journalist and you've had no training, then the problem is going to be the quality of your work. If, in the early days, you offer commissioning editors work that is not up to standard then it will deter them from looking at your ideas in the future. The warning here is against trying too soon to make a living as a freelance. Many are the staff journalists with years of experience who decide to make a go of the freelance life, perhaps after redundancy or even just because they fancy being in charge of their own lives. A history graduate with a couple of music review cuttings from the student paper is unlikely to be able to compete, except for space in a photocopied fanzine. Having said all this if you are determined that you must work as a magazine journalist and that you can't afford formal training then you'll have to train yourself. Read Chapter 4 on freelancing, read relevant books, read and analyse successful magazine journalism, study the markets, get some work experience unpaid if necessary, practise writing and interviewing even while you carry on with the day job. Invest in a mobile phone and computer. Pin two notes above your desk to remind you: 'You're only as good as your last by-line' and 'Features editors are always short of ideas'.

If you nevertheless decide to try for a job or place on a course there are certain things editors and lecturers will be looking for in candidates. The personal qualities likely to characterise journalists are well enough known (curiosity, competitiveness, plausible manner, good memory) and the skills that are needed you will be acquiring as a trainee. Beyond this the things that influence those with the power to pluck you from obscurity are, in the end, all things which show you have talent, persistence and an absolute commitment to being a journalist. So a portfolio of cuttings from student papers with perhaps a couple from your local weekly paper or arts magazine and ideally one from a regional or national would be standard. They show that other people think your work is worth publishing and that you have the nerve to persuade them to do it. They may also be evidence that you have spent some time doing work placements and this is, again, almost a standard requirement. To get a placement you need persistence and possibly contacts. It shows not only that you are keen enough to arrange the place-ment but that, having done one (or several), you really know what you are talking about when you say you want to be a journalist. Otherwise an interviewer might suspect that you think magazine journalism is all glamour and no graft, more about drink, drugs and missed deadlines than about chasing late copy, reading proofs or devising work-able flatplans. If you are applying to the abfab world of the women's fashion glossies or to a depraved den of laddishness you will have to convince the editors in your own personal way that you know enough about the content of their publications to be able to contribute. There are some aspects of journalism that can't be taught and the patience you need to interview soap starlets about their sexual preferences is probably one of them. Likewise, the imagination to think up new ways of describing the comeback of the little black dress.

Work experience

Work experience is a relatively new concept in the world of UK journalism although in the past fifteen years it has become pretty well essential for anyone hoping to make a career as a journalist, for some of the reasons given above. It can be a great disap-pointment to employers and students and most often if it is this is because there has been a lack of clarity about what is expected. This can be due to a muddle about the very term 'work experience' so it is important to have a clear idea what you mean by it. At the simplest level there is the kind of work placement where youngsters, probably still at school, go into an office for a week or so, the point of this being exploratory – to get some idea of what journalism and journalists are like, to see if it's the kind of work that might be of interest. Later, when it is clear that they want to be journal-ists, perhaps because they've had work published in student papers, they might take on longer work placements where as well as being allowed to shadow reporters they may be allowed to do some research or caption writing or try writing simple stories.

On longish work experience periods, especially over holidays when there may be a shortage of staff, students can find they are gradually entrusted with tasks of consid-erable responsibility. At a more advanced stage still, those students who are studying journalism for degrees or postgraduate qualifications will almost certainly be required to undertake periods of work experience and here what they are entrusted to do will depend on the competence of the trainee and the confidence shown in him by the editor. Up to this point there is unlikely to be much in the way of payment. My own view is that if student work is published by a magazine or paper then a lineage rate should be paid as it would for any other journalist. Editors sometimes argue that if they had to pay they simply wouldn't want to clutter up their offices with student journalists. I would agree as far as paying a wage goes, but copy that's good enough to publish is good enough to pay for. A few publishers do give their students on work experience some financial help, in recognition of the fact that they are trained and experienced enough, especially at graduate diploma level, to make a worthwhile contribution to the editorial team.

A note of caution here about what some organisations call work experience but should more honestly be called exploitation. When students have gained their vocational qualifications in journalism they are often offered unpaid work experience for weeks if not months, with the incentive that a job could well be coming up in the near future which they would be ideally placed to get if they have already been around in the editorial office. It's understandable why new journalists accept this but they shouldn't have to. Apart from anything else it makes a nonsense of that case made by some editors that they don't get enough recruits from poorer families. You already need quite a lot of cash behind you to study for a degree, then a postgraduate diploma which almost always has to be funded personally. Even quite well-off families baulk at the idea of a substantial period of unpaid labour for a profitable publishing house, especially as these kinds of jobs usually leave little time over for the part-time, cash-gathering jobs in bars or shops that students now regularly do.

Back now to work experience as part of a course. When this works well the student returns to class with renewed enthusiasm for the job, new contacts and some worthwhile cuttings. Sometimes, too, a work placement may have the effect of convincing a student that a field they'd thought about is in fact not for them. Work experience goes badly when the student expects too much of it, complains of being ignored by staffers, of not being allowed to do anything useful, or of finding too many other work experience people sitting around the newsroom at the same time. From an editor's point of view a student on work experience can seem too demanding, or not well enough informed about the content of the publication to be of much help. The faults can lie on either or both sides. Some senior staff have students assigned to them unasked by editors and simply can't be bothered finding time to help them either because they are too busy or perhaps because they feel threatened by them. Or they may not fully realise how much training and experience a student already has, they may not distinguish between the school student making initial enquiries about a variety of careers and the graduate student who is much further on in her career planning. Equally some students expect to be given juicy stories to write without having to go to the effort of thinking up any leads for themselves. That there is a problem is something that the Periodicals Training Council has recognised and it now publishes a booklet called 'Guidelines for organisation of work experience placements'.

Contacts

In this chapter it only remains to stress the importance of making and maintaining contacts. Journalists need these first as part of the reporting process, as sources of quotes, background information and ideas. In the context of getting jobs, however, the more important sort of contacts are those in a position to hire, or to commission, or even to hint that work might be available in a given office. The lucky student will know some journalists anyway but others will have find ways of getting to know some.

Work experience plays its part. Shameless phone calls asking for a few minutes time to gather advice or pitch a features idea are another way to get through the door. When it comes to making contacts your imagination and your personal level of shyness are the only limits.

Recommended reading

Association of British Science Writers (1997) *So you Want to Be a Science Writer* 2nd edition.

Periodicals Training Council (1997) 'Guidelines for organisation of work experience placements'.

Periodicals Training Council (2000) *A Career in Magazines*.

The Media Guide published annually by *The Guardian* includes a comprehensive list of magazine publishers and of training courses public and private.

Benn's Media, *Willings Press Guide* and *BRAD* are useful guides to companies which publish magazines.

3 Jobs and careers in magazine journalism

'It's a great profession, isn't it?' Bateson.
'Ours is a nasty trade,' News editor.

Evelyn Waugh, *Scoop*

The number of full-time staff journalists a magazine employs varies enormously from one publication to the next. The staff box of *Time* magazine has more than two hundred names. But *Time* is not typical. It is an international news magazine with the huge budget and huge staff it needs to fulfil its aim of in-depth global news coverage. The emphasis is on writing and reporting with high-quality photography and graphics by way of illustration. Gathering news widely for a publication with several geographically separate editions as well as at least five websites is a labour-intensive task, something which is evident from the long list of staff.

More commonly, however, magazines have what looks almost like a skeleton editorial staff, supplemented by freelances. Most often these freelances will be the writers and photographers, but in addition magazines are likely to employ a battery of casual subs when edition times are close or there's an outbreak of flu. The most senior jobs such as editor, fashion editor or features editor are usually done by members of staff or employees on substantial contracts as these are the people who determine the tone and quality of the magazine. But with the increasing trend within all journalism towards the slenderest of staffs even jobs like fashion editor or publisher can be performed on a consultancy basis by those from outside.

Almost at the other extreme is a monthly magazine such as the *London Review of Books* where the editorial team consists of about four people even though it is a dense, wordy, lengthy publication to read. This is because the editorial staff write almost none of the content. What they do is commission contributors to write reviews of books in their special fields of interest. They also edit the copy.

Consumer magazines

It's not so different on a typical consumer magazine such as *Cosmopolitan*. The masthead reveals one senior features writer, one features assistant and a contributing editor all of whom are likely to be on the staff and could be expected to write. The subs department has five in it, although it is likely that on smaller magazines there would be fewer subs and other staff such as the deputy or assistant editors would tackle some subbing. Lower down the list come the fashion writer (one of a fashion team of five) and a health and beauty editor (in a team of three). Below them again come some more people called contributing editors, which at this point in a masthead is likely to mean those freelance writers who are paid to supply a regular number of features each year. Even including non-staffers and the editorial secretaries there are, on most consumer magazines, considerably more names listed under the business functions such as advertising, marketing, promotion and publishing than there are among the writers, artists and production types.

On newspapers, by contrast, there is not likely to be a staff list published in this way at all and those papers which do have them, Glasgow's *Sunday Herald* for example, do not list all the staff and make no mention of the staff who don't work in the editorial departments.

In bigger publishing houses some staff do the same job for a number of publications. A publisher, for example, may cover four or five publications in the same field. And it's quite common in the business-to-business press for designers or subs to work on a range of titles. This makes sense as smaller publications don't necessarily generate enough work for full-time employment but the publishing house can nevertheless offer attractive full-time jobs by combining work on more than one title.

From the perspective of the young journalist who wants to work in magazines this can be disheartening. The glamour and buzz of working for a title like the award winning *New Woman* is not going to be part of the life of many writers who are more likely to be at home awaiting commissions from a range of publications. On *New Woman* there is more chance of a job as a stylist or as a subeditor. It makes sense, therefore, for those who know they want to work in magazines to ask themselves what it is about magazine journalism that appeals. Is it the opportunity to write features about sex for lads' magazines? Is it the chance to write about economic news with the luxury of weekly deadlines? Is it the attraction of writing scintillating headlines while surrounded by fashionable young creatures dressed in exotic clothes? Is it the prospect of heading towards mainstream news journalism, using the specialist press as a training ground? Is it the desire to write about a specific field which is covered properly only by magazines?

The answers to these questions will help an aspiring magazine journalist to focus on the kind of work to which he is most suited. For instance, a newshound who wanted to work on *The Economist* would be well advised, if unable to get a traineeship there straight away, to try for one of the national or international news agencies or else get into financial journalism, perhaps through financial newsletters or the business-to-business press. Someone who wants to write general consumer features needs to consider whether she is suited to life as a freelance because so much of the copy that glossy consumer publications use comes from out of house. And if that is her ultimate aim it might make sense to take a first job as a sub or an editorial assistant as a way of making contacts and learning from the inside about how such magazines work.

Career patterns

What should be clear is that a career in magazine journalism means a varied set of possibilities. For many journalists in the twenty-first century a career almost certainly will not be confined to one medium. Journalists move far more freely now between the media than once they did. Reporters and subeditors may be poached from *The Big Issue* or the *London Review of Books* by *The Guardian*, or from *The Big Issue* move to the German edition of *Sugar*. Charles Moore, editor of *The Sunday Telegraph*, worked on

The Spectator magazine first. Tina Brown, former editor of *Tatler*, and launch editor, in 1999, of the US magazine *Talk*, began her career writing for *The Sunday Times*. Julie Burchill, who started out on *NME*, moved from there to *The Face*, has also been a columnist for the *Mail on Sunday*, *The Sunday Times* and *The Guardian*, as well as founding and folding a magazine, the *Modern Review*, along the way.

There is also now the real possibility of travelling to other countries to work on local publications. There has been a British invasion of American journalism in recent years. As more companies expand their operations abroad, more opportunities for moving to other countries on behalf of UK publishers exist. And on the subject of location, aspiring journalists should note that although London is the centre of the UK magazine publishing industry there are other places such as Manchester, Glasgow, Edinburgh and Dundee with thriving magazine publishers: *Future*, the UK's fourth largest consumer magazine publisher, is based in Bath.

This means that journalists should be ready to seize opportunities wherever they present themselves. As John McKie, editor of *Smash Hits*, said: 'I got my dream job on a music magazine by casting the net wide, writing news and features and whatever else came up.' For others seizing opportunities might mean that if you work for *OK!* you could slide into television as the magazine launches a broadcast spin-off. While if you work for *The Clothes Show* at the BBC you could slip into magazine journalism through the magazine of the same name. And that's without looking at the potential for online or electronic journalism as outlined in Chapter 12.

John McKie, Editor of *Smash Hits*

There aren't many journalists who get to do their dream job but John McKie, editor of pop music magazine *Smash Hits* since December 1998, is that lucky.

Perhaps it's not fair to talk of luck, although he does. His achievement is the result of hard work, determination and an obsession with music that he's had for as long as he can remember. 'I grew up with *Smash Hits*, *Q*, *Select*, *NME*, *Melody Maker*. I read all the pop magazines,' he says. But although his older brother always wanted to be a journalist (and now is), schoolboy John had no thoughts of a career. 'When I was a kid I didn't know what I wanted to do. It was at university that I started to get a passion for journalism.' He wrote regularly for the *Glasgow University Guardian* and to no one's surprise became music editor.

From Glasgow he studied journalism at Strathclyde University where he wrote about pop when he could but also learnt to write news and features as well as picking up the essentials of law, government and production. Armed with his diploma he started to do shifts for the Scottish *Sun* and then the freelance jobs 'just came up'.

McKie also wrote and printed in full colour a glossy magazine which he called *CV*. It contained interviews with celebrities he had not published before, including ones with Marti Pellow, Harriet Harman and Jeremy Paxman. He sent the 350 copies to newspaper editors, magazine editors and section editors, particularly hoping, he says, 'that a magazine editor would pick up on it'. It helped to land him a job with the *Mail on Sunday*, first as a features writer and after a few months on the news desk, working at the hard end of Sunday tabloid journalism.

'You've got to be really tough to do that kind of hard news,' he says recalling the journalist friend who got beaten up and his own experiences of being threatened. 'I don't know if I'd want to do it again. At the time it was a challenge. I was keen to get on and I got to work on big stories.'

A stint at *The Independent* then back to the game of freelance, this time with regular shifts on the *Standard*'s Londoner's Diary. 'My aim was to do it for about six months. A diary job is a good way to get contacts and meet people,' McKie says. He did plenty of freelance work for other pages of the *Standard* and for many Scottish and English newspapers.

Just when he'd begun to think his career could do with a change of gear (and just when a 'horrific tax demand' began to loom) McKie saw the advert in *The Guardian* for his present job. His reaction was 'that would just be the best fun of all jobs. I wasn't particularly confident of getting it but I thought, I'm nearly 27 and I need to go for it now or I'll be too old.'

Emap Metro obviously thought he was young enough to do the job and he joined almost immediately. That was in November 1998. There was a handover period for his first few weeks when the acting editor put the magazine together but after that he was in charge. Not only had he never worked for a magazine before, he'd never been the editor.

'Every day I get surprised by the job, by how tough it is. You grow into it though,' says McKie. He compares his job to that of a football referee: 'That old thing about the ref having to take 500 decisions in 90 minutes. I take decisions all day long.' What he's deciding about is design, layout, pictures, stories, ideas, who gets the record company freebies, how to fix up deals with artists or wholesalers or TV programmes. He's also got to manage a team of people – which means earning the respect of those already there, recruiting new staff, nurturing talent, coping with egos or just making sure everyone gets along together.

Some people who become editors, McKie says, soon discover that they really want to be writers after all. Not him. 'I decided I really want to make a go of it.' That means he has to take on the business aspects of magazine publishing too. 'Support from the publisher is vital,' he says. So too is careful study of the competition. (The main rivals to *Smash Hits* for its readers in the 8- to 14-year-old age range are *TVHits* and *Top of the Pops*, which, as McKie says, are better than they've ever been and even the smaller competitors like *Big!* and *Live and Kicking* are getting stronger.)

So McKie now has to think about circulation figures and marketing and branding and websites. 'We are a famous brand so all eyes are on us. I have to court the industry assiduously.' The lighter side of this (and one of the best parts of the job for McKie) is getting to meet the popstars and to see them getting on to the front cover of *Smash Hits* for the first time. It also explains why he has to be involved in so many day-to-day decisions. 'Dealing with the record industry, tying in maybe a gift idea with the editorial and the cover. The editor's authority is needed for a lot of the deals we do,' McKie says.

The drawbacks of the job are that there's no time for a social life outside work. He's in the office from 9.30 till nine or ten every night and otherwise is out at record industry events. 'You need massive energy levels for this job,' he says, 'and you also need a thick skin. You have to be able to ignore the music industry slagging you off behind your back. You have to be tenacious about what you're doing and not panic if the circulation figures aren't soaring.'

Apart from going to parties where he'll meet the Spice Girls and getting popstars to make funny faces during photoshoots, the very best part of McKie's job is 'hearing a record that you know is going to be huge months before it's released'.

He also loves 'putting pages together, coming up with ideas like a Steps karaoke track on a CD cover-mount, thinking up silly jokes and funny cover lines, writing the Editor's letter'.

Sometimes he even gets to write a story. 'I try to write features if there's time. Sometimes I have to. I'm the only one in the office with shorthand.'

Who does what?

There are some job titles on mastheads which may need explaining. What is the difference, for example, between an editor and a managing editor? Each magazine will have its own system but a common one is to have an editor who is the creative whizz-kid behind a title: she's good at ideas, at dealing with people, possibly at writing and probably at editing copy; she's also good at being the public face of the magazine. Behind many such a charismatic editor is a thoroughly well-organised managing editor who does not feature so much in the limelight but who is there to make sure the magazine comes out on time and is run as smoothly as possible. Deputy and assistant editors share some or all of the tasks of the editor and in some cases will take responsibility for a particular section of the magazine: at *Marie Claire* there is an assistant editor for features and another for production. A contributing editor is probably not on the staff but is a regular freelance. A features editor or commissioning editor will, on some publications, write but more often will be responsible for coming up with story ideas and matching them to writers. They are also the people to whom freelances would pitch suggestions. News and feature writers will do exactly as you'd guess. Some magazine job titles use the word director rather than editor as a mark of seniority if there is a big team. So on *Harpers and Queen* the fashion director will be senior to the fashion editor who is senior, in turn, to the fashion assistants.

Fashion and beauty

Fashion editors and directors or their equivalent in beauty or even in a home and interiors department will not necessarily do any writing. They get their jobs because of their knowledge of fashion or make-up or furnishings. Some can and some can't write well but for most magazines the only writing required from those departments is the work of the subs in producing headlines, captions and standfirsts, usually written in consultation with the stylists who will explain what the 'story' is behind a series of photographs. Even *Vogue*, which is a kind of reference magazine for the fashion industry, offers almost no analytical writing about its main subject.

What these staffers do is research the themes and merchandise they want to promote in their pages. Research can mean anything from attendance at the seasonal clothes shows in the fashion capitals of the world, to visiting a fabric trade show in Milan, to being bought lunch by a make-up company PR executive, to trailing round stores looking at china or shoes, to talking to specialist location researchers for suggestions about where to shoot. The fruits of the research are crystallised into a 'story' idea. These stories may be more or less comprehensible (sometimes more or less offensive – heroin chic for example) but they provide a loose theme around which everyone involved (fashion team, art director, photographer, stylists, writers) can think imaginatively. The merchandise then has to be called in through the relevant press offices and models, hairdressers, make-up artists, photographers, studios, set-builders, airline tickets, hotels and so on have to be co-ordinated and booked. Once the pictures are done and the layouts designed the fashion, beauty or home staff might write the captions. Otherwise they would be responsible only for giving the subs full information about which products are included in the photographs. Publications which take this function most seriously may have a merchandising editor whose life is spent on the phone to press offices and shops checking price, size, colour and availability of the goods which feature on the editorial pages.

Travel

Some of the most envied journalists are those who carry the title of travel editor. Research for their pages may involve a few tedious press lunches but in the end you can't write about exotic holidays unless you go on them and that's what makes these people so envied. If they have a lot of pages to fill they will almost certainly have to do some commissioning and editing of copy as well, but it's not as if freelance journalists are likely to quibble at the prospect of a free holiday for four in Greece at the expense of the travel company, so commissioning here is not as stressful as trying to brief a news feature writer to travel to Scunthorpe to investigate the abuse of residents in council-run old people's homes.

Other roles

An editorial assistant may be a trainee who is learning how to do a variety of journalistic tasks or in some cases it may mean being, effectively, a secretary who can be trusted to undertake editorial tasks such as research or keying in copy.

Many magazines have agony aunts or uncles or even advisers on other kinds of topics who will answer readers' questions in print. These are, more often than not, freelance contributors from outside the staff although some of the higher circulation women's magazines do employ whole teams to deal with the agony aunt's correspondence.

At least one women's magazine, *Good Housekeeping*, has a long-established and well-regarded product and food testing department, which is devoted to doing just that. Staff here are likely to be home economists and in general, where food writing is concerned, the stylists and the cooks are freelances who work for a variety of companies both journalistic and commercial.

For other publications, whether in the trade or consumer press, the job titles are self explanatory. The crucial point to remember is that the smaller the magazine the more blurred is likely to be the boundary between tasks performed by different members of staff. On some magazines everyone may take a turn at subbing, proofing, commissioning or writing.

The publisher is another key job which journalists tend not to know much about. The publisher is responsible for the finance and the strategic planning which support the publication of a magazine. Although publishers are often drawn from the ranks of advertising and marketing staff there are notable exceptions such as Nicholas Coleridge at Condé Nast, Alan Lewis at IPC and Ian Birch at Emap. And, of course, publishers are sometimes journalists who have decided to set up their own companies of which they remain proprietors. Robin Hodge of *The List* is one (see page 207).

Also significant is that much of the writing on all kinds of magazines is done by freelance contributors. *The Spectator* has a small staff and commissions most of the material for any issue from among a team of regular columnists, commentators and reviewers. *The Condé Nast Traveller* commissions celebrities as well as journalists to review hotels and travel services.

One obvious problem, then, is that it is hard to get a staff job as a writer. Another is that on magazines where staff numbers are at a minimum it can be hard for a new member of that staff to get any training. However much a junior journalist has learnt in advance of the first job there comes a time when the regular advice of a more experienced colleague can be invaluable. Even if no one is actually delegated to do this, it will happen naturally in a good, well-staffed office but may be forgotten where pressures of time and rivalry are too great.

News

In this discussion of magazine jobs there is not much about news. This is not because there aren't good jobs involving news to be had on magazines but because news-based magazines are more likely to function like newspaper newsrooms, even if the deadlines are further apart. Careers for general news reporters tend to follow the pattern outlined above of movement between one medium and another. More often than not, though, news in magazines is related to a specific field of interest. In the business press this may be banking or insurance, in the hobby press it may be knitting or bikes or boats. In magazines like *Chat* or *That's Life!*, which feature real-life stories of the triumph over tragedy sort, most of the features are written by journalists who either work as freelances or, perhaps more typically, work for news agencies. In this case they are employees in the ordinary way but their work is sold through the news agency to newspapers or magazines which may have commissioned it or will consider it on spec.

Other magazine publishing sectors

The discussion in this chapter so far has used consumer magazines as the model, partly because these tend to be the more widely known and partly because much of what has been said about them applies to the other magazine publishing sectors. For a full discussion of these sectors see Chapter 15. Here I want to draw attention to them because of the wide range of journalism jobs they can offer.

To take the largest of all magazine publishing sectors first, the business-to-business or trade sector. This covers many more titles than the consumer field and, in 1999 at least, was thought by publishers to be riding a huge wave of success. The titles are not all well known because they are produced for circulation groups linked by a narrower range of interests (often professional) than many consumer titles, particularly the lifestyle ones. Indeed they may have tiny circulations in which case they are more likely to be called newsletters.

From the careers point of view magazines such as *GP*, *Meat Trades Journal* and *The Banker* may look as though they'd be of interest only to journalists who really want to be doctors or butchers or bankers. Not so. Many of these magazines come from large publishing companies. When they take on a trainee reporter for one magazine she doesn't have to stay there for ever. Far from it. Careers in trade magazines can move very fast as companies who have tested out an employee on the staff are likely to look favourably on promotion or internal moves to other publications. Specialist knowledge is not usually required, although it could be an advantage. What employers look for is a willingness to learn about the field and all the basic journalism skills useful to any publisher. Once the specialist knowledge has been acquired, of course, then there is no reason why it shouldn't be used to build up a special expertise as a reporter whether for other, more general magazines (an oil industry expert joining *The Economist* for example) or for other media such as newspapers, radio or TV.

The same advantage of building up expertise can go with a job on an in-house publication such as a staff magazine. You may not want to spend your entire life writing for the staff journal of an international chemical company but a couple of years doing it could leave you with a marketable knowledge of the field. Pay and conditions on company magazines can be extremely good.

Another kind of commercial publishing that can offer excellent prospects is contract publishing. A contract publisher such as Redwood produces magazines (some regular, some one-offs) for other organisations. It has all the publishing and editorial expertise and its clients will brief them as to the kind of publication they want, whether it's an in-house annual publication, or a shopper's magazine such as those available at supermarkets or which come through the mail to storecard holders. In some ways these magazines don't carry so much kudos for the individual journalist – especially if bylines are not used – but again they can provide valuable experience. Customer magazines such as those provided on airlines can have the highest standards of writing and illustration and use the best writers and photographers to freelance for them.

Another field to consider, especially for a writer who has a mission to make the world a better place, is a non-governmental organisation or public information publication. Someone who wants to write exclusively about development economics, for example, might find a job as a writer within the publications department of a charity such as Oxfam or Christian Aid much more attractive than a typical regional or even many a national newspaper, either as a career goal in itself or as a way of building up expertise in a particular field.

Money

So far I have not said much about pay. In Chapter 4 on freelance work the point is made that most (although not all) of the journalists who make fabulous sums work as freelances and that when the money reaches dizzy heights then the lucky earners have moved beyond mere journalism into the realms of showbiz. True, some of them may still be doing journalistic work but if that's all an employer wanted he wouldn't need to pay huge sums to get someone to do it. The big-name, starry journalists earn showbiz fees and pay some of the showbiz price as far as privacy is concerned. But then there are other ways in which journalism as a career resembles one in showbusiness or even the arts.

The significance of talent

Most journalists harbour notions about a mysterious thing called talent which someone either has or does not have. Nowhere is this view more prevalent than among the old school of journalists who think their trade can't be taught. And nowhere is it more clearly expressed than in the labels that are attached to individuals such as 'She can really write' or 'He couldn't write to save himself'. Substitute 'dance' or 'sing' for 'write' and you can see why the analogy works. This also helps to explain why so many journalists, particularly young ones, seem to be waiting as if for their talent to be discovered just like that of a dancer or actor. Luck, it seems to them, plays a huge part in shaping the career of a journalist. While this is true, up to a point, of the news journalist who just happens to be in the right place when a huge news story breaks, on the whole journalists create their own chances. The lucky-number attitude prevails, I suspect, because of the huge differences which exist in pay and conditions between people who are doing the same kind of job and in a trade where merit or skill or experience do not necessarily determine who earns most or even who gets promoted. In many careers there is a clearer path to advancement (all else being equal) which does not depend so much on luck and talent but more on skills, aptitude and hard work.

Test the talent theory out by asking journalists about other journalists they admire. Ask them what in particular they admire and as often as not the answer will be vague and unmeasurable. 'He writes like a dream' – well, yes, but what does that actually mean? 'She's a great editor' – again, yes, but in what sense exactly? 'She really understands her readers', but does that make someone great or merely able to read market research reports, a competence that would be taken for granted in any other commercial setting?

Of course there are great journalists. But there are also ways in which those who work as journalists are ill-served by these notions of talent and luck. For one thing it leaves many of those at the beginning of their careers uncertain about their capabilities and therefore pathetically grateful for jobs with laughable rates of pay and lamentable conditions which are tolerated because of the lingering hope of outlandish rewards or at least a serviceable gravy train at some later point in the career. I'm happy to argue that pretty well anyone with certain qualifications, reasonable intelligence and the right skills could work effectively as a journalist if they put their mind to it and were properly trained. Is journalism really so different from the civil service, or teaching or nursing or medicine or the law or retail management or commerce? In other careers people perform with different levels of success and their performance is attributed to a variety of factors. But it is not common in these jobs to act as if all the problems at work will be sorted out when a stroke of luck occurs like a lottery win.

Absorbing the craft mysteries

Another thing which distinguishes journalism, perhaps to its detriment, is the way in which preference is given in the selection of new recruits to those who have already absorbed many of the craft mysteries of the trade by doing unpaid work experience. Some work experience is definitely a good idea but you don't have to be sceptical to see that one effect of the emphasis placed by editors on work experience and on something as unmeasurable as talent is to absolve themselves of responsibility for some aspects of effective training. The risk is that certain of those craft mysteries are perpetuated beyond their useful life as they are handed on, without much question, from one generation to the next. This, I suspect, is why there was initially so much resistance to the teaching of journalism in universities from those journalists (particularly in newspapers) who did not like the idea of journalism being taught in an atmosphere of intelligent inquiry, in case the questioning undermined some of their most cherished beliefs and habits.

Recommended reading

Armstrong, L. (1998) *Front Row.*

Burchill, J. (1992) 'Nature, nurture or Nietzsche?' in *Sex and Sensibility.*

Morrish, J. (1996) *Magazine Editing.*

Periodicals Training Council (1998) *A Career in Magazines.*

Southwell, T. (1998) *Getting Away With It. The Inside Story of Loaded.*

Thurber, J. (1984) *The Years With Ross.*

Tomalin, N. (1969) 'Stop the press I want to get on'.

4 Freelance journalism

I hear from your uncle that you want to be a writer. Good. But don't expect to become a millionaire in a day. Remember that the world is not waiting to read your stuff, whatever it may be. People have better things to do. But you must work hard and by sheer persistence, draw their attention to yourself – which means write, write, and write.

R. K. Narayan, *My Days: A Memoir*

There can't be many journalists who never wonder if they would be better off as freelances than working in their regular jobs. The appeal is obvious, and freedom is the most important part of it: freedom to choose your own hours, freedom to work on stories that interest you, freedom to work with people you respect. No more rigid office hours. It sounds good but, of course, it isn't quite like that.

There are people who make a good living as freelances and almost any journalist who makes a spectacularly good living will be freelance even if that means being hired by the season rather than to do individual stories. However, the life of most freelances is not all rosy when compared with that of other journalists. Experienced former staff journalists often report their shock at discovering they have to work 24 hours a day at first to make ends meet. Whether someone can make a go of it comes down to ability, of course, as well as temperament, health and domestic circumstances.

Leaving aside ability for a moment, the significance of temperament is that if you work entirely freelance you have to enjoy lack of routine and to revel in uncertainty: not just at the level of not knowing what story the news editor will allocate today but at the level of not knowing whether you will earn anything in the next month. Then there's health. Freelances can't readily afford to turn down work, at least at the beginning of their careers and so should, ideally, be in the pink of health. Employees can make up for regular bouts of chest infection or migraine by catching up when they return to work but the freelance is vulnerable to the natural preferences of commissioning editors for freelance staff to be available on demand. Lastly there are domestic circumstances by which I really mean dependants and financial commitments: far easier to take the plunge as a freelance if you have no children and no mortgage.

Starting out

Getting established as a freelance is far harder for those new to journalism than it is for those with experience. All the advice from old hands is that if you want to be freelance it is much easier when you have a range of contacts both as potential commissioners on magazines and as potential sources of stories. This is understandable. From a commissioning editor's point of view an experienced journalist can be depended upon to produce copy to professional standards. Someone unknown (even someone with experience but who is not known to the editor) does not bring that guarantee until several pieces have been written. References or introductions can help, so if you are starting from scratch make shameless use of successful journalists you know. Ask if you can mention their names when making an initial approach to an editor to pitch an idea. Do this, however, only when you are sure you can produce publishable work.

Some novice journalists want to be freelance for the reasons outlined above or because they want to live in a particular place far away from the hub of the magazine publishing industry or even because they want to write about a subject in which they have a developed interest. This last reason is the one most likely to lead to success. The world is short of science journalists, for example, so a new journalist who has training behind him might find it relatively easy to break into the freelance market by virtue of that training combined with the specialist knowledge. The same may be said of numerate graduates, or better still those who train as journalists after working in a different field. Teaching or accountancy are the most common and this experience combined with journalism training can lead quickly to good freelance careers writing about education and money.

Otherwise the difficulty for beginners is how to convince editors to take their work and, at least initially, they may have to pitch ideas on the understanding that the editor will have a look at the finished piece with no obligation to buy. If copy is competently written for the target market an editor may be willing to offer a proper commission another time. If the copy is used a freelance fee should be paid even if the editor did not commission it. Young journalists are often so desperate to get cuttings that they accept much lower fees than the National Union of Journalists agreed rates or even no fee at all. Yet if a publication uses copy it is because the copy is of publishable standard and so there should be no reduced fee just because the writer is not yet fully established in a career.

In the case of a novice the issue of a kill-fee is more complicated. If an established journalist is commissioned to write a piece which is not used, perhaps for reasons of space, the normal practice is for what's known as a kill-fee to be paid. How much this is will depend on the circumstances and whatever was negotiated at the time of commissioning but half of the agreed fee would be normal, assuming the writer had some chance of selling the material elsewhere. If the piece is unlikely to be usable elsewhere perhaps because of timing or because the writer has an exclusive contract with one publication, then it is reasonable for the kill-fee to represent the full fee, as the work put in by the writer is the same whether or not the paper uses it. A grey area here might be if the copy was simply not good enough to be published and in these circumstances an editor might feel justified in refusing to pay.

Kill-fees are not, however, paid when a piece has not been commissioned by an editor who has merely agreed to look at copy to see whether it might be publishable. This does not count as a commission. If beginners whose copy turns out not to be usable can nevertheless get some comments on their work from the commissioning editor then they will have gained something from the experience. Most editors have no time to give this kind of help and may not even have the courtesy to let writers know what has happened to their copy, let alone advise about how to improve it. Fair enough in a way. That's not what they're paid to do.

The commissioning editor

What a commissioning editor is paid to do is to seek out lively copy from interesting writers. Many features editors say that one of the most difficult parts of their job is maintaining a steady flow of exciting ideas with which to fill their pages. The puzzle is then why so many of them are not more receptive to ideas when freelances pitch them. Not only are many of them unreceptive, some are actively hostile, some are even rude and discourteous. Even well-established freelances, not just the unknown newcomers, find this a puzzle. From an editor's point of view the problem may be that they are sent more unsolicited, unprofessional stories written speculatively than anyone could possibly be expected to deal with politely. (Although there may be the odd gem that slips by. Just because a writer is not a professional journalist does not mean his ideas are useless or his writing no good.) However, when ideas are professionally presented, even by newcomers, there seems to me no good reason for the writer not to be treated with the basic courtesy of a reply, even if it is only a standard letter. What so many freelances experience, until they are well known and valued by a particular features editor, is no spontaneous reply at all, then curtness or evasion when they try to elicit a response.

What this reflects is the curiously unprofessional way in which many publishers behave in relation to freelances. They expect professional, publishable standards of work but the majority of their transactions with freelances are undertaken without written contracts in advance and with little guarantee of anything for the journalists. There may be understandable historical reasons for this but the effect is that freelances other than those at the top, suffer greatly from the insecurity of not knowing whether or how their work will be used. In many cases there is a sense that the journalist is lucky to have her work published, that it is somehow an honour rather than a business transaction for the copy to be included in a magazine. This may be true for the student journalist placing her first or second piece but after that the feeling of gratitude should pass. Publishers are always quick to point out that they run businesses not charitable foundations, and so it is not unreasonable for journalists to expect to be treated as valued producers of the product which publishers make their money by selling.

There are some signs of change however. Recent debates about copyright have brought the subject of contracts to the fore. The NUJ now encourages its members to get written contracts before they undertake a freelance commission, even if the journalist has to write the contract out and fax or e-mail it to the editor as a record of the commissioning conversation. It's also likely that current moves towards making journalism more like a profession by standardising training will help to establish a more formal approach to the treatment of freelances.

Personal safety

A related issue about professional practice is that of safety. Here too it is common for both employers of freelances and the freelances themselves to have an almost amateurish approach to personal safety while working on a story and to the insurance implications if anything should go wrong. It goes without saying that journalists may have accidents or be attacked while working whether or not they are covering wars or riots. Even those who set out to cover wars have been known to think they are adequately covered by travel insurance (if they have thought of insurance at all!). They are not. Some organisations do now have rigorous health and safety policies which would include appropriate insurance, as well as training in risk avoidance and in first aid. But these requirements don't always cover freelances who are in any case likely to be more vulnerable as they won't necessarily have the back-up of an office team knowing where they are meant to be when. Journalists are beginning to take these issues more seriously although the macho image of the newshound has perhaps hindered progress. Advice is available from the NUJ and the Brussels-based International Federation of Journalists.

Making a living

At the top level, freelances can be extremely well treated. Some command high fees and for the London-based national magazines and newspaper supplements there can be lucrative contracts. Journalists who are in a position to command a fair deal from a good editor don't really have a lot to worry about. Except, that is, for the worry of falling out of fashion. Life on a magazine or a newspaper can be very like life in a traditional royal court. Rulers come and go and along with them come and go their favourites. The features freelance or fashion stylist who is favoured by one editor may fall from grace and find a regular contract coming swiftly to an end when that editor moves on. It follows that a freelance should ideally build up a number of regular commissioning contacts so that if one editor leaves, the writer is not left without work.

Even when a piece has been used and there is a written or verbal agreement about how much is to be paid, writers can find it difficult to get at the money. This delaying of payment is perhaps less unusual as a business practice than the lack of contracts but for the freelance who is trying to survive on modest fees it can make life intolerable to have to waste time chasing up uncontentious payments. There never seems to be a good reason. When freelances phone up to chase their fee the editorial department always blames accounts and, guess what, the accounts department always blames editorial. The loser is always the writer. Why should it take three months for an agreed fee of £150 to be sent to a writer by a highly profitable publishing company?

The other point about income is that unless writers enter the showbiz league they are not likely to be paid well. Certainly over a period of ten years or so the fees that can be expected hardly seem to have risen at all at the lower end of the range and this impression is borne out by Sally Beck who says 'A major complaint is money – the lack of and the lateness of it. Rates have been virtually static for the past five years. IPC's have dropped. Payments can take up to 12 months' (Beck 1999). At the higher end journalists tend, understandably, to be unwilling to talk about what they earn but I suspect that at the very highest end of the range fees have risen substantially in the same period. The best way to find out what it is reasonable to expect for a particular commission is through the NUJ's freelance branch. Members receive a guide to the various rates currently agreed with the various publishers.

None of this is meant to discourage young journalists from being freelance, merely to prepare them for some of the realities of this existence. The fact that pay is not high on individual publications makes it the more important for journalists to ensure that they use the fruits of one piece of research as widely as possible, targeted at different readers. Assume, for a moment, that you sell an article to a trade magazine about the fishing industry. In the course of your research you get to know quite a bit about the life of a fisherman and discover (hypothetically of course) that (a) they earn huge sums and (b) they spend a lot on cars and on drugs. Scope here for a straight news feature on the drugs angle, a motoring feature perhaps on the type of cars they like to buy, a woman's magazine article if you discovered that women are now going to sea along with their menfolk. The possibilities are, in fact, endless, and are discussed further in Chapter 8.

Freelancing on the side

So far it may sound as if working freelance is a choice willingly made by journalists but of course that's not always the case. For many journalists in staff jobs freelance work is their bit on the side, the bit which makes the difference between a living wage and an unrealistic one if they happen to work on weekly provincial newspapers. A problem can arise if the day job demands total commitment. Some papers, for example, forbid their reporters to work for anyone else even when the work they want to do overlaps in no way with their full-time job.

Other employers accept that their employees will work freelance elsewhere in their own time if there is no conflict of interest with what they are already contracted to do. Indeed for many journalists this is the established route to promotion or at least better pay. Working casual shifts or taking on freelance commissions in order to get a foot in the door of another editorial office is a normal strategy in a career where jobs are rarely advertised and usually filled by those whose work is already known to the editor.

Shifts are important. If a writer or subeditor does the kind of work that is measured in shifts then so long as they turn up for their shifts, most of what they do as casuals for other employers outside couldn't reasonably be seen as detrimental to their main job. There is a problem, however, with the kind of job where an employee is hired to be more than a presence performing a particular task. A valued fashion staffer, for example, brings contacts, experience and creativity to the magazine which it would not be acceptable for her to share with a rival while she remains on the staff.

What sometimes happens though is that even such staffers can take on freelance work which is not necessarily related to journalism or not to the same kind of journalism. The magazine sent to customers of the Standard Life insurance company contains articles by several well-known newspaper financial journalists whose home papers would not want to see them writing for other newspapers but presumably don't object to seeing them write for a customer magazine. (Other publishers would, of course, object to this and it certainly raises eyebrows among discerning readers who like to think that reporters are not beholden to outside commercial interests.) Some writers too work for other media with the blessing of their main employer. The magazine financial journalist who is invited to participate in radio or television discussions, for example, is regarded as drawing welcome attention to his publication by virtue of the expertise he is being asked to share. Or to take an example in the other direction. Maggie O'Kane, *The Guardian*'s highly acclaimed news reporter, wrote a piece for *Red* about what it was like to leave her young baby for the first time when she went back to work to cover the war in Afghanistan. The other variation on this theme is for writers to take on freelance commissions from completely different sorts of organisations: writing speeches for politicians perhaps, or copy for publicity material or books.

Freelance by necessity

Those freelances working to supplement their income could be said to be willing. Less willing are the journalists who are freelance of necessity because they don't have a regular full-time job. These may be recent graduates who are searching for a post and who are well advised to think of themselves (and set themselves up) as freelances from the minute they leave college until they find a job. Some of them will then find that they can survive successfully and stop the hunt for a job. Some just use the cuttings they acquire as freelances to help them into that first job. But there are also those who lose their jobs at the midpoint or later in their careers and have to set up as freelances because journalism is what they know how to do best. Often this proves to be a way of bridging the time before a new job is found, but again, as with the college-leavers, there are those who find they enjoy the freelance life and can earn enough to live on. These latter freelances have all the advantages when it comes to attracting good commissions because they have the contacts, the experience, the cuttings and the inside knowledge of how magazines work to be able to approach editors with confidence.

Casual subbing

So far I've talked about freelancing as if it were just writers who do it but in fact most of the editorial functions, except the most senior, those that set the tone of the magazine, can be performed by freelances. Writers are usually commissioned on the basis of individual articles, or series of articles or columns, whereas subs will be hired by the day. Indeed they have to be. Unlike writers, subs are needed in the office at specified times and so if one of the staffers is ill or on holiday it is likely that a freelance will be brought in, perhaps at short notice. Most chief subs will have a list of regular casual subs on whom they can call during busy periods and most, too, will be willing to try out new ones in order to keep their list up to date. This can be a good way to break into subbing or into a particular magazine although it's not necessarily a sure route to a writing job. Many magazine editors, while entrusting subs with the most precious of copy to edit, will nevertheless ignore the possibility that their subs could write material of equivalent standard themselves. Ultimately, whether freelance subbing can lead to commissions for writing depends on the publication and the writer. That's not a problem for subeditors who like subbing and don't indulge in daydreams about writing glory.

Paying tax

One problem for casual subs is the way they get paid. They are hired by time rather than by piece of work and this very roughly means that the Inland Revenue likes to see tax deducted by the employer, even where the sub is working for a range of different employers and is, therefore, genuinely freelance, not someone masquerading as freelance in order to benefit from more generous tax allowances. In practice this is a problem only if a sub doesn't realise it in advance and expects to be paid in full, saving up for a schedule D, self-employed tax bill to be paid at the end of the year.

Tax is a vexing topic for all freelance journalists because it is so easy to forget how much money is likely to be needed to pay that tax bill when it arrives. The temptation is there, too, to delve into whatever funds have been put aside for the taxman to tide the journalist over a bad couple of months. The advice most experienced freelances offer is to get an accountant as soon as is practical, which means as soon as you earn enough, from all sources, to interest the tax man, £4,385 in April 2000. Accountants can advise about the demands the Inland Revenue is likely to make and about whether it's necessary to register for VAT. They will advise about national insurance and how to prepare for retirement or sickness, parenthood or holidays. If you're self-employed you don't have the comfort of an employer in whose interest it is, or at least whose duty it is, to look after you.

Another advantage is that if you have a phobia about brown envelopes filled with instructions about tax, you don't even have to open them. You can just send them on to your accountant and wait for the information to reach you in a more palatable, more constructive tone. Accountants know what it is acceptable to claim in the way of allowances. They know, for example, that you may set against tax a drink bought for a commissioning editor from abroad but not one from the UK. They may even be able to explain the logic of this. They know too that certain expenses can count as legitimate business expenditure – a computer, perhaps, or a proportion of the telephone bill. And they are used to filling in all those forms so they do it without getting into an emotional state (helped of course by the fact that it's not their own money they are signing away). Lastly, what many people don't know until they hire their first accountant is that the fee for the accountant can be set against tax, making the arrangement an even better investment.

Organising your work

For young journalists this talk of pensions and accountants may seem premature but if they are going to attempt to live by freelance work then these are serious professional considerations. Some students approach freelance work in a dilettante fashion, thinking they will just do a bit of work here and there and see how it goes. Those are the ones who give up soonest and resort to staff jobs. The successful beginner journalists who make it as freelances tend to be those who are deadly serious in their intentions. From day one they are at their desks at 9a.m., on the phone pitching ideas, writing, building contacts and so on, generally behaving like any other person who is determined to succeed in a self-employed enterprise. They buy the best equipment they can afford and once the work starts to come in they are well advised to be methodical in their office habits. Records of correspondence, invoices, expenditure, ideas and cuttings should all be kept tidily so that the process of chasing up payments can be as painless as possible. And like any other journalist they should file all the versions of their stories and their notes, whether taped or written, so that legal problems can be sorted out swiftly.

However well-intentioned new freelances are things can go wrong. To begin with most feel that the problem is going to be finding enough work, not having too much to do. They accept everything that comes their way, knowing that reluctance on their part is unlikely to be rewarded with a second offer. This means, of course, that far from avoiding the unattractive jobs they may have to take them on, these being the ones that may be offered to freelances because no one on the staff wants to do them. It is difficult to get the balance right, especially at first. As the work pours in a freelance can find herself taking on far more than is reasonable because she is aware that next month there may be nothing at all on offer. Forward planning is difficult and the stress level can be high, especially for those who find they are not brave enough to take a break either at weekends or even for a holiday.

Another besetting difficulty with the freelance life is that if you work on features which require a lot of research, the amount of time spent is most unlikely to be reflected in the fee you earn. Two hundred pounds may be OK for an opinion piece that you hammer out in a couple of hours once a week but reporting is more demanding than that. It takes hours of trouble – tracking down interviewees for example, visits to get eyewitness evidence, research in libraries or on the Internet, and so on. All of this takes time. Staffers will say that they don't get enough time allocated to do proper research either and it is true that productivity rates, if measured by output of words, have risen in the past two decades to the detriment, many would argue, of serious investigative reporting or even competent thorough reporting, both of which suffer when reporters are rushed too much. So staffers have a point, but how much more keenly are these pressures felt by freelances who are merely selling a finished product, with little account taken of the amount of time their product will take to create.

There is another myth about freelancing – that freelancing particularly suits women who want to combine a career with bringing up a family. The problems with this proposition start before the first child is born. No maternity leave for the freelance. Then there is the uncertainty of income. Fine to be freelance if you are attached to someone who earns a regular sum. More difficult if both parents are freelance and not at an advanced stage in their careers. This is where temperament comes in. More clearly a problem for all is the notion that a freelance writer can just potter about doing bits of journalism between bathing the baby, cooking meals and supervising homework. Some miracle-workers can and it depends a bit on what kind of freelance work you are trying to fit in. The reality for most working parents is that a full-time job, or at least a part-time staff job, is more practical because if there is a regular income then arrangements about childcare are easier to make. Childcare is expensive and it usually has to be regular (childminders, nannies and nurseries all have their financial commitments too and want a regular not a sporadic income). Clearly this is a point that won't affect all journalists but young women journalists are so often told they will be able to do a bit of freelance when they have children that it is worth noting the difficulties.

Pitching ideas

Turning now to some of the practicalities of doing the work itself. For the sake of the discussion here we'll assume that a new freelance is used to producing work of a professional standard as it's a bad idea to offer work before you are ready to sell it on equal terms with established journalists. The main exception to this would be where you have some inside knowledge – about what really goes on in student union bars would be one example, or about trout-fishing, if that's your obsession. Another possible exception would be if a journalist had seen some of your work and suggested you submit it on the off-chance that it might be acceptable.

Assuming the work is of sufficient standard your first task is to come up with suitable ideas that you can pitch. Suitable applies in various ways. The proposal must be one that you could reasonably tackle with your experience and contacts and, unless you are already well known to the editor, one that is not going to cost the magazine a fortune in expenses. Yes, it might be interesting to talk to Cubans about the cigar trade in the light of the Clinton sex scandal but few features editors would have the budget to send anyone, let alone an untried freelance, to Cuba to have the conversations. So the ideas must be suitable for you but they must also be suitable for the magazine for which you are aiming to write. As Chapter 16 shows, one of the most significant things about magazines is the way many of them are so tightly targeted at groups of readers. They have their niches, and the successful freelance knows how to write copy which is appropriate for them.

Choosing your subject

This brings us to subject matter. If a freelance has an unusual hobby or interest she should capitalise on it by trying to write about it for the relevant magazines. Many publications depend on freelances to contribute copy, some on a regular basis. This is not a bad way for a journalist to start selling freelance work. Even if you don't want to spend your whole career writing about horses, the fact that there are several magazines devoted to the leisure riding market means that all those years you spent hanging around the local riding school could be put to profitable use at the start of your career. The more unusual your interests the more use this approach is likely to be. Football and pop music, by contrast, are much less help because so many journalists want to write about these subjects. Some will get to do it but the competition is fiercer than it would be for, say, the writer with a first degree in biochemistry who wanted to sell stories about health issues.

What the freelance writer must do then is study the publications she wants to write for, whether or not they reflect any particular interest of her own. It's not a bad idea to start with a magazine that you especially enjoy reading because then, as a typical reader, you can develop ideas based on what it is you yourself would like to read. This may be impractical if your favourite reading is *The New Yorker* or *Vanity Fair*, but if you have wide reading habits (and you should have) then there ought to be some publications you see regularly for which you feel you could write well enough to chance a proposal.

Presenting your idea

The question of coming up with ideas and developing them is covered in the next chapter. For now we'll assume you have worked up some good, relevant ideas and want to know what to do with them. The first question is whether to phone or write with the ideas. The answer is that it depends on the preferences of the commissioning editor and you won't necessarily be able to find those out in advance, although you could try ringing a secretary to ask. If I were a features editor I would always prefer a written outline of the ideas, whether sent by fax, post or e-mail. Two main reasons. First, busy people are elusive to telephone callers and if you do reach them they may be too distracted by other things to want to hear an unsolicited sales pitch from an unknown freelance. Second, it's much easier for the editor to absorb an idea at a glance if it is on paper and at the same time get a good idea of whether the freelance can write and present copy properly. From the freelance's point of view it is vital that the pitch is made as efficiently as possible and that may be easier to achieve without missing out vital points if it is sent as a carefully crafted, concise paragraph rather than recounted hurriedly on the phone.

If you are determined to phone (and time pressures may mean that is the only practical way) think about what is likely to be a good time to find the commissioning editor in a receptive mood. Avoid the busiest days before the magazine goes to press, information you can find out by phoning a more junior person than the commissioning editor. Also, unless you are exceptionally fluent, have notes in front of you to guide you through what you want to say.

If you send written ideas there are some basic rules. Make sure that the presentation and writing are immaculate. You could get away with the odd typographical error if the editor knew your work well enough to realise this represented an unusual slip rather than a slapdash approach to all your work but if you are unknown then any evidence of inattention to detail will count against you. A common fault among freelances, especially new ones, is to treat the outline of ideas much more casually than they would any writing they do for publication. This is a mistake as the letter is a sample of your work and will be treated as such by whoever reads it. So the same care is needed for both kinds of writing. A writer who is new to the publication should send a short covering letter to explain who they are, why they'd like to write for the magazine and what their experience is.

A second common mistake is to write too much. A good features idea should be capable of summary in one paragraph. If an idea is to look professional it ought to say why the writer thinks it is suitable for the target market and make clear what the angle is. It's not enough to say 'I'd like to write an article about sunbathing.' That's a topic not an idea for a feature. Better to find an angle. 'In the decade or so since doctors began to link sunbathing with skin cancer cases of the disease have risen dramatically. Why is this and are there many people who have stopped sunbathing as a result of the warnings?' That's more like an idea that could be developed into a feature. The initial idea should be kept short and simple and should include some information about how the piece would be researched, who you would interview, what other sources you would use. It should also show that you have some ideas about how the piece could be illustrated such as what could make a good photograph or where relevant library pictures are held. Your picture ideas may not be practical but will nevertheless show that you are thinking about the journalism as a professional writer should. Many features editors advise sending in two or three ideas at once, if each one is kept brief. This can give an editor an indication of the range of your ideas which might work in your favour: even if the current ideas are not wanted it may be obvious from the spread of proposals that you are thinking along the right lines for her publication and she may be inclined to look favourably at your other suggestions.

Beginner journalists are often worried about having their ideas stolen by commissioning editors to whom they offer stories. This certainly does happen and not just to novices although sometimes there is a genuine misunderstanding: an idea may have already been commissioned from someone else, which an outside freelance would not know. Given that journalists are trained to recognise stories and develop them in particular ways it is not at all surprising that more than one of them will produce the same idea for the same publication at around the same time. However, there is no copyright in ideas and so a features editor who is slightly less than scrupulous, faced with a great outline idea from an unknown freelance, just might turn it down and quietly ask a more experienced writer to tackle it. There is no obvious way to stop this happening although it is worth making clear to the editor that you've noticed and if it happens more than once to look elsewhere to sell your work. The most encouraging point to be made when this happens is that if your proposals are being lifted by commissioning editors it does at least mean your ideas are right for that publication. A slightly joky letter to that effect might produce a commission. Some editors are prepared to pay for an idea even if they then ask their own writers to develop it.

What you have to do next is wait, although probably not for too long, certainly no more than a week. If your letter has passed across the features editor's desk it has either been rejected or is waiting for a decision. That decision may never come if you don't take steps to have the letter extricated from the bottom of the pending tray and relocated at the top. You have to tread the delicate line between being a nuisance and being a seasoned professional trying to get a decision. Many young journalists err on the side of timidity, forgetting that commissioning editors are tough and entirely used to people phoning up to complain, whinge, make demands or simply to exercise their egos. You have every right to offer a piece to an editor (unless you've been asked not to submit any more) just as she has every right to refuse it without explanation. But you are a professional not someone looking for a favour so if your work is not wanted by the first magazine you'll be keen to try to sell it, perhaps in modified form, somewhere else.

One dilemma for freelances is whether to have their ideas out for consideration in different editorial offices at the same time. Where there is a tight deadline for the relevance of the piece this may be essential but it is probably best to be frank with the editors that this is the case. What you don't want is for both to accept and publish the same piece. (A writer might not mind this but editors would and the next commission might be hard for a writer in this position to secure.) With more timeless pieces the advice most features editors give is to send to one publication at a time, which will cut down on the danger of two editors using your work at the same time. If you adopt this approach it gives you a perfect excuse to demand a fairly quick decision, so that you can take an unwanted idea to another editor. In reality things are not that straightforward. An editor may simply not be able to make a decision quickly – the planning meeting for a given issue may be three weeks away – and if that's the case you will just have to weigh up whether it's better to leave it there or offer it elsewhere as well. Once you are established as a freelance it will become clear that there are no fixed rules about any of this, so much depends on the individual editors and on the quality of the relationship freelances establish with them.

The briefing stage

If an idea is accepted in principle and a commission offered then some kind of briefing discussion should take place either by phone or in person. For the first time with a new publication it is worth trying to arrange a face to face meeting so that you can get to know the person who is commissioning you. However, editors are busy and writers just have to take what time is offered.

What is vital at this stage is to get a clear brief and to make sure it is understood by both sides. It is worth writing up a note of the discussion and copying it to the editor. It may be that your idea has turned out to be the basis of a feature with a different emphasis which the editor wants, but in the excitement of having a piece accepted you think what is wanted is what you first proposed. A good commissioning editor will talk through thoroughly what is wanted in terms of the angle, the research, the quotes, the length. A good writer adheres to this and if tempted to change much of it because of what is discovered during the research process will contact the editor to talk over any proposed change of emphasis.

It is also vital to get an agreement about the fee for the piece and to have this established in writing if at all possible. Something else which beginners don't always think to discuss is expenses. These are not handouts based on an editor's generosity but a reimbursement of what you have to spend in order to write the piece. Examples would be transport costs to the homes of interviewees, drinks for the main contact, phone call costs, buying copies of the books of the author you are going to interview. An editor must be given the chance to agree to this in advance and to save aggravation at a later stage it is worth having an upper limit written into the contract or letter of agreement.

Other points to get straight at the commissioning stage are the desired length of the piece, whether side bars or boxes are needed, the deadline and how the copy is to be supplied. The writer must stick to the length where possible or phone to discuss any changes in advance. Partly this is what is expected of a professional journalist and partly this is to protect your own copy. If you submit far too much then someone will almost certainly have to cut it and they may not have enough time or attention to do it justice. A journalist knows that the deadline is sacrosanct. If there is an unarguable reason for seeking to extend it (the prime source of information has at last agreed to talk but only on the day after the piece is due), then negotiate the change well in advance. Monthly magazines are more likely to be able to allow a little leeway, depending on which section the piece is commissioned for. On weeklies it may simply depend on which issue the story is intended for.

Sending in copy

As for supplying the copy: in the old days of hard copy this would have been on paper obeying all the basic rules of presentation in hard copy – double spacing, one side of the paper only, paragraphs not to run over from one folio to another, generous margins, catchlines on each folio, 'more' or 'ends' at the end of a folio. These rules still apply where offices require hard copy or for journalists who have no alternative means of supplying their work. In the past, too, there was the option of telephoning copy and reading it out to a copytaker who typed it up there and then. Otherwise e-mail is now common, or computer disc. Fax too is possible although this is really just a new-fangled version of hard copy and still requires keying in or scanning at the magazine office.

Whichever method is used it is essential to make clear on the copy how you can be contacted during the editing period and if the story is such that the editor will want to contact someone mentioned in it, to arrange photos perhaps, then contact numbers for that person must be supplied too.

Acceptance

Once a story has been accepted by a magazine the writer more or less loses control over it unless she is a star name. There may be phone calls from the office to check facts or ask for supplementary information but it is not common for the writer to be involved in the process of preparation for press or to look at either text proofs (galleys as they used to be called) or page proofs. In some ways this is a pity, especially where complicated photo captions are required because subs can make mistakes which the writer would pick up instantly. If you know a story is complex in this way and you have the time you might offer to go into the office and check, but don't be surprised if the offer is turned down.

One of the most disappointing things that can happen to a new freelance is to have their copy used but without a byline. More distressing still is to have their work used but see someone else's name at the top of it. This sort of thing is much more common in newspapers than in magazines. The lesser crime of omitting any byline may occur because the story is short or not of much importance and the same treatment would be given to copy from a staff journalist. Sometimes, though, the name is just left off because the writer is not on the staff. For putting someone else's byline there is no acceptable explanation other than the genuine mistake. If it happens you could write to the editor of the publication and make a complaint. Whether a freelance can afford to risk offending the commissioning editor in this way is a matter for individual judgement, but it wouldn't do any harm for freelances to be more vociferous when they are badly treated whether over pay, contracts or treatment of their copy.

Unsolicited copy

Behind much of this chapter is the assumption that a writer is not going to submit unsolicited, completed articles. Editors do, just occasionally, read these but mostly they don't. Unless a magazine makes it clear on the editorial pages that it welcomes uncommissioned contributions the best advice is not to waste your time by sending them. About the only exception that might be worth a try would be to write sample material if, say, you were trying to interest a publication in taking a regular column from you. Here you would not be expecting what you send in to be used but would be aiming to give the editor a flavour of what you might be able to write on your chosen topic in a given month or week.

Conclusions

The freelance life is not for everyone but for those of a certain temperament it is a rewarding way to pursue a career in journalism. It can be a stressful existence but it can also enable a successful freelance to have more control over the kind of work undertaken than staffers usually have. In addition there are probably a majority of journalists for whom freelance work forms part of their whole career, either at particular times or throughout as a means of varying the work they do on a daily basis or merely as a means to earn more money or write about different subjects. For all who like freelancing either as a career or as a supplement to a career the future looks quite bright as publishers continue to pare down full-time staffs to the minimum and depend increasingly on casual labour.

Recommended reading

Beck, S. (1999) 'Nice idea but it's not really us', *Press Gazette*, 22 January, 1999.

Dobson, C. (1992) *The Freelance Journalist. How to Survive and Succeed*.

International Federation of Journalists *Danger: Journalists at Work*, with help card and emergency number.

National Union of Journalists Freelance Fees Guide and *Freelance Directory*.

5 Ideas and information

Reporting is the best obtainable version of the truth.

Carl Bernstein

Ideas and information are the raw materials of a journalist's craft, which involves coming up with ideas on a punishingly regular basis. Much of the rest of the job is about seeking out information so that it can be marshalled into shape for the use, or the entertainment, of the reader. Here I will look at these two processes before a brief discussion of commissioning. This is relevant in this chapter because it affects and is affected by what happens to the ideas and information: it is relevant in this book because a magazine journalist is more likely to be given some responsibility for commissioning early in a career than would be the case in newspapers.

Once again the immediate difficulty is how to say anything general about such a diverse product as magazines. How can you relate the creative and research skills needed by a writer on *More!* with those required by an investigative reporter on *Private Eye*? You can't as far as the actual ideas or the specific information are concerned. But if you think in terms of processes, rather than of end-products, then there are certain things in common. It's a question of emphasis: some tasks, a beauty photoshoot is one, require more in the way of ideas and less in the way of information research and manipulation; other tasks, an analysis of the impact of the Euro on high-street shoppers say, clearly depend on extensive research and understanding of data and information of various sorts.

For many people the range of sources of information has proliferated so wildly in recent years that they depend on journalists to guide them through the maze of nets, webs, books, advertising, broadcast media and so on. Some have argued that the accessibility of information might mean there is no longer a role for journalists. I would argue the opposite. The more information there is floating about in print or in the electronic ether, the more there is for journalists to do. Many readers, for many purposes, need information filtered by the journalist or by a publication they can trust. They simply haven't time to research at first hand everything they might want to know about and there is plenty of evidence that readers trust magazines (Consterdine 1997). Journalists can also give readers ideas about what they might want to know about, whether it's a new product for salmon farmers or guidance about car maintenance. The world is a complicated, information-filled space and part of the job of journalists is to act as navigators through this space – an important job given that many sources of information have their own perspectives which they are seeking to impose on others.

This is partly what the processes of producing ideas and researching information are about. When a writer chooses to pitch one idea rather than another, or an editor chooses to commission one feature rather than another, they are already selecting which information their readers will have access to. Even where the subject matter is the frothiest of entertainment the same holds true although it may matter less in absolute terms.

What follows will not be relevant to every journalist on every magazine but it aims to provide guidance that could be of use to any student or new journalist who is not committed to a lifetime on one publication.

Where do ideas come from?

There is a proportion of news which in a way declares itself to be just that: a city-centre bomb for example, the publication of a report about the health of schoolchildren, the death of a celebrity. As Chapter 8 shows, features are less tied to time and to the daily news agenda. So there is more flexibility as to their subject matter and the way that it is treated. This means there is more pressure on feature writers and editors to produce ideas. Using their imagination in this way is something which many journalists love. For others it is a challenge. They'd rather be given a story lead and then get on with finding out what they need to know in order to write it. Journalism needs both sorts of people. It is important, though, to realise that the creative part of news and feature writing doesn't stop when an idea for a story has been agreed. The success with which a writer tackles her research can be equally dependent on the freshness of her ideas: thinking up a new angle, finding new people to talk to, or asking them questions they have not been asked before. All of this is just as creative a process as thinking up ideas in the first place.

If we concentrate on news and features the most important things a journalist needs to produce a continuous flow of usable story ideas are these: insatiable curiosity, an excellent memory, a good general knowledge, strong powers of observation and meticulously maintained filing systems and contacts books. Story ideas are not floating chimeras that occasionally materialise in the brain of a lucky hack. Ideas for stories can be thought up by the dozen in minutes by any experienced journalist worth the name. They wouldn't all be equally marketable but the point is that the generation of ideas is not as mysterious or as difficult as beginners often think. So where to start?

The diary

Many editorial offices start with the diary. In a newsroom the diary, whether on paper or screen, is the focus around which reporters are organised by their news managers. Into it go all the regular meetings and events as well as the press conferences, visits by politicians or celebrities and so on. The diary should contain a note of every news event of interest to that publication that can be predicted. On magazines of whatever kind there is likely to be an equivalent – news-based for *The Economist*, recording the international dress shows for a fashion magazine such as the American *W*, tied to the relevant sporting fixtures for a sports magazine such as *F1*, noting the wedding dates or birthdays of celebrities in *Hello!* Freelances often create their own diaries, however rudimentary, so that they can keep track of developments in the fields they write about.

Diaries can also be used to look backwards. Journalists like to have a peg on which to hang stories. In the case of stories which are not tied to the hard-news agenda this can be expressed another way as 'an excuse to run the piece'. (This is not meant as a criticism. My own impression, though, is that journalists are far more attached to the idea that a feature needs a peg than readers, who will happily read a story with no peg at all if it's good.) By looking backwards I mean the use of anniversaries of events as reasons to run features which perhaps assess the long-term effects on a community of a tragic accident such as Aberfan; consider the mood of the nation one year after the death of Diana, Princess of Wales; a music magazine might write about the current status of Purcell in the tercentenary of his death. Instantly, a long list could be produced, the key ingredients being the date and the questions a reporter might ask about the significance of that date. Many editorial offices pay companies to produce lists of dates which are of interest in this way and there are other services to help editors compile their diaries. Arts editors make use of Fens, an online forward-planning database, or the directory *London at Large*, which has notes about which celebrities are travelling through the city. A useful agency is Celebrity Search. As a last resort journalists can trawl through the library of their own publications to find less well-known stories to update or even to run regular columns of material based around what happened fifty years ago, for example.

When looking for ideas it is important to keep in mind who the readers are and what they are interested in – know your market, in other words, and know how the magazine is to be branded or sold to that market. What image is it trying to create? Editors and senior staff often have firm convictions (perhaps unjustifiably firm in some cases) about what is right for their publication.

Staff members and colleagues

Moving on from the diary but staying within the editorial office, we'll see that ideas can arise from conversations journalists, and other staff, have between themselves. The point about other staff is minor but worth making. The ones who are not journalists – the secretaries, say, or the storemen, or the technicians, the marketing people or even the publishers – are not under the same pressure to come up with ideas all the time, nor do they necessarily meet the same people through work or at home as the editorial staff. This means they can be an easily accessible window onto different worlds where people have different concerns.

The magazine itself

One source of ideas that is so obvious it can be easily forgotten is the magazine you work for. Back issues can be exploited for stories relating to anniversaries or even just for past–present comparisons. Even in the current editions, however, there are bound to be good starting points for stories. The letters page is one, partly because an individual letter might raise an issue that your magazine ought to be covering or because cumulatively the letters might reveal a general concern among readers which could be explored.

Market research

Market research is another way in which the response of readers can be gauged and suggestions gathered about what readers would like to see. This information may not be quite as specific as a feature idea but it can give an idea of the kind of topic that is popular. Personally, though, I'm suspicious of this use of market research and I think journalists should be wary of it too, as it undermines the professional skills for which they are hired in the first place. There is much more use of market research in television than in magazines but the question remains: which focus group could ever have dreamt up the popular programmes *Monty Python's Flying Circus, Dr Who* or *Changing Rooms*? And, as John Morrish says in his guide to editing magazines, 'no survey would ever have given any support for the creation of *Private Eye* or *The Spectator*'. He notes the danger of research becoming 'an expensive distraction' if it doesn't have a clear purpose, and makes the point that research findings 'can act as a mirror to prejudice' as everyone who uses the documents will find within them material to support their own views. There is also a problem with the quality of the information: 'What people say they want is not actually what they buy . . . people do not always tell the truth to researchers' (Morrish 1996: 26–36). He is not the only person to believe that strong editorial ideas come from an imaginative, creative, confident editorial team. If an editor doesn't have this she would be better to try to build one than to spend all her time studying market research reports.

Adverts

Another occasionally good source for stories can be the advertisements, large or small, display or classified. A story may emerge from the advert itself – Benetton has capitalised on its use of controversial photographic images to make sure the press prints stories about how wrong it is to do so. Or there may be information contained in the ad which allows a sharp reporter to identify a story. To make up an example: a writer on *Bicycle Monthly* might notice in the small ads that there is a bike shop for sale in Anytown. He remembers that the UK's greatest ever cyclist lives there, where he owns a bike shop. A couple of phone calls and a visit later the writer has a big feature article with photos about the retirement plans of the famous cyclist. He's planning to cycle alone round the world at the age of 65. It's also the basis of regular features over the coming eighteen months as the magazine monitors his progress, maybe even agreeing to sponsor the trip.

From this fictional example you'll see the personal qualities referred to above have come into play. If our *Bicycle Monthly* reporter was not observant or did not have a good memory he might not have thought there was anything worth pursuing in that unobtrusive small ad.

Curiosity

The quality of curiosity speaks for itself. Journalists ought to be the kind of people who want to know as much as possible about anything and everything. They should always be asking questions and that way they will always have ideas for stories. To go back to the cycle shop example. The question that occurred to the reporter is why would Tony Wheels, the cyclist, be selling up? The answer (he's retiring to cycle the world) provokes a lot of further questions in the curious mind and out of them grows the story.

Other journalists and media

It should be apparent that there is no magical art to this. A great deal more help, however, is available so long as the writer has the approach I've just outlined. Still without leaving the editorial office, a writer is likely to refer to the work of other journalists in the pursuit of story ideas. There may be something in his own publication that could be followed up or approached from a different angle. Other comparable magazines have to be scrutinised anyway, to check they are not providing their readers with a better service, so it makes sense to apply the same curiosity to their stories in case a new angle could be used with the same material. Apart from that any other publications or indeed the broadcast media can be a source of ideas. All journalism feeds off other journalism and so the trade press, for example, will be combed by the newspapers and consumer magazines, local newspapers will be scanned by regionals, regionals by dailies.

Ideas are picked up from specialist publications by less specialist ones and so on: for example a story about hip-hop might surface in *The Source*, be taken up by *NME* and then by the national press or by general magazines. Indeed periodicals about style and the arts are regularly devoured by arts journalists on newspapers looking for story leads (Dawson Scott 1997). Academic and medical journals such as *The Lancet* are routinely studied by journalists looking for stories they can translate into terms their readers will understand. Equally newspapers will be read by magazine journalists who may spot stories which could be developed and adapted to suit their readers' interests. An announcement about mortgage rates, for example, could be developed for the estate agents' or builders' trade magazines to show exactly what effect it might have on their businesses, while *Period Homes* could research the effects on behalf of ordinary home owners.

Press releases

No editorial office is properly established until it becomes the target for press officers sending out announcements about anything from a summary of a cabinet minister's speech to the launch of a new mascara. Journalists seem to divide into those who bin press releases unread and those who merely rewrite them slightly for inclusion in their pages. (Some don't even rewrite them.)

Styling

So far it may seem as though all magazines were full of words, which of course they are not. The people who style fashion photos or create the sets for magazines about food or homes and decorating don't usually write much but they do have to generate ideas about the 'stories' for the pictures, the copy that will go with them and to help decide which merchandise to call in. Here it can be more difficult to pin down where the concepts come from although it often is simply a development of what is going on in the relevant industry. If grungy clothes in grey are on all the catwalks then grungy clothes in grey will permeate the fashion pages. And if designers of household fabrics are suddenly showing animal prints at the international exhibitions, you don't have to wait long for jungle decorating themes to hit the magazine racks. But beyond the ideas currently being pushed by designers and manufacturers, stylists take their inspiration from anywhere, whether it's the music scene, classical painting, graphic design or the latest film. (There was a plague of khaki safari kit on almost every fashion page while the film *Out of Africa* was on general release in the UK.)

Contacts

Another important source of ideas for journalists is the contacts book. At its simplest this is a record of names, addresses and contact numbers. Because journalists can't predict what stories they might work on or even which publication they might eventually join, a good contacts book is likely to be comprehensive. A reporter on a local weekly might think she'll never need to interview a butcher again after covering the launch of a brand of sausages. But eighteen months later, in her new job on *Caterer and Hotelkeeper*, she could find it useful that there is a friendly butcher who knows and trusts her as she researches stories about E-coli and BSE.

For most journalists their contacts book is their most valuable possession. They don't want to share its contents with anyone, nor can they afford to lose it. Computers can be replaced, so can mobile phones, but a contacts book is a personal creation which can't be quickly or easily reproduced. A well-organised journalist might keep a duplicate and this is much easier to do if the information is held electronically. An actual book, such as a loose-leaf personal organiser, is in some ways more reliable, as anyone will admit whose electronic equivalent has crashed taking with it all the data it contained. A book can be carried about and used in awkward places where a computer would be intrusive. Nor does it have to be woken up when all you want is to check a phone number. The loose-leaf format is essential though, as sooner or later the pages will fill up and need to be replaced.

The reason a contacts book is so precious to a journalist is because so much journalism is written around quotations (see Chapter 9). Reporters use their contacts to get quotes, to get background information and to get stories. This might be when a contact rings up and alerts a journalist to something that is going on. But it might also be that a journalist, looking for ideas, will phone contacts and ask what is happening in their field of expertise, or what the general concerns are at the moment among her colleagues. It's a good idea for journalists to keep in touch with contacts regularly anyway and to use the phone-call or meeting as an opportunity to trawl for ideas.

Public relations

In all of the suggestions so far the writer is the initiator of the idea. Life for a journalist becomes more complicated when lobbyists and pressure groups start trying to attract his attention.

It is helpful to draw a distinction between the functions of a public relations officer (or PR) and a press officer. What they do overlaps to some extent and varies from one organisation to another. A broad distinction between the two creatures is that a PR is more likely to take what's known as a 'proactive' role towards the media, which is to say she will be expected to initiate contact with journalists and try to persuade them to give favourable editorial mention to whatever product or line or person she is pushing. She will, of course, be on hand in case of emergency or adverse news about her client or employer seeping out to the press. Sometimes though, in times of crisis, a company or celebrity will call in a PR consultant who specialises in crisis management. One peculiarity about PR is that in many organisations which otherwise take their public profile seriously, no PR people sit on the Board and so are not in a position to advise in advance about the way the media will interpret certain policies. The PR staff are depended upon to deal with problems after the event but not always to comment on which managerial decisions are likely to cause problems in the first place.

More generally though, PRs are the ones with expense accounts for taking journalists out to lunch to sell them ideas. They are also the ones who organise press trips to sun-soaked resorts for the test-driving of cars or launching of new perfumes. To someone who hasn't worked in the media before the array of inducements which flow in from businesses through PR agencies or in-house PR offices can be bewildering. Is it really necessary for journalists to have lunch on the Orient Express to discover the merits of a new range in fashion watches for example? A range of sun-creams would surely do their job just as well if beauty editors did not meet it for the first time at a lavish champagne reception. At their most powerful, and useful to their clients, PRs can manage any aspect of an encounter with the media whether it is the press in pursuit of a sex scandal or a magazine editor seeking access for an interview, although the more famous celebrities are likely to have agents to look after this kind of bargaining and these agents have increasing influence over what finally gets into print (see Chapter 10). The other side of their job is less visible: preventing stories detrimental to their clients getting anywhere near the press in the first place.

More seriously, PR specialists are nowadays heavily involved in the manipulation of political and business news agendas, as Michie describes in *The Invisible Persuaders* (1998), and Anderson and Weymouth (1999) touch on in their analysis of the coverage of the European Union by the British Press. They draw attention to the argument of theorist Jürgen Habermas that 'the corporate art of public relations' is part of the process by which information in the public sphere is manipulated in favour of those whose wealth or other forms of power gives them privileged access to the media and, more bluntly, they summarise Habermas's view of PR as being 'a deception designed to exploit public opinion for political ends' (Michie 1998; Anderson and Weymouth 1999: 16). At a more trivial level, in the consumer press for example, the general point holds good that money buys influence through favourable editorial mention (see Chapter 15).

Press officers

What press officers do is usually less proactive (their word), which is to say they are more likely to react to events than to act as agents trying to get free advertising space in editorial pages. Press officers do rather less contacting the press and trying to sell a client, rather more responding to enquiries from the press. These enquiries may be for clarification of facts, or for quotes, or for access to the right person in the organisation, or background guidance about lines of thinking, requests for press releases or for books to review, tickets to concerts and so on. Press officers do take the initiative too, of course. They send out press releases, organise press conferences and photo-opportunities, collate information and cuttings. They also try to interest the press in stories relating to their organisation but in general the reporter at the receiving end of a call from a press officer feels much less pressured to respond positively. Good press officers who tailor a story to the publication are successful because once journalists realise that the material they send is likely to be of interest they are more inclined to read it.

Most journalists, quite rightly, are sceptical, if not cynical, about both sets of people, because so often what the PRs and press officers seem to be doing is preventing journalists from getting at the information they want. The ones who are good at their job are masters of manipulation in all kinds of ways that the average hack, at least at the beginning of a career, would probably never think possible (Michie 1998). What I want to suggest, though, is that a journalist when seeking ideas or pursuing research may take help from wherever it is available so long as he is sure what exactly he wants and is able to separate his agenda from that of the PR. There's no point in dismissing all press officers just because some PRs are so indiscriminately pushy as to be complete time-wasters.

Many press releases contain good ideas for stories but what regularly upsets those who have responsibility for public relations is that these will not necessarily be the stories the press officers are pushing. As ever, it's up to the journalist to ask questions of the material. For example, if a police press release glows about a fall in the number of street-crimes committed against pensioners in the past year our observant reporter might recall that following two brutal murders the previous year most pensioners in the town no longer go out at night. Yes, the crime figure has fallen but this is because of an unacceptable if self-imposed restriction on the liberty of the over-65s, not because muggers have taken to drinking cocoa in front of the TV of an evening instead of going to the pub. In this case what the press officer could certainly supply is the crime statistics and some police officers to interview or at least some quotes. In addition the press release would have alerted the reporter to the fact that there is a story to be investigated.

Many press offices are sound sources of facts and figures, and of cuttings on relevant topics taken from a range of publications, something which can be hard to pull together otherwise, especially in the heat of researching a story to deadline. Some press offices will supply photos to illustrate stories and some will also let journalists into their libraries to use their collections of books, cuttings and information. With luck the press officers will be well informed about the work of their organisation and those working in the same field. This is particularly true of well-run non-governmental organisations (NGOs) including some charities. The journalist just has to remember that any organisation or company has its own priorities when producing information. This means that when researching a story one strategy is always to ask who will have an alternative slant on this information, who might have the counter arguments, which press office will have the information to back that up. Of course, you would do this in the interest of balance and of finding people to quote but you can also do it in the early stages of research in order to find basic information. Crime reporters, for example, will nearly always talk to pressure groups like the National Association for the Care and Resettlement of Offenders or the Howard League before assessing Home Office reports, just as environment reporters will get story ideas from Greenpeace and Friends of the Earth (Schlesinger and Tumber 1994). Lobby groups, NGOs and government departments all have information offices and they are worth approaching unless you have discovered one in particular to be unhelpful or short of the kind of information you need.

Background research

For some journalists the research stage of a story is by far the most interesting. In Chapter 9 there is a discussion of how information is put together through interviewing and contacts with people and for some reporters that is the basis of most of what they write (Schudson 1995: 72). For others, particularly those working in the serious news press, research means different things depending on the story. Jessica Mitford wrote with relish about researching stories. For her the goal, when gathering background information,

> is to know, if possible, *more* about your subject than the target of the investigation does. To this end, I soak up books and articles on the subject, type out relevant passages, and accumulate a store of knowledge before seeking an interview with said target.

Journalists all have their own methods of working but Carl Bernstein points to Mitford's introduction to *The Making of a Muckraker* as being 'as good a primer on reporting' as he's ever read (Mitford 1980: 5 and 263).

Libraries

News organisations have their own libraries of cuttings and reference books and all journalists, particularly freelances, would be well advised to make sure they are registered with good public libraries too, as these can provide access to all kinds of information from electoral rolls to planning applications to out-of-print novels by the author you've just been asked to interview. Increasingly they provide Internet access too.

Electronic sources

The Internet has transformed the research process, as Tim Holmes explains in Chapter 12, and this applies equally to the search for ideas. Think of a word, preferably one for a weird activity such as trepannation. Key it into your search engine and off you go on the trail of ideas, quotes, books, contacts. The possibilities provided by the Internet only reinforce my point about how easy it is to come up with ideas for feature stories.

The careful journalist has to be sensitive to the possible pitfalls of using information acquired through the Internet, as Chapter 12 explains, but the Internet has undoubtedly transformed the work of journalists. Apart from providing access to websites it makes it much easier to conduct interviews with busy people, particularly those on the far side of the world. Telephone calls can be intrusive, or hard to co-ordinate in differing time zones. E-mail, however, allows the recipient to deal with communications at a time that suits and in a way that puts them under less pressure than a telephone interview might but is not slowed down by postal services.

Constraints on research

Research can be the most enjoyable part of the journalistic process but it can also be the most frustrating. There aren't many kinds of research in any field that operate entirely without a deadline – even Ph.D. candidates have a time limit – so not many pieces of research have the luxury of being allowed to continue until all the questions have been fully explored. However, in journalism the time constraints are usually extremely tight and often unrealistic. There are features writers who regularly write two 1,000-word pieces a day, both of which need 'researching'. Admittedly that's on a newspaper but the approach is common to much journalism. Journalists have to research their stories at such speed that they can't afford to check everything, or follow up leads which might yield a new angle. Anyone who is on the receiving end of calls from journalists who are looking for information will be familiar with their plea to talk to you that minute. Later this afternoon or even tomorrow morning is just not possible, whatever else you might have in your diary. When the topic under research is not tied to a particular day in news terms one can't help wondering why there is not more forward planning. Even in well-run offices journalists often work to time constraints which are more to do with editorial office custom than pursuit of the best story, and which are detrimental to the quality of the information which reaches their readers. Part of the cause of this is money. A reporter's time is expensive. Speculative research which might produce nothing or research which yields results slowly is, as many editors freely admit, just not affordable. That's part of the explanation for the increasing prevalence of columns based on personal opinions. These usually require no research at all.

Secrecy

Up to now this chapter may have implied that for journalists to gather information successfully is just a question of knowing what to ask and who to ask, or where to turn for written sources. This is far from true in the UK, as compared with some other western democracies, and very far from true in countries where censorship of the press is a significant political tool. The popular conception of censorship is of a process that happens after the journalist has produced the story but before it is published. In fact the restrictions start much earlier and indeed censorship at the enquiry stage can be more effective since it prevents journalists getting at sensitive information in the first place, rather than discovering information but then not being allowed to publish it.

In the UK journalists have to struggle to unearth all kinds of information to which in other countries such as the United States there would be a right of access. An example of this, which relates to a tragic story, appeared in *The Guardian* (7 October 1999: 4). In its coverage of the Paddington rail crash it noted:

> Safety warnings kept by Railtrack which could have alerted the public that trains had overrun signals outside Paddington Station before Tuesday's crash are protected by Whitehall's draconian secrecy laws . . . Members of the public cannot even ask the company . . . to release the reports or minutes of its safety committee.

So British journalists, like the British public, have no right of access to information even where, as in the above example, such information is of unquestioned public interest and may involve public money or, in some cases, public appointments. This gives rise to concern particularly in areas of public administration, responsibility for which has increasingly been shifted by government to the rather grey area of rule by quango as John Turner explains (Turner 1998: 186). The acronym quango stands for quasi-autonomous non-governmental organisation and includes such institutions as the Independent Television Commission, the Higher Education Funding Council and the local health authorities. The recent increase in their power and number has raised several issues, including how accountable they are, given that the members are responsible for spending public money but are not elected, and many of the posts are filled by government appointees without an open selection procedure. These problems may or may not be satisfactorily solved by the recommendations of the Nolan Committee.

The centralised nature of British political life, the secrecy which pervades politics and government, can make life difficult for the reporter who simply wants to find out what is going on in a particular government department. As historian Bernard Porter has noted, although there are other societies which are or have been as secretive as Britain, the British are peculiar for the depth of their secrecy: 'Not only are we secretive, we are secretive about how secretive we are' (Porter 1999: 13). The Official Secrets Acts ensure that questions are not asked freely and that those who are employed in all manner of capacities by the Crown must sign a document preventing them from disclosing any information they have gathered during their service. Stories, possibly apocryphal, abound about some of the sillier restrictions this imposes, such as the gardener refusing to reveal what plants are grown at Windsor Castle or whether Prince Charles prefers China or Indian tea.

The worrying side of this, though, is that workers in industries such as the nuclear industry are not at liberty to voice their concerns, and documents which are essential to the work of a serious news reporter are simply unobtainable. Employees in occupations as diverse as health and education are now contractually bound not to talk to the press. An account of how these restrictions can affect the work of a journalist, and one which along the way compares the situation in the UK with the USA, is provided by Marilynne Robinson in her article 'The Waste Land' about Sellafield nuclear reprocessing plant. She points out that the *sub judice* rule, which prevents open discussion of any issue about to become the subject of legal action, can keep serious issues out of the press. (The Paddington rail crash in October 1999 reminded us how little information could be made public during the two years following the Southall rail crash while criminal proceedings were under way.) Robinson gives the example of thalidomide, the drug implicated in the birth of children with serious deformities. Its manufacturers managed to keep the question of their liability before the courts for seventeen years and therefore out of public discussion until *The Sunday Times*, then under the brave editorship of Harold Evans, broke the story in defiance of the law.

In the USA the British climate of secrecy provokes puzzlement. For Americans 'a democracy without the means of public information is but a prelude to farce or tragedy' (Evans 1999). As Bernard Porter argues, great advances in access to information have been made in recent years (for one thing it is now acknowledged that the UK has secret services) but the secret services are 'expressly exempted' from the Blair government's Freedom of Information Bill: 'Secrets . . . are still regarded as the property of the secretive; there is no presumption of a public "right to know"' (Porter 1999: 15). And Evans himself suggests that the Bill will simply ensure that in the UK 'polite obfuscation and downright obstruction are amply preserved into the next century'. A conclusion which I am sure will hold whatever the final shape of the Bill which is proceeding through parliament at the time of writing.

Most journalists accept that there have to be some constraints on the publication of information. The issue is at its clearest during a time of war when in the interests of security governments traditionally clamp down on what can be published. Fair enough, perhaps, not to broadcast to the enemy that they can expect a 'surprise' bombing raid tonight or that troops are being massed on the border ready for an invasion. But things are less clear-cut when it comes, say, to reporting the number of casualties. Governments prefer to keep quiet about their own losses in case morale is affected. They also like to keep quiet about civilian casualties on the opposing side – again out of a wish to carry public opinion with them.

Privacy

There has been much debate recently about privacy, prompted by the more unpalatable excesses of the media. While it is easy to see why people should want aspects of their lives to remain private, it can also be argued that privacy laws protect the wicked from discovery. A fuller discussion of these issues is to be found in Chapter 17 and of the relevant aspects of the law in Chapter 18. For the purpose of this chapter it is important to point out that any journalist who works in news and on sensitive issues must be well acquainted with the regulations partly to know what not to do and partly to be aware of what rights do exist so that when organisations try to restrict freedom in ways beyond what is legally accepted they can be challenged. Useful guidance to the workings of local and national government is provided in the books by Ron Fenney listed at the end of this chapter. Apart from the legal restrictions on the work of journalists there are codes of practice to guide them in what is acceptable behaviour published by the National Union of Journalists and the Press Complaints Commission.

Turning ideas into stories

There are two other processes connected with ideas which need to be mentioned in this chapter. One is the pitching of ideas and the second is commissioning them. However good an idea is, it has no real value unless the writer knows how to sell it to someone else. The word 'sell' is clearly appropriate where a freelance is offering ideas to a commissioning editor but it also describes what writers on the staff of a magazine have to do. Money may not change hands for staffers in the way it does for freelances but the process of persuasion is the same. Because pitching ideas is such a vital part of a freelance's job it is covered in detail in Chapter 4.

The commissioning process

Turning now to the commissioning part of the editorial process. Magazine editorial teams are often small, and in many cases staff have to underake a variety of tasks, so it can fall to the lot even of beginners to be responsible for commissioning other writers. It's useful therefore to think about what the task involves.

By far the most grief between commissioning editors and writer occurs because of misunderstandings: the writer wrote what she thought she was asked to and the editor disagrees entirely. One way to minimise the risk of this is for the commissioner to note down briefly what has been decided at the meeting or during the telephone call and send a copy to the writer. That way misunderstandings can be caught at an early stage. The problem with this is that it is not the norm for any kind of written agreement to exist between magazine and freelance for a particular feature. Anyone who is commissioning should note down exactly what they want. If they don't know exactly then that can be made explicit. It's also helpful to say which are the essential ingredients of a story and which are less crucial but nevertheless desirable. Naturally, during the research stage, what a writer uncovers may alter the direction or significance of the story. From the commissioning editor's point of view this may not be a problem but it makes sense for the commissioning editor to encourage writers to make contact regularly during the research stage or just before writing up.

It's not easy to say what makes a good commissioning editor. Being full of ideas or knowing how to find them is clearly essential as well as knowing how to match the idea to the writer, whether staff or freelance. Just as important is being able to recognise the quality of the ideas put forward by others as well as being able to spot the strength hiding in a mediocre idea, to see how it could be developed or how the questions could perhaps be asked a different way to yield more interesting material. A good commissioner then is open to new ideas and also, I would argue, to new writers. She should be on the lookout for new talent whether this means paying some attention to the speculative letters which all commissioning editors receive or actively studying the writers who are already in print in her field to see if anyone is better than the writers she is currently using.

Commissioning editors also need a talent for pitching ideas just as freelance writers do. The bigger the magazine the more likely it is that the process of selling ideas happens in a kind of chain. The writer sells ideas to the commissioning editor who then has to sell them either to the editor or to an entire senior editorial team which may operate rather like the news conference on a newspaper where the heads of each section meet to offer their 'list' of stories.

One of the most satisfactory parts of the commissioning process can be reading the copy when it arrives; if it meets the brief exactly and is well written. There will be cases, however, when the copy doesn't meet the brief or is so bad that it has to be either rejected or sent back for rewriting and this is when a commissioning editor needs reserves of tact. Editorial judgement is important too because distinctions have to be made between the piece which can't be saved, the piece which needs reworking by the writer and the piece which needs substantial reworking by the editor or subeditors. Magazines have different approaches and money plays its part in the decision-making. If the story is important for the magazine, is it quicker to get a sub to rewrite it than to ask a disgruntled freelance to spend more time on a piece that he regards as finished? If the story is well written and could be even better, is it worth the editor's time to make the improvements? The answer really depends on the standards to which the magazine aspires and the generosity of the editorial budget. For a good account of the interventionist approach James Thurber's biography of E. H. Ross is hard to beat. It's true that the skills of a great editor such as Ross can't be taught. The mechanics of editing can, and so can some of the criteria for selection of stories. What can develop only with experience is the ability to get the best out of writers and then to work at their copy until its best qualities emerge. Legendary editors such as Ross have this ability and although it doesn't always make them popular it certainly helps to make them great.

Recommended reading

Anderson, P. J., and Weymouth, A. (1999) *Insulting the Public? The British Press and the European Union*.

Bell, Q. (1991) *The PR Business*.

Evans, H. (1999) 'Freedom of information: why Britain must learn from America'.

Fenney, R. (1997) *Essential Central Government*.

Fenney, R. (1998) *Essential Local Government*.

Michie, D. (1998) *The Invisible Persuaders. How Britain's Spin Doctors Manipulate the Media*.

Mitford, J. (1980) *The Making of a Muckraker*.

Robinson, M. (1985) 'The Waste Land'.

Thurber, J. (1984) *The Years with Ross*.

Turner, J. (1998) 'Powerful information: reporting national local government'.

Vincent, D. (1999) *The Culture of Secrecy in Britain*.

6 Writing: where to start

What is written without effort is in general read without pleasure.

Samuel Johnson

J ust as there is no such thing as a typical magazine, so there is no single way to write for magazines. What is an appropriate style will depend on the purpose of the magazine and who its readers are. To a more limited extent this applies on newspapers and accounts for the differences between, say, a lead news story in *The Independent* and the way the same story might be written for *The Sun*.

Variety of styles

In magazines things are not that simple: the material they cover is varied, the purposes for which they are written are diverse and the readerships are, in many cases, tightly defined in terms of interests, class or age. This means magazines adopt a much more individual approach to the style of writing they publish. Furthermore, there are magazines which intentionally use a style which acts almost as a way of excluding those who don't understand it. Their aim is to give readers the sense of belonging to a club or at least that the magazine is read only by people like themselves who share the same tastes in music or in fashion.

Examples can be found in magazines aimed at teenage girls and young women which use words like studmuffin, hunk, vidfest, snogfest, tongue sarnie (this is a French kiss, for those who don't know!) and so on. Alliteration is rampant (TV totty, fact files, plump up your pout, bag a boy, lassoo a lad); second syllables are abandoned (sesh for session, fave for favourite, gorge for gorgeous, pash for passion, bod for body, vid for video, ish for issue); apostrophes proliferate (L'il cutie, chillin', hoo-bloomin'rah!). In the drive for high circulations such writing could be counter-productive in that some of the slang vocabulary is not widely used even by the target age range and certainly not throughout the UK. That, however, may be the point. By reading these words as if they were the in-words in the metropolis, readers can get a vicarious sense of being part of what is cool. Using, or at least understanding, this kind of language helps readers to differentiate themselves from their less cool peers as well as from parents or other figures of authority like teachers. Turn to the hipper music or lads' or sports magazines to see no end of examples of language used in this way to draw the readers in. Apart from helping to brand readers as cool, it contributes, no doubt, to the entertainment value of the publication both by the jokiness of its tone and by the sheer fun of playing with words which has long been part of the English tradition of writing.

This use of style is also intended to differentiate the magazines one from another. Publishers see this as an increasingly important task in the crowded consumer magazine marketplace, although I'm not sure the strategy necessarily works, as all the magazines aimed at particular groups seem to pick up the same linguistic quirks probably from each other.

Which style to use

What this book can't do then is to provide a comprehensive guide to writing in the styles that consumer and lifestyle magazines use. For one thing a list of appropriate vocabulary would be out of date within a few months and in any case colloquial style is written, at its most convincing, by those for whom it grows naturally out of their own way of speaking. What any good magazine writer will learn, and any good features editor will explain, is that the writer must always have a clear idea of the market for which he is writing. Viewed positively this merely reflects what all competent writers (and speakers) do: they adjust the style of the language they use according to who they are writing for or talking to. We all do this as part of the daily communication we have with other people. So thinking of the market is not necessarily much more than good manners, although obviously it is a more difficult undertaking if you are writing for the many readers of a high-selling monthly than it is if you are talking to a few people you've just met on the beach.

Viewed less positively, however, there are some besetting problems. The first is for journalists who write for readers who are not like themselves either socially or in educational terms or even just in age. In newspapers this matters less because they mostly strive to cater for a broader range of people. But in magazines, where the readerships are identified so narrowly in the terms listed above, it does matter. If you are writing for young teenage girls it is most unlikely that you are yourself a young teenage girl, so how do you know the peculiarities of their language? You might have been a teenage girl quite recently and that would help, although colloquial language changes even in a few years, so you're likely to be out of date. Or you might have friends and family who are teenage girls. You could talk to them. You could go out deliberately to meet some, perhaps even formally through a focus group. You could read the magazines they read, watch the television and listen to the radio. The problem with this, though, is that any of these strategies brings with it a level of artificiality as well as carrying the risk of circularity: magazines are written in a certain style because that's how other journalists are writing for the same audience. And this problem doesn't just apply to a teenage readership. There's the problem of age or of class. Even if journalists are from a working-class background (and many aren't), by the time they've landed well-paid jobs on a London-based glossy they are encountering a different kind of language every day. What are they to do? How do they know the right language to use for C2, D, E readers outside London? One of the conflicts this can give rise to within a magazine office is when the various writers and editors assert that they know best about aspects of language which can never be established with absolute certainty, such as whether particular words would be used by, say, teenage boys in Liverpool.

The regional consideration is significant too. For all that consumer journalists say they try to tailor their words to their readers, they are apt to ignore the different usages that are common in different parts of the country. There is a strong metropolitan bias in almost all consumer magazines. This may be inevitable, given that London is where most magazines are based and therefore where most magazine journalists live. But it's something to consider when you hear journalists talking about the importance of knowing the market.

Some good examples of the muddled thinking in editorial offices about appropriate language were collected by Sheena-Margot Gibson. She asked a selection of editorial staff working on magazines for teenagers why they used certain slang words like 'totty' and so on. In several cases senior staff said the quoted words were not used in their publications and so were astonished when Gibson quoted page references from their current issues. More intriguing still was an air of defensiveness. Gibson was simply trying to find out where the more arcane words came from. But some editors said they were actually trying to cut back on this kind of language and one said, puzzlingly, that the word 'totty' had now been banned from the publication (Gibson 1999). The question is why they should feel the need to do that if it reflects street language. The problem, for a writer, is how to follow the vagaries of the thinking about language in a particular editorial office.

A skilful writer, with an observant eye and ear for language, can learn how to reproduce the required style. If you want to write for a particular magazine, or if you've landed a job, the trick is to study carefully the way it is written and note the characteristics in the same way you would if you were learning a foreign language. Points to watch for include rhythm, rhyme, length of sentences and paragraphs, alliteration, rhyme, vocabulary. House-style books can help and so too can the subeditors as they are the people who are charged with establishing the linguistic style of the publication, although what you do when confronted by conflicting advice from different sections of the magazine your own diplomatic skills will have to resolve.

Individual magazine styles

Style does not, however, just refer to the quirky use of language common to popular youth culture. Many magazines have their own tone – *Time* magazine is a good example of a news magazine with a recognisable style for its news pages, even if the opinion essays are allowed more variety. Other serious publications such as news or industry or professional magazines strive for what is generally thought of as a neutral voice in their news pages at least, and quite probably with features too although with features there is always, in whatever kind of publication, more scope for the individual voice of the writer to be heard. This is, of course, one of the attractions of feature writing for some journalists, and in particular one of the attractions of writing features for magazines, some of which not only tolerate but actively nurture the individuality of their writers. *The New Yorker* or *The Spectator* or *Rolling Stone* are not bought because readers want to read reportage or opinions expressed in a corporate monotone: they are bought precisely for the variety and literary quality of voices they offer.

Learning to write

One question that arises in any discussion of writing skills is whether they can, in fact, be taught. The view that writers are born not made is still common as is the notion that there is an absolute distinction between literary writing and journalistic writing.

Literary writing, the thinking goes, is creative, imaginative, of enduring quality and written by a human being blessed with some mystical quality. Journalistic writing, by contrast, is mundane, dull, lacking in creativity and written by a tired cliché-monger who has no sensitivity to the nuances of language.

The idea that writing can't be taught, is gradually going out of fashion as formal training for journalism becomes more widely accepted and as more creative writing courses are established. In the old days many good journalists managed well enough without training but what happens now, in universities and colleges, helps to speed up and formalise a process that would once have taken place in an *ad hoc* way in magazine and newspaper offices. Some writers are more naturally fluent or sensitive to language than others but that doesn't mean that they will some-how be damaged by doing a little systematic thinking about their main means of communication.

The second point, that literary writing is a separate undertaking from journalistic writing, is, I think, most easily belied by making a list of highly regarded literary writers who have also worked as journalists. Starting with Daniel Defoe, a random list might include Samuel Johnson, Charles Dickens, George Eliot, Mrs Gaskell, Arnold Bennett, Oscar Wilde, George Orwell, Tom Stoppard, Joan Didion, Tom Wolfe and James Fenton. The focus of this debate is one that underpins discussion in many areas of cultural endeavour: is there a qualitative difference between high and low culture (between literary imaginings and factual reporting for example), or is there merely writing, some of which is better than the rest? The better does not always have to be the fictional or lyrical; it might be a highly crafted piece of reportage based on detailed documentary research and extensive interviews. This is not a debate that needs to detain all readers although it does have direct ramifications for features writing at least, and will be touched on again in Chapter 8. The debate was widened beyond university classrooms by Tom Wolfe in his introduction to an anthology of American writers called *The New Journalism* and given an additional lease of life here in the UK by the increasing respect given to reportage in recent years, as exemplified by the publi-cation of anthologies such as *The Faber Book of Reportage* and *The Granta Book of Reportage*.

One of the most common reasons for newswriting to be dismissed is that it is hack-neyed and formulaic. This is sometimes true and not surprising given how much jour-nalism is written every day. Sometimes the cause is not that the writer doesn't have a way with words. It may be because of the constraints which surround the writing of news. If everything has to be done quickly, under pressure and with minimum fuss then it's quick and easy to adhere to the formulae and that may be what editors want. It doesn't necessarily follow that other kinds of writing by the same person under different constraints can't be written to the highest literary standards.

While flair, talent, genius, individual voice – whatever you want to call it – can't be taught, certain technical skills can. Some of these can be prescribed in advance of the writing, although it is much easier to indicate what to avoid than it is to give firm guidelines which will produce workable prose. One of the best ways for anyone to improve what they write is to read as widely as possible, reading with a questioning eye to analyse how writers achieve certain successful effects or what is wrong when the writing is dull. Everyone has their own tastes and so there is little point in recom-mending here particular authors, the names of revered writers are easy enough to come by. There are some books about the English language it's worth recommending because they are readable and entertaining as well as informative and these are listed at the end of the chapter.

General writing skills

It is to some of the general skills I want to turn now, hoping the reader will recognise that they don't hold good for all magazine writing but can be a touchstone. Given the scope of this book it is not possible to go into detail. Two of the most useful books for journalists are *English for Journalists* by Wynford Hicks and *Essential English for Journalists, Editors and Writers* by Harold Evans which cover grammar, syntax, punctuation and so on but always from the perspective of a journalist and using examples from journalism.

Spelling

Spelling is one technical aspect of writing that can't be taught by someone else, but a writer who is determined can usually improve it. With modern computer spellchecks it may be argued that it is not necessary for a writer to spell correctly. In fact it saves a lot of time if she can: spellchecks have limited capabilities and produce delightful misreadings thanks to the number of homophones in English; but also, if a deadline is very tight, spellchecks force more pauses for questioning over proper names than is ideal. They also don't help much at the final proof stage, when an eagle eye can spot a misspelling before it makes it into print. Someone who knows their spelling is weak and who wants to make a living as a writer would be advised to work at it, to learn the regularly used vocabulary in the same way as they might learn foreign words in language classes.

Punctuation

Another technical skill that gives endless trouble to new writers is punctuation. This can be taught and no doubt has been to all journalists throughout their schooldays: taught, learned and more or less forgotten in some cases. The apostrophe is the most confusing it seems and it wouldn't surprise me if this punctuation mark disappeared altogether over the next few years, so many are the people who are unable or unwilling to learn the simple rules by which it should be used. This is not the place to go into them. You'll know you have an apostrophe problem if you know you would have difficulty writing phrases to do with 'books belonging to many children' (children's books) or 'fleeces from many sheep' (sheep's fleeces) or something belonging to 'it'. ('It's a girl,' cried the midwife. 'Its hair is black' is one way of trying to remember this one.) The general advice here is to look carefully at what appears in print and try to understand why an apostrophe or a hyphen is used where it is, as these are the two most regularly misunderstood marks of punctuation. A full exposition of the accepted conventions of punctuation is available in G. V. Carey's book *Mind the Stop* but *The Oxford Dictionary for Writers and Editors* offers a succinct guide under the entry 'Punctuation'. Anyone who knows their punctuation is shaky must chain a copy of this book to their desk, open at the punctuation page.

Jargon

Publications like *Rolling Stone, The Spectator* and *The New Yorker* are a long way, stylistically, from the mass-market consumer weeklies and monthlies but situated halfway between, perhaps, are the professional and trade publications which use their own vocabulary although not in the light-hearted way of the teenage magazines and not to act as a badge of cool. What they use, which would not necessarily be acceptable on the pages of general newspapers, are jargon words.

Jargon often gets a bad name for reasons which are not altogether fair. What jargon means, essentially, is a set of words or ways of speaking that are used and understood by particular groups of people when talking about their shared interest. So if a group of academics are at a meeting and talk about the HEFC, the RAE, staff-student ratios, sabbaticals, Ph.Ds and FTEs no one will think them rude or incomprehensible, although if the same people were holding a general conversation at a party (it has been known!), where other guests were not involved in university life, then to use the same language would be rude as well as pointless because the outsiders would not understand.

Jargon, then, has its place and in the right context – at a meeting of colleagues, in a publication aimed at a particular group of people with shared knowledge – it is the correct language to use. In the wrong context – in a publication for a wider group of people than those who might readily be expected to understand it – jargon words go against all the principles of good journalistic writing and in particular the rule that journalism should be easy to understand.

It follows then that one of the jobs of any journalist, whether in magazines or newspapers, is as a translator of jargon. So many fields of interest these days do have extensive vocabularies of words and acronyms which would mystify those outside that journalists have to be careful not merely to reproduce the jargon. If they do they may lose their readers and, perhaps worse, they may misunderstand the story if they themselves do not understand the jargon. This is why it can be helpful to look at the task as one of translation since you can't begin the process unless you understand what you hope to translate. Another advantage of thinking in terms of translation is that it helps the writer to distinguish between jargon and gobbledegook.

The difference is that with jargon a meaning can be tracked down by the non specialist, with gobbledegook there is no discernible meaning. A definition of gobbledegook nowadays is generally that it is pompous-sounding rubbish. It may sound like official jargon (and that was once its official meaning) but when submitted to scrutiny it turns out to be more or less devoid of meaning. The writers who are most tempted to produce this are politicians, officials and bureaucrats in huge organisations such as the BBC. So prevalent was gobbledegook in official documents that an organisation called the Plain English Campaign was set up to work for improvements. Partly as a result of that, documents like tax returns or passport application forms have been made much clearer in recent years. Examples of gobbledegook are easy enough to find and *Private Eye* regularly publishes some of the worst excesses, particularly from the BBC and local authorities. For an explanation of how the style is arrived at and also avoided it's worth reading George Orwell's essay 'Politics and the English language'. Written in 1946 it shows that the tendency towards deadly obfuscation is not just a late-twentieth-century problem in English. It's also worth reading because much of what he said in the essay is accepted as gospel by writers, editors and those who teach English generally (Orwell 1946: 127). Even if you don't agree with all his points, as a journalist you will inevitably encounter those who do.

Clarity, economy and simplicity

Clarity, economy and simplicity are the three most important characteristics of journalistic writing and with good reason, even if they were not always accorded the value they are now. It was towards the end of the nineteenth century, when the mass-market publishing of journalism really began to get under way in America and Britain, that emphasis began to be given to what was regarded as the more masculine style characterised by terseness and brevity: the idea was that men were much too busy to waste time reading magazines or newspapers in which unnecessary words were employed (Garvey 1996: 178).

This has become the predominant thinking behind all of the newswriting and much of the features writing in the UK today. Readers are thought to be in a tearing hurry and to have the attention-span of grasshoppers: in the case of tabloid papers or the most popular mass-market magazines for women this means editors offer readers a large number of short stories, all screaming for attention. In the case of the more serious magazines and newspapers it means that although stories aren't necessarily short they must still be regarded as competitors to all the other stories on the page or in the publication, and display techniques are used to attract the notice of readers. I wouldn't necessarily argue with any of this – many of us do lead busy lives – but it's worth drawing attention to the assumptions that are handed on to each new generation of journalists as if there were no other way. It's worth noting, too, the extremes to which this case has now been pushed in even the most serious of radio and television journalism where interviewees and contributors are constantly being interrupted and cut short because of the acute pressure of time, making an intelligent exposition of a complicated issue increasingly difficult to find.

Nevertheless clarity, economy and simplicity are meant to prevail. By striving for clarity the journalist tries to avoid any ambiguity and not to test the reader's patience with unnecessary allusions. (This is one way in which journalistic writing differs from some literary writing where ambiguity is valued and indeed may be part of the literary point.) In striving for economy journalists aim to tell their stories in the shortest possible way, using (to generalise madly) short words, short sentences and short paragraphs. Of course all this is relative and journalism which deals with complicated technical material for a well-educated audience such as the readers of *New Scientist* can afford to use longer more abstract words than would be appropriate for the triumph-over-tragedy human interest narrative in a weekly such as *Chat*. The principle holds true though, it's just that the target audience has also to be borne in mind. In striving for simplicity the journalist is taking the most direct route through her material, keeping subordinate clauses to a minimum and avoiding anything which might distract the reader from the main purpose of the story.

We've looked at some of the reasons for the establishment of these principles of writing and these were to do with the readers. There are others which have more to do with the way journalism is produced. Journalists usually work under severe time pressure. Magazines and newspapers also set a premium by space. Copy has to compete for the limited available space and this has implications for the way journalists approach their work. These constraints do not necessarily apply to all magazines, of course, and for some magazine writers, particularly the writers of longer features, there is the luxury of being able to write to a length the material seems to merit rather than an arbitrary length decided by the page layout or the quantity and quality of other material that week.

Turning now to simplicity. New journalists, especially recent graduates, often take time to work free of a more leisured, academic style where they aim to cover all the possibilities or nuances of an argument. Journalists have to learn to be brutally selective in what they try to include in their stories. They can't put in everything they have discovered during their research and the point of what they write is not to show that they have done enough reading, as it sometimes is with student essays. What matters in journalism is that a story is told and that it is told quickly. A narrative thread is vital to most journalistic writing. One way to move towards this style is to imagine you meet friends at the bus stop and you've just heard some news. Ask yourself what is the first thing you would say about a particular incident, what sort of language would you use? Almost certainly it wouldn't be the same as the way you would describe an incident in a university essay.

Another technical point to do with simplicity has been touched on already: subordinate clauses can slow the narrative process down. By this I mean the kind of sentence that starts with the less important information first, as in this example:

> 'Having settled down in the armchair, Jemima read her copy of *The Economist* from cover to cover.'

This sentence structure is all right to use now and again, to vary the rhythm of the language or to affect the emphasis, but, because the reader has to wait so long for the subject of the sentence (Jemima) and for the main verb to appear, it does make the reader work harder than he would if it were written in the more straightforward way:

> 'Jemima settled down in the armchair and read her copy of *The Economist* from cover to cover.'

The first sentence is longer and the information is offered in a more complicated way than is necessary.

More problematic, however, and yet increasingly common, is for the subordinate clause to cause brain fever in the writer who forgets altogether what the subject of the sentence is suppposed to be.

> 'Having settled in the armchair, Jemima's magazine fell on the floor.'

The mistake here is that the subject of 'having settled' is Jemima but this gets forgotten by the second half of the sentence which reads as if the magazine had settled in the chair rather than its reader.

> 'Freezing cold and hungry, the boy's coat was no protection against the rain.'

Here the boy is the subject of the first part of the sentence but the second half reads as if the coat were.

The point about narrative does not just apply to straightforward news or news feature writing as you might expect. In those cases it is obvious that stories are being recounted but in other sections of magazines, too, the story model is used. Advice articles might use a fictional narrative thread, or real-life case histories, or be framed round a countdown to an event. Even the picture-led sections of the consumer press are thought of in terms of stories (see Chapter 3).

The advice always given to news writers does not apply to every kind of magazine work but is useful to have in mind. If you are telling a story there are six questions that will need answering at some point: who, what, where, when, why and how. In literary writing the answers to these may not all be offered at once (or even at all) but in news journalism it is usual to provide them as soon as possible. Certainly by making sure you answer these you will ensure that the essential information is given.

Retaining the human interest

Another important point about much journalism is that it is, ideally, about people. Even quite abstract information will almost always be told in terms of the people who are affected in all but the driest of magazines. So, if an announcement is made in *Press Gazette* about a radio station's closure it is likely to be written about in terms of job losses. If a new, environmentally-friendly nappy is designed, it will be featured in terms of happiness for green parents or the potential for discomfort among babies.

This point goes well beyond the simple techniques of language use – it is about deciding what is a story in the first place or at least deciding how a story should be framed. This is why interviewing is so important (see Chapters 9 and 10). In order to produce accessible narratives, people have to be involved. This gives rise to the phrase that you will hear anywhere there are journalists: 'human interest' is what makes readers read stories and journalists must therefore learn how to provide it.

When most people talk to each other or when fiction writers tell us stories they tend to use concrete words rather than abstract ones and this can be a useful guide to journalistic writing. To oversimplify: concrete words describe tangible things such as desks, chairs, people, hair; abstract words are the intangibles such as love, kindness, plans, philosophy. If a novelist simply wrote that a couple were 'in love' her career would not take off. It's when the love is described in terms of the concrete that the picture emerges: red roses are sent or red traffic-lights are ignored, a red dress is worn to attract. This is not to deny that writing about abstractions in abstract terms can be done and done well but to indicate that mostly in human interest journalism it has no place, and also to suggest that when a reporter is struggling with a piece of journalistic writing which is not working out well this might be a key with which to start the diagnosis.

A closely related point is the old one about descriptive writing needing to take account of all the five senses if it is to be vivid. Most school pupils are taught this at some stage but many forget during the undergraduate years of wrestling with argument and the exposition of ideas in their essays. Orwell makes this point in his essay. His suggestion is that a writer should not even begin to think about words until he has established as clearly as he can through pictures and sensations what he wants to say (Orwell 1946: 139).

Another test with which to diagnose problematic writing would be to look at whether too many verbs are being used in the passive voice. Again Orwell draws attention to this and he would have had all the more cause to do so if his essay had been written fifty years later (Orwell 1946: 139), as the growth of officialese in that time has been huge and it is in officialese that the tendency to overuse the passive voice is most prevalent, especially what might be called the dangling passive, which is where the subject of the sentence is not made explicit.

First an explanation of the passive voice. A simple sentence in the active voice runs: 'subject, verb, object', as in 'The dog bit the girl'. Changed into the passive voice, and with no loss of meaning this becomes: 'object, verb, subject', as in 'The girl was bitten by the dog.' The problems here for journalistic writing, if we bear in mind the points about clarity, simplicity and economy, are as follows. First, the passive phrase works almost back to front. It is slightly less clear to the reader, perhaps not in this example but in more complex sentences. The reader has to do more work to understand and as we have seen the reader of journalism can't be counted on to do anything but lose interest at the first sign of difficulty. Second then, this means the sentence is slightly less simple than the straightforward active one. Third, and this is the clinching one for journalists, the second sentence is longer than the first. It takes up more space and more of the reader's time.

This does not mean the passive voice should never be used in journalism, merely that it should be used sparingly to vary the rhythm of sentences, perhaps, or to shift the emphasis from the perpetrator to the victim of the attack in this case, from the subject to the object.

The incomplete passive, however, is more problematic and I would advise journalists to avoid it if possible. Here's an example. 'Manolo Blahnik's latest shoe designs were praised.' The crucial information here is missing, because we don't know who did the praising: was it the fashion editor of *Vogue*, a medical foot specialist or even a foot fetishist? The quoted sentence is much more interesting to the reader as soon as the identity of the praiser is known. In this example it may not seem to matter much but if you move on to items of government policy and discussion of it then you can see why a great deal of official writing is done in this uninformative way because it avoids the question of responsibility. The serious reason, then, that the dangling passive voice should be avoided in journalism, is that its use means the writer or whoever she is quoting is not telling the whole story.

There will be occasions when this kind of language is unavoidable. In the UK we have a tradition of off-the-record political briefing which functions by not assigning responsibility for statements to any individual. There may be a good case for this system (although I can't see it), but all journalists, whether in favour or not, should be aware of the way that language works to support it.

Avoiding loose ends

Where a dangling passive is used out of carelessness rather than out of an attempt at obfuscation it is an example of something else that journalists should avoid – the 'loose end'. (Literature, again, may be different as in literary writing ambiguity may be part of the effect the writer is trying to achieve.) Loose ends are merely gaps in the information the writer is providing. In the dangling passive examples the subject of the verb is missing but in other examples it may be a bigger chunk of the narrative that is missing or, and this happens more often, something is mentioned in the story which is never properly explained, leaving the reader feeling puzzled or cheated or both. As often as not this is a result of lazy reporting and not a problem of language use but sometimes the two are connected and since it is a problem that could emerge at the writing stage and should definitely be picked up by either the writer or the subeditor it is worth mentioning here.

One example is where a mother was interviewed about the effects on her family of an accident her toddler had while in the care of a nanny. The child was badly injured. The mother was quoted as feeling guilty about having left the child in the care of someone else and said she had vowed never to leave the child in the care of another again. The story concluded by reminding readers that the mother had a demanding career. The loose end here is that given the vow and given the job, what arrangements has the mother made for the child? Does it come to work? Does the father look after it? The granny? Does the mother have the freedom to work always at home? Will she ever leave it with a babysitter or is the child inseparable from its mother until it reaches adulthood? What about school? The underlying point of the story was to undermine the confidence of mothers in those whom they trust to care for their children. It left open many questions about what that might actually mean in practical terms but even within its own limited narrative did not address the questions it gave rise to.

This kind of omission is much more common than it should be in journalistic writing and arises when journalists are working too quickly, for whatever reason, or when they are not asking enough questions, not thinking through the consequences of what they write. Another factor can be that they are simply trying to include too much information. The point made earlier about journalists having to be selective is relevant here. It may be that a story contains a loose end which doesn't need developing and therefore the easiest way to deal with it is to cut the reference out altogether. In the example I've given this wouldn't have worked because it was intrinsic to the story that a career woman was the subject but in other cases it is simply a question of limiting the points that the writer is trying to make, to keep the main story as straightforward as possible.

Orwell's six rules

In his essay on language Orwell gives six rules including a reminder that no rules to do with the use of English should be regarded as absolute. The first rule, that you should not 'use a metaphor, simile, or other figure of speech which you are used to seeing in print', refers to ways of describing one thing in terms of another, as in 'She was a dove', meaning she had a peaceful manner like a dove (metaphor, where something is described as if it were something which in fact it merely resembles); 'He was like an elephant', meaning he was very large (simile, where one thing is compared directly with another); 'He's been off the bottle for a while' (metonym, meaning he has stopped drinking). All these ways of using language contribute to the richness of English but Orwell's point here is that once they become overfamiliar they lose their strength and become clichés. So 'avoid him like the plague' no longer has any vitality to it as a simile; nor does 'pretty as a picture' or 'cool as a cucumber'.

Orwell's six rules

George Orwell in his essay 'Politics and the English language', written in 1946, offered these six rules for writers of English for non-literary purposes.

1   Never use a metaphor, simile, or other figure of speech which you are used to seeing in print.
2   Never use a long word where a short one will do.
3   If it is possible to cut a word out, always cut it out.
4   Never use the passive where you can use the active.
5   Never use a foreign phrase, a scientific word or a jargon word if you can think of an everyday English equivalent.
6   Break any of these rules sooner than say anything outright barbarous.

Clichés

A cliché is an expression which has become so familiar that it has lost its freshness and therefore its strength. Whoever first used 'tip of the iceberg' or 'level playing field' or 'crystal clear' was using figurative language to try to make what he was saying more vivid. Phrases like that get taken up by other language users, though, and after endless repetition they no longer carry figurative force and simply act as verbal padding whether in spoken or written language. If we were considering worn-out figurative language only as a kind of failed attempt at last-minute decoration this might not matter, as the reader could quickly learn to ignore it. But language is not that. It is the essence of what is being written or said, as Orwell suggests: 'If thought corrupts language, language can also corrupt thought' (Orwell 1946: 137). If you agree with Orwell it's clear why clichés should be treated with suspicion or at least circumspection. The risk of using clichés is that your writing will be dreary and will therefore not be read by people who have anything better to do. More seriously, the danger of writing clichés is that they can come to shape the way you think. If you're used to writing about teenagers as bored, or footballers as brainless, or blondes as bimbos, then it takes a big effort to notice that the ones you actually talk to are none of those things. I have slipped, here, from the individual cliché of expression to the stereotyping of people or ideas but that is deliberately to demonstrate the problem with clichés: how quickly they can slide from one thing to the next and establish or perpetuate a bad habit of thought.

Two further points about clichés and journalists. From a charitable point of view it can be said that one reason why clichés creep so widely into news and news feature writing is the pressure of deadlines. Not a bad excuse, although this and some of the other points made in this chapter about the constraints of time and space should perhaps raise questions about why these pressures are so often allowed to excuse so much slack practice. From a less charitable point of view it has to be recognised that clichés are what many editors want both in the words and the thoughts of their writers. Anyone who has written for a variety of publications will know that some subeditors have a licence to inject clichés into the writers' copy. It's as if editors fear readers won't be able to follow the story or the line of thought unless they have the well-trodden mental footprints of clichés to guide them. (The magazine *Private Eye* offers its readers excellent parodies of a variety of journalistic styles including the cliché-ridden.)

Euphemisms

Closely allied to the idea of the cliché in that it also helps to deaden the impact of language and therefore to conceal precise meaning is the euphemism. Since, as I write, there is a war being fought in Europe, the examples which spring to mind are 'collateral damage' and 'ethnic cleansing', both in themselves innocuous phrases but ones which refer to the killing of human beings either by accident or design. Terms like these are not usually made up by journalists, they are used by officials and then taken up by journalists whose job really ought to be to write and speak more clearly. 'Collateral damage' is military jargon and as such has no place in an account of war written by a journalist for the general reader unless she wants to draw attention to the euphemistic way in which soldiers refer to what happens in wars. 'Ethnic cleansing' is vicious, racist murder and the adoption of a word like cleanse, which has so many other, positive connotations, assists readers in denying what it is they are actually reading about.

These are the extreme examples and there are others: 'child abuse' sounds mild enough compared with the systematic torture or rape to which it routinely refers; 'sexual harassment' sounds blandly bureaucratic compared with the actuality of the incidents reported; discussions in the UK about the rights of parents to use 'corporal punishment' on their children might be more honestly discussed if more precise words such as hitting or beating were used. In these cases journalists may try to excuse themselves by saying that the reality is too unpleasant to spell out – an excuse that would be more convincing if the media were not otherwise filled with stories and examples of cruelty and horror.

Less extreme examples of euphemism may matter less in ethical terms but they nevertheless lend an air of unreality and untruth to the journalism which perpetrates them. Those more high-minded journalists who see part of their job as being to struggle against lies and evasion should keep at the forefront of their minds the way that language contributes to exactly these twin barriers to the truth, just as it always has.

All journalists at the beginning of their careers should be encouraged to reflect on what exactly they are doing with language when they use it. It is not the job of a book like this to dictate the purpose to which language should be put but language is the tool of the trade which journalists use most and, to judge by the strong feelings that are aroused in any discussion of its use, it's a tool which is believed to carry immense power.

Political correctness

On a related note we need to look briefly at what many writers call political correctness but which could, perhaps less controversially, be called courtesy. In many publications a writer goes against the house style if he refers to women or any other group which is thought to be disadvantaged in such as way as to enhance that disadvantage. So, for example, only a well-established feminist could nowadays get away with writing about girls when she meant women.

In the early days of the struggle by ethnic minority groups and women for social equality many journalists dismissed the idea that choice of words made any difference. (This was perhaps surprising since they had staked their lives and livelihoods on the fact that words did matter.) Now, however, many of the bigger publishing houses have recognised that there is something excluding about, for example, writing which uses the male pronoun, he, all the time when the people who are being described are in fact a mixture of he and she. For that reason they recommend a variety of strategies such as always using 'they' to describe an undefined person or, as I have done in this book, varying at random the use of he and she.

When you write for a publication you need to find out from the house-style book what its policy is on this as there is still considerable variety and the phrase 'politically correct' is often used to denigrate worthwhile attempts to think about the full significance of a writer's choice of words. Of course, the prescriptive aspect of this can be taken too far but the underlying motive is, in many cases, less sinister than polite.

In her discussion of house style linguist Deborah Cameron makes clear how arbitrary are some of the precepts laid down by style books and by chief subs (see Chapter 11 and Cameron 1996). These precepts do, nevertheless, have to be accepted by those who want to write for a publication. This is where the Orwell essay can help as it has formed part of the received wisdom on language in journalism circles for many years.

One of the things Orwell most hated was pretentiousness. The journalist has to work at avoiding this in two ways – there's her own writing and then there's the writing or speech of others whose views she is responsible for reporting. If self-important or obfuscatory language is used by others it is the job of journalists, as we have seen, to translate it into everyday language that is accessible to the audience they are writing for. Orwell's essay gives many examples of how language can be used to confuse rather than illuminate in the way the writers 'dress up simple statements and give an air of scientific impartiality to biased judgements' (1946:131).

Orwell recommends choosing short words and although this advice should not be taken to extremes, it isn't a bad beginner's exercise to try to rewrite a piece of serious journalism from, say, a political or business magazine, in words of one or two syllables.

Impossible, of course, but good practice in the discipline of writing for a mass audience. The point about cutting out words, too, is a good one. Anyone who has worked as a subeditor knows how easy it is to trim down the words of someone else and yet how difficult to do the same for your own work.

Perhaps the last word should go to Samuel Johnson. He is often quoted for the following suggestion which, in my experience, proves especially helpful to writers who are struggling in the early days of features writing: 'Read over your compositions, and where ever you meet with a passage which you think is particularly fine, strike it out.' Naturally it is better if the writer can do this striking out for himself but if he fails to then he should remember there is always a sub to do it for him – the danger is that the sub might choose the wrong fine paragraph and ruin the sense.

Recommended reading

Bryson, B. (1990) *Mother Tongue: The English Language*.

Cameron, D. (1995) 'Civility and its discontents: language and "political correctness"' in *Verbal Hygiene*.

Carey, G. V. (1976) *Mind the Stop. A Brief Guide to Punctuation*.

Evans, H. (2000) *Essential English for Journalists, Editors and Writers*.

Fairfax, J. and Moat, J. (1981) *The Way to Write*.

Hicks, W. (1998) *English for Journalists*.

Orwell, G. (1946) 'Politics and the English language'.

The Oxford Dictionary for Writers and Editors.

Strunk, W. and White, E. B. (1979) *The Elements of Style*.

Venolia, J. (1995) *Write Right! A Desktop Digest of Punctuation, Grammar, and Style*.

Waterhouse, K. (1991) *English our English (and How to Sing It)*.

Whale, J. (1984) *Put It in Writing*.

7 Newswriting

'Now we've gotter write news,' said William cheerfully. William sat,
moustached and wigged, at the biggest packing-case.
'But there *isn't* any news,' objected Henry, 'nothin's happened 'cept rain.'
'Well, say it's been rainin' then,' said Douglas encouragingly.
'You can't fill a newspaper with sayin' it's rainin',' said Henry.
'Newspapers don' only say news,' contributed Ginger with an air of deep
wisdom, 'they – sort of say what they sort of – think of things.'
'What sort of things?' said Henry.
'They sort of write about things they don't like,' said Ginger rather vaguely,
'an' about people doin' things they don't like.'
William brightened.
'We could easily do that,' he said.

Richmal Crompton, *William in Trouble*

Most books for journalists assume that news is what journalism is about and a variety of definitions of news are accordingly offered. A book about magazine journalism doesn't need to repeat these since in general magazines are not in competition with the other news media to be first with anything. They sometimes are but that's not usually their prime aim. Trade or professional publications may well bring new knowledge to their subscribers – a new product or a new surgical technique – but it seems to matter less whether this information is exclusive. Magazines and periodicals are likely to be less urgent in their approach, and all the better for it, as Martha Gellhorn, legendary war correspondent and writer of news, features and fiction, believed. 'The trouble with writing for any newspaper is lack of space: I feel as if I am talking at top speed in one breath' (Gellhorn 1989: 171). Something of the same works for readers who may feel, as they read a magazine piece, that they are not being hustled from one point to the next with quite the haste that a newspaper report would employ.

Space is not the only constraint on journalists. Shortage of time is another. Time is also significant within the story itself. Almost every news intro you read in a newspaper will mention time in some way, to make clear to the reader when an event happened as well as to convey the impression that the paper is as up to date as possible. If an event took place at one minute past midnight then an evening paper (or a morning paper, supposing they still have deadlines so late) would refer to it as taking place 'early today' not 'late last night'.

Even where that pressure does not exist, on a monthly or a weekly periodical for example, it is normal to include a reference to time in almost all stories. If a new product is launched then the readers want to know when. Writers would be wrong to assume that magazine stories do not need to be precise about time if they relate to events which were widely covered in the daily news media. Each story has to be complete in its own right. Another reason for this is that many stories are covered by virtue of when the event happened. If that's recently, then good enough, but otherwise a story is most often tied to a 'peg', which means it is seen to have relevance to the readers because of a date. This may be an anniversary, for example there was a mass of journalistic material produced to mark the fiftieth anniversary of the end of the Second World War. To some this may seem an artificial requirement. If a feature about the aftermath of the war is worth reading is it really worth reading only on the fiftieth anniversary? A good question, which not only those outside journalism might ask. However, journalists do like to stick together (unless they are in a position to scoop the others exclusively) and so the peg prevails, even if ordinary readers don't accord it nearly as much importance as journalists do.

News in magazines

For the purpose of a book about magazines, though, there is no need to look into all aspects of hard news. Those reporters who cover general news, even for magazines, will find plenty of books about news to explain how to go about collecting and writing it. Here we will think of news in magazine terms, the imparting of new(ish) information relevant to the audience of a publication. In the previous chapter some general aspects of journalistic writing were covered but there remain a few to consider which relate to the newsier pages. It's also worth indicating some of the common assumptions about, and techniques of, newswriting for newspapers as the writing style on many trade and professional papers is modelled on these. So, too, to some extent are the principles of news selection.

Length

In Chapter 6 we saw that in journalism words, sentences and paragraphs are kept relatively short. This was explained as part of a striving to use words clearly and economically, without looking at some of the practical, production-related reasons for keeping things short. The first of these is to do with the length of lines typically used to print journalistic writing. Few magazines are printed with lines as long as those in books. These lines, for example, have an average of fourteen words or 84 characters in them. In *Minx* a typical story would have five words to the line (roughly 30 characters if you count the spaces between words as one character), in *Time* a typical line is about seven words (42 characters) long. A tabloid newspaper would have maybe three or four words to the line, and short words at that. This explains why paragraphs whose length is acceptable in books may seem too long if translated into journalistic print: the columns turn into long slabs of grey print without that rest for the eye provided by an indented new paragraph. The same is true of words. In short lines, long words can take over almost the whole width of the column and lead to an excessive number of lines ending with hyphens: yet another reason why journalism has a tendency towards shorter words.

Story structure

If journalism is about telling stories then one of the things which distinguishes it from more literary writing is the regularity of the way news stories are structured. The thinking on most newsdesks is that all the important points of a story should be included in the first paragraph, or perhaps the first two if the story is complicated. From then on the story should be told almost in descending order of importance, bringing in the relevant supporting evidence from quotes as soon as possible. This structural formula is usually referred to as an inverted pyramid.

Another reason for using this shape relates to the readers who, as we have seen, are assumed to be always in a hurry. They may not want to read to the end of stories but want to get the gist of an event by quickly reading the intro and first few paragraphs. An underlying problem with this model, which is not much voiced in newsrooms except perhaps when it causes problems for a trainee, is how to assess that descending order of importance. For many seasoned reporters, who have absorbed thoroughly the values of their publication, or indeed of the prevailing journalistic traditions, it may seem obvious which points are more important. Journalists sometimes refer to this as having a 'nose for news' or, more formally, 'having news sense'. Many practitioners will argue that this sense is innate and can't really be taught, even though it is possible to list the characteristics which are typical of news stories, and to analyse both the process and the outcome of news selection (Galtung and Ruge 1973).

There is another structure used regularly, although more often in features writing and in American journalism. It is what is known as a 'delayed drop' because instead of starting with a bald statement of what has happened the writer eases into the story, with some lines of description perhaps, or some other tangential information.

In this kind of intro the most important information may not be offered first but what is presented has nevertheless to intrigue the readers enough to make them read on. The introductory paragraph, or intro, is regarded by journalists as the most important by far. In striving to get it right a journalist is often in the process of identifying the most important elements of the story and many will say that, at least as far as news is concerned, once they have settled on a good first para the rest of the story falls into place. How the rest of the story is written depends on the magazine and the sort of news pages for which it is written. Broadly speaking, though, the basis of a great deal of news journalism is the quotation from verbal sources or, as Michael Schudson phrases it from the American perspective, 'The interview is the fundamental act of contemporary journalism' (Schudson 1995: 72). How quotes are acquired is covered in more detail in Chapter 9 but how they are used will be discussed here.

Facts are sacred . . . or are they?

It is an axiom of British and American journalism that news is not meant to be biased in any way and presents a balanced account of any story. This is the 'comment is free but facts are sacred' line of the late C. P. Scott, former editor of the *Manchester Guardian*, that is usually quoted to new journalism students. (Martha Gellhorn said that her own journalism tended to take the opposite stance. This may or may not be why she was, in the eyes of many, such a great reporter.) Clearly magazines and newspapers do not, in practice, take the Scott approach or, to take an extreme example, we'd never have seen headlines such as *The Sun*'s infamous 'Gotcha' which heralded the sinking of the *Belgrano* during the Falklands War in the early 1980s. Many young reporters have found it confusing to be told repeatedly and categorically by senior journalists that objectivity is the name of the game and yet to read, in every publication, reporting that is not objective at all.

There is nowadays a more open debate both among practitioners and among academic commentators about the contradiction although it is a debate which can become irrational and defensive if participants from the two groups find themselves together in the same room. Arnold Wesker, who studied the workings of journalists in preparation for writing a play, touches on the reason: 'Journalism intimidates because its currency appears to be irrefutable fact and the great myth about himself and his profession to which the journalist succumbs is that he is engaged mainly in the communication of objective fact' (Wesker 1977: 105). There is still a reluctance among journalists to recognise that, as Wesker puts it, 'fact may not be truth, and truth, if it has any chance of emerging, may rest in the need to interpret those facts.' One understandable reason for this reluctance is that there is security and simplicity in the idea that to report is merely to chronicle events using an agreed set of criteria by which to judge what matters to readers. If journalists admit that by their choice of stories or angles they are exercising not only a personal choice but their power over the way readers view the world, then by implication they carry more responsibility than most would want or admit. The tension with academic discussion of journalism practice is therefore predictable. Schudson suggests that the notion of objectivity as a professional value in journalism was from the moment it was articulated as an ideal nevertheless recognised to be a myth 'because subjectivity had come to be regarded as inevitable' (Schudson 1978: 57). Yet Wesker's evidence, and much research, suggests that what commentators observe is not always the same as what practitioners see. Rather than being defensive, practitioners might do better to acknowledge what is obvious to everyone else and continue to do their job with an open acknowledgement of how difficult it is.

Common sense (another ideological position!) ought to show how impossible it is for reporters to write anything but the simplest of hard news stories without at least an attitude of mind contributing to the shape of the final story. At its most transparent this is because reporters develop their stories by asking questions and as soon as they begin to consider who to ask or indeed what to ask they have begun to shape the outcome.

To give an example. If a bomb explodes in a city street and four people are killed the story, so far, is straightforward and can be reported in one simple sentence without any point of view slipping in (unless of course an official tries to block the publication of the story as a means of preventing the public from panicking). If, however, the reporter covering the story asks the police if the event can be linked to the Hamster Liberation Army then an element of bias has already crept in, with the suspicion that the HLA may be involved. If he further seeks quotes from the city's leading hamster-hating pressure group then their view is accorded an importance which may, or just as easily may not, be justified. (For a discussion of how linguistic choices, too, can reflect the ideological position of journalistic writing see Fowler 1991 and Cameron 1996).

The hamster example may be light but the point is serious and has attracted wide academic attention, the best introduction being Cohen and Young's reader where they make the point:

> There is a common conception of news as an objective body of events which occur and which the journalist pursues, captures in his notebook or newsreel and takes back triumphantly to his editor. Objectivity consists in reproducing the real world as faithfully as possible. But even within the boundaries of this rather simple

conception, it is obvious that it is not technically possible to reproduce all the events, to tell all the stories, to give every bit of information. So some selection must take place.

(Cohen and Young 1973: 15)

Several essays in their book examine how this selection process works, based, as it is so often, on the journalist's 'news sense', that is her skill in predicting what readers want to know. This does, inevitably, lead to bias as events are always interpreted in the light of what a given group of people perceive to be of importance and this is in turn affected by their own views about 'how things happen' in society and what that society is like. Cohen and Young are careful to point out that this bias is not *necessarily* 'impelled by a conscious machiavellianism' of the sort that censorship exemplifies (Cohen and Young 1973: 19). It can be just the result of habits of mind (or, I would add, the absorption of crafts skills and norms) which mean that journalists and editors endeavour to 'fit' events into a particular world view.

The American journalist Pete Hamill has argued persuasively against the current trend in newswriting towards 'salacious soap opera' of which the obsession with Monica Lewinsky's story and with third-rate celebrities are the most obvious examples. For him the best news writers 'provide knowable facts . . . and separate the knowable from the speculative'. He says that ought to be the strength which will enable print media such as newspapers and magazines to see off the competition from TV news and the Internet 'who cannnot or choose not to do that' (Hamill 1998: 99). The flaw in this argument is perhaps that what is actually being trusted by readers is a writer and not a medium. If a trusted, methodical, accurate writer set up a website then readers could look at her work there instead of in print. It so happens that print journalists like to think that the unregulated nature of the Web means that the material is not sifted and assessed by journalists and therefore is unreliable. Given the low levels of trust the public seem to have in what they read in newspapers it's hard to see quite where journalists like Hamill get their confidence in their own ability to gather and process more accurate information. Nevertheless, Hamill is aware that there will always be some limitations. In his plea for higher quality news publishing he argues that journalists 'must ensure their stories are true, or as close to truth as the imperfect tools of reporting can make them' (Hamill 1998: 88/89).

For Hamill that means quoting from as wide a variety of sources as possible and few news editors would quarrel with that, even if the usual constraints of time and money mean that 'as possible' takes on a less than desirable regulatory function. Academic discussion of the use of quotation in journalistic writing draws attention, as you might expect, to aspects of the practice which journalists take for granted but which observers are freer to question. Schudson, for example, notes that American journalists did not routinely ask questions until the early nineteenth century, that interviewing did not become common until the late nineteenth century and by now, according to American research into Washington reporters, 'journalists depend so heavily on interviews that they use no documents at all in nearly three quarters of the stories they write' (Schudson 1995: 72/73). He notes that journalists use quotations to establish their credentials, to demonstrate that they are doing their job properly, are in touch with the right people. The interview can be viewed positively, perhaps, as a 'means of cultural control over people in the public eye' but it nevertheless continues to raise uncomfortable issues of whether an interviewer makes news or reports it, 'of whether the journalist is reponsible to the interviewee . . . or to some other force – "truth" or the "public" or the news institution' (Schudson 1995: 88/92).

Quotations

For reporters the quotations they gather are part of the process of telling a story: they are used to gain responses to events, to report announcements, to make a case, to illustrate a predicament or to describe what an eyewitness saw. One of the frustrations for new journalists is to discover that however worthwhile a point of view or a line of argument about a particular event may be, it can't usually be argued on the news pages except through the words of people other than the reporters. There are exceptions to this: *Time* magazine labels its opinion pieces with that word at the top of the page.

The position in consumer magazines, however, is different. Some of the human interest feature articles in both women's and men's consumer magazines are written on the quotation principle as this is thought to be the best way to tell the story. But much of the rest of what is written in consumer magazines is opinion of one sort or another and that is almost certainly what readers enjoy about them. Don't look to *Company* for a balanced news item assessing the merits of a new line in bubble-bath, or even a discussion of whether bubble-bath is harmful to the skin. Don't read *Loaded* for a balanced assessment of the dangers of drinking too much beer.

Presenting the quotes

Common as quotes are the technicalities of using them can be confusing for a beginner. First punctuation. House style will determine whether the quotation is to be indicated by single quotation marks 'like this' or with double quotation marks "like this". Whichever is the style the opposite will be the case for a quotation which is used within a quotation as in this example.

> The editor said angrily to the writer: 'I told you if someone you interview says "don't quote me" then you mustn't give their name.'

In this example you will notice that 'said' is in the past tense. This is usual when a quotation is said on one occasion, when it relates to a particular event or even interview. Often, however, 'says' in the present tense will be used instead.

> The editor says 'It's quite wrong to publish the names of those who want to remain anonymous.'

Here she is reported as expressing a generally held view or policy, one which she might be expected to hold again tomorrow or next week. The present tense gives the feeling of continuity whereas the past tense, in the first example, implies that the quotation was taken from a single conversation. This is not a firm rule but a useful guide. The other thing that the present tense does is to convey immediacy, in a way that we are all familiar with in ordinary conversation. In an account of an evening out on the town a friend might say:

> 'So I go up to the bar, order my drink. Next thing the barman pours a beer over my head.'

The speaker and the listener know that the events took place in the past but the present tense brings the story to life.

This pursuit of immediacy is one of the reasons that quotations are so widely used in journalism, a point to remember when trying to decide which bits of a story should be put into direct speech (a quotation) and which should be put into indirect speech, as in:

She said she had gone into the bar and ordered a drink.

When the material gathered by interview is put together into a story by journalists it is usual to use a mixture of direct speech and indirect speech, linked together as appropriate perhaps by narrative, perhaps by linking phrases. If an eyewitness account of a big story is being given then direct quotation may take up more of the story but a less dramatic story, especially one where the interviewees have not had much that is interesting to say, will be better written with more reported (indirect) speech. The advantage of direct quotation is vividness, especially true if the speaker has a way with words, but even if she hasn't there is a liveliness about direct quotation which is lost in any other way of reporting what is said. Against that, however, it should be said that direct quotation can slow down the progress of a narrative or argument if it used too much.

Journalists therefore try to achieve a balance. In selecting which words to quote directly they seek out the most individual or personal phrases and leave the more general points or those which act more as a kind of summing up in reported speech. So, in the above example, the speaker might have said by way of introduction to her anecdote about what happened in the pub 'It was a really good night out.' This bit could be written indirectly in the interests of moving the story along as: She said it was a good night out until things went wrong in the pub. 'I went up to the bar . . .' and so on. Some writers would do this naturally but it's a point which can cause confusion among new writers and subeditors. In fact fiction writers who use dialogue have to make similar choices when considering how to tell their stories so there is no harm in looking to novels and short stories for examples of how to do this.

On the more technical aspects of punctuating quotations, I have mentioned the two different kinds of quotation marks and that their use is really just a matter of house style but a point which gives a lot of trouble is whether to put other marks of punctuation such as commas and full stops inside or outside the quote marks. There are some house styles which are slightly quirky on this point but in general the advice is to be logical.

If a full sentence is in the quotation then the full stop comes within the quotation mark.

The stylist said: 'I am not going to feature white shoes, whatever they're showing on the catwalks this season.'

Notice here, too, the use of the colon before the quote. This is, again, partly a matter of house style but is commonly used where a quote is of a substantial length. If the style of a publication is chatty and colloquial then the colon might not be used as it can be thought of as implying a longer pause and therefore a slight slowing down of the reading process. It would also not be used where the quotation is short.

The editor said 'No cigarette ads'.

This example shows too that it is correct to put the full stop outside the quotation marks, where the quotation is just a phrase rather than a sentence or even sometimes if it is a sentence but a very short one.

Things get more complicated here if there is a quotation within a quotation but armed with logic the writer should not have too much difficulty.

> The subeditor said: 'This headline doesn't work. How can the writer argue Elvis Presley is "not really dead"?'

The single quotes are put around the whole sentence. The double quotes around the quote within a quote. The question mark relates to what the subeditor is asking, not the writer and so it has to be outside the double quotes but inside the single one to show that it relates to the whole sentence. If a question mark had not been needed here then a full stop would have been used in its place, like this: dead".'

It's even more confusing if you start breaking up quotations, as journalists often do, to make clear, early on, who is talking or even just to vary the rhythm of the sentences.

> There was a lot of confusion after the press conference. 'I couldn't find the photographer,' said the reporter, 'so I just had to do the interview and hope the editor didn't want a photo.'

The second half of the quote doesn't need a capital letter at the beginning as the whole quotation is being seen as one statement. If a full stop was used after the word 'reporter' then the second half of the quotation would need to begin with a capital letter.

One final point to note about quotation is that when a lengthy quote is used it may run on for longer than one paragraph. The convention in English, although not in other languages, is that where this happens quotation marks should not be used at the end of a paragraph but they should be used at the start of the next one to indicate clearly that the direct speech continues. This does not apply if the speaker changes. A new speaker gets her own punctuation.

Other ways of writing news

The guidelines for structuring a news story – important information first, basing it around quotations – are not firm rules although they are widely used. Whether they are adhered to too strictly by news reporters is a question raised when you see the styles adopted by other media. *The Guardian*'s 'Society' section, for example, puts on its front page brief versions of the kinds of stories that fill the UK's regional papers. They are summarised and the full amusement or pathos or curiosity of the human interest in them is brought out in a way that is often either lost or even laboured too much by the conventional way of writing. There are magazines which offer digests of the week's news such as *The Week* or *The Guardian*'s 'Editor' section. *The Spectator* has long published, at the beginning, a succinct summary of the week's general news. None of these have space for the full treatment which a story is accorded on the news pages (or even in the News in Brief columns which many papers have) but it is possible that as readers become accustomed to reading these terser versions of stories fashions in general newswriting will change. Regular readers of 'alternative' magazines will already be familiar with more variety in the way news can be treated as will those who are used to reading the news pages of magazines and newspapers from other countries or even community newsletters nearer home which are written by those who haven't been trained as journalists.

What is news?

So far in this chapter we've looked at the writing of news stories but not much at what actually constitutes news in the first place. Again, for newspapers this would be a simpler task. As Johan Galtung and Mari Ruge quantify, and almost any newspaper demonstrates, there are certain conditions which hard news stories satisfy to a greater or lesser extent. These include, about any given event, its frequency, its relevance to the audience, its proximity, the extent to which it is exceptional and so on (Galtung and Ruge 1973: 70). In magazines, with specialist readerships, news could be almost any piece of information or opinion that might be of interest to the readers and that they did not know before, although even the second part of that statement shows how much scope there is for interpretation here: unless readers can be depended upon to read every page in every issue of a publication it may well be that editors have an excuse (or, more positively, a duty in the case of trade and professional publications) to keep certain types of information before their audiences. The readers and their interests have to be at the centre of a journalist's thinking. Readers of a bike magazine are likely to be keen cyclists so stories about changes in the laws which affect cyclists would be more prominent and be written about in much more detail than they might in a magazine for policemen, or car-owners, or even a general news publication. For readers of *BBC Wildlife* a news story might be about the opening of a new wildlife sanctuary. For readers of *Press Gazette* it could be the sacking of a national newspaper editor. For readers of *J-17* it might be the launch of a new range of lipsticks although this is as good an example as any of the way in which news selection is an ideology laden process, whatever journalists like to think. The news here would be little more than free advertising of a product and the perpetration of the views that, first, girls should wear lipstick to enhance their appearance and, second, that they should regularly buy new lipsticks even before the old ones are finished. There are any number of things that teenage girls might be offered in the way of news: the choice is made according to an ideological position, clear to the observer if not to all editorial staff and readers. If the topics which constitute news are so varied, it's no surprise that the approaches to writing differ too. Much the same may be said of feature writing for magazines – but that's another chapter.

Recommended reading

Cameron, D. (1996) 'Style policy and style politics: a neglected aspect of the language of the news'.

Cohen, S. and Young, J. (eds) (1973) *The Manufacture of News* (2nd edition 1981).

Evans, H. (2000) *Essential English for Journalists, Editors and Writers*.

Fowler, R. (1991) *Language in the News: Discourse and Ideology in the Press*.

Hamill, P. (1998) *News is a Verb. Journalism at the End of the Twentieth Century*.

Hicks, W. (1998) *English for Journalists*.

Keeble, R. (1998) *The Newspapers Handbook*.

McNair, B. (1996) 'Journalism and the critique of objectivity' in *News and Journalism in the UK*.

Orwell, G. (1946) 'Politics and the English language'.

Reah, D. (1998) *The Language of Newspapers*.

Schudson, M. (1995) *The Power of News*.

8 Features writing

It is hard news that catches readers. Features hold them.

Lord Northcliffe

If Lord Northcliffe's view of features journalism was positive he is not always echoed by all journalists. The view that real journalism is 'hard news' and that its opposite is 'soft features' still prevails on some newspapers. This even though Northcliffe's point has probably been true for as long as there has been mass market journalism, and in particular since the broadcast media took over the job, in most homes, of bringing in the hard news. Northcliffe's point is that hard news is much the same wherever you read it but the features create a unique tone and character. If that is partly true of newspapers it is much more true of magazines, many of which contain almost entirely features material.

To take the exceptions first. News magazines such as *Newsweek* or *The Economist* all have news pages but as they are not published daily it is not usual for readers to get their first information about big events from them. That comes from the daily press or from radio or television unless the subject is of interest only to specialists. This means that even in news magazines what is written is as background to the news or as a development of it. Accordingly, a more accurate name for some periodical newswriting would be news backgrounder, a term that is familiar on newspapers too. It's one kind of features writing, as we shall see. It's also a kind of features writing which can't be dismissed as 'soft'. A news backgrounder differs from straight hard news in that it will offer more information and greater length and space than is available for the writer to explain the issues or cite examples. So it follows that to write news features is at least as demanding, if not a whole lot more demanding, than to write news.

For the reader features may be more interesting to read because they offer a deeper and wider coverage of their subjects. Peter Preston, former editor of *The Guardian*, goes so far as to say that the public's appetite for topical features is 'ravenous' and that this goes some way to explaining why the periodicals industry is in buoyant form.[1] While futurologists like to argue that the printed word is on the way out, magazines continue to be launched and sold in ever higher numbers in Europe and North America.

What are features?

We have noted that news is written about in terms of people, as far as possible, that it tells stories about human beings, that a strong narrative thread is important and that newswriting should contain references to time. A great deal of newswriting is constructed around quotations, ideally from people as living sources but also from written sources, particularly press releases. Much of this is true of features writing but there are several differences between features and news and therefore between what writers specialising in these types of writing are expected to do.

One thing that will be obvious to anyone who reads a lot of journalism is that the distinction between the content of periodicals and newspapers is becoming increasingly blurred. I stress content because there is still plenty to separate the two kinds of publications in terms of design, paper quality and so on. But where content is concerned newspapers nowadays provide readers with a wealth of feature material, whether in the main news sections or in the burgeoning number of supplements and specialised sections they produce. This is of interest to magazine journalists because in many ways these supplements are simply magazines – the weekend colour supplements for example – or if not they may be using exactly the same kinds of stories and styles of writing as publications which are more usually thought of as magazines. Even on the traditional news pages it is true to say that much of what appears could actually be called features writing rather than news.

It's also true that the word journalism in its broadest sense has always covered a variety of types of writing including reporting, essays, descriptions of people and places, gossip, reviews, advice about how to do any number of things, comment on current events or indeed on events which are not all that current. Among all this we would recognise news by the fact that it is new information and, almost always, that it is being reported as soon as possible after the event. It's also a word that has been used in English in its more or less modern meaning for many more centuries than features. Features writing is topical as well but it is much less tied to the moment than news. Editors like to have the security of writing about the same topics as everyone else (unless they have an exclusive) and so if there is an event such as the break-up of a pop star's marriage or the murder of a 10-year-old by another child, these stories are likely to prompt hundreds of stories on related topics.

However trivial some features topics are there is a significance to the best features writing which should not be ignored. John Pilger refers to what he calls 'slow news' and says his book *Hidden Agendas* is devoted to it. The phrase is usually used disparagingly among journalists to mean a day when the 'authorised sources of information' such as governments and corporations are out of action and there has not been any act of God or calamity to interest the hard-news hacks. Pilger's positive use of the term is to describe the stories that take longer to uncover, which are less immediately tied to the daily or even weekly agenda and which are often ignored altogether by most news media. In his book there are good examples such as his revisiting of East Timor and his account of the sacking of dockers in Liverpool in 1996. Pilger's journalism is passionate and committed – passionate about humanity, particularly the underdogs of humanity, and committed to telling the truth, or at least a version of the truth different from those which predominate in most of the mass media. Even those who don't share his political convictions can learn from his methods. He asks questions about events and received wisdom that lead him to uncover new ideas and information. Viewed even just as good examples of the practice of features journalism his books are worthy of study, while for those who share his convictions he is one of Britain's current journalism heroes.

I've mentioned that features are less tied to time than news and are likely to be longer than news stories, but these are not absolute rules. A news story in *The Economist* is likely to be longer than many a feature in *That's Life!* or *Chat*. What almost holds true though is that a feature story is likely to be longer than a news story in any given publication.

Another distinction between the two kinds of stories is that in features there is often more scope for the writer to develop or use an individual style of writing as well as to allow more of the writer's personality to show through. Indeed one American textbook's definition of features writing takes this point further than most British features journalists would when it says 'A good feature story is a creative work of art.' The same book suggests that in features writing 'to make a point the writer controls the facts – by selection, structure and interpretation – rather than the facts controlling the writer' (Metzler 1986: 190). This is a useful way to begin thinking about features, where more emphasis is put on writing style and tone, even if it is rather naive about the extent to which facts stand by themselves on the page, unimpeded by anything the writer might do to them.

So far I have perhaps implied that magazines are filled with either news or features and indeed that would be one way to summarise even if it is too simple. News or trade magazines are easier to divide up in this way than the consumer magazines which contain a wide range of material, some of it written by journalists, some not. Typical things to find in these magazines are interviews, gossip pages, competitions, advice columns written by agony aunts or uncles, reviews, listings, surveys, crosswords, fashion and style pages, cookery, home interest, horoscopes, personal opinion columns or columns recounting some aspect of life, whether it's daily home life or some other kind. Many magazines carry letters pages and these are often good indicators of the tone of a magazine. The problem for monthly magazines, however, is that by the time a letter has arrived in the office and found its way into an edition of the magazine, several months may have passed because of the long lead time to publication.

Consumer magazines

It is not my intention here to explain how writers or editors produce all this material, as in many cases the way this is done is entirely individual to a publication or, as in the case of horoscopes or fiction, is really beyond the scope of what journalists are expected to do other than sub them. There are, however, a few points worth making about consumer magazine journalism.

Fiction

The first is that whereas fiction used to be a prominent part of many magazines for women and girls, it no longer is. *The People's Friend* is one which still runs romantic stories but many others have stopped. What seems to have replaced romantic fiction is realistic sex. Indeed the prevalence of articles about sex in many consumer magazines is enough to prompt the suggestion that recruits to these publications had better make sure they have learned by heart Alex Comfort's *The Joy of Sex*. Agony aunts who discuss personal relationships have been a staple of consumer magazines for centuries, even if the material they now discuss is more openly about sex and less about romance or strategic marriages than once it would have been.

Horoscopes

A second point is the popularity of horoscopes. If an aspiring journalist had a gift for writing these the success of her career would be assured, provided the fashion for them didn't change. The trouble is, as with any branch of popular entertainment, trends change unpredictably but inevitably.

Listings

An increasingly common part of a magazine's contents are listings connected with entertainment. Some magazines such as *Radio Times* and *TV Times,* are based almost entirely around listings for broadcast programmes. Yet other magazines such as *Hello!* list television programmes. Newspapers all do this too and there now text-based listings services on television. Perhaps the continued popularity of these paper lists is evidence that electronic journalism is not yet in a position to replace the more traditional paper journalism in the daily habits of readers.

Reviews

Reviews are a staple of many magazines whether their main coverage is of the arts or of politics. For some young journalists writing reviews can provide a useful way into print but the bigger and more established a publication is, the more likely it is to want to engage big names to write reviews. Reviewing rarely pays well although it can bring other rewards such as free books or tickets to events you would otherwise have to pay to see. A regular reviewer for a good publication may build up her own relationship with record or publishing companies so that even if the reviewing work dries up on one magazine, enough of the raw material continues to arrive through the post to provide ideas and subjects on which to base pitches to other publications. Reviewing is hard to break into in one way, as arts or literary editors tend to use their own coteries of writers. However, it isn't time-consuming or expensive for someone who wants to break in to write a couple of sample reviews to offer to an editor.

Josephine Monroe, television critic, *Time Out*

It's not easy, at the age of 18, to get a first job in magazine journalism if you have no training. Josephine Monroe, who is now 27, managed it though. She worked on an entertainment magazine based in south London called *Croydon Leisure*, and says one of the reasons she was offered the job so young was the fact that she 'was willing to work for seven and a half grand'. She didn't mind working for a pittance then but her initial foray into the world of reporting was short-lived. *Croydon Leisure*, the publication which had offered her the big break, folded after just four issues.

After travelling abroad for several months, Monroe was offered a place on the London College of Printing's year-long periodical journalism course. As part of it she had to do a two-week work placement and chose to go to *The Mirror*'s showbiz desk where she worked with Rick Sky, wrote several pieces that were published in the paper, and was lucky enough, she says, 'to be taken under lots of people's wings'.

As it so often does, a good work placement led to shifts. For Monroe this meant a weekly day at *The Mirror* where she became, in her own words, 'a full-time Rickette' on the showbiz desk. Among other things this meant keying in the pop-music chart listings when they arrived on a Sunday and proof-reading the pop pages for Monday's edition.

That may sound like fun but the job made Monroe miserable. 'I hated it. I found it very, very difficult and left in tears almost every day. Tabloid journalism's very hard and I'm not a natural tabloid journalist.' She felt, at that stage, she couldn't compete with the other staff when it came to bringing in the big-name stories.

Monroe decided to go freelance but soon found herself back with showbiz writing for the magazine *Inside Soap*, where she was eventually offered a job. 'It was one of those all-hands-on-deck jobs. We worked three weekends in four. Half the week we worked until midnight and often we were in the office till two or three in the morning.' It was during this time, she says, that she learned a lot about the different aspects of magazine production and got a book deal.

She left *Inside Soap* after two years because she was worried that she was getting more of a name as a soap expert than as a journalist. In the week she left she was offered regular work by *TV Times* and made her living doing this along with 'odds and sods . . . really scraping the barrel with freelance stuff'. This included writing crosswords on soaps, TV and sex under the pseudonym Cruella de Vine.

Security beckoned when *Time Out*, the London listings magazine, advertised for a television critic, and Monroe beat off the other 900 applicants to get it. 'I mentioned cable and satellite in my interview,' she says. 'I think they thought that qualified me as cable expert.'

As television critic she finds herself writing a weekly column on the cable and satellite industry, calling in tapes for review, making sure copy comes in on time and interviewing the producer or director of one of the programmes chosen to be pick of the day in the week's schedule.

She also has to have lunch a lot: 'When you've got sixty television channels to look after you have to maintain contacts. If something goes wrong you have to be able to call someone up and know they'll help in minutes,' she says.

Food isn't the only perk. She counts among the freebies she's received, cameras, Psion personal organisers, trips to Jamaica and New York and pillow-cases with pictures of George Clooney on them. In case that all sounds like too much of a good thing she points out that there are duller aspects of the job too: 'It probably takes almost a full day every week just to read the schedules to find out what's going on. That's tedious.'

Nevertheless she is well aware that by working for *Time Out* she is able to do three things which are important to her. She gets to watch television, she gets to write about the industry as a whole and, occasionally, she gets to interview someone she's really impressed by and can then write a few thousand words about them.

Monroe's advice for would-be journalists is to specialise. 'Find something that you know a bit about and can learn a lot about, whether it's housing benefit, or soap operas or French films. If you specialise you get really good contacts and it's much easier to build up a reputation in just one field.'

Interview by Dawn Kofie

Quizzes

Quizzes, which form such a staple part of journalism for women, are included as entertainment and are often written in-house by the editorial team, and with a great deal of amusement. Readers enjoy playing games like this, even if the pop-psychological approach of most of them is more light-hearted than seriously informative.

Photography

Another vital part of many magazines is the photography. The days of the general photojournalism magazines such as *Picture Post* have gone although photographers are still despatched on stories with reporters for news and some documentary work. It is rare for articles in consumer magazines to devote much space to documentary photography, although there are exceptions: the colour news magazines such as *Time*, *Newsweek*, *Paris Match* or the specialist publications such as *National Geographic*. What is increasingly popular, however, is what could loosely be called pin-up photography, whether it is portraits of bare-boobed babes for the men's magazines, of men unzipped for the women's market, of 'delish' hunks for the girls' magazines or, less lasciviously, of footballers or cyclists in the sporting magazines, of horses in the horse magazines, of model railway kit in the railway magazines or of animals and birds in the many publications now devoted to wildlife. Fashion, beauty and interiors style photos are, of course, a significant part of the content of glossy magazines but they are not photojournalism (see Chapter 14).

Opinion columns

What is true of all these aspects of magazine content which are not strictly to do with journalistic writing is that they help to create a context for the journalism. They also help to create the tone or atmosphere of the publication and this in turn, it is thought, helps to inspire the loyalty of readers.

This tone is further established by the personal opinion columns, whether they are openly labelled as such or whether they appear as a 'letter from the editor' or in some other guise. Whereas, in news, there is a tradition of journalists attempting to write impartially, in consumer magazine journalism this is not the case. Within such a magazine there may be pockets of reportage which do aspire to impartiality, but much of what surrounds these will be opinion in one form or another.

At its most journalistic it may be the sort of column that tells the story of the writer's week or some domestic incident, or it may be almost an essay on a topic likely to interest readers. It would be hard to train a writer to produce this sort of thing. If you think you can do it try it out, several times, and then test it out first on non-journalists and then, if you're going to try to sell it, on editors. The mistress of the domestic life column is Alice Thomas Ellis who wrote the weekly 'Home Life' in *The Spectator* for several years and published collections of these columns in book form. She is, however, one of our leading novelists, as well as someone who had an unusually rich home life (seven children, famous and interesting or weird friends) and so the fact that her column about daily life was so readable is not surprising. The problem with this kind of column is that while many journalists are capable of producing half a dozen of them, far fewer can sustain the effort so the material begins to wear thin.

The journalistic feature

If we turn now to what journalists would consider to be features proper, rather than all those items other than news with which magazines are filled, there is no set of formulae to learn as there is for news. Far more flexibility is allowed in structure, style and tone and, as I have noted, there is more scope for the writer's voice to emerge. (Indeed some editors would say that a voice has to emerge or the writing will remain too flat and too bland to sustain the reader over the greater length at which features are published.) There are, nevertheless, certain types of feature which are common and which can be used in many different ways and to cover many differing topics.

News backgrounder

The news backgrounder I have mentioned and this is probably the most common kind of feature. It is very much what its name suggests: a look in more detail at some aspect of a story beyond the hard news element. As I write, three bombs have exploded within a week in areas of London with large ethnic minority communities, Brixton and Brick Lane. That's the hard news. A backgrounder might look at the groups who are suspected of planting the bombs, what motivates them, how big and influential are they? Another might examine the recent record of racially motivated crime in those areas. Another might interview residents to find out what their daily experience of racism is. There are no real restrictions to the kind of question that can be asked in a news backgrounder, giving the reporter scope to think through the implications of an event and use the usual reporter's techniques to find the answers.

The interview or profile

The interview or profile is one of the most common types of magazine features, whether it is hung on a topical peg or not. Interviews may be with celebrities or with ordinary members of the public who are in the news in their own right or whose job or field of interest is in the news. There are many ways of conducting and writing interviews or profiles and for a fuller discussion of the history and techniques see Chapters 9 and 10.

The composite interview

Closely allied to the interview with one person is what might be called a composite interview feature. That is where a number of people are asked about a particular topic and their views or their stories are told in separate pieces of copy each of the same length, often with a picture at the top. The series of interviews would be introduced with a few paragraphs to explain the purpose of the piece and why it is topical. There is no limit to what this kind of feature might be about. Three examples: young men who earn their living as rent-boys; women who became Labour MPs at the 1997 election; four men who quit their jobs and got rich.

The point of composite features is to tell a story about people, what journalists call a human interest story. Many of the most readable human interest stories are those about people who are not in the public eye. Pete Hamill, in his lament about the state of journalism at the end of the twentieth century, is scathing about how overshadowed ordinary lives are by the predominance of the famous: 'The print media are runny with the virus of celebrity' is how he puts it, noting that among the celebrities who are most often written about 'true accomplishment is marginal to the recognition factor' (Hamill 1998: 79 and 80). Others feel differently, as the contents lists of most magazines show. And Lynn Barber says she writes about famous people precisely because she finds fame to be a subject of fascination in itself (Barber 1998a: xi).

Human interest stories

The term 'human interest' covers a huge range of material, and at its simplest means the telling of any story through the eyes of the people who are involved or affected by it, although often it is the people who are the point of the story rather than any independent event. An example of a typical weekly women's magazine human interest story would be an account of a woman whose teenage son caught her as she fell out of burning building and saved her life. The narrative would be broken up by quotes from her to give a vivid account of the fear and then the gratitude she felt. What the reader gets out of an account such as this is not altogether clear. For journalists it is obvious that as human beings we are all interested in what befalls other human beings. From a literary perspective it could be said that the stories journalists write are the close relations of any other stories that people like to tell and have always told each other, whether fictional or factual or somewhere in between; whether spoken, sung, filmed or written down.

In his anthology of reportage, John Carey suggests that one of the pleasures of reading accounts of the tribulations of others is that it 'places him continually in the position of a survivor' (Carey 1987: xxxv). His view is coloured by his arguable (not to say blinkered) suggestion that good reportage is largely about death and war. (Good reportage can, in fact, be written about almost anything. The preponderance of death and war in the press and in his anthology has, I would argue, more to do with the interests and, just possibly the gender, of those doing the commissioning and selecting of articles than with any absolute notion of what it might be worthwhile to read.) Nevertheless Carey is making a brave attempt to understand why it is that we should want to read lengthy accounts, which go well beyond the bare facts, of what has happened to people we have never met and never will. There would, after all, be little journalism and few journalists if nothing more had been written about, say, that famous car accident in 1997 than: 'Diana, Princess of Wales, died in a car accident in Paris early today.' Readers do want to know more, editors are paid to predict (or perhaps dictate?) how much more, and journalists do want to make a living.

Within the broad category of human interest you could certainly include all celebrity interviews and many interviews with those who are not famous if they are talking about their lives in general. One sub-division of the interview category, for example, is the interview series which is based around one aspect of the lives of a range of people. 'A life in the day' in *The Sunday Times Magazine* is the famous example of this and a tribute to its success is the number of copycat regular features it has prompted both in in the same magazine ('Relative values') and in others: for many years *The Observer* ran a series called 'A room of one's own'; *Radio Times* has a regular piece called 'My kind of day'. These are all shortish and are not designed to probe the depths of the subject's psyche. As often as not they are written in the first person, although usually as filtered through a journalist to make it readable. The point of these is, very simply, to give an insight into one or two aspects of the lives of others.

The triumph-over-tragedy piece

Another staple of human interest journalism is what is known as a TOT or triumph-over-tragedy piece. The nickname is self-explanatory: a true story is recounted about some brush with horror or death or embarrassment or disability. The gravity of the circumstances varies and the style in which it is written up varies too, according to the magazine. There are those who assume that TOTs are found mainly in the down-market press, in particular the weekly women's magazines. In reality there is no such restriction. Upmarket magazines and broadsheet newspapers all have their own ways of presenting what is in essence the same kind of story.

The personal column

If TOT stories are one step away from fictional narratives then there is newish staple of the features journalism world which is perhaps two steps away. This is the personal column in which the writer tells the story of his life week by week, weaving into it the broader narrative of those more momentous life events which can't be recounted in a joky tone just for their entertainment value. Reading these columns is like reading a novel in real time, so at each sitting there is only a limited amount that can have happened to the writer as the illness progresses, or the divorce proceeds. For many readers these narratives are much more gripping than the best fiction for the uncomplicated reason that they are true and in the most extreme cases because far from being triumphs over tragedy they provide a detailed account of the tragedy as it unfolds. Ruth Picardie dies of breast cancer, John Diamond recounts his struggle against throat cancer, Kathryn Flett tells readers about getting divorced and then being ditched by a new lover.

Some readers complain that this kind of writing is self-indulgent and too personal, but they are a tiny minority. Its supporters argue that it's the personal nature of it that makes it so worthwhile to read. John Diamond, who was already writing a regular column before he became ill, merely mentioned the diagnosis one week and found himself inundated with letters from readers who wanted to sympathise or advise, or who took strength from the writing, but who most definitely wanted to read more. It goes without saying that this isn't the kind of writing a journalist can set out to base a career on, but it should be noted as a trend because of what it says about readers.

In many cases the triumph-over-tragedy narrative does involve the account of an event whether it's a train crash or being stuck on a snowy mountain for three days with no food. Part of the piece therefore would be a simple narrative account of the event leading up to the tragedy and its eventual overcoming. Many features though are based just on the account of an event or a set of circumstances. An event such as a political demonstration might be written up as part description, part narrative, part quotation from participants or observers and with some explanation of the political purpose.

Essays

Another feature type, although one more often found in serious magazines such as the *London Review of Books* or *Prospect*, is what could almost be called the essay format. Here the writer takes a topic such as racism, the death penalty, secondary school education, begging or one-night stands and writes a considered piece based on research and reflection. The research separates this from a straight opinion piece though the distinction is not absolute. In a more essay-like article the journalist starts the research phase with a question rather than a point of view whereas most opinion pieces start from a premise with the writer researching only to find supporting evidence. By opinion pieces I don't just mean the kind of polemic that takes a stand on matters of political or ethical importance. In some of the more lighthearted magazines an opinion piece might argue the case for staying single or avoiding football matches on television.

Advice

It would be impossible to discuss features writing without mentioning the 'how to' feature. In one form or another these fill the majority of pages in magazines aimed at women and girls, and that's without including the agony columns which are filled with advice on specific problems. There are, of course, feminist accounts of why it is that females are thought to be so incompetent at leading their daily lives that they need a limitless supply of advice about how to do it. Suffice to give some examples: 'Look great naked. The lazy girl's workout for a sexy body'; 'How to find your mate a boy'. Sociologist Marjorie Ferguson argues that much of what is going on in the pages of the magazines for women and girls is comparable to what happens in religious cults: just as newcomers are initiated into the rites of a religious sect, so women and girls learn the rituals associated with the 'cult of femininity' such as how to cleanse, tone and moisturise their skin among many other things (Ferguson 1983: 5). Harmless enough advice is offered in some cases but as feminists of the more traditional sort argue, the range of topics on which advice is offered is narrowly limited to beauty, fashion, home making and sex (Greer 1999: 312; McKay 2000; White 1977: 46/47).

The recent success of men's lifestyle magazines shows that boys and men need help with learning the basics of daily life just as women have always been thought to. (Or, at least, it shows that publishers have decided there's money to be made out of telling them they need such help.) Readers of *FHM* in 1998 were taught how to wrap Christmas presents for example.

The 'how to' feature appears in almost every kind of periodical publication. Financial magazines tell readers how to purchase pensions or choose a stockbroker; parenting magazines explain the intricacies of nappy-changing; mountain-bike magazines give guides to bike maintenance. The writer's imagination is the only limit to what could be turned into a serviceable 'how-to' piece. The same could be said about features in general. There is not really a restriction on subject matter other than the preferences of the editor and the bounds of good taste: and not even those in some magazines.

Reportage

Another type of feature, reportage, is in fact the vaguest, because the word 'reportage' covers so many possibilities and forms part of so many kinds of journalism. At one level the word simply means journalistic reporting and in that sense it should cover straight newswriting too. However, most British news reporters would not think of applying the word to what they do. If they used the word reportage at all they might use it to mean something more like a news background feature, something which contains elements of descriptive writing and the other various reporting techniques. That's too simple, though, as reportage does not have to be tied to subjects which are currently in the news. Ian Jack, former editor of *The Independent on Sunday*, discusses the way the French word 'reportage' carries a weight that the English equivalent 'reporting' does not and suggests that this has something to do with the limited status of journalism in the UK: 'Reporting never did have much in the way of social status in Britain, where deference and privacy were valued more than "people poking their noses in".' This only gets worse, he argues, the more journalism becomes a branch of showbusiness. For him 'good reporting/reportage means to describe a situation with honesty, exactness and clarity, to delve into the questions *who, what, when, why* and *how* without losing sight of the narrative' (Jack 1998: v, vi).

Some of the best reportage starts not from an event that has taken place by chance but from an interest of the journalist, a question she wants to explore. Jessica Mitford's *The American Way of Death*, an exploration of how the funeral industry works, is as good an example as any. So is the more recent exploration of poverty in the UK by Nick Davies, published as *Dark Heart*. Andrew O'Hagan wrote an article for *The Guardian*'s 'Weekend' magazine which traced the journey of a lily from the field in Israel where it was grown, through the flight to London, the wholesaler, the packaging, the florist to the purchaser. In a long article such as this, a variety of subjects were touched on, giving the reader an insight into many aspects of life: commerce, mourning ritual, the logistics of the florist's trade.

One of the modern masters of this kind of writing is the American John McPhee. He takes a subject such as oranges (in *Oranges*) or the mercantile marine (in *Looking for a Ship*) or man's struggle against nature as exemplified by attempts to reroute rivers or calm volcanoes (in *The Control of Nature*). He then sets out to find out what he can about his chosen topics, using all possible methods of research, and weaves the information into fascinating narratives incorporating history, biography, economics, geography, sociology, geology and psychology (McPhee 1989). Ryszard Kapuściński is another well-known writer whose piece 'The Soccer War', about the war over a football match which broke out between El Salvador and Honduras in 1969, has found its way into anthologies. The idea for reportage may grow out of the hard news coverage of a story which a journalist then decides to revisit. A good example here would be 'Inside Iraq' by James Buchan, published in 1999, which is an account of a visit to the country several years after the war which followed its invasion of Kuwait to see what life is like in the aftermath.

What Mitford, McPhee, O'Hagan, Kapuściński (and, indeed, all the best journalists since Defoe) demonstrate is a strong curiosity. They want to know how things work, why things are done as they are, how people and places and systems fit together.

For some writers the obsession with wanting to know more leads them to do their research under cover, by joining an organisation or pretending to be someone they are not. The most famous English example of this is George Orwell's account of living at the margins of society in *Down and Out in Paris and London* but there have been several other notable examples: Gloria Steinem's account of life as a Playboy bunny (Steinem 1984: 29); Günter Wallraff's description of living as a Turkish migrant worker in Germany (Wallraff 1985); and, going back to the turn of the century, the American journalist Nellie Bly ('the most famous journalist of her time') who feigned insanity as a teenager so that she could find out what life was like in a hospital for the insane (Kroeger 1994). (The ethical questions raised by this kind of work are touched on in Chapter 17 but are in essence similar to those faced by sociologists who seek to gain access to institutions or groups in order to study them.) There are many occasions when journalists do this kind of undercover reporting in a minor way – the reporter who spends a day on the streets of London begging (Gerard Seenan for Glasgow's *The Herald*) or rather longer doing the same thing and backing up the account with research and interviews (Andrew O'Hagan for the *London Review of Books*). It will be obvious why undercover reporting is so often done at the lower end of the social and income scales: much easier to bluff your way through a day as a homeless beggar than as a stockbroker.

For the reader, features like this have the same appeal as any other journalism – entertainment or information as well as the literary pleasure, if the piece is written well, in both the way language is used and the narrative structure. Or, as one of the great journalists, Martha Gellhorn, put it:

> A writer publishes to be read; then hopes the readers are affected by the words, hopes that their opinions are changed or strengthened or enlarged, or that readers are pushed to notice something they had not stopped to notice before.
>
> (Jack 1998: xi)

Unfortunately the kind of reportage in which she specialised is not as common as it once was or as it might be, given how many millions of words of journalism are put together each month. One reason is that it is expensive to produce because of the amount of time it takes to research. Few magazines can afford the luxury of time for their reporters – a week nowadays would count as generous, at least in Britain, but a feature writer who wants to spend time investigating a subject or a group of people fully will not acquire much material in so limited a time if he also has to produce a lengthy article. This is one explanation for the increasing prevalence of the personal life or personal opinion columns: little time needs to be 'wasted' in research (Jack 1998: vii and viii).

The new journalism

This point was anticipated by Tom Wolfe in his introduction 'The New Journalism' to the anthology of the same name he edited with E. W. Johnson. Published first in 1973, and reissued regularly since, the writing it contained and the writers for whom it was a showcase, became the inspiration for many journalists, especially those who wanted to write features. One characteristic of their writing was the use of techniques more usually associated with the writing of fiction to produce articles which in many cases read like novels or short stories even though they were tightly tied to factual reporting. Another characteristic was the depth of the research they were able to undertake. They stayed with their subjects for longer than most reporters can now expect to do.

There was never really a movement called 'new journalism' but what Wolfe and Johnson did was to identify a kind of journalism aspects of which had, in fact, existed quietly for almost as long as journalism and which was becoming fashionable in the United States in the 1960s and 1970s. Some of the writers included in the anthology were or became famous: Joan Didion, Hunter S. Thompson, Gay Talese, George Plimpton, Truman Capote, Tom Wolfe himself.

The only British writer to be included was Nicholas Tomalin, a hard-news man who was killed in the Yom Kippur war. His piece, 'The General goes zapping Charlie Cong', became a model for other writers who wanted to write about media events as they really were, rather than just writing about what the media managers wanted to convey to the readers. Tomalin seems to have written down exactly the words the General used to describe why and how he was killing Vietnamese peasants. The more typical journalistic approach would have been to protect readers from the man's bluntness, perhaps in the General's interest, perhaps to spare the readers the unpalatable truth about what was really happening in South-east Asia. 'There's no better way to fight than goin' out to shoot VCs. An' there's nothing I love better than killin' 'Cong. No, sir' is the quote with which Tomalin finishes the piece (Wolfe and Johnson 1990: 227).

In his article there is virtually no comment by Tomalin apart from the briefest of asides about his 'squeamish civilian worries', and certainly none of the generous use of the first person viewpoint which has provoked not only criticism of the new journalism style but also some self-indulgent emulation from less talented writers. The article's strength is in the way it conveys the emotional reality of war. It was also important, in Wolfe and Johnson's eyes, because it proved that the techniques they had identified as characteristic of the new journalism could be used not just by grand feature writers who had plenty of time at their disposal for research and writing. Tomalin was working to a weekly deadline.

For much of the rest of what came to be called the new journalism time was an important factor. Writers had to argue for enough time to research their subjects, to stay with the people they were profiling over a period of days or weeks rather than just meet them briefly to ask a few questions. They also needed time to write, as what they were doing aspired to the condition of the best literary writing even if the writers themselves might not have expressed it in quite that way.

In search of emotional reality

The two most common criticisms of this kind of writing are, as I have noted, that it can be self-indulgent and that it makes false claims to be true. The self-indulgence criticism can be answered simply by saying that when good writers allow themselves into the story then it is for the benefit of the narrative: it is a choice the writer makes for good literary reasons. Journalism, however, like any other craft or art is not always successful. As Paul Scanlon put it in his introduction to an anthology of writing from the American magazine *Rolling Stone*: 'Until you have mastered the basics of good writing and reporting, there is simply no point in trying to get inside a movie star's stream-of-consciousness, take an advocacy position on dog racing, or invent some new punctuation' (Scanlon 1977: 9). Even among the more seasoned reporters a generally good writer may misjudge her work on some occasions or less skilful writers may attempt to use techniques which they are not capable of using well. In journalism a tradition has grown up that the story should be told in an impersonal third-person voice and so when the first person was used for telling stories rather than in clearly labelled opinion pieces there was bound to be resistance from editors. There was also bound to be a flock of journalists who seized on the technique thinking it was an easier way to write than striving for all that objectivity. So, yes, it can be lazy and self-indulgent for a reporter to write more about her own feelings than to report those of others, but that's emphatically not what the new journalism, at its best, is about. It is, instead, about trying to use every means possible to get at different aspects of reality, both the circumstances of an event and the emotional or social reality that goes with it. Sometimes, because journalism is about human beings and the things that happen to them, allowing the reporter into the story can make it that much more vivid.

Getting at the truth

The other criticism, that exact accuracy can't be guaranteed, is one which can only be countered if the reader is able to trust the writer and this is one reason why it matters if journalists are viewed as dishonest, as they increasingly are. Sebastian Junger in his book *The Perfect Storm* addresses the problem directly in the Foreword when he discusses the various sources of information he has used 'to write a completely factual book that would stand on its own as a piece of journalism' but which would not 'asphyxiate under a mass of technical detail and conjecture' (Junger 1997: xi). In writing about the deaths of six fisherman at sea he had the additional setback of not being able to interview the men to find out about their personalities or ask how it feels to be dying in a storm. One of his several approaches was to interview those who had nearly died in storms at sea. He resists the temptation to fictionalise any parts of the story, or dialogue, in his attempt to write 'as complete an account as possible of something that can never be fully known'.

The difficulty for sceptics arises when a reporter reproduces lengthy dialogue that he has overheard, as Wolfe does in the extract from 'Radical Chic' in his anthology. How can he remember everything? The answer, given by Wolfe, is that he achieved this by using 'the oldest and most orthodox manner possible: . . . arrived with a notebook and ballpoint pen in plain view and took notes in the center of the living room through the action described' (Wolfe and Johnson 1990: 412). Another of the sceptics' questions relates to passages of interior monologue which some 'new journalists' write. Gay Talese's comments on this are illuminating. He says that as a writer he used the same techniques that his mother used in conversation with the customers in her dress-shop which was a 'kind of talk-show that flowed around the engaging manner and well-timed questions of my mother'. She would simply ask 'what were you thinking when you did such-and-such' and she was a good and patient listener (Talese and Lounsberry 1996: 2–5). In other words he would ask, listen and make detailed notes.

This is where trust or faith comes in. You either believe that to be possible or you don't, but there is no real qualitative difference between trusting a reporter who writes in the new journalism style or one who writes in the more conventional way. Both kinds of writers include those whose work brings the business of reporting into disrepute as well as those who bring it respect. What isn't in doubt though is that in as far as journalism is about 'getting at the truth' there exists a variety of truths – social, psychological, emotional – in addition to the events which are the narrative framework holding them together. To get at these various truths there is no reason why journalists, like fiction writers, should not experiment with a variety of techniques. Readers will make up their own minds if editors give them the choice.

In the UK, however, readers do not often have the opportunity to choose to read the kind of feature writing which in the USA is now increasingly called creative non-fiction or literary journalism. These labels reflect the development of this kind of writing since the 1970s. Gone, more or less, are the pyrotechnics of punctuation for which Wolfe and Thompson (and indeed the new journalism) became known. Accepted, though, is the more measured, often book-length reportage of Joan Didion, John McPhee, Gay Talese, Norman Mailer, John Berendt, Tracy Kidder, Calvin Trillin, Jonathan Raban and Gabriel García Márquez among others.

It's not every aspiring journalist who wants to do this kind of writing. In the UK at least there is still a prevalent suspicion of what can be achieved and many features editors would not want to publish features written in this way – just as they would not be able to pay for the time the research and writing processes would take. (Although, as Carl Bernstein points out, Jessica Mitford achieved impressive journalistic results without a journalistic empire 'to back her up with clout and clips and cables and credit cards.) Armed with a sturdy pair of legs, a winsome manner, an unfailing ear and an instinct for the jugular she sets on her merry way' (Afterword in Mitford 1980: 262). It is, however, important for new feature writers to be aware of both the constraints and the possibilities of the genre. They may never have the freedom, as Gloria Steinem did for the piece entitled 'I was a playboy bunny', to research a piece about the Playboy organisation by training and working under cover as a playboy bunny for several weeks (Steinem 1984: 29). Or, as Pulitzer prizewinning journalist Tracy Kidder did, to follow a computer-design team to research *The Soul of a New Machine*, which in turn took over two years to write. Or, as John McPhee did, to spend several months living on Colonsay off the west coast of Scotland to write *The Crofter and the Laird*. Or, more recently, as Sebastian Junger did to write *The Perfect Storm*. But there is every sign that non-fiction has an increasing appeal for the public imagination, as the popularity of books such as Dava Sobel's *Longitude* or John Berendt's *Midnight in the Garden of Good and Evil* show, along with the popularity of confessional journalism and biography of various kinds. A further illustration of this trend is the recent profusion, on British television at least, of fly-on-the-wall documentary series such as Michael Waldman's compelling *The House*, about the Royal Opera House. There is no evidence that the public's appetite for the drama of real life has waned so it is perhaps surprising that magazine features editors have not chosen to offer their readers the literary equivalent. Much of what is commissioned is either the fantasy fodder of the lifestyle magazines (fashion, food, furniture, football and sex), straightforward news background, gossip about celebrities, practical advice about how to manage some aspect of life or else personal opinion.

Putting a feature together

Features, as we have noted, are likely to be longer than news stories. This usually, if not always, means that more material has to be researched. It also raises the awkward question of structure. News is almost always written to a formulaic structure but features writers don't have similar formulae to provide the framework of their writing and if they do make habitual use of one approach then their work will lose its edge. The truth is that what works at a length of 250 words will not be successful at 1,500.

There is no ideal way to structure a feature so the best advice is for writers to analyse ones that seem to work well in the kind of magazine for which they want to write. It is common in many publications to see case studies based on interviews used even for stories about quite abstract subjects. For a piece looking at government pension policy, for example, it would be normal in many magazines (and newspapers) to start with a real-life case study or two as a way of attracting the reader's attention. Then the more abstract discussion or the qutoes from financial experts can be woven into the whole piece. The problem is that although this is done for good reasons it has, in its own way, become a cliché of feature writing.

So there are no fixed rules about features structure although individual publications may have their own. Even where there are rules, fashions in features style seem to change more quickly than those in news, depending on the publication, its readers and the purpose for which the features are being written. It's easy to see, therefore, why journalists who like in-depth exploration of a topic choose to work on features, as do those for whom the literary aspects of writing are part of the attraction of journalism. The broader scope and wider choices of subject matter and approaches to writing up the material can seem liberating to someone used to the constraints of hard news, just as they can also seem somewhat bewildering to the beginner.

Note

1   Peter Preston, the Hetherington Lecture, Stirling Media Research Institute, Stirling University, 29 September 1999.

Recommended reading

Capote, T. (1989) *A Capote Reader*.

Carey, J. (ed.) (1987) 'Introduction', *The Faber Book of Reportage*.

Davies, N. (1997) *Dark Heart*.

Didion, J. (1974) *Slouching Towards Bethlehem*.

García Márquez, G. (1998) *News of a Kidnapping*.

Gellhorn, M. (1989) *The View from the Ground*.

Granta, published quarterly by Granta Books.

Hicks, W. (1999) *Writing for Journalists*.

Jack, I. (1998) 'Introduction' *The Granta Book of Reportage*.

Junger, S. (1997) *The Perfect Storm: A True Story of Man Against the Sea*.

Kapuściński, R. (1998) 'The soccer war'.

McPhee, J. (1991) *The John McPhee Reader*.

Mitford, J. (1980) *The Making of a Muckraker*.

Pilger, J. (1998) *Hidden Agendas*.

Scanlon, P. (ed.) (1977) *Reporting: The Rolling Stone Style*.

Sims, N. (ed.) (1984) *The Literary Journalists: The New Art of Personal Reportage*.

Steinem, G. (1984) *Outrageous Acts and Everyday Rebellions*.

Talese, G. and Lounsberry, B. (1996) *The Literature of Reality*.

Thompson, B. (1998) *Seven Years of Plenty: A Handbook of Irrefutable Pop Greatness 1991–1998*.

Wharton, J. (1995) *Magazine Journalism: A Guide to Writing and Subbing for Magazines*.

Wolfe, T. and Johnson, E. W. (eds) (1990) *The New Journalism*.

9 Interviews 1: chasing the quotes

....

I am bad at interviewing people. I avoid situations in which I have to talk to anyone's press agent. (This precludes doing pieces on most actors, a bonus in itself.) I do not like to make telephone calls, and would not like to count the mornings I have sat on some Best Western motel bed somewhere and tried to force myself to put through the call to the assistant district attorney. My only advantage as a reporter is that I am so physically small, so temperamentally unobtrusive, and so neurotically inarticulate that people tend to forget that my presence runs counter to their best interests. And it always does. That is one last thing to remember: *writers are always selling somebody out.*

Joan Didion, *Slouching Towards Bethlehem*

No matter what kind of reporter you want to be, interviewing will be a big part of your work. This is because other people's words are the building blocks of so much journalistic writing. Writers of leader columns or opinion pieces do not need to use quotes but almost all other journalism is based around quotes of one sort or another (Schudson 1995: 72). The way to get these is by interviewing.

A process and a product

....

To journalists, then, the word interview means two things – the conversation a reporter has with someone, as well as the copy into which the words are subsequently shaped. Such conversations can cover a wide range of encounters. The news reporter's two-minute chat on the telephone to get an instant quote in reaction to an item of news is the quickest. Other news coverage might demand longer discussions by telephone or face to face to get the outline of a new policy, details of a new product or more extensive views about news events. Longer briefing discussions with contacts might take place over lunch.

Then there is the set-piece interview whose purpose is to present the reader with an account of the personality of a celebrity or at least of one encounter with that celebrity. Interview features of this sort are also written about those who are not famous and often the journalist will get much more time with such a person than with someone who is in the public eye. Everyone has their own tastes, but for me too much space is allocated in magazines for predictable chats with celebrities and too little for interviews with ordinary people.

The late Tony Parker was so much the master of this type of writing in the UK that he can also be read as an ethnologist or oral historian. His work was published in magazines and newspapers, as well as books. One Sunday magazine article was titled simply 'Smith' and was a series of interviews with several women from varying walks of life all called Smith. This kind of feature is entertaining and informative in the way that any sort of insight into the lives of others is, but it can also be as significant in its contribution to the readers' understanding of current affairs as more traditional news reporting and commentary. For example, Parker's collection of interviews *May the Lord in his Mercy be Kind to Belfast* (1994) is an illuminating introduction to the conflict between Catholic and Protestant and, by extension, between any warring parties. The material is presented in a direct manner, in the first person voice of the interviewee with just a few details sketched in as background by Parker. The books of the great American journalist Studs Terkel have a similar appeal. Now in his eighties, Terkel has spent his life interviewing for radio but collections of his interviews have been published and are compelling first-hand accounts of life in twentieth-century America.

The art of extraction

One American journalism training manual defines interviewing as 'the art of extracting personal statements for publication'. The choice of 'extract', with its implication of drawing teeth, is appropriate for journalists. Another definition of news is that it is information which others don't want you to print. If you accept that, you can see why interviews do not always go smoothly. Although an interview is in some ways like a conversation, there are significant ways in which it is not. Conversations can be relaxed, meandering, repetitive, ambiguous but none the less enjoyable for the participants. A journalistic interview can rarely afford the luxury of any of this. As a journalist you have an agenda, a reason for talking to the subject, a set of questions you wish to ask or areas you wish to cover. It's likely that the interviewee will also have her own reasons for agreeing to meet you: your purposes may differ and this can be a source of tension, as Janet Malcolm outlines in her controversial book *The Journalist and the Murderer* (1990).

As a journalist you also have the pressure of time: the time you or your subject have allowed for your conversation and the time you have available afterwards for further research or writing up the results. (Radio and television journalists are much worse off, at least on live programmes, because their efforts to keep to time are on such public display.) If you are doing a story which demands interviews with a number of people you also have to allow enough time to talk to all of them as well as to get back to earlier interviewees if in a later interview something is said that needs a response. It's the focused, purposeful aspect of a professional journalistic interview which differentiates it from much conversation. An interview may turn out to be an enjoyable dialogue but the aim for the reporter is not to make or maintain friendships, even if a subsidiary aim is to make or maintain contacts.

Although the purpose is not social there obviously are sociable aspects to interviewing and for many aspiring journalists this is one of the attractions of the job. There are others, though, for whom the initial stages of developing the skill of interviewing can be trying. Someone who is naturally reticent or shy can find it takes real courage to phone a prominent person and ask them anything, whether it's the serious enquiry of a minister as to his views about the economy or the frivolous interrogation of a popstar as to which is his favourite shampoo. However, shyness is not necessarily a handicap. Provided it isn't crippling it can even work to your advantage. You are unlikely to irritate your subject by being too brash if you are shy and you may even find it easier to establish a rapport with your subject as a result. Many of the people you interview in the course of your career will be more unsure of themselves during a journalistic interview than you are as the journalist. After all, they usually have more to lose if they say the wrong thing or if you twist what they say or report it inaccurately. If you interview politicians or popstars who are used to the media you will probably find they have been trained by experienced journalists or press minders in how to get the most from such encounters. The thing to remember is not to be intimidated. You have a job to do. They have agreed to be interviewed (usually). Either of you can bring the meeting to an end whenever you like.

If more comfort is needed then consider the words of American journalist Joan Didion who has written some of the best journalism of the past forty years. She says her shyness actually helps because her subjects grow embarrassed by the silent pall her nervousness tends to cast over the meeting and that this provokes them to fill the void by saying more than they might have intended (Didion 1974 [1968]: 13). Not a technique available to all journalists for all kinds of encounter but one perhaps even worth faking if the circumstances are right.

How to assess what circumstances demand is one of the skills a journalist acquires through experience. The problem arises out of that similarity with straightforward social conversation. We no longer study the art of conversation as once was done: being good at it is supposed to come naturally (Zeldin 1998). It follows, then, that being good at interviewing is regarded as a natural skill. Against this though, any good journalist says that you must manipulate the circumstances of an interview to your advantage.

Personal attributes

Before we look at some of the techniques to use let's consider personal attributes. Shyness, we've noted, need not be an impediment, whereas overweening arrogance certainly would be. The journalist interviewer is almost always just a channel for the flow of information: an irrigation channel directs and shapes the flow of water but is not the main point of the construction, the water is. In the same way a journalist is not usually the point of the interview. The person she is talking to, or at least his words, are the point. This means an interviewer must be good at listening and also at thinking quickly enough to be able to respond with relevant further questions. Whether you are already a good listener is hard for you to know as most people like to think they are. You could try asking your friends.

Many experienced journalists say there is no such thing as a boring interviewee, only bad interviewers who encounter them. The belief behind this is one of the traditions of journalistic lore that everyone has a story worth telling. This may be true for the kind of interviews that could almost be classed as sociology or contemporary oral history, but it's too optimistic to assume that everyone you interview in the course of the mundane daily round is going to sparkle when questioned about some development in local government policy or even their latest role on the stage. Not everyone is fluent or relaxed enough to provide good quotes to order. It's up to the reporter to get the best material she can. The more imaginative the reporter and the more wide-ranging her own interests, the more likely she is to get good copy from those she interviews. (For a fascinating account of the importance of listening skills and how to develop them see Gay Talese's introduction to *The Literature of Reality*.)

This touches on another common assertion about journalism – that you must have an unquenchable curiosity about everyone and everything to be a good journalist. I'm convinced this is true. It doesn't mean you can't develop a special interest in a particular field but to interview well you must be driven by a desire to question, to find out, to fit together a picture or a narrative from what your subject is saying. Again, this is one of the attractions of journalism for many people: the journalist is paid to talk to an infinite variety of people about an infinite variety of subjects.

Finding the interviewee

Concentrating first on advice that applies to all kinds of interviewing other than the celebrity sort. Let's assume you know who you want to talk to and why. It may be that your news or features editor has suggested people to you as part of a briefing or that the person is in the news on his own account and is an obvious target. The first thing you'll need to do is get hold of the person you want to talk to either to speak to straight away or to make an appointment if time allows. Where do you start?

Easiest to get is the person whose phone number you or a colleague already have. If your interview is with someone who is at work then you can usually find workplace numbers in the telephone directory. Never underestimate the value of *The Phone Book* as even some well-known people allow their private numbers to be listed. Also try directory enquiries as new numbers may not yet be in the printed directory. (There is also a CD-Rom available which lists telephone numbers and addresses throughout the UK.) If that fails then you have to start to think creatively. Might any of your contacts know your target? Are they likely to have an agent or publisher? Do they belong to a voluntary organisation? For many journalists the detective work is part of the fun. Bear in mind that most organisations will not give out the home number of a member of staff but if you're tactful you may be able to persuade whoever is taking the call at work to contact your prey and ask him to call you back. If you leave messages on answering machines, voicemail or through colleagues it is usually worth explaining who you are, what you want to talk about and what your deadline is. Those who work outside journalism don't always realise how quickly journalists have to produce their stories. If you can't get through in person you can additionally try faxing and sending e-mails. Depending on what you want to talk about you might try asking your subject if there is anyone else who could help if he is too busy.

If and when you get through to the person who can help, you may want either to talk there and then by phone or to arrange a meeting. At this stage you are a kind of supplicant, hoping for the co-operation of the subject in an undertaking which may be of no appreciable benefit to him. It pays, therefore, to be as polite as possible and as accommodating as your own deadline allows.

Interviewing by phone

If you're going to talk by phone try to establish if it is a convenient time to talk and for how long the other person will be free. If necesssary arrange a convenient time to phone back when you will be able to talk without interruption.

Don't forget when you are interviewing on the phone that it is more difficult to build up a rapport: your friendly smile can't be detected; the fact that you are small, gentle and unthreatening is known only to you, not necessarily to the person at the other end of the line of whom you may be asking awkward, prying or embarrassing questions. The same is true in reverse: you can't see that your interviewee is responding with no irritation to your nosiness; you can't tell that he is trying to talk about a sensitive work issue just as his supervisor has walked into the office. As ever, the trick is to imagine yourself in the position of the interviewee and think how you would like to be treated. A telephone manner is as personal as conversational style but that doesn't mean you shouldn't reflect on how you tackle this aspect of your job. Make sure you don't keep interrupting. Think of ways to indicate that you are listening with interjections that don't disrupt such as 'I see' or 'That's interesting'. Journalists spend increasingly large proportions of their time on the phone rather than going out to meet people so it is worth learning how to get the most out of each call.

As a beginner this might mean making a note after a call that goes unusually well or badly and taking time to consider how you could have improved the results or what it was about your approach that worked well. In other fields where telephone calls are an essential part of the job – advertising sales or call-centres for example – the performance of staff is closely monitored and appraised, calls are listened to by supervisors and performance evaluated (Cameron 2000). This doesn't seem to happen in the newspaper or magazine industries even though young or inexperienced journalists are often entrusted with sensitive calls and could perhaps benefit from the advice of their more experienced colleagues about how to handle contacts.

When you have finished the main part of your interview don't forget to check the facts such as name, age, spelling of company name and so on. If you have a longish talk it can be easy to put the phone down having forgotten these things. If your story is controversial or complex and you're working to a tight deadline you should ask where your interviewee will be later so that you can get back to him to check things if necessary. This is always worth doing if you are in doubt, as accuracy is important. With luck your interviewee will be more impressed by your attention to detail than irritated by having to take a second phone call.

Making notes

To be accurate you need to make notes. This is true whatever kind of interview you do, but on the phone there are special considerations. The first is that shorthand can be used freely to make notes without the worry of losing eye contact. Phone work is often done from an office and so there is a desk at which to work comfortably, pen in hand. You can also spread out notes about questions and shuffle them about and refer without embarrassment to notes of previous discussions, perhaps with different sources. One problem, though, is that writing shorthand or any other kinds of notes can be difficult if you're also holding a telephone receiver in the other hand. You may even want to be making notes directly by keyboard and this needs two hands. In other jobs where the phone is a vital tool, headsets which leave hands free are the norm. Not so for journalists. Most just have to get used to a crick in the neck.

The merits or otherwise of using shorthand are hotly disputed by journalists, who divide into those who think it is essential and those who think it is unnecessary. My own view is that it is extremely useful for any journalist (I have 110 wpm) but that it would be wrong to pretend it is essential: many successful journalists don't have it. Another method of note-taking on the phone is to record the conversation on tape, using a device that can be attached to the telephone. Some telephones already have these devices built in. The pros and cons of this are much the same whatever kind of interview you do but where the telephone is concerned you have the additional temptation of being able to record conversations easily without the interviewee knowing. There doesn't seem to be any legal restriction over this, only on telephone tapping.

The polite thing would be to say at the outset that you would like to record the conversation and if you've already said you're a journalist it will be expected that you are using some means or other to make notes. But it is easy to see how the right moment for this request might pass, especially in an interview with a busy person who doesn't much want to talk to you anyway. To raise the question of tape-recording makes the enounter seem more formal and possibly more threatening than it otherwise would. Most people who are used to giving quotes will not object to a tape recorder being used although it might be more difficult to get them to speak for some of the time off the record for briefing purposes unless you make it clear that you are switching the tape recorder off when they want that.

Interviewing in person

Turning now to the interview where you meet someone in person either by appointment or by turning up on the doorstep or at the place of work. In the first case there is every chance that you will be met more or less on time but again you must establish how long your subject has to spend with you. If you're preparing a several-thousand word feature based on in-depth interviews with parents whose children have died of drug overdoses, for example, then each interview could take several hours if you want to build up the trust of your subjects and then to get the whole story from them. If, on the other hand, you are meeting a hospital consultant in her office you may have been allocated 20 minutes in her diary. Not much time and so you must make every second count. In cases like this it is worth asking if the subject can arrange not to be disturbed (except in life-threatening emergencies). To sit in the office of some frantically busy doctor or television producer while they field endless calls and then discover that your time is up is a frustration you can do without. You may learn a bit about their work through overhearing what they say and how they say it but unless you're working on a personality profile this information is of no use. If your interview is meant to be about a new medical treatment or the latest announcement about TV schedules, it's not much help to be able to observe that doctor A is always rude to colleagues or producer B is patiently polite to anyone who happens to call.

If the meeting is in an office, circumstances should be conducive to your taping the conversation if there is not too much noise. If you're there just to get a couple of quotes it may be too cumbersome to start setting up a tape recorder. However, it is easy when you start out to feel overwhelmed by the fact that someone busy and possibly important or at least senior in an organisation has agreed to see you. The risk is to be rather overawed and not assertive enough so that simple things which could help you to get the best out of the meeting don't happen just because you were too shy to ask. Remember that if someone has agreed to see you it is their choice (almost always) and although they can choose to end the interview you do at least have a right to be there asking questions.

So, if your meeting is to take more than a few minutes don't be afraid to take time to set up your tape recorder, placing it so that it records properly. Have an eye to seating arrangements so that you are at a comfortable height in relation to the person you are interviewing. If you want the meeting to be relaxed and informal because you don't intend to ask awkward questions then that will affect whether you feel sitting at the opposite side of a power-desk is more appropriate than being side by side at a coffee table for example. On the other hand, if you know you are going to be asking some difficult questions you might welcome the security of a formal set-up. In many cases you'll have no choice but always be alert to the possibilities. When someone has agreed to see you at home you may have to contend with the noises of family life or the television going on around you and there will be nothing you can do to change it. The same is true of bars or pubs, hotel lobbies or factories which can be noisy. These are the circumstances where a tape recorder simply is not much use except as a backup to the written notes you take.

Once you are in the room with your interviewee and you know how long you've got, it's up to you to decide how to play the game, depending on the kind of information you're looking for. Advice from experienced interviewers varies. Some say if you have a killer question you should get it in first so that the interviewee can relax a bit once it's out in the open. The drawback of this approach is that you might be shown the door before you have any material. Where an interview is not controversial one technique is to ensure that you cover all the ground you intend to and that you are open to other ideas and themes that may arise in the course of discussion. These may be useful to broaden the story you are working on or may be stored up as material to pursue when you have a quiet afternoon.

Research

It's worth stressing the importance of research. Most people you interview will be busy and have better things to do than waste time with journalists so to make the best use of your time you must prepare. If your story is for news or a news feature you'll know why you are talking to that individual. The preparation you must do might involve checking your magazine's cuttings files, talking to colleagues or contacts in other companies or organisations which might be affected, using the library or the electronic research sources. Prepare and make notes on questions you want to ask, probably in order of priority. As the interview progresses you may not follow this exact order. If you did it might mean your interviewing style is inflexible in that you are not listening to the responses. But your list gives you something to refer to if the talk dries up and can also act as a checklist as the meeting draws to a close. There is nothing wrong with saying to your subject that you'd just like to check your notes to make sure you have covered everything. Again thoroughness will probably be appreciated and a couple of extra minutes there and then could save you having to phone up later at a less convenient time to check a fact or two.

What to ask

What questions you ask will depend on what kind of interview you are conducting. Do you want straight factual evidence with background detail and perhaps a human angle? Do you want a few good quotes to go with a story that in essence is more or less written? Are you trying to gather background material for a profile of a person or a market sector? When you are in pursuit of quotes there is no point in asking closed questions, ones to which the answer is yes or no. That might be acceptable as a way of getting at the facts but if you want quotable material you must frame your questions to give the interviewee the best chance of expressing herself in her own language. 'What did you enjoy about your trip to Thailand?' will produce a more interesting response than 'Did you enjoy your trip to Thailand?'

The other thing to avoid (if you work for a reputable publication) is the loaded question. No one will respond positively to the 'When did you stop beating your child?' type of question and interviewees will only think the less of you for asking such a silly one (in the end though, it doesn't matter what the interviewee thinks of you so long as you do your job in a professional manner). Like all journalists you are constantly looking out for and making new contacts as well as nurturing the older ones but this doesn't mean you have to temper the questions you ask if you think a story demands some awkward probing. Your reputation as a journalist depends on the quality of your stories and your writing. Most contacts are, in the end, replaceable.

Many interviews are not conducted in the best circumstances. You may be catching a headteacher as she walks to her car and she agrees to talk for five minutes but no more. You may be kept waiting by someone with whom you have an appointment and then be told that there's not time after all unless you're prepared to travel in the taxi to his next meeting. These are yet more occasions when good shorthand pays off. Hard to tape well in a car-park in a gale or in a taxi when the driver is an unreconstructed heavy metal fan.

Off-the-record briefing

When you interview for a news report or feature you may find yourself dealing with a conversation that your source wants to designate 'off the record'. It may not be the whole conversation – perhaps just a short part of a longer discussion which the interviewee does not want to have attributed to him. Information obtained in this way can be valuable as a pointer to the fact that you're on the right track and not wasting your time with a line of enquiry, even if the person you're talking to doesn't want to go on record with a comment. It can help you to find others who might. These sorts of comments, however, do have to be treated with care, depending on the subject. If they are not attributable there is always the possibility that they are malicious or ill-informed, so you should ask yourself why the interviewee wants to talk off the record. There may be good reasons, especially as increasing numbers of employees are prevented from having any dealings with the press, even over quite trivial issues. In many cases an off-the-record comment can give you guidance about what to ask those who have formal responsibility for, say, a company or a policy.

The lobby system

Closely allied to the off-the-record briefing is the lobby briefing system where political journalists are briefed in the 'lobby' of parliament at Westminster but where the name of the individual who did the briefing is not used. For those who follow politics closely there is usually not much doubt about who will have done the talking as the list of characters is limited. Over the years there have been strenuous attempts to end a system which can easily be criticised for being anti-democratic: why should only a few well-informed London-based political newshounds know who says what and therefore who holds which kind of power?

Can you write it up anyway?

From the journalist's point of view a lobby briefing can be more use than off-the-record comments. Because many publications are using the lobby, the story can't be retracted in the same way as off-the-record, unattributable words can be. That's just one of the problems posed when interviewees start to speak off the record. At this point almost every beginner journalist will ask why as a journalist you can't just agree that the words are being spoken off the record and then ignore the agreement when it comes to writing up the story. The short answer is because this would be dishonest. The longer answer is that if you don't respect your interviewee's wishes over this you are unlikely to be able to interview her again. In some fields this might not matter but if you work in a specialist area (and particularly if you work in the trade press) you are likely to need to talk to the same people repeatedly. Your aim should be to treat them fairly. This doesn't mean you don't question them with toughness if the story merits it, or write pieces criticising their organisation when the time is right. But it does mean you need to be sure about the value of the story or the material before you sacrifice harmonious relations. And if you treat with contempt the confidences of one senior manager, say, then word is likely to get out. Others in the same industry will get to know that you can't be trusted. This is typical of the kind of dilemma journalists regularly face.

An additional word of caution for the journalist who is genuinely trying to abide by the off-the-record agreement but nevertheless wants to use the points made by an informant. If the informant agrees to that provided you don't actually attribute the words to him, you might settle on a form of words such as 'insiders say' or 'sources close to the band say'. The trouble here is that unless the pool of such potential sources is large you are in danger of naming the source by implication. Whether this matters to you is, as ever, dependent on the circumstances but it is a real danger which your source may not be alert to and to which you ought to be on his behalf. The other danger is that someone who has not talked to you may be suspected of being the source, something your actual source may or may not be trying to bring about. Journalists should always be aware of the possibility that their contacts or sources might be trying to manipulate them. It's not easy to know how to prevent this happening but a beginner reporter is particularly vulnerable in a field where there is so much received mythology about nods and winks and doing favours. Learning the rules of engagement for any given publication is one of the most difficult things journalists have to do – largely because there are no rules about what would be acceptable behaviour in all circumstances for all journalists.

Recommended reading

Barber, L. (1992) *Mostly Men*.

Barber, L. (1998a) *Demon Barber*.

Barber, L. (1998b) *The Observer*, 'Life', 8 November.

Clayton, J. (1994) *Interviewing for Journalists*.

Davies, H. (1998) *Born 1900: A Human History of the Twentieth Century – For Everyone Who Was There*.

Malcolm, J. (1990) *The Journalist and the Murderer*.

Parker, T. (1993) *May the Lord in his Mercy be Kind to Belfast*.

Silvester, C. (ed.) (1993) *The Penguin Book of Interviews: An Anthology from 1859 to the Present Day*.

Talese, G. (1996) 'Introduction' in Gay Talese and Barbara Lounsberry, *The Literature of Reality*.

Terkel, S. (1995) *Coming of Age. The Story of our Century by Those Who've Lived It*.

Wolfe, T. and Johnson, E. W. (eds) (1990) *The New Journalism*.

10 Interviews 2: chasing the stars

....

The secret to the art of interviewing – and it is an art – is to let the
other person think he's interviewing you . . . you tell him about
yourself, and slowly spin your web so that he tells you everything.
That's how I trapped Marlon.

Truman Capote

The little bastard spent half the night telling me all his problems.
I figured the least I could do was tell him a few of mine.

Marlon Brando

There is an entire genre of journalistic writing devoted to the interviewing
and profiling of celebrities – sportsmen, actresses, singers, presidents, television
presenters, minor aristocrats, rock stars, even people who are famous just for
being famous. The distinction between a profile and an interview is not entirely clear.
At one end of the scale is the profile of the star in words which could be written without
the writer ever meeting the subject. Such profiles are often anonymous and may be
written by an acquaintance of the star, but are otherwise put together from cuttings and
perhaps interviews with colleagues, friends and family. If written well these can give
an insight into the celebrity's work or life although the drawback is that so much of
the copy is secondhand and is unlikely to include fresh material in the form of revelations
or even lively quotes.

At the opposite end of the scale is the interview which does not attempt to make
any general points about the celebrity, merely to recount an encounter which took place
for the purpose of the feature. At its most pared down this may take the form of a
report, more or less edited, of the questions put and the answers given, with Q or A
being included at the beginning of each paragraph. The depth and complexity of such
interviews varies enormously from the level of the 'Biscuit Tin questions' in *Smash
Hits* (where celebrities are asked questions such as 'What's the perviest item of clothing
you own?') to the extended conversations, allowed to run over several thousand
words, made famous by Andy Warhol in his magazine *Interview*. In some magazines
(*FHM* is one) two celebrities may be brought together to have the conversation rather
than a journalist and a celebrity. From the reader's perspective this has the advantage
of allowing him to eavesdrop, as it were, on the lives and thoughts of two celebrities
at once rather than just the one, when the interview is conducted by a more self-effacing
journalist.

Why celebrities are hard to avoid

Before we consider how to conduct and write up encounters with celebrities, it's worth thinking about how and why they have become such a staple of modern features journalism. Some are portraits of people like Leonardo di Caprio or Baroness Jay – written usually because these people are in the news, and based on a meeting or possibly two plus a trawl through the cuttings, a reading of any relevant books, watching of films, listening to music and perhaps talking to enemies, colleagues or even friends. This material is then written up at varying lengths and with varying degrees of reference to the journalist's presence, a point I'll come back to. Apart from the big set-piece interviews taking up four or five pages and accompanied by specially commissioned photographs, in the weekend magazines which accompany newspapers there are smaller features based around the notion of getting to know a celebrity. The most famous and the most copied of these ideas is 'A life in the day' (see Chapter 8). These miniature interviews provide a short, readable insight into one aspect of the life of another person. The journalists are not trying to probe, but merely ask a few questions to fit a formula. This can mean the subjects are more relaxed in the way they talk. No hidden secrets are going to be revealed this way, but readers will be left with the feeling that they have had a brief but worthwhile conversation of the sort you might strike up on a bus journey with someone you've only just met rather than the soul-searching psychological exposition that might go on between old friends who spend an entire evening together. (Other examples of the formula include 'A room of one's own', 'Relative values', 'My kind of day', see Chapter 8).

It's hard to imagine someone, especially a famous someone, choosing to reveal intimate secrets to a reporter they've just met, for publication to hundreds of thousands of readers. So why do stars agree to do interviews? The answer is to do with promoting a forthcoming tour or a new album or even a policy decision. The more interesting questions are what does the journalist and her editor hope to get from these meetings and why should the reader want to read the results.

What the editors want

To start with the editors. Editors believe readers want to read celebrity interviews and so these will help to boost or retain circulation figures. The success of magazines such as *Hello!* and *OK!* which publish photographs accompanied by minimal interviews shows that this is a fair assumption. A further positive reason is that a celebrity may have a genuinely interesting story to tell and has not already told it twenty times before in competitor publications. Then there is the thrill of the chase or the scoop: some kudos attaches to the journalist who can secure an audience with a star who doesn't normally give interviews. There is also the fact that publications help to establish their brand as glamorous and in touch with what is going on in a particular world by having the shining lights of that world grace their pages. Lastly, and less positively, is the way in which one publication doesn't want to be seen to be left out of the celebrity round: if Helen Mirren is featured promoting a new film in one magazine then she has to be in all of them editors seem to think. Reporters may enjoy working with celebrities for the excitement that rubs off on their own lives. Or, more seriously, they may genuinely be fascinated by the whole business of fame (Barber 1998a: x).

What the readers want

Moving on to the reader. A good article based on an interview with a star gives the reader a feeling of greater intimacy with the subject. If you are a devoted fan of a singer such as Ian Bostridge then it's interesting to learn something of his home life, what he reads, where he studied, whether he likes being on the road for concert tours, what he particularly likes about the music of Schubert. Sometimes, too, by reading an article about a celebrity you hadn't heard of, you can be drawn to their work and in the process discover a new writer or sportsman or popstar to look out for. At their best interviews of this kind give the reader some idea of what it would be like to meet the famous person. This is why so many writers of profiles and interviews try to build up a picture of their subject so that they are combining an account of a finite encounter with background information and observation to compose what is effectively a miniature biography.

In many cases the interviewer makes no pretence that the encounter has been for more than an hour or two, perhaps in a hotel or other public place, or perhaps over lunch. In these cases expectations can't be too high. An exchange of ideas on some topical subjects, some comments about the dress and manner of the subject and some biographical background sketched in. That's about all.

What the journalists want

The psychological approach

Some interviewers are more ambitious. What they hope to get at is, if not intimate secrets, then a passably accurate analysis of the interviewee's character. This is what Lynn Barber, highly regarded and experienced interviewer in what has been dubbed the 'jugular' school of interviewing, sets out to do. She recognises that you can't make a profound assessment of someone's character based on an hour's talk but argues we do something like this in daily life: the difference is that she does it with famous people as part of her job. She is perhaps over-stating the case. When you decide whether to hire a plumber or agree to work with someone else on a project on the basis of a short meeting, you don't do a profound character assessment, you merely decide whether you trust them. This is not quite the same as voicing publicly and in the permanence of print your conclusions about how the man's childhood experiences have affected his ability to mend burst pipes.

To entertain and be funny is Barber's declared aim and her method is to choose, wherever possible, difficult characters, mostly men, and to write about the encounters with a bluntness that leaves some readers surprised that she can ever find someone else to interview. What she writes can, of course, seem brutal in its frankness. For the reader the reward is that she is able to avoid the mindless puffery that PR people seem to think makes successful press exposure for their clients.

If avoiding the puffery is a laudable aim, the danger of Barber's pseudo-psychological approach is that her own personality, prejudices and what at its worst seems like semi-digested Freudianism can get in the way of the subject. Her interview with Melvyn Bragg, for example, shows how she works on her material to produce a rather simplistic summary of his achievements and assessment of where he has been misguided in his career (Barber 1992: 86).

Her occasionally clumsy probing and summarising can be compared with the approach of American journalists such as Rex Reed or Barbara L. Goldsmith who make little comment, preferring to observe and let their subjects do the talking within the narrative framework they construct. This allows readers to draw their own conclusions about the characters depicted on the page (examples can be found in Wolfe and Johnson 1990: 72, 244 and Silvester 1993: 556).

The observer

To write a piece such as Reed's 'Do you sleep in the nude?' or Goldsmith's 'La Dolce Viva' the reporters had to spend enough time with their subjects (Ava Gardner and Viva, star of Warhol's Factory) to be able to see them interact with several other people as well as the writer. Gardner is given time to talk and her monologue outpourings, while no doubt carefully edited by Reed, provide a wealth of verbal raw material on which the reader can reflect. The biographical information is included with deftness. The point about time is important. If a reporter is allowed several hours, or a number of meetings over a period of days (as Goldsmith must have been for her Viva piece) or even weeks then the material is potentially much richer.

The promotional circus

Increasingly, however, press interviews with celebrities are arranged to a formal and frantic schedule – a film star may be flown into London from Hollywood to hold court for two days in a hotel room, each of many journalists being given about 45 minutes with the star, whose PR minder is always present. It's not clear what is meant to come out of this sort of event other than a plug for the new film.

Origins of the celebrity interview

To go back to the history of this kind of journalism. In his anthology of journalistic interviews, Christopher Silvester dates the first example of a celebrity one at 1859, when the *New-York Tribune* published Horace Greeley's interview in question-and-answer format with Brigham Young, leader of the Mormon church (Silvester 1993: 4). The first record of the word as a journalistic term in the *Oxford English Dictionary* is in 1869. As Silvester shows, this new type of journalism was not universally welcomed, while those in favour pointed to the illusion of intimacy it offered.

Another thing it does is allow a magazine to use the words and ideas of famous people who might otherwise expect to be paid. If you were to ask a scientist to write 2,000 words about the chemistry of the brain, say, then as an eminent academic she would reasonably expect to be paid, whereas if she is interviewed about the content of her new book she will not be paid (Silvester 1993: 5).

Not all interviews with famous people are about the personality of the interviewee. A business journalist might try to interview the Chancellor of the Exchequer, Gordon Brown, about the state of the economy, or a media journalist might want to talk to James Brown, former editor of *Loaded* and *GQ*, about the UK's men's magazine market.

Practicalities

The celebrity interview can be daunting. For one thing it's not possible to practise interviewing those who are in public life in advance of having to do it for real, unless you happen to have a famous acquaintance who is willing to give you a practice run. So a perfectly competent interviewer of schoolteachers, bus-drivers, parents or any kind of ordinary person in the news may find a celebrity interview much more difficult as fame, power or glamour can induce nerves in those who are not used to them. For those who make a career out of it, this problem soon resolves itself. Once you've met ten mega rock stars, including two of your own heroes, it's easier to face the next one: you know you can do it and you're no longer overawed by the expensive clothes and the entourage of flunkeys or doctors of spin. The other thing about megastars and politicians is that they have almost certainly been interviewed many times before, so they are likely to approach the job with a certain practised professionalism, even if this does mean some of them feel bored by the whole experience.

Where do celebrities come from?

To first things first. How do you get your VIP to agree to be interviewed? If you are on the staff of a magazine the problem may not be yours. A features editor may already have fixed the piece and will merely delegate to you the job of doing it. This arrangement might be the result of the star's PR handler approaching the magazine because there's a book or a film or an album about to be launched, or a politician's office may be keen to get her views on certain policies out into the open. Or it may have worked the other way, the magazine approaching the star, probably for the same kind of reasons of topicality but possibly as part of a longer-term features strategy to get, say, the right mix of cover stories or range of celebrities across the year. Either way if the agreement is in place all you have to do is confirm or arrange time and place. If you've successfully pitched an idea, or if the features editor has had the idea but not yet taken it any further, you'll probably have to do the fixing yourself.

In many cases, where a star is doing a publicity tour, this is not a problem, depending on the importance of your magazine and its reputation for the way it deals with celebrities, things you can't do much about. If your office doesn't already have the number for the celebrity then you can try various approaches: the record company, publisher, theatre, agent or other relevant professional contact of the star; your own contacts in the same field might let you have a number or address. It's quicker to phone but there are people who prefer a written approach as they feel under less pressure to make an immediate decision. A fax can be re-read and can give you space to explain exactly why you're interested in meeting the star. Also, the recipient can read it at a convenient moment whereas a phone call can get you off to a bad start if it interrupts.

Venue

If all goes well, and a meeting is agreed, you have to sort out time and place. What is on offer is likely to be 40 minutes in an anonymous hotel room whereas what you want is two hours at home. The latter is preferred because it allows you to pick up so much colourful material, ranging from how they treat their children to their taste in curtain fabric. However, the more famous the stars the less likely they are to let you anywhere near where they live. Understandable. A record company office, a dressing room, a constituency surgery or other place of work is still better than the hotel room because it allows you to get a sense of the atmosphere in which they work and can often reveal how the star interacts with other people. In the end the choice is unlikely to be yours but it's worth being prepared with suggestions in case for once it is. Where time is concerned you want as much as you can get.

Rules of engagement

There are a couple of other organisational points. In many cases celebrities specify in advance aspects of their life and work which are not to be discussed. You might as well know what these are even if you choose to ignore their wishes. This is not to recommend that you do ignore their wishes, merely to recognise that for some journalists the areas which are off limits are precisely the areas which are of most interest and so will be most vigorously pursued. One problem here for the celebrity interviewer is the increasing power of the PR. It's all very well to offend one Hollywood starlet by not sticking to the agreement about the conduct of an interview if you know you never want to interview her again. But nowadays her publicist will almost certainly be PR to a host of other celebrities and you could soon find yourself unable to get access to anyone at all for your next interview. As Lynn Barber says, editors whose publications depend on star-filled covers are powerless against the virtual monopolies created by publicists whether acting for the individual celebrities or for record and publishing companies (Barber 1998b).

The importance of research

Once the interview is set up it's time for the research. How much you do will vary according to the time available but most experienced interviewers would urge you to do as much as possible. What they mean by research is to find out, by as many ways as you can, information about the celebrity, their life, their views, their past and their work. The sources would obviously be the work itself – watching the films, reading the books, reading up about the sporting achievements – but would include looking at biographical information provided by the publicist, press cuttings, radio or television programmes and in many cases would stretch to talking to friends, family, hairdressers, anyone who could shed light on the personality of the star. For any worthwhile interview, beyond the formulaic 'Biscuit Tin' type, this part of the job is vital. The more you know about someone you interview the more interesting will be the questions you can ask. Interviewees, famous or not, are irritated if interviewers haven't prepared adequately although to be fair to journalists they are sometimes asked to do interviews at unreasonably short notice.

A further reason for being thorough in your research is that it will enable you to make the most efficient use of your allotted time with the interviewee. You won't waste 10 minutes asking where they were born, how many sisters they had or how many books they've written. All the factual information should be in your head beforehand so you can ask them the more interesting questions: 'You grew up in a family of nine sisters. Now you're grown up do you still see each other?' or 'Your wife is an airline pilot yet it's well known that you refuse to fly. Why is that?'

Indeed it's not only the facts that are useful. From reading earlier profiles by other writers you may have gathered which topics your subject is good at talking about and others that he struggles with. Some interviewers think they should know roughly what most of the answers will be before they get anywhere near the meeting. This allows them to concentrate on the way the answers are given and on developing a line of questioning according to what the subject actually says.

Asking the questions

This is an important part of any interview. Part of the preparation phase is creating a list of questions to which you'd like answers. Once you are with the subject you don't stick rigidly to this list unless you are paralysed with nerves. The questions are there as prompts and also for you to cast an eye over towards the end of the meeting to make sure the main points have been covered. But in a successful interview there will be a flow of ideas: the interviewer ought to be responsive to what is said, allowing answers to suggest new, related questions. Such a flow is not always possible. There's the time constraint, and there's the problem of the over-enthusiastic talker who can easily distract you from your purpose. Sometimes this is deliberate: if there are topics your subject doesn't want to talk about then it makes sense for him to try to be lively and eloquent about other, less controversial ones. Sometimes, though, it may be just that your subject is a rambler and your task is to try to prune him into concise, quotable replies. Either way you, as the interviewer, must be prepared to interrupt if necessary to bring your subject back to what you want to talk about.

Power games

Taking control like this can be one of the most awkward things about journalistic interviews, which is why it is vital, in the early days, to keep reminding yourself that you are a journalist with a job to do, not a fan with a hero to worship or a would-be friend with a good impression to make. When you leave the meeting you will have a story to write and your livelihood depends on it. There are many things you may not be able to control about the celebrity interview encounter but where you can be in charge then don't shy away from the responsibility of directing what goes on so that you can get the best possible raw material for your story.

The awkward question

In many celebrity interview encounters there is the prospect of broaching a difficult, awkward or embarrassing question. Advice from the experts on this varies and you need practice to see which approach suits you best. Lynn Barber, for example, says that it can often pay to get out of the way early on the difficult question, the one your subject may be dreading. They can then relax, knowing the worst is over. Others, however, recommend you wait until you've spent enough time with your subject for her to be at ease in your company and for you to have gathered enough answers to have something to write. If it's the one question that anyone would want to ask the VIP at a given moment then I suspect the Barber approach would prove most fruitful. Also, most celebrities agree to give interviews to promote themselves or their work. It's not in their interests to send you away with blank tapes.

There are ways of putting interviewees at ease where awkward questions are concerned. You could perhaps tell them at the start that if you do ask something they would rather not answer they can just raise a hand and that you won't interpret this in the finished copy as 'no comment'.

Is anything off limits?

It can happen that when the difficult question is popped the subject will say things that she would prefer were regarded as 'off the record'. What is said off the record may still be useful, but this is less likely in the case of a celebrity profile when what you want is good, informative quotable material from the subject. Lynn Barber says she ostentatiously does not switch off her tape recorder when this request is made and she doesn't make agreements about treating the material as off the record because for her purposes such material would be useless. Other interviewers don't go so far but say they would never agree to comments being labelled off the record in retrospect.

Some journalists face a dilemma about whether they can use anything that happens during the interview. If, say, you overhear one side of a phone call can you record what you heard or how the conversation affected your subject? The answer here, as ever, is that it depends on the circumstances and the importance of your future relations with the subject. In general, though, you probably should feel free to use the material: celebrities who would prefer to take a call in private can always ask a reporter to leave the room.

Another delicate problem is if the interviewee is not in control of himself because of drink or drugs. Whether to draw attention to this when writing up the interview is a decision for the journalist and editor. It may depend on what kind of publication the piece is for, and whether what is wanted is a no-holds-barred exposé of libertarian behaviour or a positive account of a man and his work.

What to ask the star

One thing which worries newcomers to celebrity interviewing is what sort of questions to ask, assuming they already have the main factual information. There is no simple answer here. Since the interview is usually prompted by the subject's career then that is a fairly safe area to discuss although the challenge is to get them to say something new or interesting. For the more psychologically probing interview, questions about childhood can produce revealing answers. In the end what you choose to ask can be as wild or random as is consistent with getting the best material from your subject.

Another worry that besets beginners is what to do if the subject is rude to them or starts to harass them. This could happen in almost any interview although it is less likely where a celebrity is concerned. What you tolerate will depend on how much you want the story and need the quotes, what kind of pressures await you from your commissioning editor if you return with nothing. The thing to remember is that you are as entitled to draw the interview to an early close as the interviewee is, but the ultimate power is yours because you are going to write up a story from what has happened. If you leave prematurely because the subject has been rude to you he is the one left with the anxiety about how you will use the material, not you. Your responsibility is to your readers, your editor and yourself. Celebrities, whether they are artists, sportsmen or politicians, can usually look after themselves or else pay others handsomely to do this for them.

Writing up the material

For a beginner the actual encounter with a celebrity can be so much a focus for nerves that what follows may not be given much thought in advance. It should be. The writing up of your material is, in the end, what will make or break you as a journalist: a good writer can fashion lively, readable copy from a dull or even disastrous meeting with a celebrity while a hackneyed writer who has seen it all before can render bland even the most sparkling personality.

Reflection

Build in some time for reflection immediately after the meeting. Don't rush to the next appointment or press conference. Set aside an hour at least to spend in a quiet place to read through your notes and sketch in details about the conversation, surroundings or events before you forget them. You might want to list what seem to be the most memorable points. Then, unless you have to write the piece the same day, you can allow your mind to absorb your material while you are thinking about other things, before you sit down to start to shape it into a readable feature.

Transcription

The next hurdle is transcription. If shorthand was your only means of recording the meeting then you must transcribe your notes as soon as possible. However good your speed, memory is an essential part of the shorthand process. You may not need to transcribe everything and as you transcribe you can be thinking about the material and making notes about what to use and how.

With tape there is less pressure to transcribe straightaway as the words don't have to be recalled to mind. It is, however, worth checking immediately that the tape has worked properly all the way through. If it hasn't, and you've just stepped out of the interview room, you may be able to salvage something by noting on paper all that you can remember. Many journalists say that the drawback of tape is that you end up with far more material than is needed. This is true: it will take about five hours or so to type up an interview that lasts less than an hour on tape, if you type every word. But you don't have to do that. As you listen you can edit and select the good quotes. And if, as is ideal, you have made written notes as well during the interview, you should be able to use these as a guide to when the best quotes or stories emerged.

Writing the copy

Once you've done your transcript and, if you're lucky, had a chance to reflect on the material the time arrives to write. For a beginner this may seem less agonising than the meeting with a star but it is nevertheless a challenging moment, especially if most of your journalistic writing to date has been the more formulaic newswriting. If you have been well briefed by a commissioning editor then you should know what is wanted and in what style. This is helpful but still leaves you with a wide choice of structure as well as of material. One hour may not seem long when you are talking to your subject, but if it goes well you'll have a lot of material. A common mistake is to assume that you just write this up in the same order as it occurred in the conversation. This may work well but there is no reason why it should. You are in charge of fashioning your raw material into something more than the mere record of a conversation, you are creating a piece which it is worth someone's while to read. Your aim is to find an angle, or point of view, or some kind of narrative around which to structure the quotes.

Sometimes, but certainly not often, this narrative might be an account of the interview process. In the hands of a skilful writer such as Hunter Davies an encounter which was unusual in some way, or one with a strong personality, can be brought memorably to life. I suspect, though, that the best examples of this kind of writing are based on lengthier meetings than average and where the writer has a chance to do more than merely perch on a hotel sofa for three-quarters of an hour.

To be there or not to be there?

One of the things the so-called new journalism in the USA in the 1960s and 1970s was trying to move away from, according to Tom Wolfe, was the blandness that deadened so much features writing and shackled its writers to a kind of numbing objectivity. It was as if interviews were written by an automaton: the fact that a meeting took place between the celebrity and a living, breathing, talking human being was somehow glossed over (Wolfe in Wolfe and Johnson 1990). He is generalising of course. Good interviews have been published for as long as interviews have been conducted by journalists but so, too, have dull ones. When journalists use the first person and allow themselves into the story the result can be tediously self-indulgent but for good writers the freedom to acknowledge their own existence can be positive.

Lynn Barber recounts that when she wrote about her former boss, Bob Guccione of *Penthouse*, for *The Sunday Times*, she made the case for using 'I' because the usual more objective 'we' sounded nonsensical when she referred back to her time as his employee. 'For the first time I felt I was writing the truth,' she recalls. For her there is no point in pretending that the subject is talking into a void (Barber 1998b: 19).

The skill, whichever voice you choose, is in the judgment. If you write up a celebrity interview in the first person remember that the reader is interested in you only as a piece of narrative furniture. Unless you are famous in your own right, readers really couldn't care less if you felt nervous in the lift beforehand or spilled your glass of wine, or hated the colour of the carpet. What might interest readers is whether the star made any effort to put you at ease, or threw your wine glass at his dog or told you repeatedly how much the carpet cost.

One of the commonest reasons for introducing the persona of the reporter into an interview is when the interview goes wrong. If it does the reporter could just give up and go home or not write up the encounter, but there is pressure to produce copy once an investment of time has been made. The story of disaster can be intriguing but it doesn't do to use this device too often and only if there is something genuinely interesting about what went wrong, perhaps because of the light it sheds on the character of the interviewee.

Another common reason for including the personal aspect of an interview is where the writer adopts the tone of the breathless fan meeting a lifelong hero. These features usually start by establishing the significance of the star both for the writer and for the reader and then move on to an account in which the reality of the star's personality is revealed and compared with the writer's starstruck fantasy. Not many of these interviews get published outside student newspapers but it is common for beginners to try this approach. A word of warning is that one of these pieces is probably enough for any single journalism career.

Inappropriate detail

A mistake which is less common is to use irrelevant information in an inappropriate way. If a journalist does an interview with someone well known but it is meant to be about the person's professional views, not their personality, it can sound strange if a reference is made to the details of the meeting. So, to take a real example, an interview with a university vice-chancellor about his views on higher education policy was rendered farcical when half-way through the writer put in a sentence about how the man took another spoonful of chocolate mousse. Perfectly acceptable in another style of interview but completely out of place in this one.

How to shape the material

Apart from these approaches, the thing to do when you start to write is to be clear about what you're trying to achieve. If your aim is merely to give the reader an impression of what it's like to meet a gorgeous soap star between takes at the studio then things are not too complicated. If your aim is a quick, amateur psychological assessment of a personality, then the structure of your finished piece will require much more thought. A theme or angle will have to be decided upon: how much basic biography is needed to balance opinions about current issues or whatever takes place as you do the interview. There is no single correct approach to the writing of celebrity interviews. For the writer it is important to keep the readers and their interests firmly in mind and to remember that while any given reader probably has a variety of interests they buy a magazine to find articles of a particular sort. For example, a reader of *Loaded* would probably expect an interview with an actress in that magazine to refer explicitly to her sex life whereas if he also reads the *Radio Times* he wouldn't be at all surprised to find an interview with her contrasting her views on working in television and working in theatre. Readers of *Good Housekeeping* are likely to be interested in how the star runs her home and whether she likes gardening, while an article for *The Stage* might look at her early career and how she made such rapid progress to stardom.

One way to start (and this advice holds good for much journalistic writing) is to imagine you meet a reader on the train as you travel back from the interview. What would you say? What would be the most striking thing to recount? Thinking like this won't automatically suggest to you a structure but it will help you to focus on what is significant. For example, if the biographical detail is fairly mundane (popstar comes from comfortable, happy, lower middle-class suburb, two brothers, early promise shown at guitar lessons), you might want to save this information until you have established in other ways what it is that makes your subject interesting today (he's just donated several million pounds to set up an orphanage in the Czech Republic). In this case you would probably fit in the biographical detail by summarising rather than by using extensive quotes.

Since there are no rules the best advice is to read celebrity interviews systematically, making notes about what works and what doesn't, why you think a writer tackled the story in a particular way and whether, with the same quotes, you would have written the piece differently. Around the launch of a film or play or album, stars usually do several interviews for a variety of publications. Pick a name and look at all the interviews with that person so you can analyse the different written treatments and perhaps form some idea of which interviewers were best at extracting good quotes. As a beginner it would be worth trying to write several versions of your early celebrity pieces to experiment with different styles and structures.

Checking the facts

The last stage of journalistic writing is in some ways the most important – the stage at which you check and double check for mistakes or for material which could get you or your paper into legal trouble. Celebrities are more likely to sue for libel than the rest of us because they can better afford the risk. They are also more likely to have reputations that merit the expense of defending them in court.

Copy approval

One question this raises is whether in the interests of accuracy it is a good idea to show the finished copy to the celebrity before it is published. The answer is that in the

UK this is hardly ever done, partly because it would be almost impossible to get clearance for a personality profile. Few of us like to read in print the words we have spoken even when they have been accurately recorded. Rare would be the interviewee who could resist the temptation to tweak a quote here or even revise a whole anecdote. A purist might say that this is the only way to print accurately what the subject thinks and says but a journalist who has to get a paper out to deadline knows that the result would be unacceptable delay.

In cases where someone insists on clearing copy in advance of publication it ought to be possible to insist that the only changes which can be made are points of factual accuracy, not slight alterations in the way something was said for stylistic reasons. My own view is that where quotes are obtained on technical subjects, medical issues for example, then it can be a wise safeguard to have the copy read by the expert who is quoted, both for the sake of her professional reputation and for the sake of the reader, who deserves accurate information.

Whatever style of copy the writer produces, for the subject the interview is part of a process of establishing or maintaining a myth about themselves. As often as not journalists want to debunk the myth or at least give what they see as a truer account of what the star is like. So the journalist tries to break down the barriers of hype by using weapons of flattery or charm while at the same time the interviewee may be trying to charm or flatter the journalist into complying with the myth (Malcolm 1990).

One final point is to ask what this round of interviews and product promotion means to the celebrities who go along with it for professional reasons. There are some who love the attention, at least to begin with, and many who tire of the process but have to agree to undergo it as a condition of the recording contract or film deal. The difficulty for many celebrities is when they are pursued by journalists even when they have no desire to give interviews. From a journalist's perspective there is an obvious appeal to the idea of tracking down a star and persuading them to give an exclusive interview. Realistically, though, this doesn't often happen except in drink-sodden dreams. Every potential celebrity-hunter should take some time to reflect on the purpose of that chase and what the effect of it is on their prey. Megastars, it is argued, benefit so much from their fame that they don't need sympathy from anyone. Does that fame mean they sacrifice the right to a private honeymoon (Zoë Ball and Norman Cook) or a private holiday (most really famous attractive women and notably Diana, Princess of Wales)?

Recommended reading

Barber, L. (1992) *Mostly Men*.

Barber, L. (1998a) *Demon Barber*.

Barber, L. (1998b) *Observer* 'Life', 8 November, 16–22.

Broughton, F. (ed.) (1998) *Time Out Interviews 1968–1998*.

Capote, T. (1987) *A Capote Reader*.

Davies, H. (1994) *Hunting People: Thirty Years of Interviews with the Famous*.

Fallaci, O. (1976) *Interview with History*.

Gabler, N. (1995) *Walter Winchell: Gossip, Power and the Culture of Celebrity*.

Lodge, D. (1999) *Home Truths*.

Malcolm, J. (1990) *The Journalist and the Murderer*.

Reed, R. (1979) *Travolta to Keaton*

Silvester, C. (ed.) (1993) *The Penguin Book of Interviews: An Anthology from 1859 to the Present Day*.

Wolfe, T. and Johnson, E. W. (eds) (1990) *The New Journalism*.

11 | Subediting and production

I liked going to work, liked the soothing and satisfactory rhythm of
getting out a magazine, liked the orderly progression of four-colour
closings and two-colour closings and black-and-white closings and
then The Product, no abstraction but something which looked
effortlessly glossy and could be picked up on a news-stand and
weighed in the hand. I liked all the minutiae of proofs and layouts,
liked working late on the nights the magazine went to press,
sitting and reading *Variety* and waiting for the copy desk to call.

Joan Didion, *Slouching Towards Bethlehem*

Y ou don't see many movies in which the hero writes a great standfirst or sensitively cuts down a 1,200-word article to the required 800. Few novels are written about the thrill of the chase for the right headline. Subeditors are the unsung heroes of journalism and if they are unnoticed by the public, their fate within the magazine office or newsroom can be worse. They are there to blame for everything that goes wrong yet when they do their job well few reporters or writers will notice. Editors will notice though because they know how heavily the success of a magazine depends on the quality of the subediting. You can produce a newspaper or magazine entirely from agency copy but you need your subeditors to work that raw material into journalism of the appropriate style and standard for your own publication. The right tone has to be ensured, the interests of the readers taken into account, the presentation suitable for the magazine worked at.

Monitoring standards

Perhaps here's a clue to why the process is called subediting. In a way the sub (the normal term for subeditor) is deputising for the editor. On a small publication all the things that subs do would be done by the editor. On a large publication the subs ensure that the standards set by the editor are adhered to in the copy.

They do more than that but essentially their job is to act as medium between writer and reader by preparing editorial material for printing. When the decision has been taken to use a piece of copy, the subs have to look at it with the eye of a typical reader – to establish that it makes sense and is clear – and with the eye of a professional journalist – to make sure it satisfies editorial criteria. Then they have to work on the presentation of the material and make sure that it finds its way into the final production process.

The point about editorial standards matters. There is plenty of criticism levelled at journalists about how low their standards of accuracy are (Worcester 1998: 47) but the standards of any publication are set by the editor and they depend on resources. It is possible to produce a magazine with no spelling mistakes let alone more serious errors. But that needs an editor who decrees that mistakes are a hanging offence, the employment of reputable writers and subeditors, and staffing levels high enough to allow careful checking and reading of proofs.

So it is not always, or not only, the individual sub or reporter who is to blame when mistakes are made. Everyone who has subbed knows there are reporters who should never be let loose with a notebook, so inaccurate or badly written is their work. As a sub you learn quickly which writers can be trusted with the facts.

It follows that subeditors have to be self-effacing. The glory in journalism goes to the reporter who gets the scoop or nets the elusive celebrity interview. That doesn't mean subediting isn't a fascinating and rewarding job, it just means that its appeal is not obvious to everyone who wants to work in journalism. This can hinder editors from hiring good subs, and most editors say they are hard to recruit. One reason for this is, I suspect, the newshound or abfab glamour image that journalism has in the popular imagination. Many of those who make excellent subs just don't want to chase fire engines and interview the bereaved or even to deal with drug-crazed models on a fashion shoot. What they like is playing with words. They like being in the office. They like messing around with page layout on their computers. They like playing spot the libel. Yet these people are more or less ignored when newcomers are being recruited. There's no denying that subs need to understand what reporters or fashion editors do, but the old idea that the only good news sub is one who has hung out with the hacks is out of date and there's nothing to stop a directly recruited trainee sub from going out as a shadow with a reporter or stylist for a couple of days to find out about their work.

If this makes subediting sound dull it's not meant to. For many journalists it is a more rewarding activity than gathering stories. And subs actually have a lot of power, collectively if not individually. That brings its own rewards and traditionally one of these has been moving up the career ladder to an editorship.

If you work in the editorial office of a magazine you are likely either to be a sub or to have to do quite a bit of subbing whatever your job title. Magazines don't employ as many staff as you might expect (see Chapter 3, page 22), particularly on the consumer glossies. But they do employ subeditors and, unlike on newspapers, almost all magazine writers may have to do some subbing at some stage during the production cycle.

The role of the subeditor

Before going into the minutiae of what subs do it's worth looking at the general role they play within a magazine office. This role varies according to the size of the staff and in turn depends on the pagination (number of pages), the frequency with which the magazine is published, the proportion of words to pictures, the proportion of staff writers to contributors and the standards set by the editor.

The people who do most of the subediting on magazines are not always called subs. They may have titles like copy-editor, copy chief or production editor, or even assistant editor. The commissioning editors (such as features editors, literary editors or health editors) may also sub or at least do some preliminary subbing on the work they have brought in.

In the days before computers, subeditors would have needed typewriters, dictionaries, type books, pens (or blue pencils), paper, paste, depth scales, set squares and rulers to assist in sizing pictures, and a good head for mental arithmetic. Now they mostly work on computers so instead of all this they need computer skills. Usually this means they know how to use word-processing packages such as Word, design software such as QuarkXpress, a package such as Photoshop if they are involved in the selection and manipulation of pictures, as well as knowing how to use the Internet as a research tool.

What subs do

Whoever does it, the subbing function is the same. The copy of a magazine that a reader picks up to read is the result of a series of processes, some of them abstract or intellectual, some of them concrete and involving different sorts of tangible objects. In many respects this sequence is like any other manufacturing production line. The raw materials (the words and pictures) come into the editorial office, are transformed by the editors and then leave the editorial office to be printed before being distributed to the consumer. Increasingly the processes are almost virtual until the last stage: that is copy, graphics, illustrations and photographs are dealt with in digital form on computers. Even when hard copy is supplied by writers or artists it is likely to be scanned into the computer system.

The stage at which a subeditor gets to see the copy will vary. On a small publication the sub, if she's in charge of copy, may also take part in the selection process, effectively to do some copytasting as it would be known on a newspaper or a news magazine. Otherwise she will be given the copy to work on once those who commissioned it have given it their approval. Before this it may have been sent back for clarification or for rewriting. Some subs, especially chief subs, do also take responsibility for copy chasing and this can be an onerous task. However the copy arrives on the desk, this is when the subbing work proper will begin.

On a magazine such as *Vanity Fair* or *The Sunday Times Magazine*, where pictures are a vital element, the photographs or illustrations for the most part will have been commissioned, probably at the same time as the words. The sub may be given the layout with the pictures to work on at about the same time as the copy. More usually the words will be available in advance so that some of the most time-consuming work can be done – reading for clarity, rewriting, checking for legal and factual errors. Then when the art department has produced a layout further work on the length and presentation of the copy can take place.

On publications not led by visuals in the same way (examples are weeklies such as *The Times Higher Education Supplement, Broadcast* or *Press Gazette*) the sub may have to commission illustrations from photographers or illustrators, or find pictures from the library, the net or agencies (see Chapter 14). Or the sub may have pictures supplied with the copy but be responsible for the layout of pages. This is similar to the way newspapers increasingly work, where individual subs often take control of particular pages.

In these cases, though, design doesn't mean the same as it does on a visual-led glossy. It means working within a limited range of options laid down by whoever did the overall design of the publication in the first place. In recent years on some publications these style options have been transformed into computerised templates which set the story length and picture size in advance. The typefaces will be more or less standard, the headline sizes, the use of rules (lines which separate stories or sections of the paper from one another), how pictures are credited – all the aspects of design that go to make up what is called the 'furniture' of the page will be pre-ordained. On publications such as these the sub has a part in the design process, if only in the limited sense of deciding which stories go where, how pictures are cropped and so on.

Subs who work on words-focused magazines need to know how page make-up works. That simply means the mechanisms by which the individual elements find their way onto the page in the right place and at the right length or size. When computers first came into UK editorial offices in the 1980s they didn't immediately bring all the changes that are now almost taken for granted. From a sub's point of view they have allowed the production process to do away with the process known as cut and paste, when paste-up artists slaved away with scalpel and Cow Gum, painstakingly inserting late corrections a line at a time before the finally approved page proof could be sent to the printer. Computers have allowed for the effective removal of the typesetting phase, among others.

Type matters

There are some terms related to type that subs need to be aware of if they are to under-stand how and why things are done in a particular way. 'Measure' is used simply to mean the width of a column or line of type. Traditionally it would have been described in units called pica ems or either of those two words alone. Before computers each folio of copy had to be 'marked up' by hand by the sub and given its typesetting requirement as in this example: 9/10 Times Roman across 12 ems. Today the sub would just key in the instruction on the computer. Hard copy also demanded a 'catchline' or 'slugline' which was an identifying word for each story. This had to be written on each folio, as did either 'more', or 'mf' (more follows), or 'ends' on the last folio after the copy. Again computers have made life easier although the term catchline is still used as a means of identifying a story in the system.

Measurement of the depth of stories on the page is now done as often as not in millimetres although at one time picas were the norm. The depth of space allowed between two lines of type is called the leading (for old-technology reasons) and is created because the space in which a letter of type sits needs to be larger than its own measurement. Where an even larger amount of space is allowed (as in nine point type on ten point leading) legibility is therefore enhanced. The word 'point' here refers to a measurement of the height of letters. It is rarely up to the sub to make the choice between one typeface and another and no sub really needs to know the differ-ence between didots and ciceros, breviers and nonpareils. Worth mentioning here though is the word 'font' which has come to mean a particular design of typeface such as Helvetica or New York or Roman, regardless of its weight (i.e. whether it is bold or italic). It's quite useful for a subeditor to know the difference between serif and sans serif typefaces. Graphic designers will choose one or the other style of typeface for a variety of reasons. Sans typefaces do tend to look more modern but they need careful handling. With the wrong leading, used over too dark a tint, for example, they can be more difficult for the eye to read. When type is used in this way it is called 'reversing out' which means a lighter colour type appears on a darker panel of grey or a coloured tint.

Computers as tools

Writers and subs in some offices are entirely responsible for keying in copy (which means a fast, accurate touch-typing speed is helpful). Where this is not the case, copy may be scanned in or keyed in by typists in the traditional way. Computer systems mean subs can produce pages which are ready to go directly to the plate for printing, eliminating the intermediary process of creating a photographic negative which would then be turned into a printing plate by plate-makers. By 1998 this system, known as page-to-plate or direct-to-plate printing, was used by several large publishing houses as well as many smaller ones. As these processes change so quickly there is little point explaining the detail of how individual systems work, although at the time of writing it would be fair to say that the most common systems used by the magazine industry seem to be Applemac and QuarkXpress.

Again from a subeditor's point of view, computers are merely a different set of tools from the ones subs would have used half a generation ago. They don't necessarily mean that headlines are better written, merely that it is much quicker for a sub to play around with type or with picture cropping than it once was. In the wrong hands computer technology can be used to produce pages that would make older journalists or those with good visual awareness weep.

Liaison with the art department

Where the magazine is picture-led a vital part of the sub's job will be to liaise with the art department. If a headline space is too short, or a picture is taking up too much space it will have to be discussed and if there is stalemate the editor will take the final decision. (Ideally, the sub will be able to provide headings in advance, for the designer to work with.) The sub can also prove invaluable to the art editor by spotting problems in the visuals.

Subbing step by step

Where things run smoothly the sub will work on the copy in a number of ways. Where there is adequate time the copy will get a first read through, just as if being read by the magazine's buyer, and the sub will note any big problems as well as ideas which might emerge for the story's presentation, if this has not been discussed at an earlier commissioning stage. On a words-led publication the story will be checked for length and the decision whether to cut on the grounds of the importance of the material will be made. The sub will then scheme the story into the page plan. On picture-led magazines, where the layout has been supplied by the art deparment, that will almost certainly have been done based on an assessment of the length or a note of what length was commissioned. When it hits the subs' desk the copy will be checked for length.

Copy-editing

Once measured the copy may need cutting by the sub. Occasionally more copy may be needed either to fill the space or to improve the copy, with additional explanations, case studies or quotes perhaps. Ideally the writer will be asked to supply additions. At this stage the sub may make notes of ideas about the presentation such as which material to pull out to run in a box or which lines to use as pull-quotes to break up the text.

The detailed copy-editing now begins. This means reading the piece with care, paying attention to the functional points (clarity and economy of expression, punctuation, grammar, spelling, accuracy, repetitions, legal pitfalls, house style) as well as the meaning of the words and the overall argument. A word here about relying on computer spellchecks. Subs must be aware that spellchecks don't pick up every problem. One obvious example is when a typing error produces a perfectly acceptable word, just one with the wrong meaning: bird instead of bard for example, which could make a difference to any discussion of Shakespeare's plays. Proper names pose problems too as one writer discovered when spellchecking a story about a Glasgow woman from the suburb of Bearsden: the computer offered up Bearskin and he didn't notice. The other common problem arises because there are many words which have different spellings in North America. (Plough in the UK is plow once it has crossed the Atlantic.) A sub's job has always included changing such words to be correct for the country of publication. Spellchecks can be customised to take these words into account and other exceptional words entered, words which are common to the particular subject matter of the magazine perhaps.

The respected writer on any publication will produce copy which requires little change other than that to do with fitting the words into the available space. Yet even good writers should have their work read meticulously, as a careful sub will spot literals (typographical errors) or inconsistencies in the copy that the writer's eye leaps over because the material is so familiar. The less respected writer presents work which is badly written, doesn't make sense, is too long and contains factual errors or legal risks. Some subs enjoy a tussle with copy like that as they find it rewarding to improve the piece. But most subs are infuriated by badly written copy and feel less inspired to write a good standfirst and headline for it. On some magazines, too, however good the copy which comes in, it will need extensive rewriting to be transformed into the written tone which is part of the publication's identity. Again this can make the job of subbing more interesting, even if it doesn't always make the magazine more compelling for the reader.

In some publishing houses extensive rewriting is the norm and is not, in fact, entrusted to subeditors. If you look at American magazines such as *Time* and *Newsweek* you'll see that their big stories may carry a list of credits for reporting, research and writing. For example, a piece from Kosovo in the 22 February, 1999 UK edition had an article entitled 'Lives in the balance' about the peace talks in Paris. The byline under the standfirst was 'By Massimo Calabresi' in largish bold type. At the end of the story three names are credited with reporting from Belgrade, Paris and Brussels. The local reporters put together dossiers of information and quotes which are then turned into full stories by the senior writers, in this case the Central Europe correspondent. This process may be carried out by senior desk editors at the headquarters of the magazine so a story with global ramifications can be put together using the information filed by reporters from anywhere in the world.

House style

Another important job for the subeditor is to make sure that the copy conforms to house style. On the whole this doesn't really refer to the tone of voice so much as the rules which govern those aspects of punctuation and grammar where a correct writer would have a choice. As far is tone is concerned this is a characteristic of the writing which is unlikely to be laid down in any house-style book but to which readers are thought to respond. Magazines for teenagers, for example, have a chatty, light tone and use lots of slang words (snogfest, studmuffin, gorge for gorgeous, totty, and so on).

A house style, by contrast, is the set of rules collected together in a book, a computer file, a loose-leaf binder or six tatty sheets of A4 stapled together about five years ago and covered in coffee-mug ring marks that lies about the subs' desk and is used as the reference point and arbitrator on fine points of copy-editing such as whether Van Gogh should have a capital v, whether King's Cross in London should have an apostrophe, whether Peking should be rewritten as Beijing; whether numbers over ten should be written as a word or in figures, whether news-stand should be hyphenated, or ice-cream or lighthouse, why Thermos should have a capital letter. The well-organised office will have an up-to-date house style which ought to answer all such queries and some style books are so well written and useful that they are sold commercially on the grounds that many of these decisions are made daily by people who don't write for journalistic publications at all and yet who might want the help of a respected journalism style book. This turns out to be a fair assumption to judge by the obvious demand from the public when they are published (Cameron 1995: 46). Notable among these is the *Daily Mirror Style: The Mirror's Way with Words*, *The Economist Style Guide*, and the *Reuters Style Book*. They reflect the material their journalists mainly work with and so in the second two examples, words to do with finance and economics prevail.

Why have a house style?

The purpose of a house style, in whatever form it is recorded, is to ensure conformity within the magazine of the kinds of points listed above where doubt would regularly arise. This may seem unnecessary on the grounds that it's the meanings of the words that count, not how they look on the page. In defence of conformity it is argued that you don't realise how much adherence to a house style contributes to a magazine's image until you look at a publication that doesn't follow one. A variety of ways of writing numbers or spelling words can become annoying to the reader because it intrudes on the reading process, so this line of argument goes, without much in the way of supporting evidence. As part of her research for the book *Verbal Hygiene* Deborah Cameron examined the various style books used by *The Times* during the twentieth century. She notes that *The Times English Style and Usage Guide* tells writers that 'inconsistency in style . . . irritates readers' (*The Times* 1992: 5). However when she asked the paper's then editor, Simon Jenkins, if he had any evidence for this he was unable to cite any at all (Cameron 1995: 37).

There are, then, those who question the need for house style arguing that it puts unnecessary and unjustifiable pressure on writers to conform to someone else's way of doing things. A more serious doubt about the arrangement is provoked by a look at the huge number of items that a house style covers and at some of the questionable pronouncements on language use that house styles often make. In her discussion of the politics of style Cameron examines the origins of certain widespread notions of what constitutes good or correct writing and notes the arbitrariness of these, many of which are perpetrated in the magazine or newspaper house styles as if they were unarguable truths not, as they undoubtedly are in some cases, the whims of the editor (Cameron 1995: 62).

One typical example, which may or may not be a whim, is from the *The Economist Style Guide*. It says the word ' "Relative" is fine as an adjective, but as a noun prefer "relation",' without giving any reason. If you check the meaning of 'relative' in any fairly modern dictionary you find the perfectly acceptable definition 'a person who is related by blood or marriage'. And yes, there in the style guide for 'hopefully' is the entry 'by all means begin an article hopefully, but never write: "Hopefully, it will be finished by Wednesday". Try: "With luck, if all goes well, it is hoped that . . .".' Note that this last example breaks a general principle in journalistic writing, which is to be as brief as possible. Notice here, too, the tone of the instruction: it is typical. The sarcasm carries a presumption of stupidity or at least inadequate education on the part of any writer who might disagree with the style book's author, even though some of the usages which are being banned (those I've quoted for example) are part of everyday written and spoken language for many if not most English speakers and even for those who don't use them carry no risk of misunderstanding when used by others.

From a sub's point of view such detailed regulation can pose problems. It's one thing to turn to your style guide to check whether your publication likes to italicise foreign words. But what would make you think to look up 'relative' or 'hopefully' if you thought they were being used correctly in the first place? The answer must be, apart from campaigning to change it, that if you work for a magazine with such a prescriptive approach to language you must read the style book carefully and re-read it at regular intervals in an effort to keep the more arbitrary decisions in your head.

Cameron explores some of the implications of the attempts of editors to control the way their staff write. While journalists would argue they are striving towards a neutral, plain language in which to report the news objectively, she argues that what they are actually struggling with is a set of stylistic values which 'are symbolic of moral, social, ideological and political values'. The puzzle, she concludes, is not that writers are prepared to accept so much prescription in what they do – after all they have their livelihoods to earn – but that they so wholeheartedly embrace the idea of there being prescription in the first place (Cameron 1995: 76/77).

Accuracy

Where it might pay some editors to be far more authoritarian is in the setting of standards of accuracy, another responsibility of the sub. The important thing to understand is that you can't be too accurate: problems arise from not being accurate enough, whether the result is a million-pound libel award or merely an irate reader's letter. In the UK this is certainly something which is giving rise to growing concern and is helping to undermine the reputation of journalists and their publications (Worcester 1998: 47).

This has serious consequences not just because it means journalists have to get used to seeing themselves listed at or near the bottom of any table of the classes of people who can be trusted. That's bad enough but if readers distrust what journalists offer them then sooner or later it might occur to them not to read journalism at all. It is also likely to mean that they are less willing to help journalists with the quotes or background information that are the lifeblood of journalistic writing. This is not to underestimate the difficulty of getting every fact in a story right but it is to argue that the decision about how accurate to be is, in the end, one of choice.

Let me illustrate. Most of us can think of reporters who have written grossly inaccurate stories but who are still in work. Editors should think about what message this sends to the other journalists working on the same paper and even to readers.

The American tradition
We could look across the Atlantic to a completely different tradition of accuracy. Anyone who has written for an American publication will have tales to tell about the

breed of journalists called fact-checkers and the diligence with which they do their jobs. If a writer mentions a river in Africa, the fact checker will look it up in an atlas – online version nowadays of course. If a writer quotes Scottish university lecturer Jenny McKay on student welfare issues the fact-checker will call to check I really said what I said, to check how to spell both parts of my name, to check that I live in Scotland and that I am attached to a university. *Reader's Digest* prides itself on the accuracy of everything it publishes on the grounds that its 100 million readers worldwide deserve to know that what they read is true.

A story about a woman who is learning to hang glide is much more interesting if her age is 80, rather than the 30 that a typing error cuts it to. At the least, accuracy is a courtesy: as a writer you are asking readers to give you their time and attention so the least you can do is produce informative or entertaining copy of the highest standard. At its most serious, inaccuracy can detract from the value of story, can cause a great deal of personal anguish to the subject of the story, or can land journalists and editors in court.

It's hard to imagine a British publication coming anywhere close to the exacting, time-consuming standards that are the norm in the USA. James Thurber writes in his biography of Harold Ross, editor of the *New Yorker* in the 1930s and 1940s:

> Having a manuscript under Ross's scrutiny was like putting your car in the hands of a skilled mechanic . . . When you first gazed, appalled, upon an uncorrected proof of one of your stories or articles, each margin had a thicket of queries and complaints – one writer got a hundred and forty-four on one profile . . . His "Who he?" became famous not only in the office but outside [and is a joke to this day in the UK magazine *Private Eye*].

> (Thurber 1984:70)

Little slips in copy could drive Ross mad, wrote Thurber: 'A couple, instead of a coupe, found in a ditch; a hippy in place of a happy bride; a ship's captain who collapsed on the bride, instead of the bridge, during a storm at sea.'

The UK approach
Mistakes like these are not always the reporter's fault, they can slip in during the keying-in process – or they could in Ross's day. Nowadays, with computer technology, there ought to be less scope for error if fewer versions of a story have to be typed out. The thoroughness of US fact-checkers can irritate reporters in the UK and probably most of all the ones who do a careful reporting job in the first place (Barber 1998b). But it can be salutary for British journalists to encounter this kind of thoroughness, even if it can also seem like a complete waste of time or worse if it means the style of a piece is ruined by a sub who cuts badly because a fact can't be checked.

If those amusing slips of the typing finger quoted by Thurber don't amount to journalistic disaster there are plenty of examples of inaccuracies which do. Two brothers who are footballers. One is charged with fraud. Let's draw a veil over the name of the publication which carried a picture of the wrong brother with the story. All right, you might say, you can't really blame a sub for not knowing there were two brothers because he knew nothing about football? Not really his fault. This won't do as an excuse though, because the name of the brother was correct in the copy and as soon as the photo with its caption carrying a different name reached the sub, his sharp subeditor's eye should have spotted that the two names were different, that something was amiss, and he should have made the appropriate checks.

I don't want to underestimate the problem of accuracy though. It can be difficult to get everything right in a story even if working conditions are ideal and obviously for reporters in the thick of a running story and working against a deadline, conditions are rarely ideal. Facts become slightly distorted and then slightly more distorted when the next person works on the story, and a chain rather like a game of Chinese whispers results, sometimes leaving a magazine's editor with a red face. The name of the murdered toddler James Bulger is one example. He never was known as Jamie but reporters for all kinds of media have persisted in using this name. Given that it is difficult to get things consistently right (we won't mention those unscrupulous journalists who makes things up), it is surprising that more publications don't follow the lead of *The Guardian* which, to the dismay of some reporters, appointed a readers' editor to look at complaints about accuracy, to oversee the daily publication of corrections as soon as possible and to write a regular weekly column of comment about the process. The serious purpose behind the appointment of a readers' editor is a willingness to recognise that the gathering and production of copy by journalists is not a foolproof operation and that if mistakes are acknowledged it goes some way to mitigating the offence (Bromley and Stephenson 1998).

Help with checking the facts

There are other aids to the subeditor when it comes to accuracy. In addition to the house-style guide a subs' desk or room ought to have special dictionaries designed for publishers which cover much of the same ground: *The Oxford Dictionary for Writers and Editors* and *The Penguin Dictionary for Writers and Editors* (Bryson 1994) are two good ones. As well as answering queries for the writer, as suggested above, these books are useful all-purpose reference books. Turning to my Bryson at random I discover that 'gorgheggio' is a musical term for a trill and that whereas Gordonstoun is a school in the Grampian region of Scotland, the similar sounding town in Grampian has the spelling Gordonstown.

There should also be a wide range of reference books or access to their computer equivalents. It would be impossible to give here a comprehensive list as it so much depends on the subject matter of the magazine. *Jane's All the World's Aircraft* would be essential for the subs working on a magazine about aircraft for example. *Crockford's* for the *Church Times* or perhaps even *Country Life*. The latest edition of *Vacher's Parliamentary Companion* for any publication that deals with government. Certainly if you find yourself working as a freelance sub on a shift basis it's worth having your own relevant, portable reference books just in case the office you go to turns out not be properly equipped. All reference books should be up to date.

Standards of accuracy vary

For the freelance sub one of the most difficult things to learn in a new office relates to the point about standards. On some magazines a sub would be expected to check most facts but on others it will be assumed that the reporter knows what she is doing and so her work will not need much scrutiny. The time allocated for work on a particular story or layout ought to reflect the care which is meant to go into a story and a sub who is new to an office needs to establish what is wanted. Many publications keep a detailed record of each story and who worked on it and made which changes. This means if a mistake does occur the guilty writer or sub can be traced.

So far I've perhaps implied that subs are saints. Not all of them are. They can be guilty of injecting mistakes into copy particularly when rewriting or cutting. They often alter words unnecessarily, make typing errors or may misunderstand the original material. This isn't always serious and we'll assume the mistakes are never made with malicious intent, but for a writer who has taken great care over the words it is justifiably frustrating to find changes made for no good reason. Worst is when copy is mauled about by an insensitive sub, usually in the interests of making it conform to the 'tone' of the magazine as a whole. To find your copy filled with deadbeat clichés, clumsy grammar and factual errors yet still carrying your name is one of the most disheartening moments of a writer's working life. It does happen and some freelances have been known to say they can't bear to read the published versions of their copy for fear of what has been done to it.

Once the story has been read and the facts checked the other important check to do is that the story is not breaking guidelines such as those laid down by the Press Complaints Commission or leaving the editor liable to a court appearance. There are several ways in which copy might be risky in this way, the most obvious being if it is libellous, if it breaches copyright or the Official Secrets Acts, or if it is in contempt of court. (For explanations see Chapter 18.) The sub is a publication's vital line of defence. Even if no one else on a small staff has any understanding of the legal pitfalls the sub must have. This doesn't mean subs have to have a law degree or even a detailed knowledge of cases and precedents as the sub is most unlikely to take the final decision about whether to publish something which would be unsafe. But the sub is the person, sometimes the only person, who will read the copy with enough care and attention to notice a risk. All subs should know exactly what might be problematic and should know exactly who to refer the question to and who is the backup if that person is not available. Legal decisions may have to be taken instantly and the fact that the editor is away from a phone means someone else senior must take responsibility.

One of the quirks of the way entry to journalism in the UK works is that magazines are more likely to employ people with no prior training and don't necessarily offer any to them immediately. So, whereas most recruits to newspapers will bring with them, or soon have, enough elementary legal training at least to make them alert to where the danger areas lie, journalists on magazines may never have this. It may be that a fashion editor on *Elle* doesn't need to know much about contempt of court but she certainly ought to know about copyright, even if it's just for the day when she decides to use a few song lyrics scattered across the page as typographical decoration. A further problem is that magazines use copy from a wide range of freelances many of whom, especially in the lifestyle and consumer sections of the market, will have had no legal training at all. This makes the sub's vigilance even more important.

Copy preparation

Once all these bigger tasks have been sorted out the sub has to tackle the more technical aspects of copy preparation. Capital letters have to be put in consistently and in any words which are trade names (Thermos, Hoover, Velcro). Small capitals (or small caps) have to be indicated where these are preferred, words put in italics, consistency checked for, repetitions weeded out, paragraph indents marked in and devices for emphasis such as bullet points (blobs) or dropped capitals. The use of quotation marks has to be harmonised. The list is too long to exhaust and the priorities not the same for all publications. The sub has to become familiar with all the conventions used by a publisher or publication and make sure the copy conforms to it.

Copy presentation

Then comes the more creative bit. Starting with picture-led publications, I've already noted that on these the sub works closely with the art department to achieve the most successful union between words, layout and illustrations. Headlines, standfirsts and captions will have to be written to fit and the photographer's or illustrator's credit included. If the story is a big one a cover line about the story may be needed for the cover. If this is the case it could be worth drafting ideas while work is being done on the story. Cover lines will inevitably be rewritten when the cover design is being looked at but it helps to sketch out ideas at the subediting stage so that there is some material to work with. The same goes for the words on the contents page. An additional factor is the need for coherence between those three elements in the magazine: readers are understandably irritated when an enticing cover line bears no relation to anything on the contents page, leaving readers to search through the whole magazine for the thing that attracted them to it in the first place. If the story is not big enough to be displayed on the cover it still needs to be clear from the description in the contents list what it is about and where it is to be found.

Headlines

There's no need to define a headline. In news copy, whether in magazines or newspapers, headlines are meant to draw the reader's attention to the story and say succinctly what it's about. At the tabloid end of the newspaper market headlines can be so joky as to be almost incomprehensible except to regular readers. On picture-led magazines, at least for the fashion, beauty and home style pages, the job of a headline is less clear. It is meant to encapsulate the mood of the pages or 'story'. Stylists, art directors and magazine staff use the word story even for a fashion shoot which carries few words except to list the prices of the clothes and the shops that stock them. By story here they mean some connecting theme around which the shoot has been devised. It might be 'Ballerina Bride' for an edition of *Brides & Setting Up Home* which features wedding dresses in the style of tutus. Or here's an example from *Company*: the headline is 'Evergreen' on a fashion story featuring clothes which are green in colour. This provides an excuse for puns about the environment and about envy all in one standfirst. Turn to the contents page and you get another pun 'Evergreen. Fashion activists go for green pieces'.

If you are a sub working on this kind of material for the consumer press you'll have to get the hang of what's needed: puns, alliteration, rhymes and jaunty rhythms are much appreciated although it is hard to convey to someone outside this world exactly how much time may be spent in brainstorming by an editorial team to come up with titles such as 'Seas the moment' for an article about cruises. It is also not easy to convince outsiders that editors on such magazines may demand that the sub or chief sub puts up at least three possible standfirsts and headings for consideration by the senior editorial team before a decision can be taken.

If the purpose of the publication is to publish written journalism which happens to have illustrations then the headline does not need to strain so hard for effect, although puns and alliteration do inevitably have their place, at least in the UK, however tiresome this might be for readers or for the subs. The usual guidelines for what makes a good heading apply to this kind of story. A headline should be informative within the constraints set by taste, legality and layout. Sometimes these constraints are so unrealistic as to make the headline writer's job into a kind of verbal torture as she wrestles to find words that will mean something and not bust (the technical term for a headline which is too long for the allotted space).

Apart from the restrictions of word length subs also have to consider house style on questions such as whether each word should start with a capital or the whole headline be capitalised. On the whole in the UK caps are avoided except for the first word but in the USA, in *Time* magazine for example, all-cap headlines are the norm for big stories and for smaller ones a capital is used for each significant word as in 'A Broken Window of Opportunity'.

The other considerations are the shapes made by the lines and how these relate to the sense of what is being written. If there are three decks, say, then a pyramid one way up or the other is not usually acceptable. So Figure 1 would be acceptable whereas Figure 2 would not. A second reason that Figure 2 would not do is that the last word in the second line should be closer to the next word in order to make the sense as clear as possible. You wouldn't put 'Mr' at the end of a line and 'Blobby' on the next, or 'San' alone without its 'Francisco', or any other words which are closely linked in sense. Nor should a line end with a preposition. However many decks there are, the principle to follow is, more or less, to be evenly ragged and that applies whether the headlines range left or right or are centred so Figures 3, 4, 5 and 6 are acceptable.

This is a three-deck headline	**This is a three deck headline**

Figure 1   Figure 2

Explanation time. Copy is said to be ranged left/ragged right when the left-hand margin is even and the right one, well, ragged (Figures 1–4). Ranged right/ragged left is the other way round (Figure 5). The word 'flush' is an alternative for 'range'. Centred is where both margins are ragged (Figure 6) and justified type means that both margins are straight as in the main text for this chapter. (These styles can be produced by a click of the mouse as they appear at the top of the computer screen.) These terms are used for all kinds of type whether in the text, the captions, the standfirsts or crossheads and pull-quotes.

And this here is a four-deck headline	*And this here is a four-deck headline*

Figure 3   Figure 4

<table>
<tr><td>

This type is set as range right

</td><td>

And this type is centred

</td></tr>
</table>

Figure 5   Figure 6

Other than that many of the things that make a good headline also make good journalistic writing. Ideally a headline should contain an active verb to give the impression of action and, if appropriate, it should describe concrete things rather than abstractions, people not inanimate objects. It should be easily understood at first glance by the kind of people who are expected to read the magazine. Once again this means hard rules can't be laid down for all magazines about what works. What's right for *Prima* ('10 easy projects for a rainy weekend', 'When dizziness is a danger sign', 'Make your home seem twice as big', March 1999), would not be right for *GQ* ('Knob freaks', 'Hidden pleasures', 'Sex Life. Pork and Ride', March 1999), or for *B* ('75% of bridegrooms try it on with me', 'My father is a rapist and Mum is one of his victims', March 1999), or *The Scottish Field* ('The Keeper's Year', February 1999).

In many cases the headlines in a picture-led magazine depend on either a subsidiary heading (known as a strapline and usually running across the top of the page) or a standfirst, to explain fully what the piece is about. One example from *Time* is 'Couture Culture' as a headline accompanied by 'When designers emphasize workmanship over theatrics, high fashion's best clients think money's no object' (1 February 1999). Or in *Scottish Field*, the headline 'Family Talents' could be about any number of families but the short standfirst which follows explains: 'Everyone has heard of Robert Louis Stevenson but few are aware that some of Scotland's most famous lighthouses and well-known harbours owe their existence to the Stevenson family.'

Verbal signposts

What is common in both these cases is that they act as so-called 'entry points' to the text. If you look at the sample spread of a magazine (Figure 7) you'll see that there are others. The thinking is that when readers turn to a page they don't necessarily read in the order you might expect: headline, standfirst, text, caption and so on. What their eyes do is jump about the page and so it may well be that a picture caption is the thing which catches the eye or it may be one of the pull-quotes. Any of these verbal signposts, therefore, must work at attracting the readers' attention enough to make them stop and then perhaps read from the start of the copy.

The other words, then, which subeditors regularly use and which need some explanation are the standfirst, caption and credit, crosshead, pull-quote, dropped capital, sidebar, widow, end symbol and page turn. To take them in turn.

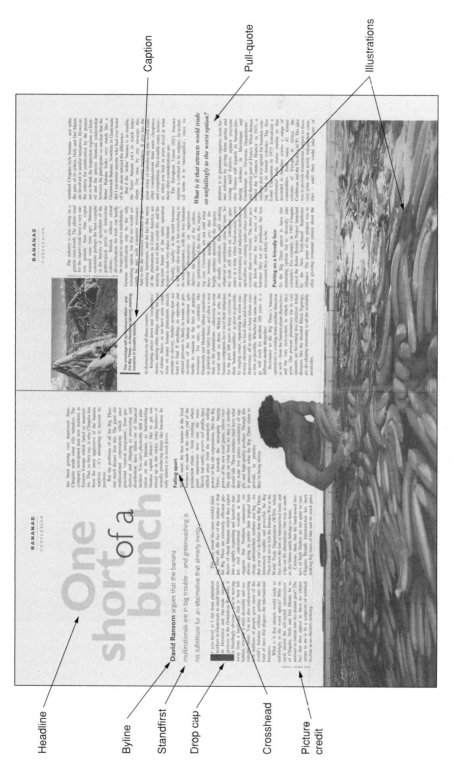

Headline

Byline

Standfirst

Drop cap

Crosshead

Picture credit

Caption

Pull-quote

Illustrations

Figure 7 A sample spread from *New Internationalist*, October 1999 © *New Internationalist*/Guardian Media Group

Standfirsts

The standfirst (or 'sell' as it is sometimes known) is the paragraph which introduces the article. It is not usually written by the reporter but by the subeditor, along with the headline and captions. A standfirst will normally include, written in the third person, the byline (or name) of the reporter. If the pictures are an important part of the spread, if they were specially commissioned for example, then there may well be a credit here too for the photographer or illustrator. Failing that there is likely to be a picture credit in small type (about six or seven point) somewhere else on the page, often in the margin and running at an angle to the main text. These small credits may even be for the picture agency or library that supplied the pictures if these are stock shots. The standfirst differs from the body copy in that it is set in a larger type which may be bolder or in a different typeface from the main text. The other thing which helps to distinguish it from the main text is that it is likely to be set in a different measure (width of a line of text) and to vary in terms of justification. So, if the body copy is justified, the standfirst is likely to be centred or ranged to the left or right.

In magazines where the words are of prime importance, features headlines may be more independent and work without standfirsts. Or these magazines may copy some newspapers by having standfirsts on their features but not their news pages.

Guidance for writing good standfirsts is similar to that for headlines and for all good journalistic writing. The more newsy the magazine the more important it is for standfirsts to seem as up to date as possible perhaps by referring to a recent event or by referring to the future, typically by asking questions about what will happen next. For example: 'Mbeki is certain to become President but how will he measure up to South Africa's father figure?' (*Time*, 1 March, 1999).

As with headlines, there is likely to be a tight restriction on the length of each line and on the overall shape which the lines produce. The guidelines here are the same as for headings and can mean that what seems like a relatively simple task – to write a paragraph of introduction to a feature – can take longer than you'd expect as the line breaks have to be manoeuvered to fall at just the right places.

Captions

The next thing is to write the picture captions. These are the words which relate to individual pictures to give information of differing kinds about them. What this involves varies greatly between publications as well as between stories. On visually-led magazines the space and shape of the captions will be determined by the art editors, which leaves no choice for the subeditor but can create problems when the space is not adequate.

Starting with a straightforward piece of reportage with commissioned photos, the captions must draw into the story a reader who is not immediately enticed by the headline. The captions must explain what a picture shows without merely describing what is in it. A good caption should somehow add to the information which the page has to offer, not merely repeat what is in the text. For some picture spreads there will be a caption to go with each picture but on others each caption may have to carry the information for more than one illustration. The important thing then is to make clear which picture is being referred to. Words like 'above', or 'clockwise from left', or 'centre' are used, perhaps enclosed in brackets, or using a different weight for the typeface. Where this is done the sub has to keep a close eye on any changes that may be made to the layout at the last minute, in case these directions become wrong.

Captions which carry information about the merchandise featured in fashion, beauty and lifestyle spreads have to be written with immaculate accuracy because readers use the information and will be put out if they discover it is incorrect. This applies to prices, sizes, shops and availability. Large companies such as Condé Nast which produce a lot of this kind of material, have merchandise departments which are reponsible for all the checking of detail, but it is up to the sub to present the information as accessibly as possible.

In newsier publications the captions are likely to be brief and functional. A typical way of doing them, where photos are usually just head shots or pictures of products, is that adopted by *Press Gazette*. It runs one-line captions which start with the name of the featured person or publication, followed by a colon and then a phrase of information or from a quote in the story. An example from 26 February 1999 is '*Nylon*: for "independent thinkers"', in a story about a new US lifestyle magazine.

There is one danger area worth indicating. Where library pictures are used to illustrate news features about subjects such as drug or alcohol abuse, prostitution, child abuse or anything vaguely criminal or distasteful, care must be taken not to imply that those who appear in an innocent photo are involved in the questionable activity. If you're subbing a feature about parents who have abused their children you can't just get a stock picture of a family. If you do then you need to have the image manipulated (in pre-computer days the easiest thing was to bleach out the faces) so that there is no danger of innocent people being branded as child abusers. An alternative is to commission a picture using photographic models and to make absolutely clear in the caption that the people in the picture are models.

Crossheads

The more text there is on a page the more likely it is that the page designer will want to see the text broken up to try to help the reader's eye move across the page without tiring of too much grey. One way to do this is by inserting what are effectively small headlines or crossheads. These can also serve the function of stretching out a piece of text to take up more space in a layout. Crossheads are usually in a bolder typeface than the text and, as with the standfirst, are likely to be set in a different way. They run across just one column of type: the thinking here is that if they ran across two or more at once the reader's eye might be misled into jumping back up the page to the next column of type. (For the same reason a picture or illustration should not be run across two columns unless it is at the top or the bottom of those columns or unless it does not take up the full width of the columns and has type ranged around it at either side.)

What crossheads contain is, yet again, a matter of house style. Sometimes it is just one word or a couple of words lifted from the following paragraph or two. It does not lift words from the preceding copy and so the careful sub will have to watch that last minute changes to the layout for whatever reason do not affect what is in a crosshead or indeed its position on the page. Across any given page or spread the aim is to balance visually the position of text-breakers such as crossheads and pull-quotes.

Pull-quotes

Another popular method of breaking up grey text is the pull-quote. This is a quotation from the text set in such a way as to stand out from the body copy, much like a crosshead or standfirst. Sometimes a pull-quote is emphasised with the use of rules above and below. A pull-quote should make sense on its own as well as intriguing readers and encouraging them to move into the text. Like crossheads, pull-quotes should always be set across one column of type only, should balance across the page or spread and should relate to text which is yet to come although not the text which comes immediately afterwards. The additional complication for the sub who is selecting quotes to use in this way is that, like standfirsts and headlines, a pleasing shape has to be created by the lines and the sense of the words must not be impeded by awkward line breaks. Lastly a pull-quote should conform to the text and if the decision is taken to omit a phrase that is in the text this should be clearly indicated by the use of ellipsis (dots as a substitute for text, three dots being the maximum in any journalistic copy).

Dropped capitals

Another device regularly used to break up the page is the dropped capital letter or 'drop cap'. It means a letter in a larger, bolder and sometimes different typeface set so that it drops down through the first three or four lines of the text which is then adjusted to range round it. The designer (whether sub or art editor) will decide whether these are to be used and whether just for the first letter of a piece or as a way of breaking up the text at other points, probably with at least one line of white space above it. From the subs' point of view there are two possible complications with drop caps. The first is if the sentence which is meant to start with a drop cap begins with a quotation and so would cause a typographical problem: a huge letter preceded by quotation marks in the same size as the body copy will look silly but equally these can't be enlarged or it puts the typographical balance of the sentence out. The answer is not to start a feature with a quote and to rewrite any opening sentence in the middle of the text where a drop cap is to be used if it starts with a quote. The second consideration is that ideally any given letter should appear as a drop cap only once across a spread.

Sidebars and boxes

In addition to the main text of an article, many features carry what are called sidebars or boxes which carry information not otherwise included in the copy. They may be set in a different typeface or measure and are often set against a tinted background. It may be factual or statistical information which relates to the subject of the article or it may be a case study of some sort. This copy must also be prepared by the sub and checked to make sure it agrees with, but does not repeat, the other information on the page.

Widows

On magazines which allow generous time for the copy preparation stage and which are not designed to look like newspapers there is some further tinkering with the copy to do. In the old days this would have been done at the page-proof stage but with computerised layouts can just as easily be done on screen. Not all editors or chief subs bother much about this but they do on publications which aim for the highest production standards.

This tinkering is to do with line-breaks and the way in which copy flows from one column to another. There are certain guidelines which are thought to enhance the look of the copy as well as its readablity. The most widely cared about are 'widows' where a paragraph ends with a line containing one short word or part of a word. When this happens copy may be slightly rewritten to extend the last line to stretch more than half way across the width of the column. Or it may be slightly cut to move the paragraph ending back by one line. Computer technology has made another solution quicker and easier. It's called kerning and means the adjustment of the amount of white space between letters and words. Computers quietly do it all the time but it is possible to over-ride what they choose to do in order to squash up a few letters or to spread them out. One of the hallmarks of amateur desk-top publishing, however, is the over-zealous use of this technique without the benefit of a designer's eye being applied to the finished lines of copy. Lines which are too generously or too tightly spaced can seem to jump out of the page at the reader, drawing attention to the wrong part of the copy. The same visual problem arises accidentally with what are called 'rivers' of white space which appear by chance in a column of type thanks to the positioning of word breaks.

A widow is most problematic if it falls at the beginning or end of a column or immediately before an illustration or at the end of a page. In these cases the rewriting must create at least a full line with which to start the next section of copy or an awkward gap will be left at the top of the next column. The same principle will apply if a short line occurs in the original copy at the top of a column. The aim is always to achieve a harmonious look to the page. If you bear in mind that graphic designers think of copy in terms of blocks of text it's clear why they don't want the shape of those blocks marred by having incomplete lines at the top or bottom of rectangles. A word of caution here for the sub though. Whenever copy is rewritten or cut there's an opportunity for mistakes to creep in. That is why not all publications take so seriously this tidying up of the look of the text.

End symbols and page turns

By the time all this work has been done on a page there remain a few details to check. The sub must make sure that appropriate picture credits have been included (see 'Captions') and that at the end of a spread there is either an end symbol or an indication of where to turn to (turn arrow). The end symbol may be no more than a black bullet or blob. Many publications, however, have a specially designed symbol that somehow reflects the title: *B* has a black blob with the letter B in white type in it.

For some publications there is no need to indicate a page turn because no article is allowed to run beyond a double-page spread. Others allow text to turn only on to the next page and so it is obvious from the punctuation and the sense of the story that no conclusion has been reached. (It is important where this arrangement prevails, for the sub to make sure that the punctuation or sense couldn't be misinterpreted, if a full stop fell at the end of a page for example. If there is any confusion some rewriting may be necessary to carry the sentence over onto the next page.) In *Prima*, which also turns only onto the succeeding page, there is nevertheless a little arrow-shaped box instructing the reader to 'please turn the page'. The more accident-prone arrangement arises where copy flows from one spread to another far away at the back of the book (as magazines are called in the trade). The risks are obvious. Thorough checking of page-turn instructions must be done at the last stage of the magazine's preparation as late alterations to the flatplan play havoc with the turned copy (i.e. the copy which is sent to the back and is known simply as the turn). It has even been known for a turn to have to be fitted in at the front of the book when late advertising appeared which had to be placed in a specified section. In some magazines all the short, newsy or diary items are interspersed with advertisements at the front and back of the magazine. Somewhere in the middle there is an ad-free zone referred to as a 'features well', where for several pages you simply find a long flow of editorial copy. The advantage of this for the editorial department is clear. It means interesting features copy or well-designed, visually striking pages can be allowed to flow from one spread to the next without the awkward interruption of adverts.

There is a further important check to make. If a publication uses an identifying symbol or tag line to distinguish its various sections then the sub needs to make sure that it hasn't been forgotten and, more crucial, that the right one has been included on the page.

Proofs

Eventually there will be proofs of the copy to look at. Proof-reading can be done on screen but many subs prefer to look at a printed version as this is closer to what the readers will be seeing. This can make it easier to spot mistakes and the very fact of reading the copy in a format different from the one in which it was subbed is another safeguard. Whether there is time will depend on the lead time (preparation time) for the magazine, staffing levels and so on. Proof-reading used to be done not only by subs but by professional proof-readers and the mythology is that they would read a text backwards so that the sense of what they read did not distract them from the words and punctuation. I've never actually met anyone who worked this way but it is true that while you do need at least one reading of a proof for sense, you also need one where the sense does not carry your eye across typographical mistakes. On an ideal subs' desk the proof would go not only to the sub who handled the pages originally but also to at least one other, who had never seen the copy before. It's amazing what a fresh eye can discover in the way of nonsense or missing apostrophes.

Proofs used to be marked up according to a standard set of signs which, in theory at least, didn't vary between publishing houses and printers. These are still used wherever hard copy is being dealt with.

Page proofs are the next stage on from what used to be called galley proofs. Galley proofs are of the text only and would not show page or column breaks or any design elements. Indeed they can be produced before any thought has been devoted to layout. Page proofs show all the elements of a page, the stories, the position of illustrations and all the other aspects of presentation discussed in this chapter. At this stage the besetting problem of overmatter (the technical term for too much copy) is likely to emerge. With computerised setting and page make-up this is much less likely to happen. If it does and yet does not warrant rewriting of the text or alteration of the layout then the overmatter can either be 'killed', which means dropped altogether, or it can be 'held over', to be kept for use on another page or even another edition of the publication.

Whether tackled on screen or as photocopies, proofs must be scrutinised for any lack of consistency or unintended incongruity: 'high-flyers' in the headline but 'high fliers' all through the text, without the hyphen and with no 'y'. After the corrections have been made, subsequent proofs are called 'revises' or 'revise proofs'.

Continuity

Page checking also has to be done with an eye to the rest of the magazine, once it is ready. Do the cover lines and entries in the contents page match each other? Are the page numbers accurate in the contents list and on the spreads themselves? The turns? The only way to be certain about any of these things is to check them at each stage.

Covers

The covers of most magazines, even of those which are designed to look like newspapers, contain several kinds of copy. There will be the publication's date, edition and logo (or titlepiece) and its barcode, the familiar black-and-white device which when scanned by a computer gives the International Standard Serial Number (ISSN). There will also almost always be some means of promoting the contents of the magazine whether in a series of short paragraphs with pictures above the logo, as is now common on newspapers and adopted by newsy periodicals such as *Press Gazette*, or in the form of what are known as cover lines. Most people refer to the logo as the masthead although there are still those who maintain that the masthead is only the box in which is listed the administrative information about the magazine such as staff, phone numbers and name and address of the publishing company (Morrish 1996: 264/6). Morrish says this can also be called a 'flannel panel' although my random queries about this have yielded no one who knew the term. This is not to suggest Morrish is wrong but merely to illustrate that some of the terms used within publishing are not universal. Whether the box containing the administrative information is a flannel panel or a masthead the chief sub will need to make sure it is kept up to date as staff leave or change job titles.

Cover lines are the phrases or even single words which tell the reader what the magazine has to offer. Some random examples are 'Poor little rich girls: when money can't buy you love', *Marie Claire*, May 1998; 'Why the scandal was good for America', *Time* 22 February 1999. For a glossy magazine which is expected to sell largely on the visual strength of its cover (see Chapter 13) the cover lines are so important as to be a subject of much discussion once the cover image has been chosen. The final words may be the result of a long, heated editorial meeting to which the sub or chief sub might have brought a selection of suggestions for each component of the magazine which were then debated by editors, deputy editors, marketing people and publishers.

Apart from cover lines some magazines, if they are perfect bound and therefore have a thick spine, will have little mottoes or joky phrases or even more cover lines relating to content printed on those spines. Again at random: *Condé Nast Traveller* goes for the straightforward informative magazine title plus 'Marseille. Costa Rica. Hong Kong. Resorts to relax in' followed at the foot of the spine by 'British Edition, June 1998, 009'; *Marie Claire* has that same basic information and then trumpets itself with the words 'The most imitated magazine in the world' (May 1998); *Harpers and Queen*, with more wit, used to print 'The non-drip glossy' on its spine.

On larger publications where the subbing is done by a team all the checks which are more to do with the mechanics of the whole magazine than with specific pages or copy are likely to be the responsibility of the chief sub, but on many magazines, particularly monthlies, there will be only one sub (or at least one staff sub) and so the responsibility falls to one person. She will have to check every last detail on the cover and all the other pages where there is editorial matter, as well as the page numbers and the headers or footers which are put on all the pages of some magazines, presumably to remind readers which magazine they are reading. This can be daunting, particularly to a sub who arrives at a magazine with newspaper experience on a big subs' table where the individual's work is always checked by more senior staff.

Copy flow

The chief subeditor, or whoever takes on that function, has to rule over the complicated series of decisions, processes and deadlines which go into the preparation of a magazine for printing. Take deadlines. Even daily newspapers have a variety of deadlines for the different pages. Magazines with large paginations and longish lead times will have much greater differences between page or section deadline times, sometimes as much as weeks. The work which individual copy or layouts demand will vary in complexity and this will all be taken into account when the production schedule is drawn up. This document (or its digital equivalent) lists deadlines for all pages and types of copy, for the various types of proof to be corrected, and for the final sending of the magazine to be printed, whether that is an in-house operation or takes place elsewhere. On glossy or big magazines with long lead times it is quite usual for the editorial work being done on any given day in the office to span several issues.

As a result a clear system is essential for the flow of copy and visual material around the office from writer or commissioning editor to the subbing, picture and art departments, to the lawyers if necessary and to anyone else (the editor for example) who might want to have a look at copy or layouts before they go to press. For anyone who trained before about 1985 this is probably best remembered concretely as a series of clearly labelled desk-trays, each holding copy and layouts with their own internal office history noted on them. Initials of the most senior staffer responsible for pages or copy would be written on the final page proof before printing, this initialising process being known as signing off. As the various stages of the production schedule are reached a dummy copy of the magazine (or its electronic equivalent) fills up with photocopies of the pages, so that whoever is in charge of progress chasing knows exactly what the latest stage is for each page.

In the computerised office files of paper are not (or should not be much) moved from desk to desk. Instead this flow of material is managed electronically even if old technology words such as 'basket' may be used to identify the files. Again, there needs to be a clear route for the flow of material however it is managed. A sub should know exactly what this is and what procedures at the computer keyboard are required to keep the flow in motion.

On magazines the last stage in this flow, as the final deadline approaches, tends to be more fraught than on newspapers perhaps because it does not occur so often. Even weekly papers or periodicals have a more relaxed day or two each week and on monthlies, although there is unlikely to be a day when little has to be done, there is certainly time to breathe and think ahead a little rather than just focus on getting the next page ready. Press day, then, on any periodical is busy and anxious until that moment when the publication has 'gone to bed', when it is in the hands of the printers and no more changes can be made.

Last minute hitches

Even at this stage and only rarely, problems can arise in the shape of court injunctions or the death of the selfsame superstar whose interview took months to arrange and whose portrait makes such a striking cover. What publishers do in these circumstances depends on how far into the printing process the magazine is and how embarrassing it will be to run the story. Pages are not all printed at once so it is sometimes possible to pull the copy, or some of it, and draw the reader's attention to what has happened. If the relevant article is short it can sometimes be pulled out altogether and other copy inserted such as a house ad (an advertisement for the magazine or another from the same publishing house). Super-efficient organisations might have files of timeless copy prepared for emergency use.

Over to the printer

Earlier in this chapter I mentioned the modern way of sending copy direct-to-plate by digital means using an ISDN line. It would be untrue to suggest that this is the universal practice at the time of writing but it is so fast and efficient compared with any other system that it is hard to see what can prevent its becoming the norm, other than the initial costs. John Morrish sums up the changes which have affected the last stage in the editorial process, the launch into the arms of printers if you like, by explaining what sending finished material to them could mean in the past and what it now does mean. He describes the final departure of whatever the editorial team releases, 'be that old-fashioned pasted-up pages and bags of transparencies, optical disks full of page layouts, words and picture handling data, streams of electronic digits down the telephone line, or even, in the near future, finished printing plates'. Transparencies (or trannies as they are affectionately known) are becoming a thing of the past now that there are digital cameras and electronic picture desks (EPDs) although where picture quality is paramount trannies are still vital.

What happens to the pages when they get to the printers is the topic for a different book. It is helpful to know enough about what happens to understand how this affects all the earlier stages in the editorial process, and to be able to think creatively about what can be achieved within the constraints of budget, time and staff. A sizeable publishing company will have a team of production experts and print buyers to advise editorial staff and to take decisions, along with the publisher, about how to make production budgets achieve as much as possible.

As we have seen, the work of writers, photographers and illustrators is transformed by the editorial team who also assemble it into layouts and instructions for the printer. Yet even when the presses start to roll the magazine is still an abstract notion and will be brought fully to life only when the task of binding is complete. Only then is the product a tangible object waiting to be picked up and held. Only then is the collection of ideas and digital instructions a magazine.

So far in this chapter the various aspects of this preparatory work have been outlined. Now let's consider briefly the way in which the different elements of a magazine are united to create this finished product, the magazine, for the readers.

Production processes

Assembling the flatplan

At the heart of the editorial production process is the magazine's flatplan. This is a kind of one-dimensional diagram of the magazine, with a square to represent each page, laid out on one sheet of paper. It enables the editorial team to see what is to appear on any given page and therefore how the sequence of articles will run. The job of creating this document is called flatplanning and is a collaborative effort between advertising director and editor.

Advertising constraints

At the flatplanning meeting there will already be two lists of constraints drawn up. First, the advertising director will have a list of advertisements that have already been sold (or nearly sold) for the issue and what positions have therefore been guaranteed to advertisers. The flatplan squares will be filled in accordingly. When the advertising team sell space their job is not just a matter of persuading companies to pay for pages and half pages. Advertisers regard some positions in a magazine more highly than others and so will pay higher rates for those spaces. The obvious example is the back cover which gives the advertisement greater visibility than an inside page. Other prime slots include the inside front cover and the first available right-hand page. In fact any right-hand page is thought to be better than pretty well any left-hand one, as a reader's eye is more likely to be drawn to it when a spread is opened up.

The flatplan also has to record whether the back or front cover, or occasionally an inside page, is to include what's known as a gatefold. This is where the width of the page is extended but folded back in on itself to fit the rest of the magazine. Sometimes there is more than one fold. Usually a gatefold is provided at the request of an advertiser but occasionally it can be used for editorial material.

Advertisers also like their material to be 'facing matter'. 'Matter' here simply means editorial material and 'facing' simply means opposite. It's probably obvious why advertisers prefer to be surrounded by editorial – it means the readers are more likely to pause on the page. In addition advertisers may list other stipulations when they book space. Make-up companies may insist that their adverts are set among the beauty pages, record companies will almost certainly want to be positioned near the music reviews and so on. No real surprises or particularly unreasonable demands there but, as Gloria Steinem found, not all requests are so easy to accommodate in the flatplan. If all advertisers had views about the content of features material near their ads it could prove impossible to get the publication out: food product ads which must be within food editorial but not within six pages of another food ad, engagement ring ads which mustn't be anywhere near stories that ask fundamental questions about the nature of romance (see page 198 and Steinem 1994).

How much space a magazine devotes to advertising varies considerably between publications and can even vary a little between issues of the same publication. The relative number of pages is called the advertising/editorial ratio (or ad/ed ratio). On business publications this is often around 60 : 40 while on consumer magazines it is likely to be the other way round at 40 : 60. As it is impossible to be sure how much space will be sold in any given issue, the ratio that is agreed by the publisher is usually set as an average over a number of issues. This means a bad month for ad revenue does not pull down the overall pagination of the magazine so much that it begins to seem too thin to its readers. Nor does an issue with a lot of advertising disappoint regular readers who expect a generous helping of editorial.

Another unavoidable restriction advertisers bring is whether they want colour or mono (black-and-white) pages. The more complicated production separation processes for colour mean that colour pages cost much more to produce. Colour pages are also more likely to attract a reader's attention. This means colour positions are charged at a higher rate. Clearly, though, it would not do for a magazine to fill with ads all the pages which have been allocated to colour and so if more colour ads are sold than expected it can mean an extra four pages of colour will be introduced into the magazine, allowing for some extra colour editorial. (Four pages because printing is done in sections which each carry multiples of four, eight or sixteen pages.) Or indeed the reverse may happen. If too much advertising falls by the wayside, colour pages may have to be dropped. This means that even for main features with excellent colour pictures the editor will not have complete control over where to place the article within the magazine.

Editorial constraints

The second list of constraints relates to the editorial material. Almost every magazine has regular columns and features that readers are accustomed to finding always in the same place. The contents page is one example. Some editorial matter too will need to be on colour pages and these will have to fit in with the ad department's requirements. Other than that the editorial team's wish-list for positions is much the same as that of the advertisers. Editors prefer right-hand pages, at least for the start of articles or for single-page articles, and they prefer editorial material to be surrounded by other editorial material. Neither side will ever get everything it wants and compromise is necessary, although publishers are apt to remind editors that it is the advertisers who pay the staffing and publication bills.

There are other flatplanning considerations. Most editors take care to ensure that there is a 'flow' to the magazine, by which they mean a logical, balanced and pleasing progression for the readers as they move from one item to the next. In a general interest magazine this might mean making sure that articles which do not have much pictorial interest are interspersed with those which do. Editorial matter shouldn't clash either with other editorial or with the adverts it is near. To make up an example: the kind of clash that could be problematic is a full-page, colour advertisement for vodka running opposite a harrowing account of a celebrity's struggle against alcohol addiction.

There is no guarantee that readers start to read a magazine at the beginning and then work neatly through the pages in order. Many people start at the back and work forward or else they use the contents list to jump straight to articles which interest them. Nevertheless editors do give these issues of flow and balance due concern because it is within their control and getting it right reflects their own professionalism.

The production schedule

Another factor at the flatplanning stage is the production schedule. This is effectively a list of deadlines for the various pages and sections of the magazine. Magazines are printed in what are called sections or formes, each of these being one sheet of paper printed on both sides which will eventually be folded and bound into the magazine. A section can cover up to sixty-four pages, according to the size of the magazine's pages. Any number of pages which can be multiplied by four, eight or sixteen can be printed as one section. So all the pages which are to be printed on one sheet, even though they may not be from the same part of the final bound copy of the magazine, will comprise one section for the purpose of printing. What goes into an individual section is determined by what is called the 'imposition'. This is the allocation of pages to the magazine's sections which will ensure that the individual pages will appear in the correct order once they are printed and bound together.

Each section of a magazine is likely to have a different set of dates for 'copy in' or 'closing', for layouts, for the various proof stages and for the various print processes. The bigger the magazine, the more deadlines.

To establish a production schedule in the first place is the work of the editor, production manager, printer and the publisher too, as the decisions have cost implications. A late closing page, for example, might be desirable in a weekly news magazine whatever the extra printing costs this incurs. To set the various dates the team effectively works backwards from the publication date, deciding how long each stage in the production and editorial process will take and then setting a deadline for each stage. It is then the job of senior staff to ensure deadlines are not missed.

Any production schedule shows how tightly interlinked the various deadlines are: if copy is late it may miss its slot for being subbed or for the layout to be done. Sending copy or layouts or film late to be printed means the time allocated for them may have been wasted and the next job may be in place. Printers, whether in-house or outside contractors, can often make up for lost time but they will charge for doing so because the work is likely to involve overtime and because machines and staff were perhaps idle as they waited for the late material. Every missed deadline has an implication for the flow of work and therefore for costs.

When decisions are being taken about where editorial or advertisements are to be placed on the flatplan, the relevant deadlines have to be taken into account, so that everything is ready at the right time and a regular flow of work is ensured both through the editorial office and at the printer.

All these competing considerations make the process of establishing a flatplan into the kind of logic puzzle found in IQ tests. The only difference is that with flatplanning some of the constraints are, of necessity, slightly flexible, depending on the importance of last-minute changes either from advertisers or from the editorial team. Where adverts fail to materialise extra copy may be needed or copy may be dropped if the decision is taken to cut pagination. This only makes the process of flatplanning more complicated. Once the essential items are established in the flatplan, however, it only remains for the editor to allocate the rest of the editorial material to the various pages that remain. Copies of the flatplan (whether paper or virtual) will then be distributed to the subbing, production and art departments.

Once the flatplan is established and the information married up with the production schedule the editorial work will get under way.

Colour

Where colour is concerned the last stage proofs are likely to be called Cromalins, the name reflecting the printing process by which they are produced. On publications with high production values Cromalins receive careful scrutiny as they give an accurate representation of the colours as they will appear in the magazine as well as showing whether the colours are correctly 'in register'.

Register refers to the success with which the areas of printed colour fit into the correct boundaries. Colour printing involves four colours of ink which are applied separately in succession. If there is a slight misalignment then the individual colours will not be properly in place on the final version and the picture will be spoiled by blurred edges where all the differing coloured portions meet. In these circumstances the printing is said to be out of register.

Every production decision has a cost implication. The quality of the ink used and of the paper on which the magazine is printed are good examples. The differing weights of paper and how glossy it is will affect the success with which colour can be printed. The paper used by, say, consumer monthlies such as *GQ* or *Harpers and Queen* is expensive but helps to establish the brand image of the magazines and is an essential support for the high quality artwork which is part of the attraction of those publications. By contrast colour reproduction of graphic material in newspapers or newspaper colour supplements which do not use high quality paper can leave the reader longing for sharp black and white pictures instead of sludgy-smudgy assaults on the eye in the name of full-colour production which is not backed up by a serious full-colour budget.

Not all magazines carry content that demands sophisticated use of colour and some make effective use of what is known as 'spot colour'. This is where one colour of ink in addition to black is used, either throughout a whole issue or on the pages printed together as one section. It doesn't compete with full colour for sophistication but on a lower-budget publication or one which is primarily about words, spot colour can bring some welcome visual variety.

Binding

As far as the finished magazine product is concerned there are other decisions which affect the look and feel of it and which are unlikely to be taken by the editorial staff alone. It is useful to have some idea of what influences these decisions. Take binding for example. The main distinction here is between publications which are saddle-stitched and those which are perfect bound. Saddle-stitching is where pages are simply folded at the seam and then stapled. This is the common method for thinner magazines such as *Prima*, *Take a Break*, *The Spectator*, *Time* and those periodicals, like *Press Gazette*, which are designed to look like newspapers.

Perfect binding, the other common technique, produces a thicker, harder spine more like that of books and is used for magazines with higher paginations and high production values which probably include the use of thick paper. This method uses glue to bind together the various printed sections which are folded so that the pages of one section fall consecutively, rather than, as with saddle-stitched pages, appearing in opposite halves of the book. Examples of perfect-bound magazines are *Vogue*, *FHM*, *Bliss*, *Cosmopolitan* and *Good Housekeeping*.

Printing

The choice about how to print a magazine will be made by the editor, publisher and print buyer and is really between offset litho or gravure printing and each is more suitable for particular kinds of work. Once the magazine is printed the pages must be folded into the right sections, bound and trimmed. Then all that remains is for them to bundled and sent on their way to the distributors, wholesalers, newsagents and readers.

Recommended reading

Evans, H. (1973 *et al.*) *Editing and Design: A Five-Volume Manual of English, Typography and Layout.*

Evans, H. (2000) *Essential English for Journalists, Editors and Writers.*

Fieldhouse, H. (1982) *Good English Guide.*

Hodgson, F. W. (1998) *New Subediting. Applemac, QuarkXpress and After.*

12 Electronic publishing and electronic journalism

Tim Holmes

Please don't be disheartened by thoughts of electronic publishing and vast on-line databases – one of the largest database hosts in the US had to start a magazine for subscribers to the system. There was no more effective way of telling them about the goodies available on-line.

John Wharton, *Managing Magazine Publishing*

Question: which print dinosaur, ink flowing through his veins, his heart still captivated by the sizzle of hot-metal typesetting and the rumble of printing presses in the basement, spoke the following words? 'Hard copy is still the heart of our business. I see no reason why that should change.' *Answer*: it was not a print dinosaur at all but Keith Jones, chief executive of Reed Business Information (RBI). Magazine journalists who love the feel of paper and the look of glossy pages will no doubt be pleased that such a senior publisher is making that case. But the electronic communications media affect journalists in more ways than the provision of new outlets in which to publish. They offer new ways of getting access to information and of communicating. This chapter is a guide to some of the ways in which magazine journalists currently use the electronic media.

Electronic publishing

Keith Jones was speaking at the International Federation of the Periodical Press (FIPP) Business Magazines seminar in September 1998.[1] RBI, along with its parent company Reed-Elsevier, is noted in the UK as one of the companies making the most of the opportunities which electronic journalism, the Internet and the World Wide Web have to offer. The company has a strategic alliance with Microsoft to help develop the MSN Internet system, and a number of its journals are available in constantly updated electronic form. RBI is by no means a dinosaur, and Mr Jones was not alone in expressing views like this.[2]

Electronic publishing, the meeting generally agreed, was important and growing but it was still far from threatening print as the dominant medium for the distribution of information. Apart from anything else, the Internet has not quite been the pot of gold which some publishers initially seemed to think it might be. A good many organisations assumed that existing magazine content could simply be put online and people would pay a subscription to get access. But the open nature of the Internet, and the demands of discerning readers, meant that this was never really likely.

The current state of and prospects for publishing, particularly news publishing, on the Internet were discussed fully in the July/August 1997 issue of the *Columbia Journalism Review* (CJR). Its findings were not optimistic. 'It appears that many people with financial responsibility for online news operations on the World Wide Web are weary of haemorrhaging cash,' wrote Denise Caruso. 'After far too many years of talk about revenue and nary a peep about profit, they would very much like for someone, anyone, to show them the money' (Caruso 1997).

It is true that most of the big publishing houses rushed to establish an online presence, and it is equally true that very few have yet discovered how to make that presence pay.[3] With so much information available for free, it is difficult to get readers to pay for a subscription, unless what is on offer is especially vital or timely or unique, and advertisers seem to have exercised their usual caution about flinging money into unproved – and, until recently, unaudited – channels.

It is hardly surprising that publishers are still finding their way around the new medium. The histories of radio and television show that the best (meaning both the most profitable and the most effective) ways of using these media were not immediately obvious to their owners, programme schedulers or advertising sales executives. It took time and a few blind alleys to get it right and there is no reason to suppose that publishing on the Internet will be any different.

As you would expect with a medium which is developing almost as fast as the technology, everything about it is changing and that includes forecasts aimed at or generated by those wanting to make money from it. Companies which were hesitant or reluctant in 1997 were being exhorted to go electronic at the 1999 UK trade show for magazine publishers, Magazines 1999. Media watchers who in 1997 thought that going online was a men-only pastime have been astonished to discover that women like it too and have followed up that discovery with the inevitable consumer-oriented online publishing offerings for women such as CharlotteStreet.com from the publishers of the *Daily Mail*. In the USA the Hearst Corporation's Home-Arts site merged in 1999 with Women.com to provide a wide range of material of interest to women, including editorial from magazines such as *Cosmopolitan* and *Redbook* which are owned by Hearst (Ramrayka 1999).

Predictions about revenue have become far more optimistic as far as e-commerce is concerned, but still vary considerably. Mintel suggested that the UK market for online shopping would be worth £1.5 billion by the beginning of 2000, while NOP's figures were 'approaching £3 billion' in August 1999 with 'current trends suggesting this figure could be as high as £9.5 billion by the end of 2000'.[4] And the signs are that in the USA women will be doing almost half of the online shopping. What this has to do with magazines is that online sites which are are not related to magazines are clearly going to provide increasing competition as a means for advertisers and businesses to reach potential customers. The forward-thinking magazine companies realise that they can either suffer as a result (and there are signs in the USA, at least, that consumer magazine circulations may already be feeling the effect) or adopt a more positive approach by taking on the competition using their established brands to attract the customers. As Liza Ramrayka points out, the popular, women-oriented sites in the USA such as iVillage (www.ivillage.com) 'can attract four to five million visitors a month ... Compare that to the average circulation of women's magazines in the US – around one million – and the marketing opportunities become obvious' (Ramrayka 1999).

Journalists and the Internet

If the business outlook is not quite as straightforward as it seemed initially, what about the effect of the Internet on providers of content, that is to say journalists? The continuing expansion of Internet publishing means the horizons of the paper-bound scribe looking to move into electronic journalism are boundless. It also means that no journalist can expect to remain untouched by the electronic media in some form. The job market is booming according to the managing director of one recruitment agency: 'Fifty per cent of the editorial positions we now handle have an online element to them . . . online recruitment is going to explode' (Urquhart 1998). As far as employer expectations are concerned, the main differences lie in what companies do with their sites and what technical skills they expect of their staff.

Definitions

Before we look at what the electronic journalist (e-journalist from here on) is expected to do, there are terms which need to be defined.

The Internet and the Web (or World Wide Web) are often treated as synonyms, but they are not. The Internet is the global network of computers, the means of distribution if you like, which supports and makes possible applications such as the World Wide Web. The Web itself comprises the thousands (probably millions) of individual pages and sites which can be called up to view or read on a computer running suitable software (the browser[5]). Sites can include text, photographs and audio and video components. Each and any of these components can be linked (hyperlinked, to be precise) to other components within the site or to any other site on the Web.

Exciting as the World Wide Web may be, the Internet supports a number of other applications. Possibly the most widely used, and therefore most familiar, function is e-mail, but also available are:

Usenet   a network of news groups using electronic bulletin boards to further discussions on a particular topic or area
Telnet   a means of accessing a remote computer and its files
Gopher   the original search-and-retrieve programme
FTP   File Transfer Protocol, another means of transferring files across the network

These and several other Internet programmes are explained in detail by Randy Reddick and Elliot King in their excellent primer *The Online Journalist: Using the Internet and Other Electronic Media*. This volume contains information (historical, practical, theoretical, ethical) useful for any journalist who is considering using the Internet – and that almost certainly means any journalist. The authors do not assume that readers will possess or wish to develop great technical skills; their starting point is an assumption that 'most journalists have little desire to become computer programmers or learn computer languages' (Reddick and King 1997: 6). As they are at pains to explain, you don't have to be an anorak, nerd or geek to acquire and use the skills an e-journalist requires. However, they stress the importance to any journalist of knowing how to access information on the Internet: 'Online access to wider sources of information means that more reporters can pursue more stories of greater interest to specific readers or viewers' (Reddick and King 1997: 5).

Now, just as the term 'electronic publishing' covers a variety of activities, so does the term 'electronic journalist'. It can mean anyone from Matt Drudge, whose eponymous Report is both gossipy and serious enough to break the Monica Lewinsky story,[6] to a far-flung stringer for a national daily tapping in copy via a modem and a flaky line. Clearly, these amount to very different sources of information, yet in some ways the distinction is hardly worth drawing: there have always been and, it is to be hoped, will always be all sorts and conditions of 'journalist'. As Ian Hargreaves, Professor of Journalism at Cardiff University, says: 'There are no qualifications for being a journalist because in a democracy everybody is a journalist.'[7] The name has never meant one thing only and the same aptitude for sorting the chaff from the wheat in printed sources is just as necessary, perhaps more so, in electronic communication.

What is more important to note here is that there are, generally speaking, two kinds of e-journalist in periodical publishing. The first, *pace* Reddick and King, uses electronic sources to research, or even uncover, stories which will be published on paper; the second does all of that, but the resulting stories are published entirely in an electronic medium.

Computer-assisted reporting (CAR)

Once an e-journalist has decided to cast off from the safe moorings of press releases, routine calls and regular beats, the Internet offers a perfect opportunity to break out of the usual journalistic cycle of sources and channels and into a new world of information and misinformation, of facts and rumours. For a journalist seeking leads, the very ease of access to anyone who wants to disseminate either truth or lies is simultaneously the Internet's greatest strength and its worst weakness. As Andie Tucker observes,

> On the Web, journalism, parajournalism and pseudojournalism don't just coexist; they invade each other, through the handy online device of the hypertext link ... Even the most respectable news site has the potential to launch the unwary surfer straight through the looking-glass.
>
> (Tucker 1997: 35)

This potential was demonstrated during the 1999 war in Kosovo, described by some commentators as the 'first online war' because so much material was published or broadcast on the Internet. In his introduction to a list of these sources, Matt Welch noted,

> [T]he Internet has allowed for scores of new information outlets to publish their version of breaking events and to spotlight their own choice of key background information ... including a Serb orthodox monk typing from a 12th century monastery, right- and left-wing groups in American, the Kosovo Liberation Army, the Serbian government and individual ex-Yugoslavs who are filling in newsgroups with reports from their neighborhoods and bitter arguments about the past.
>
> (Welch 1999)

As always, the onus for sifting and assessing material rests with the journalist doing the research, and for that person an interest in the established mores of the profession – thorough and double-checked research, balance, good writing skills, a concern for reporting accurate facts and an ethical stance – is essential. In other words, computer-assisted reporting is just reporting, with extra research tools.

Information sources

So, where does the e-journalist go for this additional information? I do not intend to rehearse all of the options discussed elsewhere (Bradley 1999; Gilster 1996; Keeble 1998; McGuire *et al.* 1997; Reddick and King 1997) but here is a brief summary, some words of caution, and some pointers to further information. In any case, the Internet is evolving so rapidly that definitive lists or rules are probably of less value than general principles.

The World Wide Web

Top of the list must come the World Wide Web. With pages put up by everyone from national governments to lone 'web warriors', a good journalist who knows how to search the Web effectively could construct an informed and reliable story on any subject under the sun without looking further than his or her browser. But, of course, a good journalist would never do such a thing; Harold Evans's dictum that 'news is people' is as true as it ever was, and 'people' still means journalists have to talk to living beings rather than passively downloading digital information.

Nevertheless, the ability to use search engines (the Internet's indices[8]) and to ascertain the reliability of the source is a skill worth cultivating. Ironically, the richest source of learning material is still print – books, manuals and specialist magazines; if you're keen to improve your Internet skills and knowledge, these are the places to start looking. Most newspapers now run regular pieces about the Internet and the basic advice must be to read whatever you can, wherever you can.

When it comes to ascertaining the reliability of information, one particularly useful Web resource is the InterNIC site. Like postal addresses which specify name, street, county and country, Web addresses, known as Uniform Resource Locators (URLs), contain several elements of direction, each of which is separated by a full stop or dot. The URL may include a national reference (for example .uk), or a generic domain-name to indicate the type of organisation – .com for a company, .org for a non-profit organisation, .net for a network, .edu for an educational establishment, .gov for a government organisation and .mil for the military. Prefixing the generic domain may be a corporate or an individual's name and prior to that will be something to identify the specific computer on which the site is hosted. Thus, for example, www.routledge.com identifies a computer known as www within Routledge which is a company.

Any individual or organisation (other than government or military) wishing to register their own domain name must register it with North American company Network Solutions, which maintains a searchable database at 'rs.internic.net/cgi-bin/whois'. The site has an online tutorial but is simple to use; simply key in the domain name (not the host computer part) of a Web address and the database will display the information it holds. For example, entering a query for Routledge.com brings up a company address in Boston, USA, along with e-mail, phone and fax numbers for administrative, technical and billing contacts. InterNIC also works for e-mail domain names, although many people using e-mail will be connected to the Internet by an Internet Service Provider (ISP) and you will only be able to look up the ISP's details. However, this may give you a starting point for substantiating the reliability of an Internet source. Of course it is not infallible, and a savvy poster of misinformation is likely to be able to sidestep this check.

Similar organisations register the domain names for European and Asian sites and there are links to them from the InterNIC site. Domains in the UK are registered with the UK Network Information Centre (NIC), which has a site at 'www.nic.uk'.[9]

E-mail

The first thing to note about e-mail is that, unlike letters delivered by the Post Office, it is not private and not secure. There are no laws to prevent anyone with access to your mail folder (for example, whoever maintains your server, or your boss) from opening it up to read your messages. That said, e-mail can be a convenient method of communication for both sender and receiver. It is faster than the post, and less intrusive than a phone call. The receiver does not have to deal with an e-mail immediately, but can respond at a convenient moment. And because it is still a new and cool medium, people are inclined to use and respond to it.

However, if a phone interview is less preferable than a face-to-face interview because you miss out on the body language of the interviewee, an e-mail interview is less preferable than the phone because you don't even get any aural signals such as tone of voice. If the subject matter is not contentious this probably doesn't matter but when you are posing a hard question it could affect your perception and interpretation of the response. McGuire *et al.* make the astute observation that,

> Online interviews also force interviewers to reveal their entire strategy upfront. This makes it impossible ... to recover from a poor first question or an incorrect assumption, or to spring a tough question at the end ... In short, an online interview may get you a usable quote, but it's unlikely to produce a revealing interview.
>
> (McGuire *et al.* 1997: 111)

Discussion groups

An alternative way of making sure you get lots of messages is to subscribe to a discussion group. There are thousands of lists covering hundreds of topics. Although Reddick and King say lists 'have emerged as potentially significant tools for journalists ... [and] can be thought of as electronic salons in which people holding similar interests gather to talk about issues of concern', they also warn that just because someone is able to participate in a news group or discussion list 'does not mean he or she has any special expertise or knows anything factual about the issue. Many news groups are filled with rumours and mistakes, particularly about current affairs' (Reddick and King 1997: 136 and 158).

Bulletin boards and virtual chat

Bulletin boards are exactly what they sound like – the digital equivalent of a noticeboard. Registered members can leave messages for individuals or the whole 'community', and those communities can be anything from a neighbourhood to a nation. A reporter on a local beat might find a local bulletin board useful for sampling public opinion, while a board put up by a government organisation will probably contain hard information for a journalist on a specialist magazine or national paper. Many special interest groups are catered for, too, some of them none too savoury.

Some journalists do find discussion groups, bulletin boards and chat useful. Paul Richfield keeps an eye on company chat for story leads and Diana Clement of *Sunday Business* finds 'the benefit of regularly checking newsgroups is the chance of an early tip-off or "meeting" a case study' (Clement 1997).

Paul Richfield, e-journalist

Paul Richfield, 36, is the American correspondent for Air Transport Intelligence (ATI), an online daily published by Reed Business Information. He was a winner in Reed's 1998 Newcomer of the Year editorial awards, for which his editor was moved to comment: 'Although coming straight from journalism school and being put into a position of well above average responsibility, he has generated a consistently high quality output.' Paul uses an IBM-compatible Pentium PC running RBI's own editorial software, which he has found simple to use.

Richfield put himself through a postgraduate masters programme in journalism at Columbia University, New York. He had been earning his living as a pilot before doing the course, so when he saw the advertisement for ATI it looked like a perfect opportunity. He was interested in aviation, but he was not fussy about going into electronic journalism.'When opportunity knocks, you take it,' he says. 'Over here, newswire reporting, which is basically what I am doing, is regarded as a first job from which you progress into more editorial writing, features and so on.

'I'm writing straight hard news for ATI and the medium does not have much to do with the content. Because our readers are in the industry we can assume a greater level of knowledge and we can use more detail but that's nothing to do with being online.'

Richfield finds that he writes very much to a formula, one which will be familiar to every news journalist. 'I need five elements to write a story. There must be an action verb; something must have happened. If nothing has happened then it's probably a feature. The story needs to have a larger significance, and in the aviation industry most things have that. I must have a quote from a primary source. I must be able to give some background, a paragraph or two in descending order of importance. And the fifth element I like to have is a differing opinion.'

It's here that the medium does make a difference, and in an unexpected way. ATI's main rival is *Aviation Daily*, a printed paper. The online journal has a lead of between 12 and 20 hours over the competition, and because this differential is a vital competitive advantage Richfield explains, 'We're pressed for time. I have to run more single source stories than I like because there's not enough time to get a second opinion.'

He also finds this pressure makes him 'more receptive than attacking' as a reporter. 'I spend lots of time rewriting press releases, although the context and interpretation of the facts is my responsibility.' The Internet is another regularly used, and important, resource. 'I use it to download information from a variety of sources,' Richfield explains. 'I find it very reliable, and it gives me an edge to know how to access databases, inter-company employee chat lines, union websites and such.'

Asked to identify an advantage of working online, Richfield considered that seeing one's work appear immediately is gratifying. His advice to someone thinking about going into a similar job is simple: 'Understand the laws which pertain to journalism, privacy and libel. And understand the difference between objective journalism and editorial writing.'

As for the next step in his career, he has a conventional move already planned. 'I'm going to a monthly magazine, where I'll be writing features and other editorial material.'

Interactivity

In that 'digital' issue of the *Columbia Journalism Review* (July/August 1997), one contributor throws cold water on the idea of interactivity. The ability of readers to contact publications and journalists in real time has been hailed in some quarters as a breakthrough in audience participation. Among other things, it can facilitate an immediate right of reply, or encourage participation in the post-publishing process. However, Andie Tucker is of the opinion that much of this interactivity is closer in spirit to *Jeopardy* (a game show in which contestants have to supply the question to an answer) than to a phone-in on the C-SPAN current affairs cable network.[10] 'Why should a website's instant poll on FDR's status be hailed as constructive engagement when the networks' overnight tracking polls on Bob Dole's status were routinely denounced as shallow or undemocratic?' she asks (Tucker 1997).

The digital reporter

Journalists who work in an entirely electronic environment are, at present, a small but growing group.[11] They range from reporters based in key overseas areas who file breaking news to specialist journals, through multi-skilled writer/photographers who compose both words and pictures and perhaps also do some layout, to subeditors who shape the copy and decide where and how to display it on the site.

If that sounds almost like the structure of a printed publication, it is – with certain key differences. The speed of work and the identity of the consumer are two of the most important.

E-publishing has one major advantage over print, an advantage which puts it on an equal footing with broadcast – as soon as something happens, it can be put on screen. This, in turn, puts the news reporter under immense pressure; a news service will have several deadlines a day and stories must be constantly updated or, better still, broken. One up-to-date lobby correspondent working for *Microsoft Network News* has given us a glimpse of both the speed with which stories appear and the new (multi)skills required of a digital reporter:

> It's no longer just a question of getting the words, bashing them into a computer terminal and pressing the send button. There's the whole multi-media approach . . .
> I now carry around a digital camera, digital mini-disk and microphone, laptop computer and mobile phone with data card that allows me to send copy without plugging into a phone socket. [When it works] there's no thrill like it. With the exception of live TV it is as immediate as it's possible to get. Within a matter of moments of filing, your story has appeared on the site.
>
> (Assinder 1997)

The other important consideration for a magazine journalist is that not so much is known about the readers (or viewers) of an electronic publication as it is about readers of conventional magazines. This is partly because the medium is still so young (no equivalent of the National Readership Surveys has yet been devised), but also because it attracts different types of readers who want different information presented in a different way.

They are also fickle, as research and observation has demonstrated: 'People on the Web like to click more than they like to scroll' (McGuire *et al.* 1997: 153). 'Surveys of Internet usage cited on the online-news list show that casual browsers outnumber active readers . . . by 65 to 1' (Pryor 1999). This has consequences for publishers, editors and, of course, journalists.

Caroline Gabriel, Editorial Director, VNU New Media

Someone who has done a great deal of thinking about electronic publishing is Caroline Gabriel, who as Editorial Director of VNU New Media has had to understand the way people use online sources. VNU, a Dutch-owned publishing group, is best known for its information technology titles. Trade journals like *Computing* and consumer magazines such as *ComputerActive* are leaders in their respective markets, but as befits a company so closely connected to the world of electronic communication, VNU has established both an electronically distributed newswire service and an expanding website.

The VNU website (webserv.vnunet.com) started as a virtual replica of the printed magazines and the newswire was primarily intended for internal consumption, keeping print journalists up to date with news from around the world, notably Silicon Valley. This has changed, as VNU, and Gabriel, have come to realise that the website is not used in the same way as the equivalent print titles, nor are the people visiting the site the same ones who are the readers of print.

'We have been surprised by the spread of VNUnet's readers', she says. 'People on the Web are more interested in more things; they are looking for something, anything, interesting to read and this is a big challenge for journalists. There's less 'stopping power', so it becomes even more important to get a grabby headline and intro. Stories need to be very concise and written for a broader, international, audience.

'I'm not sure that you want a whole new type of journalist, but you do want a new mindset. Because web-journalism is more multi-skilled – you may combine radio, tv, HTML[12] and conventional layout – there's less of a split between production and editorial. A good web-journalist will be interested in the medium, flexible (there's not much routine work) and able to work quickly and under pressure. There are three deadlines a day on Newswire. We don't demand special technical skills from new recruits but HTML could be useful, even if only for an idea of what can and cannot be done successfully. Print journalists come with preconceptions about using pictures, for example – if the story is updated regularly, then the picture should be. But it's actually harder to improve a website than a printed magazine because of the sheer weight of programming involved. Adding features or changing design is much more difficult because the technicians and programmers become involved.

'In any case, reproducing your magazine on screen is just not enough. VNU aims to get rid of "magazines" on the site altogether and have VNUnet as the brand. Some of the content will be from our magazines (and credited as such) but we will be researching and writing a lot of original material. At the moment, the Web is a good place to be for a journalist because the journalists are still in control of the medium, not advertisers, not readers. Ads are sold on the back of the number of people visiting and the only thing which attracts people is content.'[13]

The American experience

If the UK (and Europe) is still at the beginning of the e-journalism learning curve, industry commentators generally agree that the USA is, as usual, at least five years ahead; there has been an observable pattern in periodical publishing that North American trends take about this long to migrate across the Atlantic.

True to the long American tradition of teaching and reflecting on the practice of journalism (something which is still resisted by many newspaper editors, executives and even journalists in the UK), most university-based schools of journalism have begun to incorporate electronic media in their curricula.

One electronic publication which combines debate about the topic with the actual teaching process is the *Online Journalism Review* (http://www.ojr.org/) published by the Annenberg School for Communication at the University of Southern California (USC). The *OJR* is one of two online publications used by the USC to give students practice at using and understanding the medium. The other is a newswire service which feeds copy to a number of regional newspapers in California.

As a site of debate and information about electronic journalism, *OJR* is similar to the long-established *Columbia Journalism Review*.[14] An article in the issue of 11 November 1998 summarised the attitudes of several major schools of journalism. Perhaps not surprisingly, all the academics interviewed acknowledged the Internet as an important development for journalists, but they were not agreed on the best way to use it. Neil Chase, assistant professor at the Medill School of Journalism, Northwestern University echoes VNU's Caroline Gabriel.

> The first, and perhaps most important [thing about online journalism], is a simple understanding of how the Web and the Internet work, and how they are used by the audience ... The journalist must be familiar with, and comfortable with, the basics of computer use.
>
> (Raouf 1998)

Not everyone agrees that technology is the most important element in the mix. Ron Reason, director of visual journalism at the Poynter Institute, Florida, has a much more traditional take on what the training of journalists should have as its basis.

> 'Our area of focus tends to be content and philosophy of creating publications, print or Web, rather than technology,' Reason said. 'We figure someone can go to most any community college and get basic HTML training and often training in advanced programs, but few places address the editorial and ethical issues that we address as they relate to content online'
>
> (Raouf 1998)

However, there appears to be a consensus that the very least a modern journalist needs is a basic understanding of how and where to find information – and how to judge the worth and reliability of that information. Ann Brill, assistant professor at the University of Missouri School of Journalism, says:

> Without an understanding of new media, students will not understand the larger communications environment. How, for example, could anyone cover the Microsoft and Justice Department story without understanding the idea of an operating system and browser? How could a reporter write about the elections and not know how to use a database full of information about donors? Can you imagine the poor journalist covering Washington's scandals and not knowing how to access the online report or even keep track of Matt Drudge's latest rumors?
>
> (Raouf 1998)

Being able to trace back information and assess its provenance and reliability might, then, become a defining characteristic of the successful magazine e-journalist.

Job prospects in cyberspace

There is growing evidence that print journalists are being lured away from good jobs to even better ones in the e-media. For careers as e-journalists they need all the traditional journalism skills – and a few more. Some knowledge of the way the Internet works and how websites are constructed, or at the very least a willingness to learn, is important, as is the ability to adapt to a changing environment. As Julia Frazier wrote in the *OJR*:

> Success means being a Journalist Plus. Plus what? Plus a specialization: business development, e-commerce, project management. And plain old news jobs are still out there, too, especially for journalists with good HTML skills and a willingness to go where the work is.
>
> (Frazier 1998)

She also suggests that anyone serious about building a career in cyberspace should leave journalism for the better paid commercial, technical or managerial pastures.

Notes

1 'The extending boundaries of business information', *Magazine World*, 1998, Issue 18, September/October, p. 5.
2 Seminar delegates came from Crain Communications, the Economist Group, Nikkei Business Publications and Verlagsgruppe Deutscher Fachverlag, amongst others.
3 See, for example, *Press Gazette* 1 May 1998, p.12 and 29 May 1998, pp. 12–13.
4 NOP Internet Survey, 30 August 1999, at www.nopres.co.uk
5 Popular browser software includes Netscape Navigator/Communicator and Microsoft Explorer. A browser is no more than a Graphical User Interface between the user and the raw mechanics of the Internet; these two examples also incorporate the ability to send and receive e-mail, transfer files and so on.
6 See www.drudgereport.com, which also has many links to other news sites. *The Drudge Report* has also inspired numerous parody sites, which is perhaps a sign of its notoriety. For an interesting interview with Matt Drudge see www.penthousemag.com/promo/drudge; yes, it is *Penthouse*, but these pages are the soul of discretion.
7 Ian Hargreaves; lecture to journalism students at Cardiff University, 7 January 1999.
8 See, for example, www.yahoo.com, www.altavista.com, www.lycos.com, www.excite.com. UK sites include www-uk.lycos.com, www.yahoo.co.uk. Guides to the Internet explain how to make your searches more effective; learning to use the 'advanced' search techniques offered by Alta Vista and Excite is especially useful.
9 Bradley (1999) has a good section on checking the authority of data posted on the Internet; see Chapter 7. See also Appendix F in Mcguire *et al.* (1997) for the Associated Press policy for using electronic services.
10 C-Span defines part of its mission as 'to provide the audience, through the call-in, direct access to elected officials, other decision makers and journalists on a frequent and open basis'. See www.c-span.org
11 This definition is not intended to include journalists whose copy for a printed periodical is also used on a website.

12 HyperText Mark-up Language, the basic code which defines the appearance of a web page. To see what HTML looks like, load a web page, then go to Page Source under the View menu.

13 Interview with Caroline Gabriel, 12 December 1998.

14 In some respects it is better because it is purely web-based and thus all of the content and archive is accessible to the net-user. Subscription is free, and a monthly e-mail summarising the contents is pushed to subscribers.

Recommended Reading

Bradley, P. (1999) *The Advanced Internet Searcher's Handbook*.

Gilster, P. (1996) *Finding it on the Internet: The Internet Navigator's Guide to Search Tools and Techniques*.

McGuire, M. *et al*. (1997) *The Internet Handbook for Writers, Researchers and Journalists*.

Reddick, R. and King, E. (1997) *The Online Journalist: Using the Internet and Other Electronic Media*.

Taylor, D. (1997) *Creating Cool HTML 3.2*.

13 Magazine design

Tim Holmes

> It does not matter what a magazine looks like if the contents are not worth printing in the first place . . . A magazine can be a little better than its material, but not much.
>
> Ruari McLean, *Magazine Design*

In the beginning was the word, or so the Bible says, and many journalists think of words as the starting point of magazines too. But they're wrong. In the beginning is not the word but the blank page. All magazines start as a series of blank pages waiting to be filled. Think of almost any magazine and you'll think not just of words filling those pages, you'll also think of images and how these relate to the words, how these elements work together within a context: that visual context is the magazine's design, the subject of this chapter. (A detailed discussion of the actual images is to be found in Chapter 14.)

The idea of 'design' has, in recent years, been almost overburdened with significance both positive and negative. (The word 'designer', for example, is now widely used as an adjective to mean unjustifiably expensive.) Yet for the commercial world design has always been a matter of legitimate concern. In the UK the Great Exhibition of 1851 was intended to gather together the best examples of British industrial design for the edification of the general public and of those manufacturers who were thought to be lagging behind in their awareness of the importance of design. An enormous success with the public, the Exhibition generated enough money to fund the beginnings of 'Albertopolis', that corner of London's Kensington dedicated to the great national museums and the Albert Hall. It is still one of the Victoria and Albert Museum's roles to collect and display examples of the finest design in the crafts and manufacture.

The Victorian desire to spread awareness of and demand for well-designed products by consumers has lived on into the twentieth century, as the existence of the Design Council among other institutions shows. Some would argue that good design is now encountered by everyone and appreciated by all. 'Design is the greatest factor in modern life. In every home, in shop windows and in every street Beauty is making a profound appeal. Things of Beauty are now the commonplaces of life.' Margaret Thatcher said something like that when she was Prime Minister; Stephen Bayley, who writes on design and is a former director of London's Design Museum, is always saying something similar, as is Sir Terence Conran, founder of Habitat, the shop (or way of life) that helped to transform the interiors of British homes in the 1960s.

The quote, however, is from none of these people, as the idiosyncratic capitalisation might indicate. It comes from a source much closer to our present interests, Vincent Steer's book *Printing Design and Layout*, a training manual published in the 1930s.

'Let no printer remain under the delusion that the "man in the street" cannot tell the difference between designed printing and printing that merely happens,' he says. '[It] will not be long before every buyer of printing insists that the work he gives to the printer shall also be well designed and beautifully printed'

(Steer, no date: 11)

Many things have changed since Steer wrote (and had printed beautifully) those words, including the crafts of printing and typesetting. Certain standards of design are now expected, particularly in magazines and newspapers, even if it is not possible to explain exactly what 'good design' is or always to separate it out from high (meaning expensive, usually) production values. Many of us would say we know good design when we see it but we would only be highlighting how subjective the term is. This point was made neatly by Ruari McLean whose book *Magazine Design* is still one of the best introductions to the topic. He wrote that when he used the phrase 'good design' what he was actually saying was 'This pleases me, and I hope it pleases you', that 'what is "good design" in one particular context may not be "good design" in another' (McLean 1969: 3).

This means that even designers disagree profoundly about what counts as 'good'. For Neville Brody even the idea of 'pleasing' is too limiting. He is one of the best known graphic designers and typographers of the late twentieth century. He was responsible for the distinctive look of *The Face* from 1981 to 1986 where 'his work . . . questioned the traditional structure of magazines design'. For him there is no question of seeing design as mere problem solving, to do that is 'to please rather than to invent', in the sense of satisfying expectations rather than communicating with the reader in an emotive way (Wozencroft 1988: 96 and 10).

Brody's work for *The Face* has been credited with the 'reinvention of magazine language', the reflection of a new sensibility, one underpinned by the notion that to give the public what it wants is merely to give it what it is used to (Wozencroft 1988: 94–5). One of the interesting things for Brody about magazine design is the three dimensional nature of the space that has to be worked with.

Magazines are 3D items in space and time – there's a connection between page 5 and pages 56 and 57, a continuum. A magazine doesn't have to divide up space on a page like a newspaper, and the information it carries has more time to make connections between the different ideas that might be present. Why be inhibited by the edge of the page?

(Wozencroft 1988: 96)

This comparison with newspapers was made in the 1980s before it was common for newspapers to be sold with quite so many discrete parts (another kind of third dimension perhaps?). Newspaper designers were, in any case, aware of the influence on the reading public of Brody and those designers who plunged into his wake, and of the changing expectations of readers. No surprise, then, that many newspapers have made efforts to modernise and enliven the way they look in recent years. When *The Guardian* newspaper launched its revised design on 19 April 1999, the move was considered important enough to the average reader for it to be recorded in a panel at the foot of the front page. This, in turn, directed readers to a story on page 6 which described some of the changes, and the reasons for them, in more detail. Tellingly, the story was headed 'Design to create pages people want to read' and one of the key quotes came from the paper's design director, Simon Esterson, who noted: '[W]e are in a situation where magazines are very well produced. Newspapers have to try to keep up with the standards set by magazines' (Glaister 1999).

Some would say that has always been the case, but Glaister's story raises some interesting points and the headline tells us a great deal. It has long been assumed that readers have to be 'tempted' into a story, which is why the format of the classic punchy news intro under a snappy headline evolved, but here is a newspaper admitting to deploying design in addition to skilful subediting and traditional layout skills for the purpose.

What is 'design'?

At its simplest magazine design is the way in which words and images and the physical elements such as paper and binding work together. It is also, of course, much more than that, as the example of another relaunch makes clear. *Motor Cycle News* hit the news-stands in a new guise on 14 April 1999. Although there was no reference to this on the cover, the editor took space on page 2 to explain the changes, which went well beyond a different typeface or two. Emap Active, publishers of the weekly, had decided that it was not serving its readers as well as it could. As industry magazine *Press Gazette* explained: '*Motor Cycle News* has relaunched and moved more upmarket to cater for bikers who are becoming "more intelligent"' (Addicott 1999). Introducing the new look, editor Adam Duckworth told his readers, 'What I hope you'll notice is an *MCN* that's different in style, attitude and content.'

Leaving aside the attitude and the content (while acknowledging that these are of the utmost importance), the change that was most obvious was the look of the magazine. The typeface for headlines and cover lines had changed from a brashly tabloid square-cut sans serif to a sans with chiselled ascenders, taking the look away from *The Sun* and into the little-mapped territory of a tabloid magazine (or 'magloid', a phrase which seems to have been coined when Emap relaunched another of its stalwart performers, *Garden News*, a few months later). The headlines themselves changed from upper case to upper and lower in a smaller point size, both changes giving the pages a less frantic look. The body face was clearer, allowing more white to show on the page which, in turn, gave a more spacious feel. (For an explanation of the technical terms see the glossary, page 243.)

In these ways the magazine's intention to move upmarket was indicated by the look of the pages. Without reading a word most potential readers would have been able to tell that something had happened and to tell what it meant. Visual images have great power, and experienced consumers learn to read and decode them immediately, even those consumers who don't have the analytical vocabulary to explain why. There is no absolute or universal reason why a magazine like *Chat*, which targets working-class women, should have pages filled to bursting with short, bitty items and be spattered with bright colours. A convention could just as easily have evolved which meant big pictures and white space were the norm for C2DE readers and lively, information and story-packed pages were the rule for their wealthier AB cousins. (For an explanation of these terms see page 191.)

Visual conventions, like linguistic ones, are to a greater or lesser extent arbitrary and, as Jonathan Miller reminds us: 'before any significance can be attached to certain specimens of formal representation, the rules by which such representations make sense must be learned and understood' (Miller 1971: 98). The study of the way words and images work as signs and symbols is known as semiotics and while it's not a topic that interests all journalists, those who would like an introduction to it (and that is likely to include most university students of journalism) will find accessible starting points in the books by Barthes, Berger, and Williamson recommended at the end of this chapter.

Visual literacy

This understanding of visual conventions is what we mean by visual literacy. Most of our information about the outside world comes through our eyes; hearing, touch, smell and taste are all subordinate to sight. As a result, we are surrounded by images. Newspapers, books, television, films and advertising all play with images, to varying degrees and for varying purposes.

That's the main reason design is important to a magazine – it communicates the values and aspirations of a title before the potential consumer has read a word. However, it does not follow that 'design' necessarily means a highly creative arrangement of shapes on the page. As Ruari McLean noted: 'Magazine design cannot ... be generalized; it is always a specific problem. Each publication has its own problems, its own aims, its own conditions and limitations' (McLean 1969: 1). Publications (financial newsletters for example) whose purpose is merely to impart factual information to a busy reader may be best served by a straightforward arrangement of headlines and text. Readers don't have the time or inclination (such a layout implies) to bother with superfluous decoration when there is money to be made; what they are paying for is hard information, and that's what they should get. Nevertheless, there are different ways of achieving this look, and high-flying professionals are less likely to be impressed by an amateurish production which resembles a parish magazine than by one which features good typography in an unobtrusive but clear layout.

Those same readers, however, probably have interests outside their working lives. Let us say they are keen on sailing large yachts in warm but sometimes challenging weather. They may read a yachting magazine and when they pick it up they would not feel well served if it looked as plain as a newsletter. The sailing section in any newsagent shows that in magazines such as *Yachting Monthly* and *Yachting World* lavish photography and glossy paper are the norm, and usually these are accompanied by a high standard of page design.

As Neville Brody put it:

> At the root of it, design is a language just as French and German are languages. Whilst some people are able to understand design fluently, there are those who just use phrase-books. They don't understand the words they are using, but the phrase meets their need.
>
> (Wozencroft 1988: 10)

Brody was making the distinction as a comment on design practice, in the sense that the less innovative designers are the phrase-book wielders. But for those whose job is not to design but to work creatively with designers the phrase-book approach is perhaps a positive thing. Better anyway than those journalists (who specialise in words) who sometimes make the mistake of thinking that design is something separate from the prose which they so lovingly craft. Some (it's tempting to say 'the old school' but this is not necessarily so) have a more entrenched attitude and rate visual presentation as unimportant. Click and Baird attribute some of this to what they characterise as the excesses of 'screaming graphics' that made some magazines almost impossible to read in the 1960s . . . [the] de-emphasis of content by some designers to the point where they seem to be designing for the sake of design alone also presents some difficulty.

(Click and Baird 1990: 211–12)

Designers and writers do sometimes hold contrary opinions about the importance of words, and that can lead to trouble. Andy Cowles is a magazine designer whose experience ranges from *Your Horse* to *Q* and a range of magazines in between. In his view 'designers are their own worst enemies because they don't learn how to write. They can empower themselves by getting a facility with the written word and learning to appreciate the power of one word as against another.'[1] This idea is developed by Colin McHenry, a Group Art Director of Centaur Publications, who encourages fledgling designers to develop a range of skills, including 'the ability to interpret a manuscript. You need to be able to read it, understand it and get some visual ideas from it' (McHenry, quoted in Swann 1991: 132).

Covers

Nowhere in a magazine is the interaction of words and pictures more important than on the front cover. The cover has to do two key jobs for a magazine: 'It has to sell the general concept of the publication as well as to reflect, through its design, the intellectual level of the editorial content' (Swann 1991: 133). Other commentators suggest it has more personal than intellectual functions: 'It is the magazine's face . . . Like a person's face it is the primary indicator of a personality' (Click and Baird 1990: 98).

What's more, the cover has to do this more or less instantaneously, in an environment where the newsagent's customers may be milling around and where there are shelves bearing hundreds of titles including all the competing rivals in a given field. If it's doing its job really well, then the cover will tempt readers away from those rivals too, as John Morrish notes in his book about magazine editing: 'The fundamental thing is for the cover to sell the issue, both to your regular readers . . . and to other people's readers, who might be looking for a change' (Morrish 1996: 167).

This chapter can't attempt a comprehensive discussion of cover design (although some of the books recommended at the end of this chapter do). There are, however, certain guidelines which have relevance for all magazines which are sold on the newsstand rather than by subscription. It's worth remembering for these publications that about a third of all the decisions to buy a magazine are made on the spur of the moment in a shop and that readers take, on average, between two and three minutes to choose from the hundreds of titles in front of them; the average time spent by a potential purchaser on appraising each women's magazine cover is three seconds.[2] According to research carried out for the Periodical Publishers Association, the cover is a publisher's main method of enticing shoppers to buy and every other cover in the shop is trying to do the same thing.[3]

Guidelines for cover design

- Use a strong image, though not necessarily a photograph; sometimes type can work well.

- Make sure the titlepiece (sometimes now called the masthead) is clearly identifiable. This doesn't mean the whole word has to be visible but enough of its distinctive lettering should be there to make it clear to readers which title they are looking at.
- Make sure cover lines are legible from 2–3 metres. Some publishers refer to this as the floor test. If you throw a magazine on the carpet you should be able to read the cover lines without bending down.
- Promise a clear benefit to the reader.
- Offer something for beginners or new readers.
- Create strong links to the contents page. Readers are irritated if the fascinating story heralded on the cover is impossible to find in the contents list, perhaps because it is given a different title.
- Deliver everything you promise.
- Put the emphasis on the left-hand side of the cover as that is the part which will show when the magazine is on the average newsagent's shelf. The other important site is the top, which is why you won't see many titlepieces positioned at the bottom of the page.
- Plan the cover as early as possible and spend as much time on it as you can. Some publishers now recommend deciding on a cover first and then commissioning the features to go with it. It's even been said that some editors like to think up the cover lines first and then order the features.[4]

These guidelines are not all relevant to all covers. News-based publications often choose to look rather like newspapers, by adopting some of the conventions of newspaper design such as using a lot of type on the front page. *Press Gazette* is one example although it is printed on heavier, glossier paper than a newspaper. Other sorts of magazines, too, adopt a newspaper style, although *Melody Maker* opted to change to a glossy magazine format in October 1999 saying that for its target teenage readers the newspaper format no longer carried the right appeal.

Titles which are largely sold by subscription or which reach the reader unrequested as part of a weekend newspaper package have the freedom to be more adventurous in their designs as the cover is not necessarily the selling point, although it still has to do the job of tempting the reader to open the magazine. Depending on the target readership the covers of newspapers' supplement magazines may be much simpler, minimalist almost, with perhaps just a picture and one or two words to draw attention to the cover story. Readers will be getting the magazine anyway, they don't make a purchasing choice based on the magazine's cover lines and that gives the designer greater freedom to concentrate on the visual aspects of the design.

Writing good cover lines (the name for the words on the cover, sometimes called barkers or screamers) is a craft in its own right. There is a temptation to try out clever word play, as in some headlines, but in Morrish's view this should be resisted:

> They are there to tempt and intrigue and invite further scrutiny. They should be positive and enthusiastic. Above all they need to be short, snappy, colloquial and absolutely straightforward . . . Readers need to look at the line once to understand what it means.
>
> (Morrish 1996:174)

A further point is that, generally speaking, the more downmarket a title is, the more words and individual pictures there will be on the cover to the extent that papers like *Chat* or

Take a Break can become what one designer called a 'visual nightmare'. Unfair, of course, as it's all a matter of taste and designers, editors and publishers go to a lot of trouble to make sure that they are creating the kinds of covers that will bring them readers.

Whatever kinds of covers are under discussion, a designer who recognises the importance of the verbal elements which contribute to the success of a cover is more likely to be able to influence the outcome. So too is a writer who appreciates the principles of good design and some of the ways in which designers are trained to think. Designer Andy Cowles is not the only person who believes that, 'the best editors are those who understand a visual language', the ones who, if not fluent in the language of design, perhaps, at least carry the phrase-book.

Looking for the reader

Peter Booth is Associate Design Consultant of the recently relaunched (and redesigned) *Classic Cars* magazine, and he puts neither writer nor photographer nor designer at the heart of the matter. 'You have to think of it from the reader's point of view,' he says. 'It can be very easy to get into a particular way of writing, or for an editor to expect to see a feature presented in a certain way, but the full impact must be considered. Maybe the reader sees it or would like to see it in a different way. It's important to think about that.'

He also believes that the designer has a responsibility to introduce new ideas to those whose primary language is not visual.

> I like to get people to look at different designs and see what it 'says' to them. This is quite easy to do now. Experimental layouts can be created quickly and the process can be seen immediately on screen. It is important for journalists and editors to develop visual awareness. Writers have tended to think only of the words, although it has changed since the days when an editor would just hand over a package of words and pictures and say 'fit that'. Then the possibility of changing the words around to make a better overall design was never even considered.

Emap Active designer Peter Comely agrees, but thinks that people can learn to appreciate the visual for themselves. 'You can train yourself to become aware of how things look in magazines and on TV or in films. Design has become so important in everything we see or buy,' he says. For him one of the most important things is attention to detail and he thinks too many journalists overlook things like lines of type out of alignment, or a missing 'end blob' at the finish of a story. He says he is lucky that the magazine he works on (*Land Rover Owner*):

> has had very little design input in the past, so the editorial staff are just appreciative of anything I do to make it look better. But one thing which is really important is forward planning and an organised work style. It's vital to think of the feature and the magazine as a whole, and that's much more difficult, if not impossible, when you're constantly working right on the deadline and in a rush.

What, then, can a word-loving magazine journalist, adept at headlines, standfirsts, captions and copy, do to improve on an underdeveloped visual awareness? Some guidance is essential if only to ensure that you're thinking about the right things and asking the right questions. Talk to art editors and graphic designers about why they make the decisions they do. If they can't spare the time try to sit in on some art room discussions. Read some of the books listed at the end of this chapter, all the time trying to learn about the visual conventions which magazines follow or, in some cases, deliberately try to challenge and flout.

This still doesn't explain how to 'do' design, and in any case, as Ruari McLean was experienced enough to acknowledge: 'what the public will buy can be guessed, but cannot be predicted, any more than the winner of the 2.30' (McLean 1969: 5). Nevertheless, one of the best ways to start to try to understand the process of designing a magazine is by breaking down a page into its various elements and considering why each is important.

Paper quality

Paper is, literally, the basis on which everything else rests. But what kind of paper? The weights, grades and finishes are legion. Should it be glossy, matt or like newsprint? Thick or thin? More or less white? (If you think all white paper is 'white', you haven't been looking closely enough.) Some of these decisions will be limited by the budget; paper can be the single biggest item of expenditure for any magazine and learning how to judge and price it is a skill which is left to specialist buyers in the larger publishing houses. Other choices will be determined by the type of publication. Glossy stock will not suit a news magazine which runs long stories – the reflections make it harder for the eye to read – but may be essential for a fashion title whose main purpose is to show high-quality photographs. In addition to practical considerations, the look and feel of paper carries its own message to potential readers: thin and flimsy signifies low quality, thick and glossy signifies luxury. The way in which the magazine will be used must also be taken into account. At the time of writing *Radio Times*, which receives intensive, if short-lived use, is produced with too poor a quality of paper for its cover and in many households this means the cover detaches itself within a day of the magazine arriving in the home.

Paper size

It's not just the quality of paper which counts, size is another variable. Magazines are produced in a variety of formats, each with their own strengths, limitations and significance. A big page allows the use of larger pictures; a small one allows the magazine to be slipped into a pocket or handbag but limits the kinds and shapes of illustrations. Paper size will also determine the number and width of columns which can be used on a page. The more columns there are, the more possibilities are open to the designer to combine widths for either text or pictures, thus adding to the variety of shapes in a layout. Think also of what different numbers of columns 'mean' – four on an A4 page indicate 'news', while a single column of text floating in a sea of white space (that is, an area of the page which carries no text or illustration) on a double-page spread is something else entirely – an essay-like feature perhaps.

The grid

Magazine pages are designed on what is called a grid, a skeleton plan which allows consistent placing of elements such as columns, page numbers, running heads and repeated rules. The word is used in two ways: first, to describe the abstract pattern to the placing of columns etc.; and second, as the physical thing with which a designer works – paper in old technology, a computer screen for most designers now. (The physical grid shows, on paper or screen, what decisions have been taken when the abstract grid was created.) Devising the grid (in the abstract sense) is probably the single most important stage in determining how a magazine will look, and some commentators give it a heavy weight of significance. In a study of *Elle Decoration*, Barbara Usherwood cites Robert Craig, an American design historian, in support of the grid's symbolic importance. Craig, she says, 'stresses the semiotic connotations of quality associated with use of the grid: "professionalism, concern with detail, carefulness, thoughtfulness, exactitude"' (Usherwood 1997: 186).

Type

Typesetting is one of the most complex and arcane areas of design and the study of type – typography – is a fascinating discipline in itself whose current traditions can be traced back to the fifteenth century. Most journalists don't need to know the detail but ideally all journalists should familiarise themselves with these basic points.

The style(s) of type selected for any given magazine will be subject to many variables. Legibility is important on almost all publications, and at the simplest this means a title aimed at young or old readers will need larger type than one intended for teenagers. But legibility is also affected by the form of the typeface. There are thousands of typefaces to choose from, with new ones being introduced all the time. To make a beginning, however, you need to understand only that there are two main forms – serif and sans serif. A serif typeface has pointed embellishments finishing off the strokes of letters which make the shape; a sans serif face does not, as these examples show:

TIMES IS A SERIF FACE   Times is a serif face

HELVETICA IS A SANS SERIF FACE   Helvetica is a sans serif face

Most designers agree that large blocks of copy are easier to read if set in a serif face. Sans serif, on the other hand, is effective for headlines or for shorter blocks of copy which need to be distinct.

Another print design axiom is that type is easier to read if set in lower case (small letters; capitals are referred to as upper case). This is because when we read we do so by recognising the shapes of words, rather than by spelling them out letter by letter. Lower case typesetting makes much more recognisable shapes and so is held to be less tiring on the eye.

The width of a piece of typesetting is also crucial, which is why the width of columns must be decided in conjunction with the selection of a suitable size and form of typeface. Columns should ideally contain between 50 and 70 characters (these include letters, spaces and punctuation marks). Any more and it becomes increasingly difficult for the eye to follow; any less and words become broken up and the spacing may fall apart. Other variables include the justification (alignment of line endings and beginnings) and leading (the space between lines); both of these have a great impact on the legibility and the overall look of the page. (For more information on these points see Chapter 11).

Layout

At its simplest, layout design could be characterised as determining the dynamic relationships between various elements on the page – type (both greyish text and blacker headlines), photographs or illustrations (whether colour or mono), and the colour of the paper itself. By arranging these elements in various shapes and juxtaposing them so that, for example, a horizontal form is balanced or challenged by a vertical form, a designer can create pages which look attractive and interesting. Walker suggests a further exercise to demonstrate the importance of these basics: 'Note the interaction, study how balance has been achieved, pay particular attention to the white space, cut up pages and rearrange them, see how a simple change of position of one element can transform a design' (Walker 1992: 30).

Before cutting up those pages, try to analyse how your eyes move over the page. Most people tend to start in the upper left corner, then move right and down; the typical movement is often represented as a Z-shape. This can give a clue as to where the most important element of the page or spread might go. There are no rules about what that 'important element' is – it could be a photograph, a headline, a block of text or even white space. The key is to decide the hierarchy of importance of the different elements, and then use them appropriately. Always remember, though, that rules are often broken, and just as 'good writers don't always use only simple declarative sentences . . . good magazine designers don't always put the starting element in the upper left' (Click and Baird 1990: 216).

The use of 'white space' as a positive design element is nothing new. Although many laypeople seem to think that it started in the 1960s or 1970s, Russian designer Alexey Brodovitch began to devise 'new rules of page composition organised around three elements – text, photography and white space' for *Harper's Bazaar* in the 1930s (Bauret 1999). Vincent Steer's manual for typographers states that a successful trainee will be able to combine the technical skills of a printer with artistic sense. Among the former are 'the principles of type selection and the methods of distinguishing one type from another' while the latter include 'the basic laws of design and the best way to train the mind to visualise; the use of white space and the disposition of margins' (Steer, no date: 12).

Colour

The choice of colours for paper and ink can affect more than the straightforward look of a page. Like all other design choices these carry additional significance. To take the example of women's magazines, at Christmas many of these will carry covers with lots of red on darker backgrounds than in summer when paler colours are the norm and there is plenty of candy-floss pink lettering. The connotations here go beyond what looks good on the page in a particular month: the red brings with it the cheery mood of Christmas celebrations; the pastels remind of beaches and summer sunshine. These are broad generalisations and ones which might make a brave art editor, anxious for a publication to stand out on the news-stand, think of adopting the unconventional approach. It all depends on the publisher's interpretation of the psychology of potential readers: would more readers be put off a publication which stood out from the throng than would be attracted to it in the first place by its being more noticeable?

From a technical point of view, it is worth knowing that 'normal' colour is achieved through a four-stage printing process, as part of which the image is separated into shades of magenta (process red), cyan (process blue), yellow and black. These shades are then recombined as the paper passes through the four stands of the printing press; look at a four-colour image through a magnifying glass and you will see the dots which make up the image. This works because of a mix of physics and perception. How 'in printing, nearly all colours can be obtained by mixing yellow, magenta and cyan inks in their correct proportions', is explained in Alastair Campbell's designer's handbook; following this, the brain interprets the mix of fine dots which we see through the magnifier as a solid image (Campbell 1985: 88).

Occasionally a designer (or perhaps an editor) will want to use a special colour which cannot be achieved through the four-colour process. Gold or silver, for example, can't be made truly this way, nor can the currently popular fluorescent oranges or yellows seen on front covers. In these instances the designer will specify a fifth colour (or even a sixth, if feeling particularly extravagant) – at extra cost, of course.

Conclusions

Vincent Steer, in summarising what he saw as the primary truths of design back in the 1930s, truths which still influence today's designers like Peter Comely, wrote: 'To become a qualified typographer only requires patience and study . . . In short, the key to complete mastership of the art of Printing Design and Layout lies in attention to detail' (Steer, no date: 12). That was only partly true sixty years ago and it will still be partly true whenever you happen to be reading this. This functional view omits the creativity of the best designers, the willingness of a Neville Brody to challenge the accepted ways of working, the accepted visual tools. It also overlooks (quite understandably for its date) the wider significance of graphic design. According to designer and editor Jon Wozencroft 'design is a . . . great deal more pervasive than is suggested by its primary function of preparing artwork for the printer, or even blueprints for an architect' (Wozencroft 1988: 159). You could argue that since almost everything we see is mediated in some way by conscious design decisions then the designers of consumer magazines in particular wield considerable influence over readers and, as a consequence, over the visual choices (in clothes, home decoration, etc.) those readers make in their own lives.

Notes

1   Andy Cowles, speaking at the conference on design and communication held by publisher Emap Active at the Business Design Centre, London, 2 February 1999.
2   Figure from Yolanda Green, Capital City Communications, 1999.
3   'Magazine Retailing: Beyond 2000' published by the Periodical Publishers Association, November 1998.
4   Among them Andy Cowles, Ian Birch of Emap Elan and Nick Gibbs of Future Publishing.

Recommended reading

Barthes, R. (1973) *Mythologies*.

Berger, J. *et al.* (1972) *Ways of Seeing*.

Click, J W. and Baird, R. N. (1990) *Magazine Editing and Production*.

Hebdige, D. (1988) 'The bottom line on Planet One: squaring up to *The Face*', in *Hiding in the Light*.

McLean, R. (1969) *Magazine Design*.

Steinberg, S. H., revised Trevitt, J. (1996) *Five Hundred Years of Printing*.

Walker, R. (1992) *Magazine Design: A Hands-on Guide*.

Williamson, J. (1978) *Decoding Advertisements*.

Wozencroft, J. (1988) *The Graphic Language of Neville Brody*.

14 Magazine illustration and picture editing

Tom Ang

> Pictures, to be sure, are more imperative than writing, they impose meaning at one stroke, without analysing or diluting it.
>
> Roland Barthes, *Mythologies*

For many magazine readers the photographs and illustrations are one of the main reasons for buying the publication. This may not be welcome news to writers and obviously doesn't hold good for all publications, especially those which concentrate on information and news. But for periodicals as diverse as *National Geographic*, *BBC Wildlife*, *Vogue*, *Period Homes*, *Classic Cars*, *Country Life*, *GQ*, *MBUK*, *Heat*, *Hello!* and *Top of the Pops*, the pleasure readers get from their purchase is as much to do with looking as reading. Readers want to indulge themselves by lingering over photographs of the highest quality. This gaze is one reason magazines still thrive even in an era of television and film. You can pause over, cut out, pin up or keep on file images from magazines in ways with which television can't compete, though the Internet might one day be able to.

News periodicals such as *Paris Match*, *Time*, *Newsweek* and *Stern* owe much of their appeal to the quality of the photographs, although here the purpose is to offer an additional, complementary and often more emotive and dramatic dimension to the coverage of current affairs and news. The heyday of using photographs in this way was in the middle of the twentieth century when magazines such as *Life* in the US and *Picture Post* in the UK flourished by providing photojournalism which sought to entertain as well as to inform. The photographic essay has lost its prevalence in favour of the television documentary but, nevertheless, still photographs of news events can be more evocative, more informative and infinitely more shocking, or funny, than news footage, again because the viewer controls the length and quality of time devoted to it.

The distinction between what counts as an illustration and what as a photograph is increasingly fuzzy. In any case the word illustration can be used in two rather different ways, both relevant to this chapter. In the context of a magazine it most often means a kind of artwork (drawing, watercolour, computer graphic, map, cartoon). But the word can also be used in a more general sense to cover any pictorial material that accompanies a text. In this sense it includes photographs but for the purpose of this chapter it will be used mainly in the former sense.

Just as photojournalism has been nudged aside by television news, so were illustrations by artists nudged aside by the arrival of photography. There are still illustrations to be found in many magazines and newspapers. These may take the form of cartoons, line portraits and caricatures, drawings of people or places featured in the text, or artworks created to relate to a text by capturing a mood or the essence of an argument. Fashion drawing, which was once the only way to show readers what the chic were wearing, has all but disappeared from women's magazines even though it can still be used to great effect.

There is another type of image which can be the amalgamation of both photography and illustration – what is called collage by some picture editors, composites or photomontage by others. In its traditional meaning collage refers to any picture made from scraps of paper or other odds and ends pasted together but it has come to mean, too, pictures assembled from a variety of sources and is now gradually being applied to some uses of photography. As digital technology has made easier the alteration of photographs so it has become more common to make substantial changes to the images which the photographer has seen through the lens.

Minor changes to photographs in the sense of retouching are nothing new, of course, and big publishers would have had staff whose job was to eradicate facial hair or enhance the breast curves of fashion models by means of a very fine paintbrush and a negative. Digital technology has simply made the process quicker, cheaper and easier, and it can provide far more radical changes. Heads can be placed on bodies that don't belong to them, frowns replaced with smiles, Asian car workers converted into Caucasians. Naturally this kind of thing is controversial. Readers may complain that they expect photographs to show only what is 'real' in the sense of what the photographer could actually have seen on one occasion through the lens. Photographers, too, can reasonably find fault with a process that alters their work while keeping their bylines. (There are also implications for copyright and moral rights when this happens.) One way round the controversy is to credit any photograph which has been substantially changed as a manipulated picture (calling it a photo-montage or collage), particularly if it is not clear from the image on the page that anything has been altered.

Photography or artwork? Who decides?

The decision about which kind of illustrative material to use will be made in different ways on each magazine, depending on the size of its staff and its policy about visual material.

On a few periodicals, particularly those which look more like newspapers and place most editorial emphasis on print (*The Times Higher Education Supplement* is an example), the subs will decide whether to commission artwork or photographs or whether to find existing pictures either from the publication's own library, through an agency or from a photographer's own stock.

On most magazines the choice is likely to be made by the art or picture editor. On a largish magazine the picture editor may well be responsible for commissioning or finding photographs at the request of the art department, while the art editor will commission his or her own illustrations. Some magazines, *BBC Wildlife* is one, will have staff whose whole job and professional expertise is searching for pictures. Depending, again, on the kind of magazine the picture editor may be in a position to suggest features ideas, perhaps on the basis of photographs she has been shown by photographers, who bring in their portfolios in the hope of attracting commissions.

Kirsten Sowry, picture researcher, *BBC Wildlife*

Working as a picture researcher for a magazine about wildlife means Kirsten Sowry never knows what weird creature's portrait she'll have to track down next. It could be a woolly monkey or a jumping spider. Whatever it is she has to find the best quality image available as the magazine's main selling point is its use of colour pictures of wildlife.

There's more to the magazine than that of course. The pictures are part of a magazine, says Sowry, that creates awareness about conservation and the environment. For her that is a positive part of her work. 'It's a very worthwhile magazine. Working here definitely gives me a sense of purpose.'

Not every magazine has a picture researcher but for one which depends so much on the quality of the photographs and where these are not always easy to find, a picture researcher is essential. The only pictures the magazine commissions are portraits of people. All the wildlife pictures are from libraries or photographers' collections.

What the job involves is finding out from the magazine's art and features staff what is needed – a honey badger perhaps. Then Sowry has to liaise with photographers, photographic agencies or photographic libraries. 'A lot of libraries and photographers are now developing their own websites,' she says. 'This means you can log onto a site and research the picture you want. Some allow you to buy and download a high resolution image, so if it's a last-minute request you can get it fast. We always prefer to have the transparency as we need the best reproduction. If the reproduction house has only a digital image for guidance it's more difficult to get the colour right,' she says.

For Sowry the contact with people is a valued part of the job. 'I love it when the photographers bring their work in to show me,' she says. She also sees the general variety of the work as a plus, whether it's looking, talking or logging. 'It's really important that each transparency has some kind of reference number and is logged on our computer system. I need to be able to tell immediately where an image is, whether we still have it or it has gone back to the supplier.'

She has clerical help for all this and just as well. The fee for a lost or damaged original transparency is a flat £500 so only those with tidy minds and desks will make good picture researchers. A less obvious part of her job is syndication.'The *Daily Mail* might phone me and say they want to use the picture of polar bears that we had in one of our issues. They'll want to know who to contact and how. I might then act as an agent.'

Sowry's interest in photographs goes back to her teens. She did an art and design course when she left school which included photography. A degree in photomedia at Plymouth left her 'really interested in photographic libraries and how they work'. So much so that she knew she would rather make picture research her career than work as a professional photographer.

After travelling through India, Thailand and Australia she got a job at Tony Stone Images, a leading photographic library in London, where she worked for two years until the call of Bristol, her home town, grew too strong. Her current job was advertised in the local paper and although it was initially to cover someone's leave she now has a permanent post.

For the future, she says, there are various possibilities. 'I'd quite like to be a picture editor, actually to have control over the pictures and make decisions about which ones are used. Here that's a joint decision between the editor and the art editors. I have quite a lot of input but not the final choice.' And she says she'd also like to work as a freelance picture researcher in the future. 'But I'm very happy to be here,' she says. 'I enjoy the work and I've learnt so much about wildlife.'

Interview by Anna Levin

It should be clear that whatever the set-up on a publication the picture editor and art editor work in collaboration even if not always in close harmony. Like all editorial staff they need to have negotiating, selling and diplomatic skills to resolve differences of opinion and a thick skin helps too, for those times when other members of the team are not convinced by the vision of one individual. It will usually be the art editor who is responsible for the overall look of a spread and for the appearance of the whole magazine. The picture editor is part of the interdependent team which supplies the raw materials.

When photographs are to be shot specially for the magazine it's likely several staff will contribute to the creation of the concept and then to its execution. Typically this might mean the editor, the fashion editor, the art editor and the picture editor along with their junior staff. Where the story is a more journalistic one, such as the coverage of a news event, then the commissioning editors will need to be involved. Ideally, for big stories, the photographer and writer will work on the story together but sometimes one part is supplied before the other can be commissioned. From a photographer's point of view a rare but welcome event is to be commissioned to produce a photo-feature where the photography is pre-eminent and will be accompanied on the page by the barest of captions. Specialist photography magazines such as *Photo Reportage* (France) or travel titles such as *Geo* (France, Germany) and *National Geographic* do this. Some of the weekend newspaper colour magazines still carry this kind of story.

Before we look in more detail at the factors which influence picture selection it's worth being aware of the distinction, as designer Ruari McLean put it, between informative illustration and decorative art. Clearly an ideal example of the former would also be the latter but he was making the point with reference to *Reader's Digest* where illustrative material has to earn its place by enhancing the reader's interest or understanding (McLean 1969: 340). On other publications illustrations can be used in a slightly less integrated, less demanding way, perhaps as a tool of the layout artist who wants to break up blocks of text on the page. Sometimes the pictures may be the dominant element while words take second place.

Whichever approach is adopted the task of the picture editor (and/or art editor) is to get the best possible illustrative material into the publication. There will be constraints of budget, time and the availability of artists, photographers or agency pictures. What follows is intended to give journalists on magazines an elementary understanding of that process. This will be useful for anyone who works in magazines but of particular importance to writers and editors on smaller publications who may take on some picture editing reponsibilities, including picture research.

Photographs or illustrations?

As we have seen, the distinction between photographs and illustrations is becoming more blurred. A good example here would be a photograph which is manipulated through the computer to look as if it had been painted in water-colour. Is it then an illustration or a photo?

There are other, technical, ways in which the distinction between photographs and illustrations has been eroded. It used to be that photographs would have been supplied to the picture or art desks as prints, negatives or transparencies while illustrations would have arrived as finished artwork on paper or board. Now either can be supplied in digital form and is likely to arrive at the magazine on a CD-Rom or removable media such as Zip, MO (magneto-optical) or other disk, or be sent direct by telephone, down an ISDN (Integrated Services Distribution Network) line or other wire service, ASDL for example. This change means that the artist or photographer is responsible for ensuring that the digital file is in a form suitable for the magazine. This may mean more than just the correct file format and could possibly include detail such as image sizing, resolution and even the definition of colour space to ensure the file is compatible with the publisher's colour management scheme. Artists and photographers are now expected to carry out some of the functions which would formerly have been the job of pre-press technicians.

There is another important change brought about by technology. The traditional model of magazine production described the process as a chain of contributions and interventions through design and pre-press production to printing press and then to distribution. This model, which was always somewhat simplistic, is now out of date. Before digital technologies much of the material that went into the making of a magazine could physically be in only one place at a time. A print of a photo could not be simultaneously on the editor's desk and in front of the caption-writer unless, unusually, there were multiple copies. Digitisation of the pre-production processes means that the photo or drawing can now be worked on by several people at once. And this is a further reason for the blurring of boundaries between the work undertaken by different staff members. The subeditor will now be expected to design a little, the picture editor to write captions and the art director to specify picture formats.

The process of picture editing

Picture editing is, essentially, the process by which photographs and illustrations are created, selected and assembled from a variety of sources. It's helpful to think of it as taking place in four steps. First, is the formulation of aims; second, the sourcing of pictures which may be done by commissioning original photography or illustration, or from existing picture or art collections; third, the images gathered must be edited and assembled or organised ready for the fourth step, which is preparing the images for production. (It is these last two steps which are now becoming one.) A brief outline of each step follows.

Aims

There are usually two sets of aims for the picture editor. There is the specific project (the individual layout or sequence of spreads) and there is also the overall purpose of the publication or even the publisher. So, for example, the aims of an upmarket fashion magazine such as *Harpers and Queen* are clearly different from those of a trade publication such as *Media Week*. A publisher such as Condé Nast with a stable of glossy monthlies will not have the same corporate aims as the publisher of the radical monthly *New Internationalist*. These aims, although they may not be explicit, can influence picture-editing policies. At a simple level a company might, for reasons of corporate PR, wish to distance itself from anything controversial: this could affect the choice of photographer in fashion shoots, the kind of 'story' which is portrayed, whether the models can be photographed with their breasts bared. What is at issue here is the ethos or ideological background to the publication. This has general implications for all staff, including the picture editor. For some companies, budgets must be adhered to even at the cost of editorial quality. For another publication the most important thing is to publish the best innovative work at whatever cost.

Sourcing

Whatever the picture-using environment, a great deal of a picture editor's skill and effort is knowing how to get hold of the required images. If pictures are to be sourced from libraries and agencies, a picture editor must be able to find the best as quickly and cheaply as possible. Specialist publications may have staff picture researchers (see case study, page 172) but a general-interest magazine may hire a picture researcher for one feature if the research for the topic is specialised. If images are to be commissioned, a picture editor, often working with the art director, has to select the right photographer or illustrator for the job. To do this well the picture editor needs a network of contacts and experience of working with a range of photographers as well as an awareness of the contemporary art scene.

Assembly

The selection of a small number of photographs and illustrations from a choice of possibly hundreds is what most people think is a picture editor's job. Many people think it is a job they themselves would be able to do and indeed anyone with basic visual literacy could probably pick out the one good photograph from an offering of otherwise mediocre work. However, it takes experience and confidence for a picture editor to be able to spot the gem whose brilliance is revealed only with deft cropping or when set imaginatively in a layout. Like talent scouts in search of future stars, good picture editors have the ability to spot potential. They also know how to watch the budget.

It should be clear that a picture desk must be well organised and have efficient filing and storage systems. Where these housekeeping points are neglected problems will arise. A typical picture desk handles tens of thousands of pictures each year from dozens of different sources. A well-run desk needs to maintain a controlled inflow of pictures, to sort and store these ready for use, to make sure that caption information is supplied and not mislaid, and to return the pictures promptly to their sources once they are used.

An additional task has arisen thanks to the growing practice for publishers of magazines and newspapers which commission photographs to negotiate (or wrest) the rights to allow them to re-use or sell on the pictures they have bought. This means that picture desks also operate as picture agencies.

Production

Once they have been selected, photographs and illustrations must be fitted into the production cycle. They will need tagging with caption information and then they may need to be marked up, retouched or scanned into desk-top publishing systems before they can be worked on by layout artists. Even if a picture has arrived electronically (downloaded through satellite links or ISDN lines) it may need colour correction and cropping. Part of a picture editor's responsibility is to ensure that photographs and illustrations are of good enough technical quality for the publication.

Commissioning illustrative material

When presented with a story idea to illustrate, the picture desk has to decide which would be more appropriate – photography or illustrative artwork. There are several factors which influence the choice.

First, to commission an artwork or caricature may be just as expensive as commissioning a photograph although it depends on the fees charged by individuals. Typography used in a decorative way may be the cheapest alternative but calligraphy or specially designed type is more expensive.

Second, artwork can be done without reference to a real subject or by using photographs as reference points whereas a photograph needs the sitter to be available if it is a portrait. Other subjects may have to be shot on location, which raises costs and takes longer.

Third, there is the risk that commissioning photographs or illustrations can go wrong, most usually if the brief has been misunderstood. If the subject of a portrait changes her mind, the photographer would be left with nothing while an artist might still be able to produce something usable. Fourth, photography is often slower whereas a good cartoonist or artist can run up an illustration in ten minutes or less. Last, artwork is particularly effective if a story does not need an illustration that shows an actual scene or person but is instead used to invoke a mood or give a visual interpretation of an argument or concept.

Once the choice has been made, the picture or art editors need to be clear about a number of points. They must decide what it is essential to include in the image and distinguish that from what it would be good but not essential to cover. They must establish the deadlines and a budget for film, processing, printing, travel and subsistence, materials and research. Reproduction rights must also be agreed.

There are also organisational points which need to be checked. Do all production staff know the timetable for the delivery of images and their processing for publication? Have all possible (and improbable) permits, visas and permissions been cleared? Is there any back-up in case of disaster? Is there any way in which the photographer or illustrator might cause problems for the reputation of the magazine by their behaviour, beliefs, personal habits or dress? Is the commission in writing, and does this include all the negotiated agreements?

The art of commissioning well, and this is true for writers as well as artists and photographers, is to be as informative as possible about what is wanted and which, if any, of the stipulations may be regarded with a degree of flexibility. Those who commission visual material must be sure that what they are asking is manageable, making clear the required level of quality, the key facts of the story and how images will relate to them. They should also discuss what might go wrong. An artist should have clear instructions about size and format. A photographer may need guidance about choice of film or other technical matters.

Selecting the right pictures

Once the pictures have reached the picture desk the best must be chosen for publication. For artwork this is usually simple enough: because it can be specified with more precision than photography it is usual for just one piece of artwork to be submitted. If the art director doesn't like it then it might have to be altered or done again but there is unlikely to be anything comparable to the photo selection process. Here, from the dozens or so images provided a tiny number have to be chosen. Artistic considerations are important here but there are several technical considerations for photographs too, as the following list shows.

Technical standards for the selection of photographs

Film. Contrast should be normal; graininess should be low; colour rendering characteristics and colour balance should be normal unless variation in these is appropriate to the image and its task.

Processing. Standard process for normal results; non-standard where appropriate such as cross-processing for high-contrast colour; maximum density in shadows; clear highlights; digitally processed images should be free of printer artefacts such as uneven coverage, barring, mis-registration, etc.

Exposure. Should be correct or appropriate for task; normally, mid-tones in subject should be reproduced as mid-tones in photograph.

Image quality. Good sharpness with details resolved to good contrast; rich tonal quality or variety of colours; a good depth of field which should be at least adequate for the subject; good colour correction and correct colour reproduction with no fringeing; no ghosting or internal reflections on images due to stray light reflecting around inside the lens; the overall technical standard of the photograph should be adequate for the size at which it will be used on the page.

Orientation. The camera should be properly aligned to the subject so that, for example, the horizon should be horizontal or level, and vertical subjects should be vertical in the picture; the image may need to be portrait or landscape in shape to fit the space it has been allocated.

Finish. Prints should be spotless with any minor blemishes retouched.

Information. Pictures should be clearly identified with the name of the photographer or agency, date, location, title of the event and names of subjects; a model release form may be required.

The picture edit

Most discussions of picture editing start here. But by the time this stage is reached much of the hard work has already been done and if it has been done thoroughly the edit hardly feels like work at all. When asked how they choose the best photograph from a selection of good ones, most picture editors will shrug their shoulders. One attempt at a definition of a great photograph is that it possesses the three qualities of resonance, history and revelation. We'll look at these in turn.

First, resonance. This is used to mean a visually emotive quality that emerges from the structure and composition of the photograph but which could not be predicted from the contributing components. Resonance arises when the photographer organises the material in a way that suits both the subject of the photograph and what is being said about the subject. It is a partnership between composition and content and gives a photograph a lasting impact on the mind. Next, history. A great photograph acquires a historic dimension when it comes to represent a significant event. It may have importance as a historical record, whether as evidence or because it somehow captures the mood of a moment. Finally, revelation. A great photograph is in some way revelatory. Its content lifts it out of the ordinary by offering new insight.

Non-technical factors in picture selection

In addition to the technical factors outlined above, several other, non-technical, considerations influence picture editors.

Subjective response

Picture editing is a subjective process. Technical decisions are, in a sense, objective, as certain requirements have to be met, but a picture editor still has to decide which technical standards to apply. There are certain responses to photographs which are held to be more or less universal, for example response of nausea to a photograph of the victims of a massacre. More usually, though, tastes, cultural background and life experience shape the viewer's responses to an image. Experienced picture editors (and photographers) know this. Here are some examples.

Narrative

The dictum that a picture is worth a thousand words carries the implication that photographs can be used to tell stories and when photojournalism was in its prime, photographs were expected, almost literally, to tell a story, with only the barest of prompting from a caption or text. Today the preference continues to be for photographs that tell a story. However, the potential of a picture to do this almost always needs some support from text: words can be used to increase a picture's narrative strength. It's also true that a strong picture may take the text's story in a different direction from the copy. The strongest picture from a shoot in a war zone may, for example, show people with big smiles. If the reporter was concentrating on the country's misery then a different picture would have to be chosen or additional copy written to take account of the happy faces.

Expression

One quality in a photograph that usually needs no textual support is the expression on a person's face. Choosing the right expression may be hard because the camera catches in one instant a person's constantly changing expression. This may then be used to represent the whole of a complex character: yet one smile cheaply won for the camera may mask years of suffering.

The choice of expression is an uneasy balance between two considerations. On the one hand a picture editor will try to find the shot with the facial expression that seems in some sense most 'true' to the person. On the other, an expression, any expression, is assumed to be true if the camera has caught it. What matters is that the photograph shows the expression which best fits the story.

When judging facial expressions picture editors will look at various factors. The eye nearest the viewer should normally be in focus as this mimics what we do naturally: when we look at a face we focus on the eye nearest our face. Catch-lights (or specular highlights, the reflected image of the light source) in the eye give animation to the face. The mouth is also important, as it is the part of a face that people normally look at after the eyes. If the hands are in view they can be evocative – gripping each other tightly gives away an underlying tension. Portraits may show more than head and shoulders; the body's posture and the position of other parts of the body will contribute to the image by the information they offer. The way that a subject is lit also shapes the viewer's interpretation.

Eroticism

Eroticism has long been used as an ingredient in the production of art and artefacts and photography. It means that a photograph or illustration which may produce a sexual response is likely to be preferred over one that will not.

Exoticism

A photograph showing something exotic, that is, having a strange, bizarre or an unusual attraction or allure, is likely to catch the eye of a picture editor. This may seem obvious but less obvious is the way culture and context determine what is considered exotic. Pursuit of the exotic can thus cause cross-cultural problems. A feature for a European magazine about tropical rain-forest dwellers may show the naked bodies of nearly nude tribes-people going about their daily lives. For many European readers such photographs would be acceptable as an accurate record of how people dress in a distant country but for Third World readers the pictures might equally be seen as degrading. Different cultural responses have to be taken into account by picture editors, especially by those working for magazines with an international distribution.

Composition

A photograph's composition is the arrangement of its parts in relation to each other and to the whole. Many photographers think that to be clever or innovative is the sure way to a picture editor's heart. Not at all. For most published pictures unusual styles of composition are not wanted and conventional ones, as outlined below, are preferred.

Elements of composition

Orientation or 'format'. This refers to which way the longer axis of a rectangular image runs. The vertical or portrait orientation places the long axis vertically and the horizontal or landscape orientation has the long axis running horizontally. Picture orientation or format is essentially a way to crop or cut down the roughly circular image of normal vision into a practical shape. In practice, landscape format pictures are much more common even though almost all books and magazines are vertical in format. This has implications when pictures are commissioned for a cover or a full page.

Lines. Horizontal lines (such as the sea's horizon) and vertical lines (such as the sides of tall buildings) can influence the image. On the whole, horizontals and verticals should be parallel to the sides of the picture.

Symmetry. An image exhibits symmetry if half of it is mirrored in the other half. This property is important in picture composition: viewers often respond well to bilateral symmetry, which is where the image is divided into two main mirror images of each other. Perfect symmetry tends to make a picture look and feel static and weighted down although this can be used to good effect in landscape and architectural photography.

Thirds. Pictures in which the centre of interest lies about a third or two-thirds along the main axis often appear balanced and well composed.

Apparent depth. Because they represent a three-dimensional world, photographs always contain three-dimensional information. This is, of course, more apparent in some pictures than in others as a sense of depth or receding distance. The effect is achieved in a variety of ways.

- Scalar perspective. The further away from the viewer an object is, the smaller it appears. This is particularly true for objects such as the human body, or parts of it, which are so familiar that the viewer's interpretation of the image scale is almost automatic. One effective compositional technique is to place an object very close to the camera with the next nearest object much further away.

- Converging parallels. This is a special case of scalar perspective where the distance between the lines appears to decrease as the image scale gets smaller.

- Depth of field. This usually works in conjunction with the above scalars as they help interpret the variations in image sharpness. Otherwise, it is difficult to know whether an object that appears out of focus is in front or behind the plane of good focus. A shallow depth of field can increase the apparent sense of depth as the background falls out of focus rapidly.

- Overlap. An object can overlap and cover up part of another only if it is the one nearer to the viewer, and this is another way to show receding distance.

Apparent movement

Visual clues and cues about movement not only suggest depth in a photograph but also bring vitality to the image. Visual clues include blurring and multiple images. Blurring is caused by the image being 'spread' over the film like butter: it can apply to either the main subject which moves against a static background or the background which is blurred against a sharp image of the subject. Stroboscopic flash or multiple exposures create multiple images that display some of the steps making up a movement. Visual cues to movement are graphic elements that suggest, rather than depict, movement. A winding road suggests movement through a landscape, as do symbols such as arrowheads or speed flashes. In general, pictures with a sense of movement in them are preferred to those without.

Colourfulness

Photographs full of bright colours attract attention. As always, what works best depends on the intended use. Consideration has to be given to the effect a photograph's colours will have on the design of the page as a whole, in relation both to other photographs and to the use of coloured type. One colourful shot can unbalance the page, especially if black and white illustrations are also being used nearby. The use of coloured type on a page can be effective: the type's colour can be matched to a colour in the photograph or be chosen to complement or contrast with it.

Croppability

A croppable picture is one that can lose parts of its side, top or bottom edges to improve the way it fits into a given space. Croppability improves the versatility of a shot. Empty areas around the main subject may appear to be wasted within the composition but looked at from the demands of a page layout, such areas are valuable. Pictures may also be cropped for reasons other than fit, usually to improve their impact by focusing on one area of the image while losing other distracting parts of it.

Other factors

Depending on how a picture is to be used, the following factors may also need to be taken into account during the edit.

Markers of date or time

Almost any element in a photograph has the potential to give away the date or time the photograph was taken. Here are some of the most common clues.

The date of a picture may be revealed by the clothes, for example. Fashions easily give away era as do faces, make-up, hair-styles, beards, even facial features. Advertising posters, cars, buildings, street furniture such as streetlamps, traffic lights, bollards and bus-stops, and any publications such as newspapers, magazines and books which are in view. The technical quality of both image and film may also suggest an approximate date.

Time or season may be apparent from the state of deciduous trees and flowering plants as can the coats or plumage of animals and birds. Sunlight and shadows or stars can also be clues as to time.

Markers of locality

Much travel and landscape photography is an attempt to capture the *genius loci* (or spirit of the place), be it a village square, the copse of a wood or a concrete townscape. Locality markers in photographs may be used as clues about where the picture was taken, making captions less necessary. For example, a photograph of a green valley with sheep grazing could be taken in many parts of the world. To indicate where it was taken it needs a locality marker such as a European church spire or an Asian yurt.

Effective locality markers include styles of architecture, dress, artefacts, transport, facial features, well-known topographic features such as Mount Fuji, well-known man-made features such as Angkor Wat, or natural features such as animals and vegetation.

Locality markers may have to represent an entire country or even become iconic shorthand for it: the Eiffel Tower stands for Paris or France for example. Digital technology has made it possible to key such icons into a picture.

Identifiable people

Publishing a photograph of identifiable people (other than those who have agreed) can cause problems depending on three things: the use to which the photographs are put, the content and tone of captions and the circumstances in which the photograph is taken. There may be issues of privacy. Or there may be legal problems over libel or model releases (these are the documents signed by the subjects of a photograph to give permission for the picture to be used). To take these in turn.

Usage. Photographs can be used in a variety of ways to tell different kinds of stories. In the context of news and current affairs there are fewer problems although picture editors must watch out for images showing identifiable people who are doing illegal things or even just things they may not want publicly displayed. The further from news you move towards news features and features pages in general, the more care is required. Pictures are more likely to be used as general illustrations of a phenomenon rather than a specific event, more likely, too, to be drawn from a library. A classic mistake here would be to illustrate an article about drug abuse among teenagers with a stock shot of identifiable teenagers in the street. They would have just cause for complaint because of the defamatory implication that they were drug-users.

Captions. Factual captions cause, or have the potential to cause, fewer problems than opinionated or critical captions. The difference is plain: 'Mother with her four children' has less potential for offence than the objectionable 'Evil temptress playing with children'. While 'Prostitute goes shopping with her family' may well be factually accurate, a picture-editor would need sound reasons to offer this as caption material to the subeditors. (One reason might be that the picture was taken specially for a feature on the family life of prostitutes and the subject had agreed to be interviewed and photographed in this role.)

Circumstances of photography. There are photographs which capture a person's private moment as an incidental feature of a street scene. These are less likely to cause trouble for a picture editor than a snatched shot of a celebrity who is trying to retain some privacy for himself. This is partly because the unknown individual may not mind or if he does will soon realise there is nothing much to be done if a picture appears without his permission. In the UK at least, celebrities in public places are not specially protected from the unwanted attention of photographers although the Press Complaints Commission guidelines give some indication to photographers about what is regarded as acceptable. The picture editor's job, in consultation with the editor and possibly the publisher, must be to weigh up three things: the public interest, respect for the privacy of the person depicted, whether famous or not, and the need to maintain or boost circulation figures.

Where ordinary people are concerned it is common for standards of intrusion into grief to become more permissive as the distance between the event and the place of publication is increased. So, for example, picture editors of British newspapers might refrain from using a harrowing close-up picture of a mother grieving over a child killed in a railway accident in Birmingham. But they would not think twice about using a similar picture of a mother who has lost her child in a ferry accident in Bangladesh (Galtung and Ruge 1981; Taylor 1991).

Sequencing

Pictures work with their context – in a page layout or an exhibition – but they also work with each other. Photographs in a picture essay, for example, may be printed in a sequence that assumes the reader will look at them in order. So a country doctor's working day might be dramatised by the picture layout to enable the reader to re-create the sequence of events.

Censorship

While a picture editor may be expected to know the censorship laws in her own country, photographs which are taken in foreign countries or perhaps by foreign photographers may bring problems as the laws about privacy and decency or the censorship policy differ between countries. As publications, or at least publishing houses, become increasingly international, with multinational syndication of photographs becoming the norm, so picture users and distributors are safest if they restrict their material to stay within the most stringent censorship laws found in their distribution area.

National security

In almost every country it is illegal to publish photographs that threaten national security although what is construed as a threat varies. Even in the liberal-minded West censorship may be tight: damage to the national interest by photographers during the Gulf War was all but impossible, for example, so controlled access to the fighting.

Conclusions

In conclusion then, it remains only to emphasise that the way a magazine looks is vital to the way in which it attracts readers. The overall design, the layout of individual pages and the illustrative material such as drawings or photographs all play their parts. Magazine readers seek different things from their magazines but they can tell from the look of it whether one is right for them to buy or to read.

Recommended reading

Ang, T. (2000) *Picture Editing (Second Edition)*.

Copyright, Designs and Patents Act 1988, Chapter 48.

Berger, J. and Mohr, J. (1982) *Another Way of Looking*.

Fulton, M. (1988) *Eyes of Time: Photojournalism in America*.

Galtung, J. and Ruge, M. (1981) 'Structuring and selecting news'.

Giles, V. and Hodgson, F. (1990) *Creative Newspaper Design*.

Meggs, P. B. (1989) *Type & Image*.

Ritchin, F. (1990) *In Our Own Image*.

Taylor, J. (1991) *War Photography*.

Taylor, J. (1998) *Body Horror*.

15 The business of magazine publishing

> I'm there to make money. Everything we do has to make money.
> Mandi Norwood, Editor-in-chief, *Cosmopolitan*

> There were to be no editorial concessions to commerce; we were going to write about all the stuff we liked and if no one else liked it then so be it.
> Tim Southwell, Editor, *Loaded*

It is unusual for journalism students to pay much attention to the business aspects of magazine publishing. This is perhaps a fair reflection of how things are in many editorial offices. One good reason for this is the understandable desire on the part of many journalists to retain their independence, something they feel might be compromised if they got too involved with what many see as the slightly grubby world of advertising revenue.

In reality such independence begins to be compromised the minute a reporter accepts her first freebie, whether it's lunch with the PR for an electronics company or a bottle of champagne delivered to the desk by a make-up company; the minute she agrees to write an advertorial feature or to include in a fashion spread a dress from a big advertiser rather than one from a new designer. The impulse to independence is a worthy one and most journalists would prefer not to think about the financial aspects of their publication, especially if that means being pressurised to give a positive mention to a product in the editorial pages to clinch an advertising deal or avoid offending an advertiser. Apart from the personal conscience of the journalist the credibility of the magazine can be damaged if readers begin to suspect there is too close a liaison between advertisers and journalists. Credibility is particularly important in the business-to-business sector of magazine publishing but consumer magazines, too, as we shall see, pride themselves on the trust their readers place in what they publish.

Editorial recruits to magazines do need to have some understanding of how magazine publishing works if for no other reason than that they need to know where the jobs are and what these might involve. If you don't know what business-to-business or contract publishing mean, and if you think newsletters are what the vicar sends out once a month, then you'll be missing out on a huge range of titles which might employ you. Whereas newspapers tend to be openly visible to the world on the news-stands, there is a majority of periodical titles that hardly appear in public except when readers subscribe to them. In the UK there are getting on for 9,000 periodical titles of which almost 3,200 are consumer publications and the remainder are categorised as business-to-business, professional or learned academic journals. A further reason for the importance of some understanding of the publishing business is that advertisers have had, and continue to have, greater influence on what gets featured in magazines than they do in newspapers (Clark 1988: 345). This is not to say that advertisers have no influence over newspapers, as can be seen in almost every local weekly or, more seriously, in the way described by Blake Fleetwood in *Washington Monthly*. He notes widespread changes in the USA which mean 'editorial, advertising, circulation and promotion are all co-ordinated around the goal of marketing a product. Instead of worrying about whether this is a good story, editors ask whether the proposed story will connect with the reader's lifestyle' (Fleetwood 1999). His examples bear out the findings of commentators such as Curran and Seaton who argue that the power publishers ascribe to advertisers means the advertisers are 'a *de facto* licensing authority' (Curran and Seaton 1997: 34). (For a fuller discussion of the political economy of publishing and other mass media see Herman and Chomsky 1988 and Schudson 1984.)

A final reason for looking at the business background is that any new magazine journalist will be endlessly exhorted to have the reader and the reader's expectations clearly in mind when writing a story. The people who think they have the clearest idea about these things tend to be those whose job involves money; they are the ones who have to convince advertisers that the product is reaching those readers in substantial enough numbers to make it worth their while buying space in. In order to convince advertisers they have to do detailed research into who is buying (in the case of consumer magazines), why they are buying and, of course, what they might want to buy that an advertiser might want to sell. Sometimes the advertising salespeople or the publisher have rather blinkered views based on the generalisations put together by market researchers but these can be useful pointers to what the readership wants. Can be: but as any serious businessman knows, the only dependable information is about what the public has actually bought. You can't predict for sure what they will buy in the future.

It's probably obvious what advertising salespeople do. They sell space in magazines to advertisers and the revenue they raise goes a long way to covering the costs of publication and providing profits. The job of a publisher (the individual with this as a job title rather than the publishing house) is slightly less clear to the outside world, partly because it varies between publications. It is possible for a journalist to work on a magazine for years and never meet the publisher, even though some of her decisions will be relayed to the editorial office, probably through the editor, and probably suggesting ways to save money. The publisher is the controller of the purse strings, not necessarily on a day-to-day basis but certainly in general. She is likely to be senior to the editor in the management hierarchy and ideally is the point of contact (and perhaps even arbitrator) between advertising director and editor. In small companies, the publisher is often the proprietor too. In large companies there might be several publishers, each taking charge of a group of magazines, perhaps ones with the same field of interest, the equestrian titles at IPC for example or the teenage girls' titles at Emap Elan.

Consumer publications

Back to that question about business-to-business publishing. What most people immediately think about when magazines are mentioned are consumer publications, that is the ones which give readers information, advice and entertainment which relate to the time when they are not at work. This wasn't quite an accurate definition in the days when magazines for housewives were regarded as the trade press for those who worked at home (Garvey 1996) but if 'leisure interest' can encompass the field of home interest, whether for full-time housewife or weekend-only homemaker, then it's a useful enough definition. Under the 'consumer' umbrella would come all those titles related to hobbies or special interests such as cars (*Classic Cars, Autotrader*), boats (*Paddles*), fish (*Koi Carp*), windsurfing (*Windsurfer*), pets (*Reptile World*), sport (*Shoot, Cycling World*), and embroidery (*Stitches*). What links all these publications is that they carry adverts that aim to encourage readers to buy something whether it's forks for a mountain bike or the latest in scuba-diving equipment. Where titles are not clearly about one activity or interest they are likely to be about lifestyle: most of these are for women and girls but since the early 1990s several new ones have been aimed, with spectacular success (*FHM, Loaded, Front, GQ*), at the men's market. Winship points out that for all the talk of 'options' for women that surrounded the launch of *Options* magazine, the only real choice 'the magazine offers are, first and foremost, between one set of goods and another' (Winship 1987: 39). What Cynthia White asked in her study of women's magazines in the 1970s, how far they 'support acquisition as a primary goal in life, thereby relegating other possible goals' is still pertinent today for all lifestyle magazines (White 1977: 63). That's the point of them and whether you regard that as a strength or a weakness probably depends on whether you are an advertiser or a reader and, possibly, how green-tinged are your politics.

Business-to-business publications

The business-to-business or trade or professional press refers to all those publications whose aim (in addition to making money) is not to provide general news to a wide audience, but to provide news in a limited field to a tightly targeted audience. Some of these publications look like newspapers (although usually printed on glossier, heavier paper) but can nevertheless be classed as periodicals. A good example is the journalists' weekly trade magazine *Press Gazette*. The adverts *Press Gazette* carries might be to do with purchasing but on the whole are not. Display ads tend to be for jobs. Classified ads tend to be placed by those seeking jobs. In a typical issue there might also be adverts publicising journalism awards or announcing new services or even new publications. (Display adverts are the ones which are bigger and more strikingly laid out, usually with some graphic design element, and with rules to separate them. Classified ads are the small ones which are laid out in columns, grouped together by subject.)

Range of trade publications

The range of trade publications is enormous whichever indicator you choose to use. Some of the titles you might not have heard of before, unless you know someone in a particular industry, include: *The Dram* (for the Scottish licensed trade), *Campaign* (for the advertising industry), *British Baker, Forestry and British Timber, Convenience Store, Insurance Age, Beauty Counter, The Dentist, Drapers Record, Commercial Motor* and *Euromoney*.

While subscriptions account for about a quarter of the trade press circulation, a majority of these publications is in fact circulated free of charge on what is called a 'controlled circulation' basis. This means readers qualify to be sent a copy under whatever terms the publisher establishes: so, to make up an example, if a publisher decided that politics lecturers had enough in common and were likely to have enough spare cash to make them attractive targets to advertisers, then *Politics Lecturer Monthly* might be launched and sent free to all politics lecturers in the UK, a list of whom could be compiled by contacting politics departments in universities, by advertising, by buying access to the mailing lists of other companies such as, in this case, academic bookshops. The great selling point to advertisers of controlled circulation publications is that the readership is very precisely targeted. There should be no 'wastage', that is people who get to see a publication but for whom a particular advert is of no relevance. An advert in *Farmers Weekly* about chicken-feed will be of interest to some readers only – the ones who keep poultry – whereas everyone who reads *Poultry World* would be a likely target for chicken-feed information. Which would turn out to be the more cost-effective publication for an advertiser would depend on additional factors, however, such as cost of the advert, total circulation of the magazines, their penetration into the target market, how well established the magazines are and what reputation they have among farmers.

Circulation

A couple of these terms may need explanation. Circulation differs from readership because a copy of a magazine will almost certainly have more than one reader. Indices for this are drawn up by publishers so that they can tell you how much bigger the readership is than the circulation. For example, *Geographical Magazine* says that 14.6 readers see each copy. For *Classic Stitches* the figure is even higher at 15.1 and *Classic Cars* gets 18.1. Whether low scores indicate a magazine which isn't popular, one that is a bargain purchase or one that is so good readers must have their own copies is probably the subject of intensive research in circulation departments. Some of the low scoring consumer magazines are *The People's Friend* (2.4 readers per issue), *It's Bliss* (title changed to *Bliss* in 1998, 1.9 readers per issue), *Fiesta* (1.5) and *Big!* (2.0). That this really doesn't reflect popularity is clear if you look at figures for *Reader's Digest* which is the UK's third best-selling consumer title but which has a reader per issue figure of only 3.3, or *Top of the Pops* magazine which sells more than half a million copies but attracts only 2.4 readers per issue (PPA 1998: 16, 30, 31). A study of these figures is instructive in many ways. Women will not be surprised to note that whereas women's magazines get their own womanly categories, magazines which are quite clearly aimed at a male readership such as *Loaded*, *FHM*, *Maxim* and *Fiesta* are categorised as 'general' by the National Readership Survey. *Parents* magazine, which makes considerable efforts not to exclude male parents from its pages, nevertheless appears in the women's monthly data (PPA 1998: 30, 31).

Penetration

Another term that needs explanation is penetration, which refers to the percentage of potential target readers who actually buy the publication. So if half of all mothers in the UK bought a made-up title called *Mothers' Weekly* then its penetration would be described as 50 per cent. Clearly a controlled circulation trade or business-to-business magazine should be able to get close to 100 per cent penetration, give or take those recent newcomers to the particular trade who are not yet on the mailing list.

Newsletters

Closely allied to these are the titles categorised as newsletters, which may have tiny circulations, perhaps even in the hundreds (Buchan 1998: 12), and charge their readers the full-cost price for publishing as they carry no advertising. The service newsletters provide, although it seems expensive, is tailored exactly to the need for information that those readers have, which must be why the annual turnover of this type of publication was estimated at £75 million in 1998 (Peak and Fisher 1998: 83). 'Subscribers are paying for exclusive information; the fewer who get that information, the more exclusive it is' (Buchan 1998: 12). A typical example is *Music and Copyright*. Its subscription rate is £795 for 23 issues annually and it is regarded as essential reading for music business executives.

Contract or customer publishing

A further category is contract or customer publishing. This is where a company or an organisation pays a publishing house to produce a publication for it. Sometimes these are in-house magazines for distribution to the staff of a large company, or they may be provided by an airline to all passengers in their seats. Redwood Publishing is such a publisher and it produces magazines for a wide range of high-street names such as Boots, Early Learning Centre, Safeway, as well as for Volvo and the AA's magazine, sent to all members through the post. Emap publishes *The Garden* for the Royal Horticultural Society to send free to its members. How far these publications resemble what (perhaps optimistically) might be called the editorial objectivity of consumer magazines depends largely on what the contractors wish, as they are paying the bills. Some of them have genuinely interesting editorial which doesn't exclusively connect with the company's products, others are little more than vehicles by which a company extends methods of advertising.

Contract publishing is a relatively new undertaking, having begun in the 1980s, and by the mid-1990s the market in the UK alone was estimated as being worth £127million (*Magazine World*, December 1997: 8/9). The top four, and six out of the top ten UK magazines in terms of circulation are all customer magazines of one sort or another.

In-house journals

In-house journals for big companies may of course be produced and published in-house and not involve a contract publishing house. Whether this is the case is likely to depend on the size of the company and whether it can afford to have a team of journalists working to high enough standards. International companies which have an in-house publications team can provide their huge staffs with well-written, glossy publications which fulfil some of the function of all in-house magazines, that of keeping staff informed about company news and developments. At their best these can be quite good places to start a career, the good companies offering far better salaries and more opportunities to travel than a new journalist might encounter on an ordinary trade or consumer magazine. On the other hand, it does mean that everything you write for the first couple of years is, effectively, a kind of puff for the company. At their worst these publications may be produced at well below professional standard and the promotion of the company is the only noticeable characteristic.

The alternative press

Lastly, there are many magazines which are, effectively, produced by amateurs or at least by people who don't expect to make money or draw salaries out of their efforts. The most publicised sort are the pop and football fanzines, which nowadays usually look sharper than they used to thanks to computer technology but which only fifteen years ago might have been produced with a typewriter and a photocopier. There have also always been literary and political publications which are produced for the sake of the subject rather than for profit. Broadly, this area of publishing is referred to as the alternative press but it is a label that describes a huge variety of publishing enterprises and there is no simple definition, as Chris Atton demonstrates in his essay 'A reassessment of the alternative press' (Atton 1999).

The fruits of these alternative publishing labours, which now are often called 'zines', may be distributed in a variety of ways: by an individual with a carrier bag, by post, or they may depend on subscriptions or even just donations from supporters. Then there is *The Big Issue*, which can't necessarily be called alternative, in that its circulation throughout the UK of 266,000 puts it well out of the usual alternative press range and is in fact a circulation that many commercial publications would be happy with. Its distribution system is well known – copies are sold to homeless people who then keep the profit when they sell them on to customers in the street.

For smaller publications, whatever their subject matter, the technology certainly makes it possible to produce quite sophisticated magazines on relatively small budgets. The struggle they are most likely to have is with distribution.

More professional are the magazines which an organisation such as a charity might publish in order to disseminate a message to the outside world and these, although not in any way commercial, may carry the highest production standards.

Newspaper supplements

One of the huge changes in magazine publishing over the past three decades is how much this kind of material has become a regular part of what newspapers do. *The Sunday Times* launched its colour magazine in 1962 and since then there is hardly a Sunday or a Saturday newspaper that hasn't followed suit. And this magazinification, if I can call it that, is not confined to the parts of newspapers which so obviously look like other consumer magazines. As Brian Braithwaite points out: 'Newspapers, particularly the tabloids, are increasingly becoming magazines, not only in their day-to-day features, but with their Saturday and Sunday supplements' (Braithwaite 1995: 158). He's referring to the enormous expansion in the number of pages all newspapers devote to copy which is not hard news. Some older newshounds are dismissive of this material saying it is 'too soft' but it can be of just as much interest and importance as any news story. This expansion has been led, it is true, by the trawl for advertising revenue.

We have already seen that however much influence advertisers have over what gets published that influence is greater in consumer magazines than in newspapers (Clark 1988: 345). Curiously though, readers are thought not to develop such intimate dependence on the magazines which come with newspapers as they do with lifestyle ones they buy from choice (Consterdine 1997). For magazine publishers this finding lends strength to their sales pitch to advertisers. For some readers, by contrast, it means that the newspaper supplements are, or at least were when Clark was writing, less like catalogues offering goods to buy than many of the lifestyle magazines.

This aspect of magazine publishing is now so commonplace as to be almost unworthy of comment: information about where to buy the goods featured in editorial fashion and home pages gradually crept into women's magazines (Winship 1987: 40). For a long time some kind of photographic set has been created through which the stylists tell in pictures a story such as grunge chic, where all the featured clothes look like they're being worn by vagabonds. But in many magazines this process has now been pushed to the extent that there are always several pages where what is on offer are small pictures of the goods alone (the garments, or handbags or tableware or even guns) with captions bearing the price and stockist. And *PS*, launched in February 2000, features only goods which can be ordered from home. The main difference really between this and a catalogue designed for home shoppers is that the magazine merchandise will come from a variety of suppliers instead of just the one company. The logical progression here is for the magazines to sell and promote goods in their own right. Newspapers have begun to follow suit. Is there perhaps cause for concern from readers when papers and magazines become retailers of what they also review, as several publications now are.

The commerce of publishing

To return, now, to the business of publishing magazines for commercial gain there are some aspects which it is essential for newcomers, whether to trade or consumer magazines, to know about.

Revenue

It is often forgotten by readers that the cover price of a consumer magazine does not cover the cost of publishing it, let alone provide a profit. That's why the adverts are there and one way of looking at this, popular with advertisers and publishers for obvious reasons, is to see the advertising as a subsidy of the editorial material. The alternative to advertising, they argue, would be government subsidy, with all the dangers of censorship and control that this would carry. (They ignore, of course, the shaping of editorial content that goes on to please advertisers.) Another possible alternative is to charge the reader the full cost of the publication. From the perspective of journalists and readers the picture is not quite so rosy as advertisers suggest because they are not a neutral force. Their power and influence over editorial is enormous and inevitably how they choose to use it does not necessarily serve the best interests of anyone other than themselves.

Leaving that discussion aside for the moment, let's look at some figures. The proportion of the revenue of a magazine that comes from sales as opposed to its advertising differs between titles and also between sectors of the market. Consumer magazines get 38 per cent of their income from advertisers and 62 per cent from sales. (Brian Braithwaite has pointed out that if readers were bearing the full cost this would mean a doubling of the cover price in the case of *Cosmopolitan* of which he was publisher (Winship 1987: 38).) Business and professional magazines by contrast take 82 per cent from advertising and 18 per cent from circulation (PPA 2000). This is because, as we have seen, much of the business-to-business sector is distributed free. According to the PPA, the financial characteristics of the sector are that revenues are growing and magazine publishing houses are highly profitable. It is also evident that a successful entrance to the publishing business can now be made far more cheaply as computer technology has led to a reduction in production costs (PPA 1999: 10).

For publications which are sold, the cover price is important. It should be low enough to ensure that target readers are not deterred and high enough to bring in maximum profit or to contribute to the branding of the magazine as a luxury product. This may, in itself, be a selling point. The price therefore has to reflect not only what the market will bear but also the cost of the direct competition. It's often assumed that the higher the circulation the better but this is not quite the case. For expensive glossy magazines the number of readers is less important than their quality or at least their spending power. If as an advertiser your aim is to market an expensive perfume or brand of watch then you don't need to reach a lot of people who can't afford those things, what you need is to reach the few people who can. When *Vogue*'s founder, Condé Nast, said in 1909 he was creating the magazine as a lure for certain advertisers, it was then a relatively new way of thinking about magazine advertising (Clark 1988: 321). It seems familiar enough now, though, when the job of a publisher has changed from selling products to those who might want to buy, into selling potential buyers to the advertising industry (Clark 1988: 377). Any sceptic who is in doubt about how far along this road lifestyle magazine publishing has travelled needs only to look at what publishers and advertisers say about the industry when talking among themselves: 'The magazine environment delivers a reader in the right frame of mind to be receptive to advertising' (Consterdine 1997: 6). This phrase 'delivers the reader' is a constant refrain in any discussion of the commercial aspects of magazine publishing and for new journalists has a chilling ring to it. Whereas they thought their job was going to be the delivery of exciting editorial to eager readers who might glance at an advert as they make their way through the magazine from one article to the next, the reality is that with many publications it is the readers who are being delivered.

Identifying the reader

One effect of this is that there has grown up a whole industry based on identifying who readers are and who they might be. You won't work for long in magazines without hearing readers referred to as predominantly ABC1s or C2DEs or some other combination of letters and numbers. What this refers to is the market research categorisation of the population according to their social and economic status. The gradings were devised by Research Services Ltd in 1946. There is no point in quoting the actual income levels fifty years later but the social distinctions looked like this.

Grade A   is the highest level of income.
Grade B   is the next level down.
Grade C   is split into two to distinguish socially between sets of workers who earn roughly the same money but do different kinds of work. C1s are the non-manual (clerical) workers. C2s are the skilled manual workers.
Grade Ds   are unskilled manual workers.
Grade Es   are those on low incomes who are retired or unemployed.

So from Condé Nast's point of view only the As were needed, and possibly a few aspirational or wealthy Bs. He did not need or want to attract the rest of the population. This would have affected, and still affects, the kind of advertising a publication might accept. Just as the highest number of readers is not always the goal for a publisher, neither is the highest number of adverts. If you flick through a copy of *Vogue* today it is clear not only that the ads would be of little interest to those on low or even middle incomes, but that the ads themselves are a contribution to the lavish feel of the magazine's editorial. A cheap, badly drawn or unappealing advert could detract from the overall look of the magazine. A publication can regulate the number of adverts by charging more as it's the revenue total that matters, not the number of pages bought.

The A to E categorisation is regularly used by advertising departments when persuading advertisers to buy space and is also a handy shorthand way for the editorial staff to think of their readers. For both, of course, there are other considerations in any readership profile. Age is perhaps the most obvious, gender another. Geographic location may be another. In fact the knowledge which can be amassed about a given readership can be startling to the newcomer. Take this example from the media pack for *More!* Target age for readers is 16–24 and the median age is 20.5 years. Almost half of them wear cK perfume and go out three to four nights a week. Most of them live at home and are single. Almost three-quarters of them have been on holiday in the past year and 71 per cent of them always buy travel insurance. Readers spend an average of 112 minutes reading each issue.

These figures are arrived at by various organisations. One is the National Readership Surveys, which collects and publishes statistics about readerships for the benefit of newspapers and magazines. One of its indices is the OTS or 'opportunities to see' score which measures the number of readers who will read some part of the title during its currency. Another organisation is the Audit Bureau of Circulations, an independent organisation which measures and monitors the circulation of magazines and newspapers in the UK to give what's known as an ABC figure. It publishes its figures every six months and the results can produce dismay or elation depending on how they compare with the previous figure. At *FHM* a leap in circulation of 217.6 per cent in the second half of 1996 was a cause for great celebration at Emap.

To complement the NRS and ABC figures the Quality of Reading Survey was launched in 1998 by the PPA, among others, to get at even more data, such as how long individual readers spend on reading a particular magazine, how many times they open the magazine at a particular page (this gives a PEX or 'page exposure' score) and where they get their magazines from. Companies also spend small fortunes on market research specific to their own titles. For journalists this can sometimes lead to the disheartening experience of an editorial meeting where the magazine is looked through page by page with statistics about reader interest and reader satisfaction attached to each article. All of this kind of research has its place in the business of publishing but most journalists treat it with some scepticism because its accuracy, given the modest size of the research base, can't be counted on.

A further point to note about revenue, as you hand over your £2 for a copy of *Minx*, is that only about half of that money will make its way back to the publisher. The other half goes on distribution, to the wholesalers and the retailers. This explains why publishers are so keen to get readers to take out subscriptions and why they are prepared to offer sizeable inducements in the shape of discounts or gifts. *Private Eye*, to take one example, costs £1.20 an issue which would work out at £31.20 for all issues over a year. A subscription is therefore a bargain to the reader at £19. A further advantage for the publisher is that a subscription guarantees an amount of income over the year, even during the weeks when a casual, news-stand purchaser might forget to buy or be away on holiday. This makes financial planning more secure. Against this has to be set the cost of postage and of advertising for subscribers. For this reason in the United States, which traditionally sees a much higher proportion of consumer magazines sold by subscription, there is now a move towards increasing news-stand sales.

Distribution

The method of distribution is something that can never be far from the magazine editor's mind as it has a bearing on the presentation of the publications. At its most obvious a magazine which depends on news-stand sales must have as eye-catching a cover as possible and its cover lines (the words) must be intriguing. If, on the other hand, a publication arrives unasked for and unpaid for as a controlled circulation magazine which everyone in a particular industry must read, then the designer is under less pressure as there is no immediate competition for the reader's attention at a point of sale. A news-stand magazine must also assume that when it fights for space on the shelf only the left-hand side of the cover will be visible as other magazines will usually be placed in front, concealing the right-hand side.

In fact the subject of distribution is enough to bring publishers close to exasperation (and probably distributors too). One reason is that the traditional shops which supplied us with our magazines, the confectioners, tobacconists and newsagents (or CTNs as they are known), have seen their business drawn away by new kinds of retailers such as supermarkets, convenience food stores, garages and so on. Publishers may find these new outlets unwilling to carry the range of magazines that the CTNs once did, and this affects the smaller circulation, specialist publications. Yet the market is fragmenting as more titles are launched at smaller target markets putting additional pressure on the space which is available for display in any shop of whatever kind.

Furthermore, in magazine publishing the so-called supply chain is more complex than it is for newspapers. First there is the publisher. Then there is the distributor. This may be the equivalent of an in-house circulation department (direct distribution). Or it may be through a separate distribution division in which the large publishers have a shareholding (e.g. IPC through Marketforce, Emap through Frontline or the National Magazine Company through Comag). Lastly there are the companies which are paid by publishers to do the distributing for them.

The next stage in the journey of magazine to reader is through the wholesaler. This area, like distribution, is increasingly dominated by huge companies such as W.H. Smith. The wholesalers are the ones who take orders from and deliver to the retail outlets. As they increase in size efforts to keep costs down and profits up are made by cutting the number of depots from which deliveries are made. This introduces economies of scale but the fear is that it mitigates against the kind of personal touch that enables retailers to cater for quirky, specialist markets.

Subscription sales, which could provide one solution and are certainly growing, are nevertheless kept down by the high cost of postage. Competition for readers is fierce, because although more people are reading magazines than a few years ago 'the consumer is much less brand loyal and is buying from a pool of titles rather than a limited short-list' according to PPA research (PPA 1998: 10). This reader gets the nickname 'repertoire reader', one of whose characteristics is that he buys on impulse. Irritating, that, for publishers who used to be able to depend on a number of devoted fans for a particular title.

One strategy the publishers of monthly magazines use to secure the money of the repertoire buyer is to get into the newsagent first. It used to be normal to buy an April edition, say, in the last four or five days of the preceding month, that is, March. But in the past year or two these dates have crept forward so that the April edition of most consumer magazines is actually on sale throughout March and some are on the news-stands in the last week of February.

Promotions and cover mounts

In other attempts to counteract this fickleness, or grab the attention of the impulsive buyer, publishers sometimes seem to take leave of their senses so daft are some of the promotional free gifts (or cover mounts) they offer. At one end of the quality scale a magazine like *Time* offers inducements to subscribe such as a watch with the word Time in the *Time* magazine logo on it or travel luggage or electronic personal organisers.

Some magazines offer tokens which can be exchanged for presents such as a free CD (*Smash Hits*). The advantage of tokens is that they induce people to buy and then more copies have to be bought for the reader to save enough tokens. One early 1999 edition of *Smash Hits* had tokens, little card pictures of popstars to cut out and keep, a free CD holder and a packet of hot chocolate powder, all held in place with a plastic bag. This arrangement is called 'bagging' and is necessary when the free gifts are of awkward shape or are so desirable that they might otherwise be ripped off in the newsagents shop by dishonest customers, desperate to own yet another bright pink, inflatable picture-frame. Another possible reason to bag is if raunchy material is on offer. So the edition of *More!* with its separate booklet entitled 'Men unzipped. Find out what's inside their minds and their trousers', was carefully bagged to stop girls peeking without buying.

The drawbacks to bagging a magazine are that it may deter new readers who can't flick through to get an idea of what's inside. One advantage (to the publisher at least although I'm not sure they would put it like this) is that the reader can't examine too closely the gift on offer.

Gifts can range from the practical and appropriate – a CD with *Classical Music* to demonstrate some of what's talked about in the editorial, nail varnish for a teenage girls' magazine – to the awkward – a trowel stuck to the cover of a gardening maga-zine which was so heavy that it pulled the copies off the news-stand onto the floor. There's no doubt that one-off purchases are made as a result of these inducements, particularly if they really do have some value, such as the Penguin paperbacks offered by *Marie Claire* in early 1999. For some magazines, computing and classical or dance music ones, a gift is more or less essential now. But there is considerable doubt in the trade about whether they have any lasting effect on circulation. Marie O'Riordan, publishing director for Emap Elan, has spoken of the danger of readers becoming immune to 'gifting' and Margaret Hefferman, publishing director of *Big!* and *Smash Hits*, has said she thinks 'the promotional gift war is detracting from the real issue . . . the content on the inside of the magazine' (*Press Gazette*, 19 February 1999: 7 and 21 August 1998: 6). These views were echoed vehemently by Mandi Norwood, then editor-in-chief of *Cosmopolitan*: 'I absolutely loathe it that I have to be involved in discussions about scented candles' (J. Gibson 1999: 7). She has a point. Everyone likes to get something for nothing but publishers would go out of business if they really provided that, so many promotional gifts are useless as well as tacky and are likely to attract only those buyers who are devoted collectors of kitsch.

Prizes

One further way publishers try to attract readers is with prizes in competitions although, again, no one seems convinced of their value as circulation builders even if they may contribute to the satisfaction that a reader gets from the magazine. Competitions do, however, have a further value as they can assist publishers in their search for data about readers.

Brand extension

For almost as long as there have been consumer magazines there have been ways for publishers to make money out of their products other than merely from advertising and sales. The technical name for much of this is 'brand extension' and that can mean selling through the pages of the publication anything from cheap T-shirts to expensive leather desk diaries bearing the magazine's logo. What it typically means, in the trade press, is the organisation of exhibitions or conferences based on the subject matter of the publication. It might mean the publishing of directories or books in a particular field; *The Economist Style Guide* is one example, or the *Time Out Guide to London*, or the burgeoning number of websites that relate to magazines.

One new, specialised and potentially lucrative example of brand extension is nick-named masthead television, which is the term used for television progammes which develop out of a magazine title. (For several years this has worked the other way round – television programmes such as *The Clothes Show* or *Teletubbies* spawning glossy publications using the same kind of material as the parent programme.) In April 1998 the ITC regulations which prevented magazines being developed into television programmes for channels 3, 4 or 5 were relaxed and experiments are under way (*Uploaded* is one, *Zest* another) to see if the flavour of a magazine is transferrable into television terms and if it is how it can best be done.

In the current highly competitive marketplace of the late 1990s brand extension can no longer be regarded as a source of a little extra money to be earned from a small, peripheral sideline. Susan Young of Carnyx Publications says that the events organised under the auspices of Scotland's media magazine *The Drum* now earn more revenue than the publication, although the exhibitions, seminars and awards activities clearly need the brand name of the magazine to attract custom. And when Mandi Norwood took on the new title of editor-in-chief of *Cosmopolitan* she revealed to an interviewer that only about 60 per cent of her time would be spent on editorial activities, the rest being brand extension work (J. Gibson 1999).

None of this is surprising, especially as so many of the big media companies are keen to have interests in more than one medium. The BBC is best known for its radio and television products but through its publishing arm it has now built up a large stable of successful publications including *Radio Times*, *Top of the Pops*, *BBC Wildlife* and *BBC Gardener's World*. And not all of its magazines are directly related to individual programmes. *Family Life*, although it is now defunct, was an attempt to produce a general interest lifestyle magazine without relying on such a connection. Emap too has cross-media interests. The company started in 1947 as a publisher of provincial news-papers, moved into magazines in the 1950s, launched a radio station, Kiss100FM, in the 1980s and it owns several radio stations. In early 2000 Emap restructured to group its activities by subject (music for example) rather than by medium.

Brand extension clearly works in two directions. On the one hand it is a way of offering additional goods or services to readers for which they pay like any other customer. On the other it works as a promotional tool for the magazine itself. New readers may be attracted after they attend an exhibition organised by a publisher or when they purchase a trade directory, or these things may just help towards a general raising of public awareness. Like any licensing agreement this kind of brand extension needs careful monitoring: editors should try to keep control over the name that is such a valuable asset in the marketplace and perhaps try to stick to the kind of merchandise that reflects the expertise and subject matter of the publication.

Promotion

Promotion of a magazine title or brand is something in which senior editorial staff often have to be closely involved. It can mean being interviewed by the broadcast media about either the magazine or its field of special interest. So, for example, the editor of *Jane's Defence Weekly* is likely to be invited by radio and television current affairs programmes to comment on stories about the arms industry. And the editors of society magazines like *Vogue* or *Tatler* were in big demand to comment when Diana, Princess of Wales died. Or it can mean making sure a magazine is constantly getting publicity – ideally good, positive publicity but sometimes more controversial publicity too, just so long as the paper is being talked about.

The importance placed on this kind of work by publishers is shown by the citation for Alexandra Shulman when, in 1996, she won the accolade of magazine editor of the year from the Periodical Publishers Association. She was praised most for being 'a clever and imaginative editor who gets her title talked about ... with almost every issue containing at least one story which has been picked up by the other media'.

Getting a title talked about can backfire as James Brown found when the March 1999 issue of *GQ* hit the news-stands. Its article '200 most stylish men of the 20th century' included the Nazis, to the understandable outrage of right-thinking people, including the Anti-Nazi League (*GQ* March 1999: 56). Brown resigned.

Advertising

Back in 1900 newspaper proprietor Lord Northcliffe could seriously advise his staff on the *Daily Mail* 'Don't go out after your advertisers. Wait for them to come to you' (Clark 1988: 322). Any newspaper or magazine publisher which took that view today would soon close down. During this century the competition for advertising revenue has intensified so that aggressive sales teams are now dedicated to the task and have the full array of market research tools at their disposal when trying to work out ways to clinch a deal. Advertising directors are now responsible for bringing in the vast sums of money (or revenue) which the editor is then responsible for spending. At *FHM*, for example, the income from advertising is more than £6 million a year.

Delivering the reader

In a journalists' utopia that would be all there was to it: the revenue would be spent by the editor on whatever she chose to fill her magazine with. In the real world, however, and in the absence of a multi-millionaire sponsor with no agenda and a bulging bank account, the editor has to spend the revenue in such a way that the advertising director will be able to raise as much revenue as possible. This is the part of the job that many journalists would prefer to ignore, although unless they lead a cushioned existence on a very successful magazine, they ignore it at their peril as I noted on page 191. If they work for a commercial organisation of any sort their job is not really, or not exclusively, about producing accurate analysis or perfect prose on whatever topic takes their fancy; their job, at least in the eyes of the publisher, is to 'deliver' readers so that the advertisers will flock to buy space and pay handsomely for getting it. This in turn will deliver profit for the benefit of shareholders or proprietors.

Keeping a distance

This may seem an extreme view but it's a realistic one. No wonder the question of magazines and money arouses strong feelings. Susan Young, who edits a monthly business magazine among others, says: 'The advertising department is the most important part of my company' and magazine publisher Eve Pollard has said the most important thing she learned when she moved into that role from newspapers was 'Be nice to advertisers' (Morgan 2000). While John Morrish, in his book *Magazine Editing*, acknowledges 'There is no more vexed issue than the relationship between the editor and the advertising department. A certain distance is desirable if the independence and integrity of the editorial department is to be maintained.' He goes on to describe what causes the vexation. Advertisers spend a lot of money with magazine publishers and are therefore inclined to expect favours, particularly if, as advertising salespeople like to imply, they have influence over editorial. This should be resisted, says Morrish, while acknowledging that 'few editors will pass through their careers without at some point or other receiving a threat of the removal of advertising for some slight, whether real or imagined' (Morrish 1996: 94). And Jeremy Seabrook notes that it's not only favours, it's the right to approve and 'provocative' editorial material (Seabrook 2000: 108).

An editor is faced with the task of satisfying two sets of customers, whereas in many industries one is seen as quite enough. An editor has to attract readers as well as advertisers because, on the whole, you can't have one group without the other. This shouldn't necessarily cause any conflict: a good consumer or trade magazine which has found its target market should find it easy enough to attract advertising.

Conflicts of interest

But things are not that simple as American journalist Gloria Steinem explains in her account of her days as editor of *MS* magazine in the United States. She makes an important point that Morrish evades, which is that the demands of advertisers cast a pall over the editorial staff on consumer magazines. Advertisements can be attracted by a magazine provided its journalists are producing editorial that supports only the idea of consuming more goods and provided its target audience has money to spend. At almost its most shamefaced this means inserting favourable comment about the actual product into editorial copy. More subtle, in fact so subtle as to be the norm, so subtle as to attract little academic or press comment, is when the editorial team provides the kind of context which Steinem calls 'supportive editorial atmosphere or complementary copy'. What this means is that to attract shampoo adverts a magazine has to publish articles about hair care, to attract adverts for cookers or food products, there have to be articles about the cooking and preparation of food (although not, usually, about the adverse aspects of this such as food poisoning or the conditions in which battery hens live). As Steinem argued repeatedly with potential advertisers, there is something daft about this. Someone who is on the lookout for a new brand of mascara won't be deterred from reading an advert for one just because it is placed next to an article about people who choose not to wear make-up at all or even one about education policy. Unfortunately the advertisers she met didn't see this point: no recipes in *Ms* magazine meant no adverts for food. 'It isn't just a little content that's designed to attract ads; it's almost all of it,' she comments (Steinem 1994: 131). Although, according to a leading specialist in consumer research, Joseph Smith, 'there is no persuasive evidence that the editorial context of an ad matters' (Steinem 1994: 152). In fact, in Steinem's view, the opposite is true: 'The greatest factor in determining an ad's effectiveness is the credibility and independence of its surroundings' (Steinem, 1994: 165) and she cites research from the *Journal of Advertising Research* which concluded 'the higher the rating of editorial believability, the higher the rating of the advertisement' (Steinem 1994: 152).

Editorial mentions

Some of the ways in which advertisers influence editorial copy are explicit, for example agreements to take out a series of expensive ads if good editorial coverage is given to a particular product, perhaps not even the one that is being advertised. Where this is a product that might have been mentioned anyway perhaps there is no harm done but the line, in most editorial offices, is just not that clearly drawn. Which clothes will be featured in a fashion spread is a good example. Of course fashion directors say they have complete autonomy but if you study carefully the featured clothes and compare them with the advertisers you will notice that the same names recur. Richard Shortway, then publisher of American *Vogue*, was frank about the link between editorial and advertising: 'The cold, hard facts of magazine publishing mean that those who advertise get editorial coverage' (Clark 1988: 338). This point is illustrated in almost any edition of any consumer magazine.

Betraying the trust of readers

One reason that this matters is the confidence which readers place in the guidance offered by magazines. Research commissioned by the PPA concluded that readers enjoy a strong relationship with a favoured magazine and that a bond of trust grows up between reader and magazine. 'This creates a particularly powerful and trusting relationship' (Consterdine 1997: 5). Teenage girls buy spot-creams they have read about in *Bliss*, teenage boys buy bike equipment they have read about in *Dirt* magazine, parents buy toys they have read about in *Parents* magazine. They do this because magazines catch them in the right mood. This effect is described with engaging honesty by one advertiser as being that the quality of trust in the relationship between reader and editor creates 'an aperture or opening to the reader's mind and heart . . . through which we advertisers can establish communication' (Consterdine 1997: 40). If what was in magazines were not influential then advertisers would not bother booking space. A mutual understanding is required. Even if the commercial pressure on editorial staff is not overt, the evidence for it is nevertheless there.

Consider, for example, how many years it took for most women's magazines to introduce any kind of health warning into their reporting about sunbathing. Long after reputable research linking sunbathing to increased rates of skin cancer had been published and absorbed by readers of serious newspapers, magazines for women and girls were (and are) undiminished in their admiration for a golden tan. It's as if they couldn't risk the loss of advertisement revenue from suncream manufacturers. Now, of course, suncreams are sold as a way of avoiding the harmful effects of the rays but as any dermatologist would tell you the best advice about exposure to the sun is simply to avoid it by staying in the shade. But if everyone did that then an industry would collapse and lifestyle magazines would suffer a loss of revenue, so the serious questions are not much raised in magazines which depend on this kind of advertising.

Meeting the demands of advertisers

Yet it's not just in this way, which some might argue is fairly innocuous, that advertisers try to exert control. They want a supportive environment in the positive sense but they may also want a right of veto, and this obviously can have a more negative effect. To borrow one or two of Steinem's examples. She quotes the insertion orders which accompany agreements to place adverts in particular publications: cleaning products should be adjacent to editorial about children or a diamond company selling engagement rings insists that its ads are well separated from 'hard news or anti-love/romance themed editorial' (Steinem 1994: 156). (She points out that this kind of demand poses unrealistic logistical problems at the flatplanning stage, quite apart from the ethical ones for editors.) At one level this can seem funny, trivial almost, but there's a serious side to it. How many lifestyle titles find space for controversial (other than sexually explicit), challenging articles or reportage? Some do on some occasions but most don't.

Thus many potential topics of interest to readers are squeezed out of the pages of consumer magazines. For all they are called that many of them contain little material that calls particular products or services into question. Fashion coverage is, by and large, reduced to stylish photographs and captions, and the absurdity of some of what appears on the catwalks is accepted unquestioningly. Rarely is there any interesting analysis of the designs, let alone the political economy or the history of fashion. The absurdity or even on occasion the offensiveness of what appears on the fashion pages is offered so solemnly to readers it would seem that editors have failed at birth to pick up the usual allocation of critical faculties.

Steinem describes the sense of liberation she felt as an editor when she took the decision to stop taking adverts altogether. It wasn't just that the magazine didn't have pages of irrelevant material to detract from the editorial. It was the fact that the advertisers could no longer bring other sorts of pressure to bear. She had found them very conservative so that they would, for example, be unwilling to advertise cars in a feminist magazine even though she could demonstrate how many millions of dollars a year were being spent by her women readers on cars.

It has to said though that her liberation was partly made possible by the fact that in the USA there is a higher proportion of magazines sold by subscription than at the news-stand. For a while, even so, it looked as if the future of *MS* was in doubt unless it began to take ads again but in mid-1999 its relaunch was announced after new backers had been found.

Gloria Steinem's account is instructive because many magazine editors are unwilling to admit publicly how far the demands of advertisers influence what they publish. An exception is Sey Chassler who was editor-in-chief of *Redbook* for several years. 'Most of the pressure came in the form of direct product mentions ... We got threats from the big guys ... blackmail threats. Advertisers want to know two things "What are you going to charge me? What else are you going to do for me?"' (Steinem 1994: 161). And more recently, the novels *Streetsmart* by Nicholas Coleridge, Condé Nast UK's managing director, and *Front Row* by *Vogue*'s Fashion Director, Lisa Armstrong illustrate how these relations work.

Some editors will deny that they ever meet the advertising people in their company; for them there is an invisible wall between the two. In some cases this may be true but in reality it probably shows the extent to which the editor in question has subconsciously absorbed what it is that advertisers are looking for. There are a few exceptional magazines, which survive financially because they have a loyal readership or proprietor, but on the whole these are the ones with a more serious intent.

Some editors contend that their readers are highly sophisticated and won't be taken in by advertising. Anecdotal evidence is against this. Most women, for example, think the make-up credits on fashion photos mean that the actual products have been used to create the look. Yet most often the faces are made up by the make-up artist using her own palettes and then the PR from a company (obviously one which spends a lot on advertising in the magazine) comes in to look at the picture and suggest which products by her company could have been used to achieve the same effect.

Steinem's research showed that while readers do care about the influence of advertisers 'most of them were not aware of advertising's control over the words and images around it'. And Consterdine's research for the PPA bears this out. He notes that readers of consumer magazines are likely to feel a strong affiliation with their chosen title and that the stronger this is 'the higher the level of endorsement that the advertising receives' by virtue of appearing in that particular publication. This endorsement is even stronger for 'advertorial' or the 'advertisement features' which are discussed briefly below.

Encouraging consumption

Yet this, in the end, is why there are so many magazines which encourage readers to spend more money (whether on hair-care products, vacuum-cleaners, nose-trimmers, personal pension plans, nappies, wallpaper or cars) and why there are so few which are devoted to an alternative. Put simply, this is why there are consumer magazines but almost no anti-consumer ones. (*Which?* is not anti-consumer although it certainly performs an alternative function by genuinely testing and researching the performance of goods and by not being beholden to advertising for survival.) That's understandable enough although not good for those who want to read intelligent, unpartisan debate or reportage in magazine form.

In one generation some of the UK's best magazines of this sort have folded: *New Society* and *The Listener* are two examples. This is partly offset by the increase in the number of supplements and magazines that newspapers push out, but the territory is not quite the same perhaps because the community of interest among the readers of a given newspaper is so much less defined. Less understandable, perhaps, is that the lifestyle consumer magazines don't allow more space for the discussion of ideas or for general reporting on issues. The truth is that where lifestyle magazines are concerned the aim is to 'create a desire for products, instruct in the use of products, and make products a crucial part of gaining social approval', in the case of women's magazines this often means catching a man and pleasing him (Steinem 1994: 154).

Advertorials

There is another aspect of magazine advertising which causes journalists and many readers more heartache than any other, and that is what is called, particularly by those who frown on the practice, 'advertorials', or more euphemistically, 'special features'. These are pages for which an advertiser pays, as with any advertisement, but which are designed and written in the same style as the magazine's editorial, often by the magazine's editorial staff or freelances working to the same standards. They are, in Consterdine's words, 'a halfway stage between editorial pages and normal display advertisements. Readers can be very interested in and learn from advertisement features' (Consterdine 1997: 53). However necessary the business-minded may argue that advertorials are, they can't ignore the point that advertorials are pretty close to being an attempt to fool readers into thinking that they are reading objective editorial matter and that the goods featured in the advertorial enjoy some kind of endorsement from the magazine.

The endorsement matters because, as we have seen, readers of lifestyle magazines, at least, regard their regular magazine as a trusted and loyal friend. This is not just surmise. Consterdine notes the touching naivety of readers, although as his report is for the industry he doesn't put it quite like that: 'There is a strong implied endorsement by the magazine' was the finding of a survey for the National Magazine Company and in 1996 research for IPC showed that readers 'assume the editor has been involved in the selection of the product shown in the advertisement feature, and this implies researching the products and choosing the one that's best for readers', and the closer the match between editorial style and the advertorial style, the stronger the endorsement

(Consterdine 1997: 54). Even if we're prepared to believe that most reputable magazines would not enter into an advertorial agreement with a company whose products were thought to be faulty or fraudulent, there is nevertheless huge influence being exercised over what subjects and what themes readers get to read about. Simply put, if American Express gets endorsement by association from advertorials in glamorous Condé Nast magazines, the service provided by other companies is not available for serious comparison unless they want to spend equally huge budgets on buying an equivalent endorsement. An objective assessment by the magazine's editorial team of the relative merits of different types of plastic money is unlikely to be offered. It is perhaps too strong to say that readers are being duped but, in the words of Consterdine: 'the magazine's own brand values feed into the advertorial, and they in turn feed into the readers' perception of the product' (Consterdine 1997: 54). Industry guidelines say these advertorials are meant to carry a kind of health warning (or perhaps more appropriately a truth warning) clearly on the page to indicate an 'advertising feature' or 'special advertisement feature'. In practice they don't always carry this and even if they do it's not at all clear that readers recognise the implications of it unless they've worked in newspapers or magazines.

Advertorials can cause problems for journalists if the writer does not want to work on material that might compromise his integrity as an objective reporter. Some publishers always use freelances for advertorials while others pay their staff extra for working on them and bylines are not used. The PPA does issue its members with a set of guidelines to cover the preparation and use of advertorials but how thoroughly they are observed is open to question (Morrish 1996: 96).

Morrish also draws attention to the business-to-business press and the way that publications which concentrate on the promotion of new products are increasingly wont to ask companies to pay for the additional cost of using photographs in colour rather than black and white. Again there are guidelines as to the way these should be labelled.

Ad-get features

Closely allied to the advertorials are what some publishing houses call ad-get features, others call special sections or special supplements. For these a theme or topic is proposed as a basis for the advertising department to sell space. At its least dubious this might involve *The Times Higher Education Supplement* alerting book publishers to the dates on which it is going to carry features and reviews on a particular topic, cultural studies say, and inviting them to advertise in that week's issue in the knowledge that those working in the cultural studies field are more likely to buy the paper that week, but with the advertisers having no say at all in which books get reviewed or what features are written around them. The reason I say this is less dubious is that here the topic is one which would be covered anyway by the paper. Things get slightly murkier when topics are chosen just because they are likely to bring in advertising rather than on their own merit. And murkier still when the editorial which accompanies the ads is altered or even written from scratch to include favourable mentions for the advertisers.

Matters of taste

One further problem that advertisements can sometimes cause is if they are offensive to readers, perhaps by being too sexually explicit or showing images of violence or blasphemy. If this happens readers can complain to the Advertising Standards Authority.

The appeal of advertising

In this discussion of advertising I have so far ignored most of the positive aspects of this way of funding magazine publishing. Publishers certainly believe that readers like to look at ads and that these are seen as an essential part of the whole product. 'Relevant advertising is valued by readers, and is consumed with interest', writes Consterdine in his report for the industry on how advertising works. I feel compelled to write that this goes against all the informal anecdotal evidence I have ever encountered. If you do cut out the ads in a magazine before reading it then the chances are that you'll be discarding almost half of the pages in the average weekly or monthly consumer magazine. This ratio of roughly 40 to 60 is known in the trade as the ad–ed ratio. In business-to-business publishing the ratio of advertising to editorial is roughly the reverse.

Where advertising is viewed positively is when it contributes another dimension to the strengths of the editorial. A good example is *Vogue*, which is devoted largely to fashion coverage and has high production values for all its photography. It insists on the same from its advertisers and so a four-page advertising spread from Armani, say, brings to the reader yet more glamorous, high-quality fashion pictures than the editorial budget alone could justify. At a humbler level the adverts in lots of magazines, such as hi-fi or sports titles, serve a useful basic purpose: if you buy a house for the first time and have no idea where to buy furniture or fittings then the classified ads can be of help and with hobby magazines the adverts quite definitely provide a service to readers in suggesting where to shop.

For readers and journalists, whether they like to make use of ads or question their influence (or most likely do both), the unmistakable fact is that if advertising revenue dries up then staff are sacked and the magazine disappears. As Clark notes, the relationship between magazine and advertiser is symbiotic – no advertising means no magazine, just as no magazine means no advertising message delivered to readers (or indeed readers delivered to advertisers). Ellen Gruber Garvey shows that the tension between advertising and editorial emerged early in the history of the mass-market magazines as vehicles for consumer culture. By the early twentieth century 'A question emerged. Was the reader accepting an unwanted pile of ads in exchange for a lowered price for the literary matter of the magazine? Or was the reader being bribed by entertainment to read ads?' (Garvey 1996: 169).

What does give rise to legitimate concern is not so much that advertisers exert some influence on editorial but how strong that influence is allowed to become. As Vincent P. Norris wrote 'The role of the publisher has changed from seller of a product to consumers, to gatherer of consumers for advertisers . . . The role of the reader changes from sovereign consumer to advertiser bait' (Clark 1988: 377). And, one has to add, the role of the journalist in these circumstances is little more than the hook on which to hang the bait unless they work for publications where the content is the prime purpose of publication.

Recommended reading

Armstrong, L. (1998) *Front Row*.

Braithwaite, B. (1998) 'Magazines: the bulging bookstores'.

Clark, E. (1998) *The Want Makers*.

Coleridge, N. (1999) *Streetsmart*.

Garvey, E. G. (1996) *The Adman in the Parlor. Magazines and the Gendering of Consumer Culture, 1880s to 1910s.*

Morgan, J. (2000) ' "There is money out there', Pollard tells launch hopefuls'.

Packard, V. (1981) *The Hidden Persuaders.*

Reed, D. (1997) *The Popular Magazine in Britain and the United States 1880–1960.*

Schudson, M. (1984) *Advertising, the Uneasy Persuasion: Its Dubious Impact on American Society.*

Seabrook, J. (2000) *Nobrow: The Culture of Marketing The Marketing of Culture.*

Steinem, G. (1994) 'Sex lies and advertising'.

Turner, E. S. (1965) *The Shocking History of Advertising.*

16 The magazine industry

> The whole history of the magazine business is attended by continual
> deaths of titles as they run out of editorial steam or fail to deliver
> the right audience at the right price to their advertisers.
>
> Brian Braithwaite 'Magazines: the bulging bookstores'

The magazine industry is increasingly dominated by large companies. Not surprising, perhaps, but it's not that long since the arrival of new computer technology brought with it the hope that so cheap and easy would it become to produce magazines that anyone would be able to do it. For some this meant a real possibility that a new democratised magazine publishing industry would open up its arms to smaller, minority interests. It hasn't happened although a company such as Future Publishing demonstrates how quickly a new commercial publisher can, in just a few years, become one of the UK's largest companies. Fanzines and alternative magazines are launched and survive, as they always have, because someone cares passionately enough to work for nothing. Subscribers buy them in spite of the paper quality because the subject matter is of interest. But there has been no burgeoning of a half alternative or non-commercial press (Atton 1999), the success of *The Big Issue* being a notable exception.

The main players in the UK market in addition to Future are, in the consumer market, IPC, National Magazine Company, Condé Nast, D. C.Thomson, H. Bauer, Emap, G&J of the UK, Reader's Digest and BBC Worldwide. And in business publishing, Reed Business Information, Emap Business Communications, Haymarket Business Publications, Miller Freeman and VNU Business Publications (Consterdine 1997: 6).

In early 2000 there remains a certain amount of optimism in the magazine publishing industry, in spite of some disastrous showings in the 1999 circulation figures as well as deteriorating world economic conditions. Between 1990 and 1999 circulation of magazines in the UK increased by 156 million, which represents growth of 13 per cent and revenues grew by 113 per cent. Since the mid-1980s the number of titles published in the UK has increased by well over one third and there are new titles launched almost every day although there are also closures. In the same fortnight that Emap Metro launched *Heat* in 1999, IPC said it would close *Options* and had just announced redundancies for 200 staff. In the USA there are thought to be around 100 launches a month and a survey of the whole US industry concluded that it was 'enjoying strong profits driven by growing advertising volume'. The business-to-business sector, too, was seen as very healthy.

Worldwide there are also hotspots of activity. In the CEE (Central and Eastern Europe) countries, where the economies are doing well, as in the Czech Republic, the consumer magazine industry is said to be booming and local versions of *Elle*, *Harper's Bazaar* and *Cosmopolitan* are thriving; in 1998 Poland saw the launch of *She*, *Marie Claire* and *Votre Beauté*, and Romania now has a version of the glossy magazine *Elle*, courtesy of Hachette.

What the number of titles doesn't tell you is the number of copies sold and although over a decade or so this figure has risen, there is evidence that sales may be beginning to drop, at least for some individual titles. This is partly what you'd expect in a volatile market – consumers may have less money to spend either on magazines or on the products advertisers are trying to push. An additional factor, which some commentators say publishers are ignoring at their peril, is what the Periodical Publishers Association calls in its report *Magazine Handbook 1998–1999* 'robust increases in cover prices'. Profit margins have increased, and run at somewhere between 6 and 12 per cent a year. Yet cover prices have increased much faster, and that can spell trouble for the circulation department.

Fragmentation of the market

What is clear is that the market in the UK is fragmenting. Titles proliferate as the publishers chase smaller bands of readers who share a common interest or 'tightly defined target audiences' as the advertising teams call them. Who would have thought there could ever be a publication for men called *Stuff* which was simply about the kind of gadgetry that middle-class younger men without children have the spare cash to buy?

Indeed this close targeting is regularly referred to by those involved in the business side of magazines as one of the industry's strengths. Publishers like to say there is a magazine for everyone – whatever an individual's interests or workplace needs. A survey of any large news-stand suggests this must be true, so varied and so many are the titles on offer. But there is one statistic that is absent from the upbeat industry annual surveys: about half of the UK's women never read a women's magazine. This point is made by Brian Braithwaite, who worked for many years as a publisher of women's magazines for National Magazine Company. His view is that what is on offer to readers – women readers at any rate – is not as diverse as it could be. He criticises publishers for duplication: 'Too many titles are devoid of originality or innovation . . . The future has to lie with innovation, not parrot publishing' (Braithwaite 1995: 158). He argues that the leaders in any given sector (*Hello!*, *Marie Claire*, *Cosmopolitan*) were mould-breakers in their time but that publishers now seem to be more willing to produce copies of what works than to break new ground. His criticisms have been echoed by editors and commentators who worry that where an idea (celebrity gossip, most embarrassing moments, explicit sexual material) is seen to be successful in mainstream consumer magazines, the material is then allowed to take over the editorial pages almost to the exclusion of anything else. One example is the extent to which sex is used as bait for readers, even readers who are not yet out of childhood.

Secrets of success

Braithwaite firmly believes that a good magazine depends on the vision of a strong editor: 'We need big editors with big ideas', and he gives as examples what he calls the superstars Tina Brown and Helen Gurley Brown (no relation). Good 'editorial technicians' are needed too but these are not enough to ensure success. His point here is part of a recurring debate in the consumer magazine world: how far should a magazine be designed around the findings of market researchers and focus groups to fill a 'gap in the market' and how far should a magazine be launched because someone has a good idea which will generate its own market even if potential readers did not realise in advance that they wanted such a publication.

Sometimes a certain amount of mythology grows up around this sort of issue. The magazine *Loaded* enjoyed spectacular success after its launch in 1994 and sure enough the copycat publications came rolling off the presses soon afterwards. Tim Southwell, who was originally its deputy editor and became editor in 1998, recounts that the idea was a brilliant hunch on the part of launch editor James Brown while he and a couple of friends were on a wild football bender in Barcelona (Southwell 1998: 2). No amount of asking boys of 18 what they wanted in the way of a glossy monthly magazine could have come up with the idea as it finally emerged from IPC.

However, it's only fair to say that publishers had already noticed there was a gap in the market for magazines aimed at young men. Alan Lewis, who became editor-in-chief of *Loaded*, had worked on several of IPC's music titles and was on the lookout for ideas for a men's title. 'If I'm totally honest the whole idea of us starting a men's magazine was ad-driven,' he is quoted in Southwell's account of the first two years of *Loaded*'s life (Southwell 1998: 16):

> *GQ*, *Arena* and *Esquire* had been around for a while but they weren't at the top of anyone's list of important cultural happenings. Nonetheless, they were steady and contained loads of ads that we [at IPC] weren't getting – clothes, fragrance, booze, cars etc.

His point is echoed by IPC Publishing Director Robert Tame: 'IPC had had a feeling that there's a fairly good advertising market there. But you can't go to it just because there's a market there, you've got to go to it with a proposition' (Southwell 1998: 35). This may well be the secret of the success of *Loaded* – the coincidence of a good market-driven proposition with a strong, original journalistic idea. That would certainly bear out Braithwaite's point about diversity and perhaps explain some of the deaths in the women's magazine market where a failure to provide anything new or with which to maintain a differentiated identity can lead to a title being killed off with little ceremony and could well account for the pretty dismal set of circulation figures seen by women's magazines in the first half of 1999.

The reality is, though, that consumer magazine publishing is a volatile industry. If *FHM* were to lose circulation and cease in five years time it would not mean that the title was a failure, merely that it was a creature of the mid-1990s, the moment when it was highly successful. So while it is correct to note that some magazines die because they probably should never have been born others die because they have reached the end of their natural life.

From a publisher's point of view births and deaths can be expensive. In early 1999 IPC spent at least £2.5m on the launch of a new title for men aged between 24 and 35, called *Later*. As Braithwaite notes 'there are rich rewards to be made if the publisher gets it right or alarming losses if a new launch misses the target' (Braithwaite 1995: 156). He gives the salutary example of *Riva*, launched into the women's weekly market in 1988 with an investment of £3.5 million. Within six weeks it was closed. No wonder he describes the magazine industry as paranoid.

What Braithwaite doesn't explore in his discussion of the consumer magazine industry is what helps to drive the lack of diversity – the power of the advertisers. Many commentators have noted that the dependence of publishers on advertising gives business interests ultimate control over what gets published (see Chapter 15). It's easy to imagine magazines for women (and indeed men or children) which would look different and have a different agenda or tone from the ones which prevail. Occasionally such magazines emerge onto the news-stands and some survive for several years: *Spare Rib* lived for fourteen years, longer than many a more commercial magazine; the glossy women's magazine *Working Woman* lasted for about a year in the mid-1980s and one reason for its failure, undoubtedly, was the conservatism of advertisers.

Robin Hodge, independent publisher

Robin Hodge is in the rare position of being an independent publisher. In 1985 he was one of the founders of *The List*, the fortnightly events guide for Edinburgh and Glasgow. It's still going strong in spite of competition from other entertainment publications. So strong, in fact, that it's now in the process of diversifying into other media, just like its bigger rival publishing companies. It's part of the group which in 1999 launched Beat 106, a radio station in Scotland, and there are electronic online projects underway.

Looking ahead, exploring possibilities for expansion and development, is all part of Hodge's role as publisher. Otherwise the work revolves around money and organisation. 'My job is to co-ordinate activity and make sure the different elements of what we do hold together well,' he says. 'I have to ensure that each issue is published on time, that it's a comprehensive and reliable guide to what's going on, that the features are written and designed to as high a standard as possible, that the advertising sales effort is thorough and professional, that the copies are distributed promptly and efficiently to the shops and that the bills are paid.'

To begin with, though, back in 1985, being publisher meant also taking responsibility for all those things that no one else wanted to do. 'With money so scarce it was easier to find people to write and design than to sell advertising space or drive the delivery van,' says Hodge. Gradually as the business built up he was able to bring in more staff so that by the early 1990s he was able to take on the role of editor as well as publisher.

The editorial side of journalism is what had originally attracted him. As a student of politics and economics at Durham University in the mid-1970s he was editor of the fortnightly student newspaper. 'The student press was much more political then than it is now. It was such fun working with friends and tackling issues that concerned us that I thought it would be great if I could earn a living that way,' says Hodge.

Many of his friends thought so too and also became journalists, most of them foreign correspondents because, as Hodge recalls, 'the other routes into mainstream journalism at that time were limited and quite frustrating'. Those were the days when news reporters had to serve at least two years on provincial papers learning to write in a very formulaic style. 'It was difficult to get the chance, at a young age, to write about a subject that interested you. You had to become a hack.'

That didn't appeal to Hodge so he found himself working for the Edinburgh book publisher Canongate, doing every kind of task – advertising sales, publicity, production, editing. Eventually, in the early 1980s, he became a director of the company.

Next came *The List*, the idea of a group of friends who wanted to stay in Scotland if that didn't mean sacrificing interesting careers. 'We thought that there was a need for a publication that focused on all that was happening in Glasgow and Edinburgh and on the new creative talent that was beginning to emerge. We thought by publishing a magazine we could both get the jobs we wanted and help encourage growth and development in the arts in Scotland.'

At the time they were 'very naive' about the practicalities of launching a magazine, and assumed 'that the world would rush out to buy it'. They were sure they would be rich and successful in no time, so much so that they didn't even get round to preparing a proper business plan. 'We thought that kind of stuff was dull,' says Hodge. Nor was there a dummy issue.

They managed to sell 4,000 copies of the first issue. Trouble was that meant tipping the other 11,000 they'd printed into a skip. Hopes that circulation would grow fast were unfounded: sales even went down as the intial interest provoked by a launch fell away.

Other problems soon emerged. 'It was a real struggle to publish on time as we were overambitious about what it was feasible to research and write in the available time,' Hodge admits. 'We often missed our printer's deadlines and were late getting the magazine into the shops. This didn't help with circulation – a guide to events that happened yesterday is obviously not a must-have purchase.

'We assumed advertising revenue would come rolling in and that we would be able to choose to publish what we liked best. The reality is that any new publication takes a long time to be successful as advertisers like to wait until they are sure it has a well-established readership before booking into a new title. There is only a limited amount of revenue about.'

In time circulation did begin to grow slowly and steadily so that now, after fourteen years, it's regularly approaching around 18,000. 'It's still a challenge to make each issue as strong as possible,' says Hodge. 'We're competing with countless glossies who have deep pockets, high-quality printing presses and easy access to celebrity interviews. We have to fight our corner with much more limited resources.'

As publisher he has to worry about the increasing competition in the entertainment and lifestyle fields from magazines and from the newspaper magazine supplements. One source of satisfaction for Hodge, however, is to see the number of successful writers and editors on other publications who started out at *The List*. 'The magazine has helped launch the careers of many talented writers and editors, which is something I'm proud of.'

He's also pleased that *The List* has managed to retain its independence. 'With so much of the media controlled by huge corporate conglomerates with vast resources it can be quite uncomfortable at times and we have to dodge and weave occasionally to survive. We are fortunate to be in control of what we do.'

Interview by Mark Robertson

The future
....

From a commercial point of view today, however, there does seem to be a spring in the step of some publishers, particularly those in the business-to-business field. As consumers spend less on newspapers they spend more and more on magazines. Research is telling advertising agencies that whatever they spend on television advertising will produce even better results if campaigns are linked in with magazines, partly because (research again) readers are in a more receptive frame of mind than viewers: they are more likely to concentrate on their magazine whereas television viewers are notoriously likely to be doing other things too (Consterdine 1997: 64, 68). This finding emphasises the extent to which the various media now intertwine: with neat reciprocity three out of the six best-selling consumer magazines in the UK in July to December 1998 were television listings titles, between them selling more than four million copies weekly.

Futurologists suggest that the number and diversity of titles will continue to grow as social trends create the right conditions for such growth (Consterdine 1997: 9). When they make this kind of prediction the Henley Centre stargazers are drawing attention to a number of things. What they call the growth in the 'knowledge society' will, they say, entail an increasing demand for information. The 'continuing fragmentation of social identities', particularly among the young, presumably means they will want a wider range of magazines as badges of and guides to those social identities. There is a reference, too, to the 'polarisation between income groups and consequent increase in the diversity of lifestyles, needs and aspirations'. (Not every reader will share this rose-tinted vision which seems to mean that as the rich get richer and the poor get poorer everyone will need ever more consumer magazines. Good news for publishers perhaps but not for the rest of humanity.) The Henley Centre's report *Media Futures* also refers to the demand for specialist titles from the babyboomers as they move into retirement. It's not clear whether this means specialist in the sense of having editorial specifically about growing old or whether there are leisure and lifestyle issues that are of such unique concern to the greying babyboomers that they will want to read whole publications devoted to their coverage. (Incidentally the fifth best-selling magazine in the UK, *Saga*, is aimed exactly at that grey market. It outsells all other UK monthly magazines except *Reader's Digest*, and that is perceived, although perhaps unfairly as a grey-market title.) Lastly the 'continued expansion and fragmentation of leisure interests across society as a whole' is cited as a further provoker of more, and more diverse, titles (Consterdine 1997: 9). As with all predictions the best advice is to treat them as guesswork and wait to see what actually happens. But for those who run any kind of business the sort of predictions made by the Henley Centre are at the very least useful pointers to what could happen.

Brand extension

What is not in doubt is that there have been recent developments in the way that magazines earn money or 'develop revenue streams'. Many magazine publishers now use a publication's title as a brand name on the strength of which to set up exhibitions, conferences, directories, databases, direct mail and, increasingly, electronic publishing operations as well as ways to sell branded goods. If this all seems peripheral it's worth noting that in a sector of UK industry worth about £5.4 billion, at least £1.9 billion of that is not from sales of either copies or advertising but from these brand extension activities.

The international dimension

Another marked trend in magazine publishing is towards globalisation as companies move across national borders to expand their operations. This can mean a variety of things. It is not a new trend, merely one that has speeded up in recent years as publishing houses grow and become part of multinational conglomerates and as many industries, wherever they are based, have increasingly looked abroad for new or expanding markets.

At its simplest it means that a publisher with a successful magazine in the USA, say, will launch versions of its magazine in other countries. Condé Nast did this with *Vogue* and other titles in its stable. As recently as 1998 it launched its Russian version of *Vogue* and announced its first moves into the Portuguese market with the purchase of *Sposabella*.

Its chairman, Jonathan Newhouse is reported to be looking at global opportunities as far afield as Japan and China. *Cosmopolitan* began life with Hearst magazines in the USA in the late 1960s, came to the UK in the early 1970s and is now published in many countries, including India. In the reverse direction, Gruhner & Jahr set up G&J of the UK to bring *Best* and *Prima* over from their base in Germany.

When companies look abroad, they can do it in a variety of ways. Condé Nast has a British branch to look after its British titles (*Vogue, Tatler, GQ, Condé Nast Traveller, House and Garden, Vanity Fair* and *Brides & Setting Up Home*) and the National Magazine Company, publisher of *Cosmopolitan*, is owned by the American Hearst Corporation. Big multinational companies such as this can own outright magazines in a number of countries. Emap bought the US company General Media's automotive group of magazines in early 1999 and Miller Freeman is investing in US business-to-business interests. Future Publishing bought Italy's biggest publisher of computer and videogames magazines in the spring of 1999. Even small companies can operate across national boundaries. *Hello!* magazine is published by a small family firm in Spain which built on the success of the original ¡Hola! by launching in Britain. Sometimes companies from one country license companies in other countries to produce versions of the parent title. One advantage of this system is thought to be that it ensures the characteristics of the local market will not be forgotten when editorial content is being prepared.

Increasingly, however, companies are entering into partnership agreements with foreign companies. In some cases this is because the legislation in the new country demands partnership with local industry if it is to allow a foreign company in. In Brazil, for example, foreign ownership in a new company can only account for a maximum 20 per cent of the value.

This can mean job opportunities abroad for UK journalists. Kevin Hand, chief executive of Emap, has said he hopes staff will be able to benefit from recent international expansion plans: 'My dream is that you can start working anywhere in England and then be able to move around two or three countries' (*Press Gazette*, 16 October 1998). In 1998 Emap began developing a new international division to work on recent purchases in Australia, Singapore and Malaysia where it is investing somewhere between £600 million and £800 million. In any case it was already a truly international company – a fifth of its 5,000 staff being based abroad (*Fact File 1998*, Emap). When Attic Futura decided to take its teenage title *Sugar* to Germany, it sent along a British journalist as editor.

This isn't always the pattern though. Companies moving into foreign markets have to remember that national and local tastes differ and this is likely to mean a substantial number of local staff are recruited. Thomaz Souto Corrêa of Editora Abril in Brazil made this point to American editors: 'Magazine brands are not Coca-Cola, the same product, the same formula around the planet. Rather they are a creative mixture of ideas presented in an original way to a specific audience' ('Crafting the deal around the globe' *Magazine World*, December 1998: 2). The local publisher's job is to 'adjust and recreate the brand's formula to the wants, needs and desires of the local reader'.

Anyone who doubts this has to do no more than compare Condé Nast's American and British magazines for brides. The styling of the fashion pages (too many tacky tuxedos for British tastes), the tone in which the copy is written, even the kind of topics that are covered have clear differences.

It's not just the consumer magazines which are moving into global markets. A title such as *Business Week* has twenty licensing arrangements worldwide and has been active internationally for several years (*Magazine World*, July 1998: 10). Commentator Charles McCullagh of DeSilva and Phillips in New York says business-to-business publishers 'go global for the same reason consumer publishers do: to increase revenue, to remain competitive, to satisfy advertisers, to strengthen and protect a brand, to improve a domestic edition and to gain market share'. He notes that the speed of development is very fast indeed: 'Countries that were not on most publishers' radars in 1994, now have become potentially lucrative markets', giving the examples of Russia, China and Argentina. The difference between this and consumer publishing is that there are not that many subject areas in the business-to-business sector, other than oil, gas, telecommunications and computers, that are truly international. Here it is technology not lifestyle which leads the editorial way.

Conclusions

According to *World Magazine Trends* (1998/1999) there is cause for optimisim in the the fact that many magazine markets have great potential for growth. In Asia and Latin America, in particular, this is partly due to increasing literacy as well as improving infrastructure for distribution. The report notes, however, that there is no room for complacency as financial markets struggle to come to terms with the turmoil begun in late 1997. Equally problematic is the assessment for North America and Western Europe that 'in most countries in these regions magazine readership is pretty much as high as it is ever going to be'. The reasons are to do with demands on the time of individuals and one suggestion for dealing with this is further expansion into the new media as a way of competing for readers and advertising revenue. However, this is not to sound any kind of death knell for print journalism. The report concludes: 'While printed products will remain at the core of most publishers' business for many years to come, the new media will encroach more and more on their activities.' Encroach on but not kill off, complement but not replace, is the optimistic view. If publishers are justified in their belief about the loyalty of readers to brands then there is nothing to fear from the digital world, was the prevailing view at the PPA's May 2000 conference. A much less discussed threat to their businesses, but one which publisher Felix Dennis has dared to suggest, as noted in Chapter 1, is that as more people begin to think about the environmental consequences of mass consumption then magazine and newspaper buying may suffer.[1] It's one thing to use up trees in order to produce information we all need, but quite another to use them up in order to promote new brands of lipstick or the sagging careers of minor popstars.

Note

1 Speech at Magazines 99 conference organised by the Periodical Publishers Association, May 1999, London.

Recommended reading

Braithwaite, B. (1998) 'Magazines: the bulging bookstores'.

Morrish, J. (1996) *Magazine Editing*.

Reed, D. (1997) *The Popular Magazine in Britain and the United States 1880–1960*.

Zenith Media *World Magazine Trends* (1998/99 edition), published by the International Federation of the Periodical Press (FIPP).

17 Issues of conduct

....

Journalists justify their treachery in various ways according to their temperaments. The more pompous talk about freedom of speech and 'the public's right to know'; the least talented talk about Art; the seemliest murmur about earning a living.

Janet Malcolm, *The Journalist and the Murderer*

Many journalists would disagree with American reporter Janet Malcolm, at least in public, but there is no doubt that the interests of journalist and subject rarely coincide except in the simplest of publicity transactions – and those are not usually the stuff of interesting journalism. Questions about what is acceptable behaviour for a journalist are rarely to be answered simply. And what makes this perplexing for a beginner is that there is no clear answer to the question 'How far can I go?' in pursuit of a story or a quote: is it ever acceptable to break the law, or a code of conduct, or merely to break the bounds of good taste? What if your employer asks you to do any of those things? Do you have the right to refuse? This chapter looks at these questions, and some of the issues related to them.

Anyone who doubts there is a problem about how some journalists behave should look at the proof. Public perception may not be evidence but if it can be allowed as an indicator then there are reputable opinion polls which reveal how low journalists are rated in terms of honesty and trustworthiness (Kellner 1991; Worcester 1998). The usual reaction of journalists is to laugh it off but some are beginning to take the problem seriously. Ian Jack, former editor of *The Independent on Sunday*, now editor of the magazine *Granta*, argues that while reporters have never had much social status in Britain things have got much worse over the past twenty years (Jack 1998: vi). He attributes the decline to the way journalism has become part of the entertainment industry and to the cost-cutting which is characteristic of a competitive market. The worry is that if the readers don't trust journalists then they may choose to withdraw their co-operation from reporters and may even stop reading journalism altogether.

There is further evidence of a problem: the existence of more than one code of conduct attempting to define what is acceptable behaviour. The codes from the Press Complaints Commission, the National Union of Journalists and the Teenage Magazine Arbitration Panel, while not identical are intended to rein in the worst excesses of behaviour. They also give clues about what journalists get up to. If journalists always behaved well then there would be no need for such codes. But journalistic endeavour is too varied to simplify into a universal statement of proper conduct of journalists. Some journalists are engaged in preserving the democratic process, in seeking out fraud, or in describing social realities. Others are engaged in promoting the careers of celebrities or in helping to create a market for blue mascara. So although there are ethical questions about how journalism is produced, these are not the same for all journalists.

It may be that journalists on consumer or trade magazines are not faced with the same doubts about their behaviour as those who work in hard news. It is noticeable that most of the more extreme examples of questionable practice from journalists do seem to revolve around news. Nevertheless, some magazine journalists write news and all magazine journalists should be aware of what some of the ethical issues are. News brings its own pressures to do with deadlines, speed of work, competition between both reporters and publications and, it has to be said, the machismo style of many newsrooms. Any journalists who are prepared to think in terms of morals may find their work threatens to compromise their beliefs more or less often. This is why it's important for beginner journalists to reflect on the implications of what they've chosen to do.

I can almost hear the shout across the editorial office that if reporters spent time worrying about morals they'd never write any stories. This is a common position but a weak one for two reasons. First, journalists have an impact, good or bad, on the lives of their readers. Readers of magazines, in particular, trust what they are told in their favourite publications. People who feature in stories may have their lives ruined as a result, whether by intention or by accident. The pressure group Presswise documents cases, including several of mistaken identity, that have left the lives of ordinary citizens in tatters. As Belsey and Chadwick note, 'if harms can be measured on a scale of distress, some cases of invasion of privacy may cause more distress than certain kinds of injury to health' (Belsey and Chadwick 1992: 9).

Second, some journalists lay claim to the high moral ground in defending behaviour (sneaked tapes or photos of people in bed together) that most of us would be ashamed to admit. When 'journalists' do this kind of thing they set themselves up as moral guardians. They decide what is acceptable behaviour for the rest of us: if we stray for a second, and are even slightly famous, then the wrath of the tabloids will be upon us.

Compromising positions

Many journalists do, of course, have high standards. For some that is one reason for becoming a journalist in the first place. They talk of democracy, accountability in public life, of honesty and truth, of leaving the world a better place. They look at their skills and talents and realise that writing for a good magazine or newspaper is the best way for them to make a living while making a contribution to society. The talented, the fortunate, or those who don't need much money to live on, may well be able to pursue a career without ever compromising their ideals. It is true, though, that for others the ideals do have to be compromised.

The extremes are well known and can be read about in several books notably the account of *The Sun* newspaper and tabloid culture given by Peter Chippindale and Chris Horrie (1999). At the tabloid end of the scale it seems there are no lower levels to which to stoop. Going through the dustbins of politicians is one example. Doorstepping politician's wives whose husbands are spending the night with a mistress is another. The merciless deception and hounding of staff and patients in hospitals where the famous lie dying is yet another, memorably described by Alan Bennett in his account of the last illness of his friend Russell Harty. 'Now as he fought for his life in St James's Hospital one newspaper took a flat opposite and had a long lens trained on the window of his ward' (Bennett 1994: 50). A less extreme example and perhaps more typical behaviour was when the cleric due to marry a moderately famous couple who wanted their wedding to be private was phoned by a reporter seeking the location and pretending to be a relation of the groom.

There are reporters who would refuse to do some of these things and might try to get out of others. But almost any reporter can expect to be asked to do some things that would raise the eyebrows of the ordinary citizen. Why, for example, do journalists assume they have the right to ask to interview people who have recently suffered a tragic bereavement or been victims of a crime? The better sort of news editor will argue that his staff have every right to ask for an interview but should not persist if asked to leave. Other news editors will insist that reporters keep on asking and that they try to get pictures too. The journalists' case is that people often want to talk when they are in a state of shock, they want to share their emotions and their memories of the dead person. To which the devil's advocate responds: are journalists the best people to talk to in these circumstances? Their aim, if they are any good as reporters, is not to soothe a troubled soul but to extract the most exciting story.

This point about intrusion into grief is made by Janet Malcolm when she says the journalist is 'a kind of confidence man, preying on people's vanity, ignorance, or loneliness, gaining their trust and betraying them without remorse' (Malcolm 1990: 3). Her observations about the transaction between reporters and reported are more usually made by outsiders, but Malcolm is an experienced and successful journalist so she can't be lightly dismissed. While public figures may be able to look after themselves, for the ordinary journalist working with ordinary folk, there often is, or ought to be, what Malcolm calls a moral impasse. 'The wisest know that the best they can do . . . is still not good enough. The not so wise, in their accustomed manner, choose to believe there is no problem' (Malcolm 1990: 162).

This reflects the approach of much traditional journalism training, at least in the UK, which for many years did not formally recognise the need for journalists to worry about whether their behaviour was morally acceptable. Now, in universities at least, there is usually some kind of debate. This doesn't mean reporters who study journalism at university are any less willing to be reliable staff for their editors, it merely means that they have thought through some of the issues before they hit the streets. This can be invaluable whichever end of the moral spectrum they veer towards.

Student journalists are now encouraged to think about how they might behave in terms of 'moral dilemmas' and 'ethical questions'. This is somewhat disingenuous as to some extent the ethical dilemmas are sorted out before you become a journalist. You choose journalism over advertising or PR because you are more interested in truth than deception, but recognising there might be times when you have to do things to people that you would not want to have done to yourself. It is for this reason I dare to suggest that momentous phrases like 'moral dilemma' are occasionally used by journalists when they mean merely that their conscience is pricking them. A dilemma implies that you might make either of two choices. In most cases journalists know which choice they are going to make (thanks to their training, their commitment to an employer or their fear of getting fired) so there is no dilemma, just an awareness that they are behaving badly when they relentlessly pursue the innocent for no serious purpose, or when they make up a quote, or lie about who they are.

Pretence

The question of pretence often arises and it illustrates the usefulness, or otherwise, of codes of conduct. Undercover reporting means pretending to be someone you are not. It may be harmless enough: pretending to be a tennis fan in order to write a piece of reportage about Wimbledon or dressing like a beggar for a month.

The justification falters when the journalist pretends to be someone else in order to access information they couldn't get any other way. In the examples above the journalist could, after all, just interview fans or homeless people. If you pretend to be a junior hospital doctor in order to get into the ward to read the case notes of a celebrity, then you have entered a dubious moral realm. Yet all reporters can think of examples that merit the deception. If an old-people's nursing home is under suspicion for mistreating its patients what better way to find out the truth than by getting a job as an orderly for a few weeks?

The PCC code of practice offers guidance but there is vagueness. Take point 11: 'Journalists must not generally obtain or seek to obtain information or pictures through misrepresentation or subterfuge.' In the case of the tennis example what harm could be done? But it's the word 'generally' in the clause that seems to provide the freedom. Does it mean most of the time, or most journalists, or most publications? Is it all right to do it sometimes but not often and, if so, how often is acceptable? The answer comes in a separate part of the clause which states 'Subterfuge can be justified only in the public interest and only when material cannot be obtained by any other means.' A little clearer perhaps, until we turn to the definition of public interest which provides the exception. This, we learn, includes 'Preventing the public from being misled by some statement or action of an individual or organisation.' For most circumstances, where wicked deeds are suspected, that may be adequate but what about the popstar who merely wants to pretend he's on holiday when in fact he's at a drying-out clinic?

What about journalists who attempt to set people up to commit crimes they might not otherwise have committed, the so-called 'stings'. That's a kind of subterfuge. Journalists would argue that the police do this all the time, but what they forget is that broadly speaking the police have a mandate from the rest of us to keep the peace and tackle crime in society. Journalists have not. Do they have a right to frame someone, particularly someone who is not in his own right a public figure but merely the teenage son of one?

Another kind of pretence is more widespread. It is where a journalist interviews several people and then draws together the quotes to make it appear as if the words came from one person whose name is invented. As a practice this doesn't worry all journalists, provided the quotes were genuine in the first place, but I'm not sure that readers feel so relaxed about what is, after all, a deception of them. The PCC code says nothing about this practice.

Children

The PCC does offer guidance about the treatment of children by journalists but again these are imprecise and inequitable. How old is a child? Why should 17-year-olds at school attract more protection than those who are not? Why should children under 16 be protected at school but not outside school, where parental consent is to be sought only if the interview is in connection with the child's welfare. If young people should be free to complete their time at school 'without unnecessary intrusion' what would constitute 'necessary' intrusion?

Codes of conduct

One unarguable benefit of the existence of the codes is that journalists who are asked to do things they feel uneasy about can try quoting the codes as a reason for refusing. Some journalists even have the PCC guidelines written into their contracts of employment. For them the code can be a useful protection from rogue editors. For other staffers, though, and for freelances, the guidelines are open to interpretation by editors and may indeed be ignored. If a journalist wants to question what he is being asked to do (persist unreasonably in trying to get interviews with the eyewitnesses for example) then he often risks his livelihood. What both the NUJ and the PCC codes depend on is the notion that the end (exposure of a villain) can sometimes justify the means (breaking into his private office) that would otherwise be questionable.

Journalists as moral arbiters

The problems with the ends and means argument are first, that some journalists take this to mean that they are free to break the law or at least behave badly so long as *they* think they have a good reason. Second, this implies, yet again, that they are in some way licensed to act as moral and almost legal guardians for society. Not everyone would see that as necessarily a bad idea and there is a way in which the public humiliation that the press can provide is distantly related to the public humiliation sinners used to get in church when their sins were denounced from the pulpit. My aim is to draw attention to assumptions which underly some of the activities of journalists. If their role as moral arbiters (ferreting out fraudsters, paedophiles, drug-dealers and so on) were more openly acknowledged, then perhaps a more rigorous selection and training would be recommended. Perhaps more consistency would then emerge in their thinking. It isn't logical to look at media output as if it all comes from one source but if you allow yourself to do that for a moment there are some contradictions. To read the tabloid press (and the broadsheets which hang on to the coat-tails of the tabloids) you'd think that extra-marital sexual encounters were only for deviants, that one-night stands were beyond the pale and that oral sex was the province of the prostitute. Meanwhile in another part of the media forest, there are several lifestyle magazines for women and men, girls and boys which fill their pages with advice about how to have as much sex as possible. Another topical example: many newspapers are so fierce in their condemnation of paedophiles that they publish photographs and names to help parents know who their children should avoid. Meanwhile other 'journalists' on magazines for young teenage girls publish photographs that would delight the average paedophile and are encouraging behaviour that can only make girls more vulnerable (McKay 2000).

Privacy

Then there is the awkward question of privacy. How far should journalists be allowed to intrude into the lives of those they want to write about? Should there be a distinction between public figures and private individuals and, if so, how do you distinguish between the two? The tension here is the old one about freedom: when does my freedom to act impose on your liberty to act? In journalism terms this tension is between, on the one hand, those who want reporters to have the freedom to research and write stories as part of the underpinning of the democratic process, even if this means some intrusion on private lives, and, on the other hand, those who feel that an individual has the right to a private life and that even his professional life should be scrutinised only in the most restrained way. In a serious investigation a reporter can't be sure she has a story until, perhaps, the invasion of privacy has taken place. Getting proof may be the point of the doorstepping or the long-lens photography from an adjacent building. Where serious misdemeanours are revealed in this way there is little public outcry.

The cases which cause outrage and which could, in the end, lead to stringent curbs being put on the press are the ones where no criminal activity is discovered or even suspected: why should a woman, however famous, not be free to exercise in her gym without secret cameras taking pictures of her? Why should a footballer not be free to use the services of a call girl if he wants to, without this being revealed in the press? Why should magazines have the right to publish photographs of film stars having bad-hair days and wearing awful shorts? Why should the UK royal family's latest recruit by marriage, the Countess of Wessex, find eleven-year-old pictures of herself frolicking on the beach being used to boost the circulation of a tabloid newspaper, *The Sun*? The impotence of the PCC is only highlighted by the fact that an apology was forced from the paper in this case, probably because she was a member of the royal family: others who are damaged by the press may get nothing, especially as they have to weigh up the probability that the damaging material will be reproduced while their complaint is being considered.

The tale of Diana, Princess of Wales is well enough known, and although photographers have been exonerated from causing her death, almost the most chilling story to emerge from the tragic events in Paris in 1997 was the hour-by-hour account of the last three days of her life published in *The Sunday Times*. It revealed the extent to which she was a prisoner of her fame and good looks, hunted and haunted by journalists who made their living by the pursuit. One of the justifications journalists offered for their mercilessness is that she courted the press herself on some occasions but it would have been surprising if she hadn't, and would have taken almost super-human restraint, given that the press were already writing about her every twitch. Diana is the most unscrupulous example of someone who suffered at the hands of the rat-pack, as the more extreme reporters are nicknamed, one irony being that as she was happy to oblige the camera, there wasn't even any real excuse for intrusion. Put simply, hers was an image exploited for financial gain by publishers all over the world. The DJ Zoë Ball is another public figure who has grounds for complaint about the way reporters pursue her and twist the slightest incident in her life into a melodrama (Ronson 1999). This is what happens to many public figures for no other reason than profit. Even journalists who don't hunt their prey like paparazzi are implicated if they work on, or edit, magazines which buy the pictures and the copy.

In a case involving Diana's brother, Earl Spencer, the PCC found that just because you choose to invite one set of reporters to write about and photograph your house, it does not mean that another set of reporters can freely hide in the bushes outside a clinic to take unauthorised pictures of another family member who is ill. Yet journalists frequently argue that anyone who is in any way in the public eye has, effectively, forfeited their right and that of their family to freedom from intrusion. The trouble with this argument is that it could mean that in the long run there will be a shortage of people willing to shoulder the burden of public office – or, less important though it may be, of becoming a Radio 1 DJ.

Hypocrisy

Journalists defend some of the more questionable things they do as being part of a crusade against hypocrisy, yet some of them seem unable to look with candour at their own behaviour. There may be journalists who have never claimed a pound more on expenses than they actually spent, or who have never had too much to drink or been near a drug. Some, but not most. Hypocrisy is as prevalent in editorial offices as it is everywhere else. Minor human weaknesses are exaggerated by journalists to the point of destroying lives, while systematic wickedness goes unreported, as John Pilger and many others have demonstrated (Pilger 1998).

In the news press (especially, but by no means exclusively, the tabloids) and in a wide range of consumer periodicals, the apparent prurience of the British is exploited as an excuse to print sexually titillating material which will boost circulations. A good example of hypocrisy creeping in is with magazines for young teenage girls. Editors of these use arguments about sex education and empowerment to justify their generous use of sexually explicit material. No one doubts that some of this is informative but that doesn't explain the extent of it or the contextual tone it creates. When being frank editors will admit that it's all about sales (McKay 1998) and it would be interesting to see whether the publishers' public devotion to the good causes of education and empowerment would survive were these shown to push sales down rather than up.

The lifestyle sector's obsession with sex (whether explicitly, in articles about sex, or implicitly, in articles about other topics which in turn depend on a particular attitude to sex) has been good for sales even if it has attracted some adverse comment. Most of this has been focused on magazines for adolescent girls, because it seems to be more acceptable to question material which is aimed at a youthful and therefore more vulnerable audience. (Females, also, are thought to need more protection than males in this respect.) Arguments about the way sex is used in magazines for grown-ups naturally stumble at the question 'Why shouldn't a 28-year-old read what she wants?' The diet of diets, dubious health advice, sex, fashion and celebrity tittle-tattle that typifies many magazines for women may attract condemnation but there's not much to be done about it unless you have the resources to set up a new magazine with richer content.

One line of 'post-modernist feminist' argument is that it doesn't much matter what's in magazines for women because of what Joke Hermes calls 'the fallacy of meaningfulness'. By this she implies that the pleasure women get from reading magazines is transitory and forgettable (Hermes 95: 143). Critics of the general content of consumer lifestyle magazines, whether for men or women, might take comfort in the hope she's right. Her arguments are echoed by Angela McRobbie, who suggests 'girls and women are now "knowing" enough to recognize how they are persuaded to consume' (McRobbie 1996: 189). The difficulty with these arguments from the academy is that the research done for publishers finds the opposite. It shows that readers build up strong feelings of trust in their magazines (Consterdine 1997: 16), something which could only happen if they believed and remembered what they read.

When feminists criticise the newer magazines aimed at younger men for their adolescent blokishness (at best) and unreconstructed misogyny (at worst), they know that the soaraway circulation success is all the justification publishers and journalists need. It's interesting, though, that in the case of sexually explicit editorial for men much less attempt is made to justify its inclusion in terms of health education. Lads are free to dream about what they'd do to the unclad glamour girls in their favourite magazines, without having to wade through endless articles about thrush or STDs first. (This is an observation not an endorsement.)

One further way journalists may demonstrate hypocrisy is in relation to payment not to contributors but to the ordinary people who have stories to tell, eyewitness accounts to give or even expert explanations and comments to share. The PCC guidelines say that criminals or witnesses in criminal trials should not benefit financially from those circumstances. No need to question that but journalists often express their disdain for the idea that others should be paid for their time and efforts. Perhaps their approach is the necessary corollary of the altruistic, high-minded seeker-after-objective-truth model of news reporting but it overlooks the fact that even this sort of journalism is nevertheless a commodity and that ordinary eyewitnesses or commentators provide journalists with their raw material. Some of the women's magazines recognise this and have no hesitation in paying people modest sums to tell their stories of tragedy overcome. Yet 'chequebook journalism' gets a bad name when huge sums of money are handed over.

In respect of payment the position of *Hello!* and *OK!*, the good-news gossip magazines, is more open. They pay huge sums to those who agree to feature in their pages, especially for exclusive access to an event such as a wedding or the first picture of a new baby. Even they are not immune to sniping, however: as the prices charged by stars for their pictures rise, there is an occasionally voiced worry from one magazine that the other has gone too far this time.

News values

Many of these examples imply that questionable journalism arises only out of exploiting the innocent or at least the naive, but there are sins of omission too and these often reflect basic questions about news values. When reporters get wind of stories they don't pursue because of the embarrassment these might cause to their contacts, their government or even their friends, they are undoubtedly behaving in a questionable way. Stories may lie unpursued because they don't fit the picture of reality that a particular publication supports.

Ian Jack, among many others, is worried, as we have seen. He says 'the craft of what the late Martha Gellhorn called ʻserious, careful, honest journalism' has entered its own small crisis'. He sees a trend away from reportage towards pages dominated by frivolous journalism with its emphasis on showbusiness and its pathological fear of 'the spectre of the reader's boredom' (Jack 1998: vii). Photographer Christopher Shewen gave a typical example in *New Internationalist*:

> On the same day in May 1998 two things happened. Geri Halliwell quit the Spice Girls and war broke out between Ethiopia and Eritrea. One story got full front-page coverage in Britain, the other a few meagre words buried in the deadground of a couple of broadsheets. The career change of a transient pop star cuts more media ice than half-a-million troops squaring up for the biggest current land war, between two of the poorest countries on earth. This is called the 'cuddliness factor' – spice is cuddly, a major war in Africa is not.
>
> (Shewen 1999)

His criticisms of daily press news values could be made the more strongly of a range of magazines except those, like *New Internationalist*, which are devoted to coverage of the poorer countries of the world. You won't read much about social or political issues at home or abroad in the average lifestyle magazine.

Shewen's point, like Jack's, is that the news agenda is being trivialised. Whether you call it the process of 'dumbing down' or the rise of 'infotainment' there is no denying that gossip about celebrities, however minor their names, however speculative the story, does seem to occupy a growing amount of space not just in those magazines devoted to it (*Hello!*, *OK!*) but also in publications that might be expected to carry other items as well or even instead.

Perhaps celebrity tittle-tattle is more dull than it is harmful. The *Hello!* approach is innocent enough: if you buy it for the story of a footballer's wedding you can be sure the words and pictures haven't been acquired in an underhand way. Compare this with publications at the rougher end of the trade where the slightest incident in a star's life (arriving too late to be served at a restaurant in the case of one) is twisted out of all recognition into an account of a sex-crazed couple driving miles through the Scottish night in the hope of buying oysters (Ronson 1999). This kind of story is probably no more than irritating to a star who has grown used to being treated in this way, but it is of no justifiable interest to readers especially if it isn't even true. Sociologist Todd Gitlin, in an edition of *Brill's Content* devoted to a debate about gossip, cites the more serious case of actress Jean Seberg who eventually killed herself after a story appeared suggesting the baby she was carrying was not her husband's. It was in fact his, she had a breakdown and lost the baby before committing suicide.

An extreme example perhaps. There obviously is space and demand for light stories but Gitlin argues that the problem lies in the way 'the gluttonous media' is unwilling to draw boundaries. Gossip has been allowed to spill out of demarcated gossip columns: 'With news annexed to the entertainment business, tabloid logic rules, gossip isn't left in its place ... Gossip displaces news. Gossip unbounded has grown into a national – make that global – game of Trivial Pursuit' (Gitlin 1999). Journalist Pete Hamill agrees, citing the whole 'salacious soap opera' of the Monica Lewinsky story as an example which puts journalists to shame (Hamill 1998: 15). He condemns the way the mass media devote so much time and space to celebrities. He even identifies a sub-genre as 'necro-journalism – the journalism of dead, or near-dead, celebrities' of which Diana Princess of Wales is the greatest ever example with Marilyn Monroe a close second.

In defence of her trade the successful American gossip writer Liz Smith says 'gossip is one of the great luxuries of a democracy. It is the tawdry jewel in the crown of free speech. You don't read gossip columns in dictatorships.' She may be right, but you could not hope for a better example of the pomposity to which Janet Malcom draws attention. In any case, against Smith I would argue that dictatorships are often founded on, and maintained by, the wide and malicious circulation of half-truths and outright lies. With her other defence – that she's made an enormous amount of money out of gossip and 'it beats being a news reporter by a country mile' – she is surely closer to the truth (Smith 1999).

If too much frivolity in journalism really is a problem then it is nowhere more so than in the lifestyle magazines created around specific themes as a way of attracting well-defined kinds of readers and 'delivering' them to advertisers. Anyone who wants to work for this kind of magazine should think in advance about the general context within which all her work will be set. A general reporter on a newspaper will cover a range of subjects which means that even if one causes a frisson of distaste she'll be on to the next story before the day is out. In magazines it's different. The same subject matter, treated in roughly the same way, constantly recurs. Could a radically green environmentalist work for a magazine company, most of whose profits derive from adverts for cars? Could someone with strong religious beliefs work for the magazines for women which portray as a norm a way of life they find offensive? Could a feminist bear to work for *Loaded* or a vegetarian for *Meat Trades Journal*?

Equally, anyone who wants to work in consumer magazines at the moment needs to think through her approach to sexually explicit copy. Can she write it for one thing? (If so her career is made.) Is she happy that the publishing company she works for hopes to make a profit from the publication of what some would regard as soft porn? Publishers long ago discovered that sex sells. The resounding success of the newer men's magazines shows this to be true and many mainstream women's magazines have now replaced their traditional emphasis on romance with a modern emphasis on sex.

So explicit is some of what is produced for adolescent teenage girls that publishers have also been forced to discover that sex offends. In 1996, to try to convince the world that they are not as irresponsible as concerned parents and politicians began to suspect, the Periodical Publishers Association helped to set up the Teenage Magazine Arbitration Panel (TMAP) as a response to public criticism of the contents of magazines like *J-17* and *Bliss*. The TMAP drew up guidelines for publishers although there is nothing much to act as a deterrent either in the guidelines or in the sanctions available for the Panel to use against offending editors (McKay 2000).

If that's not a problem (which for most journalists it wouldn't be) is there a difficulty in working for a publisher whose mainstream magazines aimed at men move beyond the merely erotic into the realms of sado-masochistic cruelty and violence towards women?

Journalists have to earn their crust, a fact they remember whenever they're asked to do something they would rather not do whether it is on grounds of taste or conscience. For most there is no difficulty, or they wouldn't be in the job in the first place, but a problem of conscience is no less acute for being a small, private one rather than a large, public one. It would probably be true to say that many journalists with strong moral convictions of whatever sort aspire to starting their own magazines or to working on magazines published by organisations whose work they support: magazines, that is, which have a purpose beyond encouraging readers to spend their cash.

There are two further aspects of the work of magazine journalists which regularly cause a heartsearch if not anything quite so strong as a moral dilemma. The first is peculiar to the specialist magazine reporter, the second is the more widespread problem of the freebie.

Specialist reporting

A specialist reporter is one who concentrates his writing in a particular field (or 'beat', the US term) such as football or the environment, or beauty or crime or pensions. Many magazines are devoted to specialist fields of interest and so there are many journalists on trade papers who spend most of their time writing about a small group of companies or activities, and who therefore get to know a relatively small group of people as contacts or sources of stories and quotes. The potential for conflicts of interest is easy to see. Contacts are useful assistants until the day arrives when the reporter has to write a negative story about the contact's company or organisation. That's when the contact can put pressure on to have a story left out or, at the very least, can decide to offer no help in the future (see Tunstall (1971) for a full discussion of specialist reporting).

Freebies

The difficulty raised by the culture of freebies so prevalent in the UK is also one of reciprocity as I have outlined elsewhere in this book (Chapter 15). It may not always be so crude as an offer of certain goods in exchange for editorial coverage but it comes close, even if the general effect is more cumulative. A literary editor, say, will look with particular favour on authors from a publishing house that insists on sending any books requested, even from the back catalogue, and which provides expensive lunches at regular intervals. This probably wouldn't ensure a good review but it might be enough to ensure that a review appears. This kind of exchange may seem innocent enough but it can easily blur the edges of impartial journalism, as a few British editors have realised. (In some other countries the offer of gifts, hospitality or inducements to journalists would simply not be acceptable.) On a few publications reporters are not allowed to accept hospitality and the company pays their way.

One obvious thing that can make freebies a little (if not very) corrupting, particularly for reporters working in the more glamorous fields such as fashion, music or motor industries is the discrepancy between their own incomes and those of the people they are surrounded by as part of their job. Anyone who is living on an ordinary reporter's salary is bound to warm to designers who make sure they always have respectably expensive clothes or cars to borrow, or who enable the reporters to eat, drink and travel in ways they could not otherwise afford. The regulatory bodies, curiously, have little to say about the exchange of gifts, the PCC confining itself to guidance for financial journalists who are enjoined not to make private use of information they acquire in confidence as part of their job.

Conclusions

In this chapter I have tried to show how journalists on magazines may be faced with issues of conscience as they go about their work. Some of these relate to the context in which their writing appears and the editorial concept of the publication for which they work. Others reflect a journalist's individual beliefs and practice. The more spectacular lapses from human decency are more common among hard news reporters and may sometimes occur without malice, being rather the result of thoughtlessness, mistaken identity or just the constraints under which journalists work. There are various codes of practice which offer guidance to reporters and these can provide support for journalists as well as restricting how they operate. It seems to be true, however, that when publications breach guidelines such as the PCC's the punishment doesn't reflect the magnitude or the effect of the crime and when journalists breach the guidelines they still seem to keep their jobs. As one agency reporter put it: 'Perhaps the best protection a reporter has if asked to do something really crass by an editor is the knowledge that he can lie to the newsdesk just as much as he can lie to the public.' I'm not advocating that reporters lie to their editors but merely recalling the wisdom of Mrs Do-as-you-would-be-done-by.

The intense competition for readers and the rivalry between journalists perhaps make it inevitable that stories will sometimes be bent or invented. But the more often this happens the less worthy of respect will be magazines and newspapers, television and radio journalism. As Todd Gitlin puts it: 'A press that infantilizes its public forfeits that public's respect, or deserves to' (Gitlin 1999).

The reason any of this matters is that good journalism matters. As a society we need reporters to be asking questions on our behalf, to be describing events and situations on our behalf as well, of course, as to be entertaining us. That's why it gives cause for concern to see journalists being so vilified (and justifiably so) over the reporting of trivia, and at the same time being bound by restrictions (see Chapters 5 and 18) when it comes to reporting the things that really do matter.

Recommended reading

Belsey, A. and Chadwick, R. (1992) *Ethical Issues in Journalism*.

Brill's Content, May 1999 edition.

Chippindale, P. and Horrie, C. (1999) *Stick it Up Your Punter*.

Curran, J. and Seaton, J. (1997) *Power Without Responsibility*.

Hammill, P. (1988) *News is a Verb*.

Knightley, P. (2000) *The First Casualty: the War Correspondent as Hero and Myth-maker from the Crimea to Kosovo*.

Malcolm, J. (1990) *The Journalist and the Murderer*.

Pilger, J. (1998) *Hidden Agendas*.

Snoddy, R. (1992) *The Good the Bad and the Unacceptable*.

Sparks, C. (1991) 'Goodbye Hildy Johnson: the vanishing "serious press"'.

Tunstall, J. (1971) *Journalists at Work*.

Wilson, John (1996) *Understanding Journalism: A Guide to Issues*.

18 The magazine journalist and the law

Anthony Richards

J ournalists who don't know the law are a danger to their publications. While some, through ignorance, run their publications into danger, others unnecessarily suppress potentially good stories because they have wrong ideas about what may be published. Subeditors in particular must know their media law. They are the main line of defence. Any transgressions which get past them may prove costly. Subs must carefully examine every piece of copy from a legal point of view and raise queries with reporters in any cases of doubt. The reporter, in turn, needs to look carefully at his subbed copy to ensure that the sub has not introduced any errors which were not there originally.

Many decisions on questions of law (sometimes, whether a story should be run at all, if there are doubts about its legal safety) have to be taken hurriedly by editorial staff as the publication is going to bed. A final publish-or-not decision is unlikely to fall to the subeditor alone, but would be referred up through the chief sub, if there is one, to the editor or even the publisher.

Magazines have traditionally been produced on paper but the Internet has signalled a revolution. Many magazines now appear online either as electronic versions of a paper original or as a new kind of magazine altogether, one that is created for electronic transmission only. But the same basic legal principles apply to material transmitted through the Internet, and to publication of material downloaded from the Internet, as apply to material obtained from any other source and published through any other medium.

We will look now at aspects of the law as they affect magazine journalists. First, where the law comes from.

Sources of English law

Statutes (Acts of Parliament) will have passed their various stages through each House of Parliament and received the Royal Assent – nowadays a mere formality. They are of supreme authority and binding on the courts. Statutes may or may not apply to Scotland or Northern Ireland. Some statutes (or some sections of a statute) may not come into effect until an appropriate statutory instrument (see below) has been passed.

Delegated legislation (made by a subsidiary body under power delegated in a statute) comes in three forms.

1 *Statutory instruments* contain regulations put before Parliament by a government minister.

2 *Orders in Council.* These tend to consist largely of constitutional matters put forward by the Privy Council. Few are likely to affect the work of journalists.

3 *By-laws.* Local authorities and certain other bodies have power to make local laws within specific authority.

Laws of the European Union. Membership of the European Union requires UK courts to observe European treaties and decisions of the European Court, and to apply EU legislation (Regulations and Directives), even if in conflict with statutes.

Regulations apply generally throughout member states. They are immediately binding.

Directives, too, are binding, but the mode of implementation is left to the member states themselves.

Judicial precedent. Decisions on legal points by judges in the superior courts create precedents which must be followed by inferior courts when dealing with similar cases.

Decisions of the European Court of Human Rights. As a signatory to the European Convention on Human Rights, the UK is bound to give effect to the Court's decisions, which are thus an indirect source of law. When the Convention is incorporated into English law under the Human Rights Act 1998 (expected in autumn 2000) cases under the Convention will be heard in UK courts.

Civil and criminal law

Criminal law is concerned with wrongs against the sovereign, anything from parking on a yellow line to murder. Civil law is concerned simply with disputes between citizens, perhaps to obtain compensation (called 'damages') for injuries suffered in a road accident or an order (called an 'injunction') to restrain one person from, for example, assaulting or pestering another, or, another common example, to get a divorce.

A person may find himself in trouble with both the civil and the criminal law over the same incident. A motorist who causes an accident may be both prosecuted in a criminal court for careless driving and sued in a civil court for the injury and damage which he caused.

The criminal courts

Magistrates' courts

Virtually every criminal case starts life in a magistrates' court where three types of case are heard.

Summary offences
Cases which *must* be tried by magistrates. They are generally the least serious.

Either-way offences
Cases which *may* be tried by magistrates. They may, alternatively, be tried by a jury in the Crown Court. If the accused intends to plead not guilty he may insist that his

case is tried by jury. Otherwise it will be tried by the magistrates, unless they decline
to hear it because of its apparent seriousness. Theft, burglary and indecent assault are
three examples of either-way offences. Where a person accused of an either-way offence
is convicted before magistrates he may be sent to the Crown Court to be sentenced if
the magistrates feel that he deserves greater punishment than they have the power to
give him.

Indictable-only offences

Cases which *cannot* be tried by magistrates. Because of their seriousness they can be
tried only in the Crown Court. Murder, rape and robbery are three examples. In some
areas – experimentally, at the time of going to press – such cases were going directly
to the Crown Court under the Crime and Disorder Act 1998.

Committal proceedings

If the offence is indictable-only, or if it is an either-way offence which is not to be
tried summarily, the magistrates sit as 'examining justices'. They decide whether the
prosecution case is strong enough to warrant trial in the Crown Court. They will not
hear oral evidence, but will base their decision on written statements by prosecution
and defence witnesses and arguments advanced by lawyers for the two sides.

In some cases (called 'paper committals') the accused will have consented, through
his lawyers, to the case's being sent to the Crown Court for trial, and will indicate
which of the prosecution witnesses he requires to be present. In such a case, the magistrates will not study the witness statements. In some cases the prosecution may *require*
the case to be transferred to the Crown Court. These are cases alleging serious fraud
or serious sexual or cruelty offences against children.

Appeals

A person who is convicted before magistrates may have his case reheard by a judge
sitting with magistrates in the Crown Court. That court's decision is final on any question of fact. If the Crown Court finds the accused guilty it may impose any sentence
which the magistrates could have imposed.

If the accused wishes to argue that he was wrongly convicted by the magistrates in
law (that is, he does not dispute the facts, but argues that, on those facts, he was not
guilty of the offence charged) he can appeal to the High Court (the Queen's Bench
Divisional Court) 'by way of case stated'. The magistrates set out in a 'stated case'
the facts of the case and how they applied the law.

This procedure is open also to the prosecution. So a person who has been acquitted
by magistrates on a legal point may later be convicted by decision of the High Court.
If the legal point is one of general public importance either party may, if leave is
granted, take the case to the House of Lords.

Magistrates

Most benches of magistrates, when trying a case, consist of at least two (more
commonly, three) magistrates. Most are not legally qualified and are unpaid, except for
travel and subsistence. They are advised on legal points by a clerk. Some courts, especially in large cities, are presided over by stipendiary magistrates (likely soon to be
called 'district judges'). These are experienced barristers or solicitors who sit as professional magistrates. They are paid a salary and try cases sitting alone.

The Crown Court

The main Crown Courts such as the Old Bailey and Winchester try the most serious cases, such as murder, before the more senior judges (usually High Court judges). Others, presided over by circuit judges, recorders or assistant recorders, try lesser offences. The cases will have been committed to the Crown Court by magistrates' courts, except where an accused has been committed by means of a 'voluntary bill of indictment' – an uncommon procedure.

If the accused pleads not guilty he will be tried by a jury. If he pleads not guilty to some counts but guilty to others, a reporter must make no reference to the pleas of guilty while the trial on the other charges is proceeding. As in the magistrates' court, the prosecution must prove the accused guilty. It will call witnesses, each of whom will be *examined in chief* (the prosecution 'counsel', or barrister, will ask them questions aimed at proving the accused's guilt). The witnesses can then be *cross-examined* – counsel for the defence (or a suitably qualified solicitor) will put questions aimed at shaking the credibility of their evidence. Finally, he may be *re-examined* – prosecuting counsel may ask questions to deal with points raised in the cross-examination.

The same procedure applies when the defence presents its case. The accused may give evidence. He cannot be compelled to do so, but if he does not the jury may draw its conclusions. The respective counsel (prosecution first) then address the jury, and the judge sums up. He must tell the jury that they must take directions on law from him, but questions of fact are their exclusive prerogative. He must always explain to them the *burden* of proof (that the prosecution must prove the accused's guilt) and the *standard* of proof (that the proof must be beyond all reasonable doubt).

Appeals

A person convicted in the Crown Court may appeal against his conviction, or sentence, or both, to the Court of Appeal (Criminal Division). His appeal will be heard by three senior judges. On an important legal point either the defence or the prosecution may, if leave is granted, appeal to the House of Lords.

The main differences between English and Scots law

The civil courts

In Scots civil actions, for 'claimant' read 'pursuer' and for 'defendant' read 'defender'.

Scotland is divided into six sheriffdoms, each of which is further divided into sheriff court districts. Each sheriff court district has its *sheriff court* – roughly the equivalent of a county court. An appeal from a sheriff court lies to the 'sheriff principal' (though for certain small claims appeal lies only on a point of law) and beyond that to the Inner House of the Court of Session – and ultimately, with leave, to the House of Lords.

A serious civil action will come before the *Outer House of the Court of Session* and will be heard by a Lord Ordinary. The *Inner House of the Court of Session* hears appeals against decisions of the Lords Ordinary, and also against those of inferior courts. The Inner House has two Divisions: the First, presided over by the Lord President, and the Second, presided over by the Lord Justice Clerk. (A Lord Ordinary may seek the guidance of the Inner House before deciding a case.)

In defamation, Scotland draws no distinction between libel and slander. Scots law draws much from Roman law, rather than from the English common law. Roman law looked to injury to the feelings rather than to the reputation, and Scots courts will take account of *convicium* (invective or abuse) especially when deciding questionsof malice. However, for the pursuer there are strict rules of pleading, especially when an innuendo is relied upon.

The criminal courts

The Scots approximate equivalent of the magistrates' courts are the *district courts*. As in England and Wales, these may be staffed by lay or stipendiary magistrates. The *sheriff courts* (see above as to their civil jurisdiction) deal with crimes of a more serious nature, while the most serious offences are tried by the *High Court of Justiciary*. (Note that whereas the 'High Court' in England and Wales is the highest first-instance *civil* court, the High Court in Scotland is the highest *criminal* court.)

The High Court is presided over by judges of the Court of Session. Unlike in civil cases, there is no appeal to the House of Lords.

Children who are adjudged to require a 'compulsory measure of care' (and this includes offenders) are referred to a children's panel, to be arranged by a local officer called a 'reporter'. Only by leave of the *Lord Advocate* (roughly the Scots equivalent of the Attorney-General) may court proceedings be instituted against children – and only in the Sheriff Court or the High Court.

The *Procurator Fiscal* – a public officer similar in many respects to the District Attorney in the USA – directs the inquiry into an alleged offence and also decides whether to prosecute and, if so, what mode of procedure to adopt. He may choose either the *solemn procedure* or the *summary procedure*, depending on the gravity of the alleged offence. In the solemn procedure, carrying more severe maximum penalties, the trial is before a judge and a jury of fifteen, the verdict being by a simple majority. The summary procedure involves a hearing before a judge alone.

Fatal Accident Inquiries (or FAIs) are roughly the equivalent of English inquests. Such an inquiry may be held if it appears that a death may have been sudden, suspicious or unexplained.

Civil courts

Magistrates' courts

Magistrates exercise civil jurisdiction in hearing matrimonial and allied cases in the Family Proceedings Court: separations of spouses, custody and maintenance, and paternity orders where men are alleged to have fathered children whose mothers seek maintenance.

Magistrates have also an administrative function in granting, revoking or transferring liquor and gaming licences.

County courts

Most county court cases are for money owed, or for damages for injury resulting from civil wrongs, usually road or industrial accidents. Whether such cases are tried in the county court or the High Court will depend usually on the amount of money likely to be involved, but sometimes on the complexity of the case. All divorce petitions are issued in county courts. Most are undefended. Defended cases may be transferred to the High Court.

County courts also deal with property and tenancy disputes, equity cases (for example trust funds) and, within financial limits, wills and intestacies. Some have jurisdiction in bankruptcy. County court actions for relatively small sums (£3,000 in 1999) are usually heard in arbitration: a more informal procedure, in private, where costs are not normally awarded. Major county court cases will be heard by a circuit judge, others (mostly in private) by a district judge. Regulations introduced in 1998 were designed to streamline proceedings (in both the county court and the High Court), thus reducing costs and waiting times.

The High Court

The High Court consists of three Divisions, whose jurisdiction is in many instances broadly similar to that of county courts, but on a larger scale.

The *Queen's Bench Division* has unlimited jurisdiction in contract and for civil wrongs, often awarding huge damages in cases such as medical negligence and libel. The Division also exercises a general supervisory jurisdiction over other courts and tribunals, and deals with cases of contempt of court arising from publications.

The *Chancery Division* deals in the main with cases not involving money damages: those dealing with property rights, tax law, probate, trust funds, business associations and non-pecuniary remedies such as injunctions.

The *Family Division* hears some defended divorce petitions, though these nowadays are rare. Since the Family Law Act 1996 much time is devoted to questions arising from that Act in relation to mediation before divorce, parental responsibility, custody and maintenance, and domestic violence. The Division also hears appeals against decisions by magistrates in Family Proceedings Courts.

Appeals

An unsuccessful party in the county court or the High Court may appeal to the Court of Appeal (Civil Division). From there, the unsuccessful party may, if leave is granted, appeal on a legal point to the House of Lords.

Coroners' courts

Nearly all cases in these courts are inquiries into deaths where there may be some doubt as to whether the cause was natural. The inquest is held to determine the identity of the deceased, how, where and when he died, and certain particulars which the coroner is required to supply to the Registrar-General. If it can be shown that the inquest was not fairly conducted, a High Court order can be obtained to quash the verdict and arrange a fresh inquest before a different coroner. Inquests are also held, rarely, to decide whether ancient gold or silver which has been found buried or hidden is 'treasure' and belongs to the Crown.

Tribunals

Numerous tribunals decide various rights to benefits etc. The tribunals most commonly covered by journalists are industrial tribunals, which deal with, among other matters, cases of unfair dismissal, redundancy and discrimination at work on grounds of race or sex.

Admission to courts

All courts must sit in public. A court cannot exclude the press and public simply because it thinks that the case before it should not be published, or to spare a person embarrassment. (But a court may exclude the public, though not the press, while a child is giving evidence in a sex case). Members of a court cannot hide their identities from the public. However, any court may exclude both public and press if it considers justice cannot otherwise be served, or if it has power by statute to exclude the public (for instance, a criminal court trying a case under the Official Secrets Acts) or where a witness might be intimidated.

In youth courts the press, but not the public, have a right of admission. In family proceedings the press have a qualified right of admission. Some courts have special power under rules of court to sit in private, for example courts dealing with patents, welfare of children, certain nullity of marriage cases and cases involving persons of unsound mind.

Coroners' courts must sit in public unless the coroner decides that an inquest or part of it should be heard in private for reasons of national security.

Admission rights to various tribunals vary, and it is necessary to look at the appropriate procedural rules for a particular tribunal in order to discover rights of admission.

Libel

A libel action can be cripplingly expensive and the outcome wildly uncertain. Awards of damages can be unpredictable when they are assessed (as they still are at the time of going to press) by juries. Costs of libel cases are always enormous. The losing side usually has to pay them, but rarely will the successful party recover all its costs, so a magazine will almost invariably lose financially even if it wins its case.

Juries' verdicts, too, are unpredictable. Much may depend on how the jury construes the disputed words. The list of unpleasant things which you might write about a person is endless, but immorality and dishonesty are the most common imputations giving rise to libel actions.

Mistake no defence

It is no defence to plead that the defamatory words were published by mistake. The law is concerned with what was in fact published and the meaning which it might convey to the reader, not with what the journalist *intended* to publish or with the meaning which he *intended* to convey.

Nor is it a defence that you are reporting a mere rumour, even if you say it is untrue. A racing correspondent reported an allegation by punters that a jockey had 'thrown' a race in collusion with bookmakers, adding that the allegation was quite untrue. Nevertheless, damages were awarded.

Innuendo

Double meanings can be costly. Often the 'other meaning' can arise through circumstances unknown to the journalist but known to certain other people. In 1928 the *Daily Mirror* published a picture and caption of a couple who had just announced their 'engagement'. Unknown to the newspaper and the 'fiancée', the man was already married. His wife was awarded damages. In order to marry he could not be married already. So people who knew that she and he had lived together would conclude that they must have cohabited outside wedlock.

An inference is a meaning capable of being drawn by *anyone*. In 1945 a newspaper reported that a bomb-damaged house belonging to a councillor had been repaired by the local council to a better standard than the house next door. This was factually correct, but the newspaper could not prove the likely inference – that the councillor had pulled strings to secure preferential treatment for himself.

Judges have evolved four tests to decide what is defamatory, asking if the words tend to do any of these things:

1 Lower a person in the estimation of right-thinking members of society generally? Here lies the benefit of trial by jurors – they are drawn from all walks of life.

2 Expose him to hatred, contempt or ridicule? Many obviously damaging statements will give rise to hatred or contempt. Satirical writers and cartoonists make a living from ridiculing prominent people, but good natured ribbing is one thing – imputing misconduct is quite another.

3 Disparage him in his office, profession, trade or calling? Anything suggesting that a person is incompetent at his job, or has behaved in a way unbefitting it, falls under this head. When a critic 'pans' an actor's performance, or a sports writer 'slags off' a footballer, clearly the person criticised is disparaged in his profession. If sued, the magazine's defence would almost certainly be fair comment. Note, however, that merely to state incorrectly that a person has ceased to carry on his profession, perhaps through retirement, does not *disparage* him in it, even if it may cause him financial loss. It may, however, give rise to malicious falsehood (see p. 235).

4 Cause others to shun or avoid him? If a hypothetical reasonable person would be less inclined to associate with the plaintiff after reading the words in dispute, this test is satisfied.

'Referring' to the claimant

Defamation is concerned with damage to a person's reputation, that is, what other people think of him. The words of which he complains must therefore be reasonably capable of being understood (if by only a few people, or perhaps by only one) to refer to him, or to a small group to which he belongs. To publish, for instance, that 'all lawyers are thieves' would not enable any lawyer to sue the publisher for libel unless there were something in the story pointing towards him.

When cruel practices in 'a certain factory in the south of Ireland' were alleged, it was held that sufficient clues had been included to enable a reader, familiar with southern Ireland, to glean which factory was meant. And when a woman was stated to have been raped 'by Banbury CID' all ten male officers in Banbury CID recovered damages.

You cannot libel a local authority, but a disparaging story about a council may well reflect on identifiable members or officers.

Referring with insufficient particularity to an offender – 'Harold Newstead, Camberwell man' – proved to be an invitation to all the Harold Newsteads in Camberwell to sue the publisher for libel.

A work of fiction is usually obviously fictitious, so the portrayal of a 'baddie' in such a work should not normally incur any risk of libel of a namesake. But there have been cases where the character and the namesake have had so much in common that legal action has been threatened.

Publication

The defamatory words must have been 'communicated' to at least one person other than the claimant. In media cases, there can be no difficulty in proving publication, but some points must be borne in mind.

Every repetition is a fresh publication. Where a story appears in several publications, each publication can be sued.

There is a common misconception that, once a defamatory story (for example that a politician has been having an affair with a prostitute) has been broken, the story somehow becomes common property and – because the politician does not appear to have taken or threatened any action against the publication which broke the story – it is fair game for everyone. He may be wary of taking on a big national newspaper knowing he would have a costly fight on his hands, but he may more readily sue a smaller publication because he knows the high costs of fighting a libel action might persuade the publishers to settle out of court.

There is a one-year limitation period. A claimant for libel must commence his action within one year of the publication appearing, though the court may in exceptional circumstances extend this period. So although a defamatory story may have escaped through lapse of time, a journalist must be careful not to repeat the allegation, otherwise the twelve-month period will begin again. This is worth remembering when past material from a cuttings file is being used.

Defences

If the claimant proves the above matters he is entitled to succeed, unless the publication can make good a recognised defence.

Justification

Except where the Rehabilitation of Offenders Act 1974 applies (see below) it is a complete defence to prove that the words are true. But they must be true in both *substance* and *fact*. A story alleged that a solicitor had trapped a girl for 'sex', when he merely slapped her bottom but did not have intercourse. The story was true in *substance* (that he was a lecherous man) but not in *fact*. Conversely, a story alleged that a councillor's house had been repaired by the council to a better standard than his neighbour's. The allegation was true in *fact* (this was not disputed) but not true in *substance,* because it implied that the councillor had misused his position on the council.

The publication must prove the truth of any inference created by the words in question (as in the above example) and also any innuendo. We have seen how the *Daily Mirror* reported that a couple had announced their 'engagement'. This was true. But the newspaper could not prove the innuendo: that the woman with whom he had until recently been living could not be his wife. The full 'sting' of the words must be proved. Thus it is dangerous to call a person a 'thief' if the only evidence is one conviction for theft. 'Thief' implies that the person *habitually* steals.

If a story consists of more than one allegation and not all are proved to be true, the defence will not fail if the most serious one is proved to be true and no real harm is done by the others.

In pleading justification the magazine bears the burden of proof. If the defence depends on the evidence of a 'star' witness, what happens if that person dies before the case comes to trial? A journalist should always carefully preserve his notebooks and other evidence; but what happens if important exhibits become lost, or the judge rules them to be inadmissible?

The claimant in a libel action is often a celebrity. He may captivate the jury, who may regard the press as intrusive and scandal-mongering. And where justification is pleaded unsuccessfully, damages are likely to be all the heavier.

Where the publication has disclosed a previous criminal conviction which is now 'spent', the defence of justification will fail if it is shown that the claimant's criminal past was disclosed with malice. The Rehabilitation of Offenders Act 1974 lays down a table of periods after which convictions become 'spent'. The main ones are:

- where the offender was fined, five years;
- imprisonment for not more than six months, seven years;
- imprisonment for more than six but not more than thirty months, ten years.

Privilege

The law accepts that there are occasions when journalists, in reporting matters on which the public have a right to be informed, need protection, provided that they produce fair and accurate reports. One such occasion is the reporting of proceedings in courts of any kind. Here, the protection is *absolute privilege*. If the report is fair (not one-sided), accurate and published contemporaneously (in the next available issue) there is a total protection, regardless of any question of malice. If not published contemporaneously the protection is *qualified privilege* (that is it is protected if it is a fair and accurate report and is not shown to have been published with malice). Qualified privilege protects also reports of various other kinds of gatherings and official statements. These include:

- parliamentary proceedings and parliamentary papers (documents published by order of either House of Parliament and reports to Parliament);
- proceedings of local councils and their committees, if heard in public;
- tribunals and inquiries, if held in public;
- public meetings: bona fide gatherings to discuss matters of public concern, such as election meetings, residents' association meetings;
- statements for public information by certain official bodies, including the European Parliament and the police;
- general meetings of public companies;
- findings and orders of bodies regulating professions (such as the General Medical Council) and sport (such as the Football Association).

In all the above examples (except parliamentary proceedings and papers) the publisher will lose his protection if he does not publish, at the request of a person who has been criticised, a reasonable letter or statement of explanation or contradiction, or if he does so in an inadequate manner. Note, though, that this is not an *apology*. If the story was fair and accurate there is nothing for which to apologise.

The Defamation Act 1996, which provides the above protection, also sets out various types of report where no such letter or statement need be published. These include fair and accurate reports of proceedings of courts and parliaments outside the UK, notices issued for public information by judges or court officers anywhere in the world, and information from public registries (for example companies, and births, deaths and marriages).

There is a privilege at *common law* if the publisher and *all the readers* have a common interest in the subject matter. If, as in most cases, it is possible for a publication to be read by someone who does not have such an interest, this defence will fail.

A story contained allegations against a former politician. The court agreed that the publisher had a duty to publish, and the readers to receive, the allegations, but the court was not satisfied that the 'nature, status and source' of the material was such that it should be protected. In 2000 this defence was successfully used by a newspaper in Leeds.

Fair comment

Comment appearing in magazines includes editorial columns, writers' columns, reviews of plays, books, sports reports, road tests on motor vehicles, and readers' letters. A comment differs from a statement of fact in that a comment cannot be right or wrong – one can only agree or disagree with it. The law protects the free expression of opinion if it is honestly held and expressed without malice on a matter of public interest. Spending of public money and provision of public services are essentially matters of public interest. Opinions differ on whether this extends to the moral indiscretions of public figures, but expressed judicial opinion is that such matters are of public interest if they reflect on the person's suitability to remain in office. But the facts on which the comment is based must be true or privileged. It is not sufficient that the writer *believed* the facts to be true. A privileged fact would be, for example, a jury's verdict or the findings of an official inquiry.

Editors must be careful, when publishing criticisms of a person's actions or words, to avoid any suggestion that he had an improper motive for making or speaking them. Damages were awarded when a TV commentator suggested that a referee's decision to send a player off during a Wembley cup final was prompted by a desire to get his own name in the FA record books.

Malice, in the context of both fair comment and qualified privilege, means any deviation from the objective, or any ulterior motive. If an editor wanted a textbook reviewed, it would be unwise to give the task to someone who had himself written a book on the same subject. A criticism may be in harsh terms, but the use of invective may provide evidence of malice, as when Nina Myskow wrote of the singer Charlotte Cornwell: 'She can't sing and her bum's too big.' (Note that it is permissible to quote the allegation in a subsequent report of the case, as this is.)

Consent to publication

There is a general legal rule that he who consents to a wrong cannot afterwards complain about it. If an MP calls a press conference to deny a rumour that he has a homosexual lover, he obviously consents to publication of the rumour together with his denial of it. If a damaging allegation is made, for example against a company, it is important to ensure that any consent to publication comes from someone who has authority to speak on the company's behalf.

Offer of amends

Under provisions of the Defamation Act 1996 (the implementation of which was deferred) a publisher who is sued for libel may make an offer of amends whereby he offers to publish, in an appropriate position, a suitable correction and apology, to pay the complainant's costs and, possibly, to pay a suitable sum of damages. If the offer is not accepted the defendant may, if he chooses, rely on the offer as his defence. If he does so he cannot put forward any other defence. This procedure is not available if the defendant knew or had reason to believe that the words referred to the plaintiff and were both false and defamatory of him.

Slander

Defamatory words published in any medium will give rise to libel, not slander (which concerns transitory, usually spoken, words). However, a journalist needs to take care how he phrases his questions, and to whom he addresses them, when investigating a person's alleged misconduct. The subject of his inquiry could otherwise sue for slander.

Malicious falsehood

Much rarer than libel, this consists of an untrue, albeit not defamatory, story of a kind likely to cause financial loss (an incorrect report that a solicitor has retired from practice). Publication will be deemed 'malicious' if the reporter does not check it out.

Contempt of court

A person who is involved in a court case, whether it be criminal or civil, is entitled to expect that its outcome will not be influenced by prejudicial media stories. When writing about crimes in respect of which court proceedings are in progress, or may shortly be started, journalists can be at risk of publishing material which may influence the outcome of a trial. In 1949 the *Daily Mirror* wrote of a man who had been arrested on suspicion of murder: 'The vampire confesses.' The Attorney-General, who in practice institutes virtually all proceedings for this kind of contempt, is concerned to ensure that accused persons who may appear before juries are tried on the basis of the evidence in court, not on reporters' speculative stories.

Liability for contempt in criminal cases starts when a person is arrested, when a warrant for his arrest is issued, when a summons is issued, or when he is orally charged. At this point proceedings become 'active' under the Contempt of Court Act 1981. Publication after this time of material which creates a 'substantial risk' that court proceedings may be seriously impeded or prejudiced can result in a heavy fine or, very rarely, imprisonment. Your intention, as an editor, in carrying the story is irrelevant, though you have a defence if you can show that, having taken reasonable care, you had no reason to believe proceedings were active.

A description, or picture, of the accused may amount to a contempt if a question of identification may arise. Eye-witness quotes may similarly cause prejudice.

The risk applies until the accused is acquitted or, if he is convicted, until he is sentenced. However, once a jury has given its verdict it is very unlikely that a background story would be likely to influence the judge when passing sentence. When the accused has been sentenced, proceedings cease to be active until he lodges notice of appeal, if he does so. But, again, as an appeal from the Crown Court will be heard by experienced judges in the Court of Appeal, there can be little risk of serious prejudice here.

Criminal proceedings will also cease to be 'active' if an arrested person is released without charge (but not if he is released on police bail); if the person named in a warrant is not arrested within twelve months; if a charge is ordered not to be proceeded with; or if an accused person is found to be unfit to plead or to be tried.

It is rare for contempt proceedings to arise in respect of civil proceedings, since most of these are tried before a judge sitting alone, and the risk of prejudice is therefore minimal. Furthermore, the liberty of the subject is not at stake.

Civil proceedings become active when an action is set down for trial or a date fixed for the trial. They continue to be 'active' until the case is over, or until it is withdrawn or abandoned. It is not a contempt under the 1981 Act to discuss in good faith a matter of public interest which figures in 'active' proceedings, if the risk of impediment or prejudice to those proceedings is merely incidental to the discussion. There was no contempt in publishing an interview with a woman who was contesting a Parliamentary by-election as a 'pro-life' candidate at a time when a doctor was on trial for the alleged mercy killing of a Down's Syndrome baby.

Even if proceedings, civil or criminal, are not 'active' it is possible to be in contempt at common law if one publishes a highly prejudicial story with intent to influence court proceedings – as when *The Sun* described a doctor as a 'real swine' at a time when the newspaper knew that he was likely soon to be arrested for alleged rape.

Restrictions on reporting courts

....

1925. It became unlawful to take photographs in court or of persons involved in a case while in the ill-defined 'precincts of the court'.

1926. It was made illegal to publish evidence from a divorce case. One may name the parties and witnesses, report allegations, etc. in respect of which evidence has been given, and report points of law and their outcome, and the decision of the court and any observations made in giving it. Similar restrictions apply to the reporting of proceedings before magistrates in the Family Proceedings Court. The 1926 Act also prohibits the publication, in a report of any court proceedings, of any indecent details which are likely to injure public morals (unless the publication is directed solely at the medical or legal professions).

1933. Special courts ('juvenile courts', now called 'youth courts') were set up to deal with cases involving youngsters. (The age range is now 10 to 18.) A report from a youth court must not include a juvenile's name, address, place of education or work, any other identifying particulars, or any picture of him. This applies regardless of the capacity in which he appears in court, even if, for instance, he is a witness. If and when the relevant provisions of the Youth Justice and Criminal Evidence Act 1999 are brought into force a ban on identification (name, address, etc.) of a juvenile 'involved in an offence' will apply even before the youngster's court appearance. (This ban can be lifted by 'any appropriate criminal court'.) The 'youth court' restrictions under the 1933 Act can be lifted (a) to avoid injustice to the juvenile, (b) where a juvenile who faces a serious charge is on the run, or (c) to the extent specified by the court, if the court considers it is in the public interest.

1967. Parliament decided that evidence from committal hearings should not be published, as it might influence jurors who sit at the subsequent trial. The restriction was re-enacted in 1980. Oral evidence is no longer given in these hearings, but it is unlawful, unless reporting restrictions are lifted, to report anything that is said, or anything else except the names of the court, the magistrates, and the lawyers; the identities of the parties and witnesses; the charge(s) on which the accused appears, the decision to commit him for trial, to which court and on what charge(s), any adjournment; whether he gets legal aid; any arrangements for bail (but not reasons for refusing it); and whether an application was made for lifting the restrictions. The restrictions apply from the accused's first appearance in court. (There may be several adjournments before his eventual committal for trial.)

Reporting restrictions will be lifted if the accused so requests. If there are more than one accused and they do not all want a lifting, the court may lift the restrictions only if satisfied that it is in the interests of justice to do so.

1976. In that year it became an offence, once a person had been accused of a rape offence, to publish any material which might identify the woman, called the 'complainant'. The restriction applies for the rest of her life. In 1988 a further restriction was added – that, once an *allegation* of a rape offence had been made, it is unlawful to publish the woman's name, address or picture. At the time of going to press a Bill before Parliament proposed that the total restriction should bite as soon as the *allegation* is made. A 'rape offence' means not only rape, but attempted rape, aiding or abetting, counselling or procuring it, inciting a person to commit it, conspiring to commit it, or burglary with intent to rape. It is now legally possible for a man, too, to be a rape victim.

The complainant may be identified:

- if the court permits it so that witnesses may come forward to assist the defence;
- if the court considers the restrictions to be a substantial and unreasonable curb on reporting the case, and that it is in the public interest to lift them;
- if the complainant consents in writing to being identified, unless it is shown that she was pressurised into consenting.

1992. The restrictions on reporting rape offence cases were extended, subject to the same exceptions, to a range of other sexual offences, including unlawful sex and indecent assault.

Powers of courts to restrict reports

Juveniles

We have seen that a juvenile appearing before a youth court may not be identified. If he appears in any other court he may be identified unless the court makes an order (a 'section 39' order) which imposes restrictions in similar terms to those of the automatic ban in the youth court. Such an order can be made only in respect of a juvenile, and the juvenile must be still alive. Such orders should not be made automatically, and can relate only to proceedings before the court which made the order.

Note that if a person's identity is protected, whether by statute or by court order, a journalist must be careful to avoid 'jigsaw' identification, that is, identification made possible by the clues in the journalist's own story, or by comparing it with reports in other publications. When reporting offences where a child who is related to the offender is the victim, journalists have been advised to identify the offender but give no indication of the relationship to the child. Many publications still seem, however, to prefer to report the case anonymously, stating (incorrectly) that the accused 'cannot be named for legal reasons'.

'No names'

A court may, under section 11 of the Contempt of Court Act 1981, prohibit the publication of any 'name or other matter' appearing in a case. But such an order cannot be made unless the 'name or other matter' has been withheld from the public throughout the proceedings.

Postponement

A court may direct that all, or part, of the case before it shall not be reported until some specified future time if it considers that publication immediately may prejudice the case in question or any other case which is being heard or shortly to be tried. The High Court has held that such an order must be no more draconian than necessary.

Mitigation

Where the defence, in a speech in mitigation of sentence, attacks the character of a third person, the court may prohibit reporting of the allegation if it was not made during the hearing.

Copyright

Print journalists will be concerned with 'literary' and 'artistic' works. Editorial copy is 'literary'. Even compilations, such as football league tables, come under this heading. 'Artistic' will include photographs, sketches, cartoons and graphics. Copyright lasts for seventy years from the end of the year of the author's death. If the author is not ascertainable, or if the copyright belongs to a corporation (as in the case of most newspaper and magazine articles), copyright runs for seventy years from the end of the year of publication.

A person will infringe copyright if he copies or reproduces a copyright work in any form. A journalist who 'lifts' a story from another publication will no doubt 'rejig' it in the hope of disguising his misdemeanour. He may fail, however, if the original story contains an error which the rewritten version repeats. And, in any event, one can usually recognise one's own story, whatever efforts have been made to disguise it. Don't confuse a 'lifting' with a 'follow-up'. You can always follow up a rival's story, unearthing your own material. A judge once said that there is no copyright in news, but there may be copyright in the way in which it is presented.

Ownership of copyright

Copyright in a work belongs to its creator, unless it was produced in the course of an employment. In that event, it will belong to the employer, unless the author's contract provides otherwise. Where, however, the author of the work is a freelance, he owns the copyright unless he assigns it to the publisher. The writer of a letter to the editor implicitly authorises the publication to which he sends it to publish his letter on one occasion only. Many publications reserve the right to shorten letters. Even where no such right is reserved, the judicial view has been towards a right to shorten, unless the writer of the letter has stipulated that it is to be used in full or not at all.

Fair dealing

There are occasions when it is permissible, to a limited extent, to quote from a copyright literary work, or even to reproduce a copyright artistic work, with acknowledgement.

When criticising or reviewing. What would be 'fair dealing' for this purpose has never been judicially quantified. Basically, when reviewing a book a critic may quote from it for the purpose of making his point. It may not be so much a question of *how many* words as *which* words he quotes. If, for instance, in reviewing a thriller, he were to give the game away, this would exceed fair dealing.

Reporting current events. It is permissible to quote from a copyright work where the words relate to a current event – again, within limits. For instance, if a cabinet minister sends a letter of resignation to the Prime Minister a brief quotation from the letter setting out his reasons for resigning would be likely to be protected as fair dealing. But when *The Sun* set out in full the text of a private letter from Prince Philip on Prince Edward's resignation of his Royal Marines commission, this far exceeded the bounds of fair dealing for reporting the Prince's resignation.

Moral rights

An author enjoys certain 'moral rights', namely (a) to have his name on his work (but this does not entitle a reporter to a byline), and (b) not to have his work treated derogatorily (but this does not preclude a sub from altering a reporter's copy). A further right, enjoyed also by a reporter, is not to have his name put on someone else's work. A newspaper fell foul of this rule when it attributed to Dorothy Squires an account of her married life, despite a line in small print saying that the story was 'as told' to a reporter.

Commissioned works

Where any work has been produced under a commission since 1989, the copyright belongs to the person commissioned. So a wedding photographer has the copyright in the wedding photographs. He is under an obligation, however, not to make them public and thereby betray the trust placed in him by the person who commissioned the pictures. If he does so without permission he will be liable in damages, and so will any publication which uses the pictures. It is therefore important, when borrowing a picture, to ascertain who produced it. If it is a snapshot from the lender's family album, the lender can authorise its use. But if it has on the back a photographer's stamp (for example if it is a school photograph) it will be necessary to get the photographer's consent, and no doubt pay him a fee. If the school 'commissioned' the photographer, its consent may also be needed. If the photograph were produced before 1989 the copyright would belong to whomever commissioned it.

Spoken words

Copyright in a report of spoken words belongs to the first person to reduce them to writing, unless the speaker reserved copyright in his speech before making it. But, as fair dealing permits limited inclusion of copyright material for reporting current events, to this extent a reporter could report the speaker's words despite his reservation of copyright.

Confidentiality

A servant is duty-bound not to betray his master's secrets. A spouse is similarly bound. In 1962 the Duchess of Argyll obtained an injunction to stop her ex-husband, the Duke,

from revealing secrets of their marriage. Sometimes an injuncti⸺
a 'kiss-and-tell' ex-lover. In 1988 a judge refused to strike⸺
woman identified only as 'T' to stop disclosure of ⸺
a young woman. Basically, the tests will be (a⸺
(b) would disclosure be likely to damage⸺
was it communicated in breach of ⸺
is 'yes' an injunction is likely⸺

1 The public inter⸺
   matter conf⸺
   asserti⸺

Useful addresses

ı
or
sec⸺
Right⸺
for refu⸺
which so⸺
look forwa⸺

Privacy

Although the UK i⸺
the setting up of the⸺
and the threat of leg⸺
could well shackle inve⸺
ought, in the public inter⸺

The PCC's Code of Prac⸺
a person's religion, sexual o⸺
to respect for his or her priv⸺
Following the death in 1997 o⸺
not to use any more 'paparazzi' ⸺

Doorstepping journalists who ob⸺
under section 137 of the Highways A⸺
premises for a particular purpose, at⸺
photographs, could be sued for trespass

Association of British Science Writers, 23 Savile Row, London W1X 2NB, tel. 020 7439 12⸺
absw@absw.demon.co.uk

Audit Bureau of Circulations, Black Prince Yard, 207–209 High Street, Berkhamsted,
HP4 1AD, tel. 01442 870800, http://www.abc.org.uk

British Society of Magazine Editors, c/o Gill Branston Assocs, 137 Hale Lane, Edgware
HA8 9QP, tel. 020 8906 4664, bsme@cix.compulink.co.uk

Campaign for Press and Broadcasting Freedom, 8 Cynthia Street, London N1 9JF, tel.
4430, http://www.architechs.com/cpbf

Freedom Forum European Centre, Stanhope House, Stanhope Place, London W2 2⸺
7262 5003, http://www.freedomforum.org

International Federation of Journalists, IPC, Boulevard Charlemagne 1, Bte 5,
tel. 32 2 238 0951

International Federation of Periodical Publishers (FIPP), Queen's House, 55/56 Lin⸺
London WC2A 3LJ, tel. 020 7404 4169, http://www.fipp.com

International Institute of News Safety, Don Mackglew, c/o National Union of

National Readership Surveys, 42 Drury Lane, London WC2B 5RT, te⸺
http://www.nrs.co.uk

National Union of Journalists, Acorn House, 314–320 Gray's Inn Road
tel. 020 7843 3706

Periodical Publishers Association, Queen's House, 55/56 Lincoln's Inn F⸺
tel. 020 7404 4166, http://www.ppa.co.uk

Periodicals Training Council, Queen's House, 55/56 Lincoln's Inn F⸺
tel. 020 7404 4168, training@ppa.co.uk

Press Complaints Commission, 1 Salisbury Square, London EC⸺
http://www.pcc.org.uk

PressWise, 25 Easton Business Centre, Felix Road, Bristol B⸺
pw@presswise.org.uk

Reporters Sans Frontières at 5, rue Geoffrey Marie 75009 Par⸺

Teenage Magazine Arbitration Panel, c/o PPA, Queen's House⸺
WC2A 3LJ, tel. 020 7404 4166, http://www.ppa.co.uk

UK Newsletter Association, Queen's House, 55/56 Linc⸺
tel. 020 7404 4166, ukna@ppa.co.uk

Glossary

....

ABC – the Audit Bureau of Circulations, the independent organisation which audits and publishes the sales figures of newspapers and magazines

ABC figure – the audited circulation figure for a magazine or newspaper from the *Audit Bureau of Circulations*

ABCDE – categorisation of the population by market researchers based on their social and economic status: A is high and E is low

ad – *advertisement*

ad–ed ratio – the ratio of space in a magazine filled by advertising and editorial material respectively

ad-get feature – editorial material prepared specifically to attract advertisers

adjacency – the position of an *advertisement* next to certain editorial material for which publishers can charge higher rates

advertisement – written or pictorial material which is included in a magazine for payment by the advertiser

advertisement feature – see *advertorial*

advertising revenue – money a publication earns from advertisers who buy space on its pages to advertise their products

advertorial – copy and pictures paid for by advertisers but prepared to look like editorial material. The more formal name is *advertisement feature*

agony column – regular feature where readers' letters about personal problems are answered. Usually written by an agony aunt but there are some agony uncles

angle – the way of approaching a story

art editor – person who is responsible for the visual aspects of the magazine

artwork – the illustrative material ready for printing

ASA – Advertising Standards Authority

ascenders – the parts of letters such as k, f and d which extend above the basic *x-height* in a *typeface*

author's corrections – changes made to *copy* by the author once setting has been done

author's proof – a *proof* sent to the author for correction

back issues/numbers – issues of a magazine published before the one which is current

back of the book – pages in a magazine that fall after the *centre spread*

bad break – describes a word which has been hyphenated clumsily in order to fit into a given space

bagging – the practice of enclosing a magazine in a transparent plastic bag. Keeps *cover mounts* safe and prevents browsers from reading before buying

banner – a *headline* that extends across the whole of a page or spread

bar code – on a magazine's cover the black and white serial number which can be read by computer

bastard measure – type that is set to a *measure* that is not standard for a given publication or page

beat – more commonly used in the USA: a journalist's specialist field of interest

binding – the way in which pages are united to produce the finished magazine

bleed (bled off) – where the printed matter extends to the edge of the page

body copy – the main text

bold – version of a *typeface* in which the letters appear thicker and darker than in the standard version

book – another word for the magazine

box – area of type that is surrounded by rules to create a 'box' shape on the layout. Sometimes called a panel

brand extension – the use of a magazine's title (or brand) by a publisher to expand into other areas of business such as *masthead television*, exhibition organisation or selling goods as diverse as bedlinen and cheese

browser – software used to navigate the *World Wide Web*

business-to-business – the current name for the trade press. These are publications which concentrate on work and professional interests rather than leisure and lifestyle

bust – a *headline* or *standfirst* busts if it is too long for the allocated space

byline – the name of the writer as it appears with the story

camera-ready – the elements of a page ready to be photographed for printing

caps – short for 'capital letters'

caption – words that accompany a picture or illustration

CAR – computer-assisted reporting

cast off – to work out how much space a piece of copy will occupy

catchline – a short word used to identify a story during the editorial process but not printed. Called a slug-line in the USA

centre spread – the middle two facing pages of a magazine. Also called the centre-fold

centred – type that is set as if from the centre of the column so that the margins on either side of the type are equal in width in any give line. This produces ragged margins in a column of type

chapel – the name for a branch of the journalists' and printers' trade unions, led by a mother or father of the chapel

character – an individual letter, number, punctuation mark, symbol or space

chief sub – the senior *subeditor* who is in charge of the subediting process

circulation – the number of copies of a magazine issue which is sold or otherwise distributed

classified advertising – small *advertisements* grouped together on the page or 'classified' by subject matter

cliché – a phrase that has grown dull through over use

close/closing – time at which a page or a publication is finally sent to the printers

close up – instruction to reduce the space between characters, words or lines of space

coated paper – paper that has been treated to give it a glossy finish, suitable for high-quality printing

editor – the most senior journalist on a publication. The person responsible for the editorial content

editorial – material in a magazine generated by journalists and not by advertisers. Can sometimes mean an opinion piece by the editor or editorial staff

editorial mention – inclusion in editorial material of the name of a product

e-journalist – a journalist whose work is published electronically. Also a journalist who uses electronic means to conduct research

embargo – a request not to publish before a specified time. Applies to information that is released to the press in advance

end blob or **symbol** – characteristic symbol used by a magazine to denote the end of a story

expenses – out-of-pocket expenses incurred by journalists or photographers while on assignment. Also known as 'exes'

facing matter – position in a magazine opposite editorial material (or 'matter'), favoured by advertisers

fanzines (or 'zines) – amateur magazines produced out of devotion to the topic (such as a rock group or a football club) rather than with a view to making money

finishing – the processes such as *binding* which take place after printing

FIPP – International Federation of the Periodical Press

fit – to cut copy so that it fits an allocated space exactly

flannel panel – the place where the magazine gives its address and other contact information as well as the list of staff and the copyright notice. Sometimes also called the *masthead*

flatplan – the one-dimensional diagram of a magazine used in planning to show what will appear on which page

flatplanning – the process of producing a *flatplan*

flush – type that is set so that one margin is even, as in 'flush left', meaning the left margin is straight while the right one is *ragged*

focus group – group of people brought together by market researchers to discuss a particular topic

folio – page

font or fount – name given to the range of *characters* in one *typeface*

four-colour – the printing technique that uses four colours to produce colour pages

fragmentation – term used to describe the effect on the market of the proliferation of titles in a particular publishing sector

freebies – gifts or inducements sent to journalists by organisations seeking publicity through *editorial mentions*

freelance – someone who is self-employed, usually working for a range of publications

full out – where type is set across the full *measure* (width) of the column

furniture – the regular features that appear in a magazine. Also used to mean the graphic devices used to indicate differing sections of the magazine

galley proof – proof of typeset copy which is not yet assigned to a *layout* and so is produced as a single column of type

gatefold – an extra page which folds out, usually from the cover. Most often used for *advertisements*

gone to bed – the publication has been sent to the printers and no more changes are possible

graphics – illustrative material

grey market – potential readers of magazines who are older than those typically thought of as *consumer magazine* purchasers

grid – established shape for the design of the pages of a magazine which determines such things as the width of columns and margins

gutter – the vertical space between columns or between two pages in the same spread

halftone – a way of representing light and shade by using black dots of differing size

handout – information supplied as a *press release*

hard copy – *copy* supplied on paper, either typewritten or handwritten

headline or heading – words in larger or distinctive type which attract the reader to a story

hold over – instruction to keep *copy* for use at a later date

house ad – *advertisement* by a *publisher* in a magazine it owns

house journal – a publication given to the employees of an organisation bringing them news and information about its activities

house style – the collection of guidelines about English usage and editorial policy established by a publisher for a publication as a way of ensuring consistency

imposition – the way pages are arranged for printing so that they will be in the correct order after the folding process

imprint – the details of the printer and publisher which a publication is legally obliged to include

indented – line where the type starts a few character spaces in from the margin to which the rest of the column adheres

in-house – taking place within a publication's own publishing house

insert – loose sheet or sheets of paper, usually an advertisement, inserted into a magazine after binding

insertion orders – requests from advertisers about where in a magazine their *advertisements* are to be positioned

Internet – a global network of computers which supports several applications including e-mail and the *World Wide Web*

intro – usual term for the first paragraph of a news or feature story

inverted pyramid – describes the typical way in which a news story is written, with the information included in descending order of importance

ISDN – Integrated Services Digital Network. A means of transmitting editorial material, using an ISDN telephone line

justified – typeset copy in which both left and right margins are *flush*, i.e. without indentations. Justification is the process by which this is achieved

kill – to drop a story

kill-fee – fee paid to a journalist whose story has been commissioned but is not used

landscape – describes pictures which are wider than they are deep

layout – the design for a page

lead – the main story on a page or in a publication. Also, an idea for a story or a tip-off for one

leading – pronounced 'ledding' this is the space between lines of type, originally achieved by the insertion of bars of metal or leads

libel – a defamatory statement in permanent form

light box – a box with a translucent surface and an internal lamp on which transparencies can be viewed

line drawing – an illustration that uses lines rather than shaded areas

lineage – fee paid to a journalist which is assessed on the basis of the number of lines of text used in the publication

literal – a typographical error. Also known as a *typo*

logo – commonly used to describe a magazine's title design as it appears on the cover and any other page or merchandise where it may appear. See *titlepiece*

loupe – a small magnifying glass held up to the eye through which to view *transparencies*

lower case – small (not capital) letters

mark up – to indicate the *typeface*, size and *measure* in which copy is to be set by the printer

masthead – now a common term for the *titlepiece* or *logo* of a magazine which used to refer only to the place in a magazine, usually near the beginning, where its address and contact information are published as well as the *staff box*. See *flannel panel*

masthead television – television programmes developed around a magazine brand

matter – typeset copy

measure – the width of a piece of typesetting

media pack – information prepared by the publisher for advertisers giving details about a magazine's circulation and readership

merchandising – information about stockists and prices included in consumer articles

MF – abbreviation for 'more follows'. MFL means 'more follows later'

model release – document signed by a photographic model authorising the use of pictures in which he or she appears

mono(chrome) – printed with one colour, usually black

mug shots – portraits showing head and shoulders only

NCTJ – National Council for the Training of Journalists

news agency – an agency that supplies stories and pictures to a wide range of media organisations

newsletter – *business-to-business* publications with small niche readerships to which they supply specialised information

niche market – a relatively small group or sector of potential purchasers of a publication, usually with a shared specialist interest

nose – the beginning of a story or *intro*

NRS – National Readership Surveys

NUJ – National Union of Journalists

NVQ – National Vocational Qualification

off the record – words spoken to a journalist which the speaker does not want to have reported or at least attributed to her

OTS – stands for 'opportunity to see' and is one of the indices used by the *National Readership Surveys*. An OTS score measures the number of readers who will read some part of a title during its currency

overmatter – typeset material for which there is not enough space on the *layout*

ozalid – a type of *proof*

page proof – a *proof* of the whole page showing text in relation to *layout* and presentational material such as *headline, standfirsts, captions*

page rate – the cost of a page of advertising in a magazine. Also used for the amount of money an editor can spend on the editorial content of a page

page traffic – term used by publishers to describe how well read a page is

page-to-plate – name for the process of sending copy directly to the printing plate without intermediate stages

pagination – the number of pages in a magazine

paparazzi – photographers who take pictures of celebrities without their consent

par – a paragraph

passed for press – stage at which authorisation has been given for printing to begin

peg – reason for publishing a story at a particular time

penetration – describes the proportion of a publication's target *readership* which is reflected in its *circulation* figures

perfect binding – the *binding* system using glue which creates a hard, squared *spine*. Usually used on thicker magazines printed on good quality paper

pex – an index used by the *QRS* to measure page exposure, or the number of times an individual reader opens an issue of a magazine at a particular page

photomontage – a picture created from more than one original or heavily *retouched*

picture byline – a *byline* that includes a photograph of the writer

picture editor – person who commissions and selects photographs for a publication

picture-led – publication where the visual material takes priority over the words

pix – abbreviation for pictures

plate – the name for the printing plate, whether made of metal or plastic, from which pages will be printed

point – the unit of measurement used in *typography*. One point is roughly ½ of an inch

position – on a magazine refers to the site where particular elements will be placed. Editorial positions are where editorial material is found. Advertisers pay higher rates for certain special positions such as the back page, *facing matter*, first right-hand page or even 'first fragrance'

PPA – Periodical Publishers Association, the trade organisation for *publishers*

PR – abbreviation for someone who handles public relations for a company or person

press release – written (or electronic) announcement of news by an organisation

print run – number of copies printed

production schedule – the list of times at which various editorial and production processes for a magazine are to be undertaken

profile – an article that describes a person or, more rarely, an organisation

progressives – *proofs* pulled at each stage of the colour printing process

promotion – means other than advertising by which a publication is brought to the attention of the public

proof – a typeset version of the *copy* which can be used for checking. As a verb it means to read a proof carefully, checking for mistakes

proof reader – someone who reads *proofs*

PTC – The Periodicals Training Council, the *publishers'* organisation which has responsibility for training matters

publisher – a company that publishes printed material. Also the name for the person within a magazine publishing company who takes overall responsibility for the commercial aspects of a publication

pull-quote – a few words taken from the following text and set in a contrasting type to be used as a visual device to break up the text as well as an enticement to read the story

QRS – stands for Quality of Reading Survey, a source of data for publishers launched in 1998 to complement the *ABC* and *NRS* figures

ragged – with an uneven margin

range right (left) – type that is *flush* or straight on the right-hand side (left-hand side) of the column

rate card – the information for advertisers about the rates a magazine charges for advertising space

readership – the number of readers of a magazine. Distinct from *circulation*, which is the number of copies sold or otherwise distributed

register – the alignment of the coloured inks on the printed page. If a page is 'out of register' the pictures and the lines within them look blurred

repertoire buyers – those readers who don't remain loyal to one publication

reportage – reporting. May also mean extended feature articles which include descriptive writing

repro house – place where colour pictures are scanned and married up with *layouts* ready for printing. Also known as a colour house

retainer – regular payment to a *freelance* to secure a commitment to the publication

retouch – to enhance the quality of, or otherwise alter, a photograph

returns – copies of a magazine that are returned unsold to the *publisher* by the retailer

reversed out – type printed in white on black or on a tinted background

revise – a *proof* to be checked after corrections to a previous proof have been made

river – white space that forms by chance during setting and which creates a distracting gap running down a column of type

roman – the standard style of type, as compared with *bold*, where the letters are thicker, or italic, where they are finer and sloping

rough – a 'rough' sketch showing a suggested *layout*

rule – a line separating columns of type or surrounding illustrations

saddle-stitching – means of *binding* the pages of a magazine by folding and then stapling

sale or return (SOR) – an arrangement for the publisher to take back copies of a publication which a retailer can't sell

sales revenue – income derived by publishers from sales of copies of magazines as opposed to income from advertisers

sans serif – typeface whose letters don't have *serifs*

scanner – computer equipment that translates *hard copy* or illustrations into digital form

schedule – collective name for all the *advertisements* a company will place with a magazine over a specified period of time.

scheme – to make a plan of a page *layout*

section – that part of a magazine which is printed on one sheet of paper before being folded and trimmed and bound into the magazine. Sections can be of any number from four to sixty-four pages but must be divisible by four

sell – paragraph of copy to entice a reader into reading a feature article. Also known as a *standfirst*

separations – the parts into which a colour picture is separated before printing begins

serif – the small embellishing strokes at the ends of letters in serif *typefaces*

shoot – a photographic session

sidebar – a complementary story or additional material relating to the main text which is placed in a *box* or panel at the side

sitting – a photographic session or shoot

slander – a defamatory statement which is spoken

small caps – capital letters in shape but of the same size as the lower-case letters in a given *typeface*. LIKE THESE

special feature – another term for *advertisement feature*

spike – the old word for the metal spike on which unwanted *copy* was stored

spine – the bound edge of a *perfect-bound* magazine

splash – the main story on the front page of a news magazine

spot colour – a colour other than black which can be used throughout a publication or on individual pages

spread – two pages that face each other

staffbox – the list that appears in a magazine of its staff members and contributors. Often includes the *imprint*

standfirst – text in type larger than the *body copy* and usually written by *subeditors* which introduces the story to the reader

standing artwork – *artwork* which stays the same from one issue to the next

stet – literally 'let it stand'. Used to indicate that a correction which has been marked should in fact be ignored

stock – the grade of paper used for a magazine

strapline – subsidiary *headline* that expands on the main headline and runs above it

style – abbreviation for *house style*

style book/sheet – the document in which *house style* is recorded

stylist – person who organises a photographic session

subeditor (or **sub**) – the journalist responsible for checking, editing, *fitting* and presenting the *copy* on the page

subscriber – reader who pays in advance for a specified number of copies of a publication

subhead – a subsidiary *headline*

syndication – selling on to other publications of material used by a magazine or agency

take back – instruction to take words back to the previous line

tint – shaded panel over which type can be printed

titlepiece – the correct name for the name of a magazine as it appears on the cover (although this is regularly called a *masthead* and a *logo*). Masthead is often said to be the wrong term but it is now common as in the phrase 'masthead programming'

TMAP – Teenage Magazine Arbitration Panel. Organisation set up by *publishers* to monitor the material which appears in magazines aimed at girls in their early teens

TOT – stands for 'triumph over tragedy' and refers to a type of feature article which tells a real-life story in which the subject overcomes difficult personal circumstances

transparency – a photograph in film form, also known as a tranny

turn – the term to describe the section of a story which is continued on a page other than the one which carries the majority of the *copy*. Indicated to the reader by an instruction such as 'Turn to page' or what's known as a turn arrow

typeface – the letters in a given family of type

typo – a typographical error. Also known as a *literal*

typography – the craft of using type

u/lc – short way to write '*upper and lower case*'

unjustified – column of typeset copy where one of the margins is uneven

upmarket – market research term for a *readership* with larger disposable income or higher social class. See *downmarket*

upper case – capital letters, e.g. ABC

upper and lower case – mixture of *capital* and small letters

vox pop – stands for *vox populi* which means voice of the people. A story where the reporter canvasses opinion from ordinary members of the public

website – a grouping of several pages together from the *World Wide Web*

weight – the thickness or boldness of letters in a *typeface*

white space – area on a page with no words or illustrations

wholesaler – the intermediary who organises the delivery of publications to retailers

widow – a line of type at the end of a paragraph which has only one syllable or one short word in it. If it falls at the top or bottom of a column the text may have to be altered to remove it

WOB – stands for 'white on black' and means where the usual arrangement of black type on a white background is reversed so that white words appear on black. Also known as *reversed out* type

World Wide Web – electronic network of computer files

x-height – the height of the lower-case letter x in any given *typeface*. See *ascenders* and *descenders*

'zines – see *fanzines*

Bibliography

The bibliography is divided into three sections: books, journal articles and papers; newspaper and magazine articles; and electronic sources. Authors with multiple works may appear in more than one section.

Books, journal articles and papers

Anderson, P. J. and Weymouth, A. (1999) *Insulting the Public? The British Press and the European Union*, Harlow, Essex and New York: Addison Wesley Longman.

Ang, T. (2000) *Picture Editing (Second Edition)*, Oxford: Focal Press.

Armstrong, L. (1998) *Front Row*, London: Coronet.

Atton, C. (1999) 'A reassessment of the alternative press', *Media, Culture and Society*, 21: 51–76, London: Sage.

Ballaster, R., Beetham, M., Frazer, E. and Hebron, S. (1991) *Women's Worlds: Ideology, Femininity and the Women's Magazine*, London: Macmillan.

Barber, L. (1992) *Mostly Men*, Harmondsworth, UK: Penguin.

Barber, L. (1998) *Demon Barber*, London: Viking.

Barrell, J. and Braithwaite, B. (1979) *The Business of Women's Magazines: The Agonies and the Ecstasies*, London: Associated Business Press.

Barthes, R. (1973) *Mythologies*, trans. A. Lavers, St Albans UK: Paladin.

Beetham, M. (1996) *A Magazine of her Own. Domesticity and Desire in the Woman's Magazine, 1800–1914*, London: Routledge.

Bell, Q. (1991) *The PR Business*, London: Kogan Page.

Belsey, A. and Chadwick, R. (1992) *Ethical Issues in Journalism*, London and New York: Routledge.

Bennett, A. (1994) *Writing Home*, London: Faber.

Berendt, J. (1994) *Midnight in the Garden of Good and Evil*, London: Chatto and Windus.

Berger, J., Blomberg, S., Fox, C., Dibb, M. and Hollis, R. (1972) *Ways of Seeing*, Harmondsworth, UK: Penguin.

Berger, J. and Mohr, J. (1982) *Another Way of Looking*, London: Writers and Readers Publishing Co-operative.

Bradley, P. (1999) *The Advanced Internet Searcher's Handbook*, London: Library Association Publishing.

Braithwaite, B. (1995) *Women's Magazines: The First 300 Years*, London: Peter Owen.

Braithwaite, B. (1998) 'Magazines: the bulging bookstores' in A. Briggs and P. Cobley (eds) *The Media: An Introduction*, London: Addison Wesley Longman.

Bromley, M. and O'Malley, T. (eds) (1997) *A Journalism Reader*, London: Routledge.

Bromley, M. and Stephenson, H. (eds) (1998) *Sex, Lies and Democracy: The Press and the Public*, London and New York: Addison Wesley Longman.

Bromley, M. and Stephenson, H. (2000) 'Ordinary people question and make up their own minds: new paradigms for the self-regulation of the press after the death of Diana', Association for Journalism Education Conference Papers 1, London: AJE c/o City University Journalism Centre.

Broughton, F. (ed.) (1998) *Time Out Interviews 1968–1998*, Harmondsworth, UK: Penguin.

Bryson, B. (1990) *Mother Tongue: The English Language*, London: Hamish Hamilton.

Buchan, J. (1999) 'Inside Iraq' in *Women and Children First, Granta 67*, London: Granta Books.

Burchill, J. (1992) *Sex and Sensibility*, London: Grafton/HarperCollins.

Cameron, D. (1995) *Verbal Hygiene*, London: Routledge.

Cameron, D. (1996) 'Style policy and style politics: a neglected aspect of the language of the news', *Media, Culture and Society*, 18: 315–33, London: Sage.

Cameron, D. (2000) *Good to Talk?*, London: Sage.

Cameron, J. (1967) 'Journalism: a trade' in M. Bromley and T. O'Malley (eds) (1997) *A Journalism Reader*, London: Routledge.

Campbell, A. (1985) *The Designer's Handbook*, London: Macdonald.

Capote, T. (1967) *In Cold Blood*, Harmondsworth, UK: Penguin.

Capote, T. (1989) *A Capote Reader*, London: Abacus/Sphere Books.

Carey, G. V. (1976) *Mind the Stop. A Brief Guide to Punctuation*, Harmondsworth, UK: Penguin.

Carey, J. (ed.) (1987) *The Faber Book of Reportage*, London: Faber.

Carey, J. (ed.) (1995) *The Faber Book of Science*, London: Faber.

Carey, P. (1996) *Media Law*, London: Sweet and Maxwell.

Carter-Ruck, P. (1997) *Carter-Ruck on Libel and Slander*, 5th edition, London: Butterworth.

Caruso, D. (1997) 'Show me the money', *Columbia Journalism Review*, July/August: 32–3.

Chippindale, P. and Horrie, C. (1999) *Stick it Up Your Punter! The Uncut Story of The Sun Newspaper,* London: Simon and Schuster.

Clark, E. (1988) *The Want Makers: Lifting the Lid off the World Advertising Industry: How They Make You Want to Buy*, Harmondsworth, UK: Penguin.

Clayton, J. (1994) *Interviewing for Journalists*, London: Piatkus.

Click, J. W. and Baird, R. N. (1990) *Magazine Editing and Production*, Dubuque, Iowa: Wm. C. Brown Publishers.

Cohen, S. and Young, J. (eds) (1973) *The Manufacture of News. Deviance, Social Problems and the Mass Media*, London: Constable.

Coleridge, N. (1988) *The Fashion Conspiracy*, London: Heinemann.

Coleridge, N. (1999) *Streetsmart*, London: Orion.

Consterdine, G. (1997) 'How magazine advertising works II', Research Report 40, London: Periodical Publishers Association.

Cookman, B. (1993) *Desktop Design: Getting the Professional Look*, London: Routledge.

Copyright, Designs and Patents Act 1988, London: HMSO.

Crompton, R. (1927) 'All the news' in (1984) *William in Trouble*, London: Pan Macmillan.

Curran, J. and Seaton, J. (1997) *Power Without Responsibility: The Press and Broadcasting in Britain*, 5th edition, London: Routledge.

David, A. (1988) *Magazine Journalism Today*, London: Heinemann Professional Publishing.

Davies, H. (1994) *Hunting People: Thirty Years of Interviews with the Famous*, Edinburgh: Mainstream Publishing.

Davies, H. (1998) *Born 1900: A Human History of the Twentieth Century – For Everyone Who Was There*, London: Little, Brown.

Davies, N. (1997) *Dark Heart*, London: Vintage.

Dawkins, W. and Inman, C. (eds) (1998) *Inside the FT: An Insight Into the Art of FT Journalism*, London: FT Republishing.

Dawson Scott, R. (1997) 'Getting noticed. How arts journalists decide what goes on the arts and entertainment pages', unpublished M.Litt dissertation, Strathclyde University.

Defoe, D. (1978) [1724–26] *A Tour Through the Whole Island of Great Britain*, Harmondsworth, UK: Penguin.

Delano, A. and Henningham, J. (1997) *The News Breed: British Journalists in the 1990s*, London: School of Media, London College of Printing and Distributive Trades.

Department of Culture, Media and Sport (1998) *Creative Industries Mapping Document*.

Didion, J. (1974) [1968 US edition] *Slouching towards Bethlehem*, Harmondsworth, UK: Penguin.

Dobson, C. (1992) *The Freelance Journalist. How to Survive and Succeed*, Oxford: Butterworth Heinemann.

Ellis, A. T. (1986) *Home Life*, London: Duckworth.

Evans, H. (1973 *et al.*) *Editing and Design: A Five-Volume Manual of English, Typography and Layout*, London: Heinemann.

Evans, H. (2000) *Essential English for Journalists, Editors and Writers*, London: Pimlico.

Fairfax, J. and Moat, J. (1981) *The Way to Write*, London: Elm Tree Books/Hamish Hamilton.

Fallaci, O. (1976) *Interview With History*, Boston: Houghton Mifflin.

Fenney, R. (1997) *Essential Central Government*, London: LGC Communications (EMAP Business Communications).

Fenney, R. (1998) *Essential Local Government*, London: LGC Communications (EMAP Business Communications).

Ferguson, M. (1983) *Forever Feminine. Women's Magazines and the Cult of Femininity*, London: Heinemann.

Fieldhouse, H. (1982) *Everyman's Good English Guide*, London: Dent.

Fowler, R. (1991) *Language in the News: Discourse and Ideology in the Press*, London: Routledge.

Frayn, M. (1965) *The Tin Men*, London: Collins.

Fulton, M. (1988) *Eyes of Time: Photojournalism in America*, New York: New York Graphic Society/Little, Brown.

Gabler, N. (1995) *Walter Winchell: Gossip, Power and the Culture of Celebrity*, London: Picador.

Galtung, J. and Ruge, M. (1973) 'Structuring and selecting news', in S. Cohen and J. Young (eds) *The Manufacture of News. Deviance, Social Problems and the Mass Media*, London: Constable (2nd edition 1981).

García Márquez, G. (1998) *News of a Kidnapping*, Harmondsworth, UK: Penguin.

Garvey, E. G. (1996) *The Adman in the Parlor. Magazines and the Gendering of Consumer Culture, 1880s to 1910s*, New York and Oxford: Oxford University Press.

Gellhorn, M. (1989) *The View from the Ground*, London: Granta Books.

Gellhorn, M. (1993) *The Face of War*, London: Granta Books.

Gibson, S-M. (1999) 'An analysis of the use of language in today's teenage magazines', unpublished MA essay, Napier University, Edinburgh.

Giles, V. and Hodgson, F. (1990) *Creative Newspaper Design*, Oxford: Focal Press.

Gilster, P. (1996) *Finding it on the Internet: The Internet Navigator's Guide to Search Tools and Techniques*, London: John Wiley & Sons.

Gordon, A. D., Kittross, J. M. and Reuss, C. (1996) *Controversies in Media Ethics*, New York: Longman.

Granta (1998) *The Granta Book of Reportage*, London: Granta Books.

Greenwood, W. and Welsh, T. (eds) (1999) *McNae's Essential Law for Journalists*, 15th edition, London: Butterworth.

Greer, G. (1999) *The Whole Woman*, London and New York: Doubleday.

Griffiths, D. (ed.) (1992) *The Encyclopaedia of the British Press 1422–1992*, London: Macmillan.

Guardian Media Guide (see Peak and Fisher).

Habermas, J. (1989) *The Structural Transformation of the Public Sphere*, Cambridge: Polity.

Hamill, P. (1998) *News is a Verb. Journalism at the End of the Twentieth Century*, New York: Ballantine.

Hartley, J. (1996) *Popular Reality: Journalism, Modernity, Popular Culture*, London and New York: Edward Arnold.

Hazlitt, W. (1930–4) 'The Fight' in P. P. Howe (ed.) *William Hazlitt: The Complete Works*, volume xvii, London and Toronto: J. M. Dent & Sons.

Hebdige, D. (1988) *Hiding in the Light*, London and New York: Comedia published by Routledge.

Hennessy, B. (1993) *Writing Feature Articles. A Practical Guide to Methods and Markets*, Oxford: Heinemann.

Her Majesty's Stationery Office (1988) *Copyright, Designs and Patents Act 1988*, London: HMSO.

Herman, E. and Chomsky, N. (1988) *Manufacturing Consent*, New York: Pantheon.

Hermes, J. (1995) *Reading Women's Magazines: An Analysis of Everyday Media Use*, Cambridge: Polity Press.

Hicks, W. (1998) *English for Journalists*, London: Routledge.

Hicks, W. (1999) *Writing for Journalists*, London: Routledge.

Hodgson, F. W. (1998) *New Subediting. Applemac, QuarkXpress and After*, Oxford: Butterworth-Heinemann.

Jack, I. (1998) 'Introduction', *The Granta Book of Reportage*, London: Granta Books.

Jack, I. and Marlow, P. (1997) 'Those who felt differently' in *Unbelievable, Granta 60*, London: Granta Books.

Jobling, P. and Crowley, D. (1996) *Graphic Design. Reproduction and Representation since 1800*, Manchester: Manchester University Press.

Johnson, E. W. and Wolfe, T. (eds) (1990) *The New Journalism*, London: Picador.

Jones, N. (1995) *Soundbites and Spin Doctors: How Politicians Manipulate the Media – and Vice Versa*, London: Cassel.

Junger, S. (1997) *The Perfect Storm: A True Story of Man Against the Sea*, London: Fourth Estate.

Kapuściński, R. (1998) 'The soccer war' in *The Granta Book of Reportage*, London: Granta Books.

Keeble, R. (ed.) (1998) *The Newspapers Handbook*, London: Routledge.

Kidder, T. (1982) *The Soul of a New Machine*, Harmondsworth, UK: Penguin.

Knightley, P. (2000) *The First Casualty: The War Correspondent as Hero and Myth Maker from the Crimea to Kosovo*, London: Prion Books.

Kroeger, B. (1994) *Nellie Bly: Daredevil, Reporter, Feminist*, New York and Toronto: Random House.

Lodge, D. (1999) *Home Truths*, London: Secker and Warburg.

London Review of Books, an Anthology (1996) London: Verso.

McAleer, J. (1992) *Popular Reading and Publishing in Britain 1914–1950*, Oxford: Clarendon Press.

Macdonald, M. (1995) *Representing Women: Myths of Femininity in the Popular Media*, London: Edward Arnold.

Mcguire, M., Stilborne, L., McAdams, M. and Hyatt, L. (1997) *The Internet Handbook for Writers, Researchers and Journalists*, New York: The Guilford Press.

Talese, G. and Lounsberry, B. (1996) *The Literature of Reality*, New York: HarperCollins, now Addison Wesley Longman.

Taylor, D. (1997), *Creating Cool HTML 3.2*, Foster City: IDG Books Worldwide.

Taylor, J. (1991) *War Photography*, London: Routledge.

Taylor, J. (1998) *Body Horror*, London: Routledge.

Terkel, S. (1995) *Coming of Age. The Story of our Century By Those Who've Lived It*, New York: New York Press.

Thompson, B. (1998) *Seven Years of Plenty: A Handbook of Irrefutable Pop Greatness 1991–1998*, London: Gollancz.

Thurber, J. (1984) *The Years with Ross*, London: Hamish Hamilton.

Tinkler, P. (1995) *Constructing Girlhood: Popular Magazines for Girls Growing Up in England 1920–1950*, London: Taylor and Francis.

Tomalin, N. (1966) 'The General goes zapping Charlie Cong' in T. Wolfe and E. W. Johnson (eds) (1990) *The New Journalism*, London: Picador..

Tomalin, N. (1969) 'Stop the press I want to get on' in M. Bromley and T. O' Malley (1997) *A Journalism Reader*, London: Routledge.

Tucker, A. (1997) 'Why web warriors might worry', *Columbia Journalism Review*, July/August: 35.

Tunstall, J. (1971) *Journalists at Work*, London: Constable.

Turner, E. S. (1965) *The Shocking History of Advertising*, Harmondsworth, UK: Penguin.

Turner, J. (1998) 'Powerful information: reporting national and local government' in R. Keeble (ed.) *The Newspapers Handbook*, 2nd edition, London: Routledge.

Twyman, M. (1998) *The British Library Guide to Printing: History and Techniques*, London: The British Library.

Usherwood, B. (1997) 'Transnational publishing. The case of *Elle Decoration*' in M. Nava, A. Blake, I. MacRury and B. Richards (eds) *Buy This Book. Studies in Advertising and Consumption*, London: Routledge.

Venolia, J. (1995) *Write Right! A Desktop Digest of Punctuation, Grammar, and Style*, Berkeley, California: Ten Speed Press.

Vincent, D. (1999) *The Culture of Secrecy in Britian 1832–1998*, Oxford: Oxford University Press.

Walker, R. (1992) *Magazine Design: A Hands-on Guide*, London: Blueprint (Chapman and Hall).

Wallraff, G. (1985) *The Lowest of the Low*, London: Methuen.

Waterhouse, K. (1991) *English our English (and How to Sing It)*, London: Viking.

Waugh, E. (1990) [1933] *Scoop*, Harmondsworth, UK: Penguin.

Welsh, T. and Greenwood, W. (1999) *McNae's Essential Law for Journalists*, London: Butterworth.

Wesker, A. (1977) *Journey into Journalism*, London: Writers and Readers Cooperative.

Whale, J. (1984) *Put It In Writing*, London and Melbourne: J. M. Dent.

Wharton, J. (1995) *Magazine Journalism. A Guide to Writing and Subbing for Magazines*, London: Periodicals Training Council.

White, C. (1969) *Women's Magazines 1693–1968*, London: Michael Joseph.

White, C. (1977) *The Women's Periodical Press 1946–1976. Report for the Royal Commission on the Press*, London: HMSO.

White, J. V. (1982) *Designing for Magazines*, New York and London: R. R. Bowker.

Williamson, J. (1978) *Decoding Advertisements*, London: Marion Boyars.

Willings Press Guide (1998 and updates), Teddington, Middlesex: Hollis Directories.

Wilson, J. (1996) *Understanding Journalism: A Guide to Issues*, London: Routledge.

Winship, J. (1987) *Inside Women's Magazines*, London: Pandora.

Wolfe, T. (1968) *The Electric Kool-Aid Acid Test*, New York: Bantam.

Wolfe, T. (1983) *The Right Stuff*, New York: Bantam.

Wolfe, T. and Johnson, E. W. (eds) (1990) [1973] *The New Journalism*, London: Picador.

Worcester, R. M. (1998) 'Demographics and values: What the British public reads and what it thinks of its newspapers' in M. Bromley and H. Stephenson (eds) *Sex, Lies and Democracy: The Press and the Public*, London and New York: Addison Wesley Longman.

Wozencroft, J. (1988) *The Graphic Language of Neville Brody*, London: Thames and Hudson.

Zeldin, T. (1998) *Conversation*, London: The Harvill Press.

Zenith Media Worldwide (1997) *UK Media Yearbook*, Zenith Media.

Newspaper and magazine articles

Addicott, R. (1999) 'MCN goes upmarket' *Press Gazette*, 16 April: 4.

Assinder, N. (1997) 'Their eyes glaze over despite my cry "you'll all be using it soon"', *Guardian* 'Media', 24 March: 6.

Barber, L. (1998b) *The Observer* 'Life', 8 November: 9.

Bauret, G. (1999) 'From Russia with love', *Guardian* 'Weekend', 10 April: 33.

Beck, S. (1999) 'Nice idea but it's not really us', *Press Gazette*, 22 January.

Bracken, M. (1998) 'So, how DO you make money on the World Wide Web?', *Press Gazette*, 29 May: 12–13.

Buchan, A. (1998) 'The Cinderella Sector', *Press Gazette*, 2 October.

Clement, D. (1997) 'Online advantages of journalists', *Press Gazette*, 18 April: 15.

Duckworth, A. (1999) 'The start of something great', *Motor Cycle News*, 14 April: 2.

Evans, H. (1999) 'Freedom of information: why Britain must learn from America', *Guardian Media*, 31 May: 4.

Farrelly, P. (1999) 'Reed-Elsevier still seeking dream deal', *Observer* Business Section, 31 January: 3.

Fleetwood, B. (1999) *The Guardian*'s 'Editor' section 17 September, quoting from 'News at a Price' in *Washington Monthly*.

Gibson, J. (1999) 'She's sticking with sex', *Guardian Media*, 1 February: 6–7.

Gitlin, T. (1999) 'Why gossip can be hazardous', *Brill's Content*, May: 109.

Glaister, D. (1999) 'Design to create pages people want to read', *The Guardian* 19 April: 6.

Johnson, A. (1997) 'Net uncertainty for trade titles', *Press Gazette*, 7 November: 11.

Johnson, A. (1998) 'In search of those Net profits', *Press Gazette*, 1 May: 12.

Kellner, P. (1991) 'Nobody trusts us and that's bad news', *Independent*, 7 August.

McIver, K. (1998) 'US hotlines', *The Times Interface*, 13 May.

McKay, J. (1998) 'Dear Tony, can reading stuff like this make me pregnant?', *The Scotsman*, 19 November: 16.

Magazine World (1998) 18, September/October: 5, London: International Federation of the Periodical Press.

Morgan, J. (2000) ' "There is money out there", Pollard tells launch hopefuls', *Press Gazette*, 25 February: 9.

O'Hagan, A. (1998)'A floral tribute', *Guardian Weekend*, 2 May: 10.

Pilger, J. (1999) *The Guardian*, 7 September.

Porter, B. (1999) 'Boarder or day boy', *London Review of Books* vol. 21, no. 14, 15 July.

Ramrayka, L. (1999) 'Are women the future of the web?', *Guardian Online*, 9 September: 3.

Reeves, I. (1999) '*Guardian* will make last-minute decision on new-look front page', *Press Gazette*, 16 April.

Ronson, J. (1999) 'Zoë and an ordinary dream', *Guardian Weekend*, 25 September: 8.

Shewen, P. (1999) *New Internationalist*, October.

Smith, L. (1999) 'Why gossip is good for us', *Brill's Content*, May: 107.

Urquhart, L. (1998) 'From print to pixel', *Press Gazette*, 23 October: 14.

Magazine World, London: International Federation of the Periodical Press (FIPP), care of PPA.

Press Gazette, Croydon, UK: Quantum Publishing.

World Magazine Trends 1998/1999, London: Zenith Media for FIPP.

Electronic sources

www.brillscontent.com

www.drudgereport.com

www.penthousemag.com/promo/drudge

Frazier, J. (1998) 'Job prospects for the online journalist', *Online Journalism Review*, 7 December, www.ojr.org

Raouf, N. (1998) 'Cross-training journalists', *Online Journalism Review*, 11 November, www.ojr.org

Smith, R. W. (1995) 'Speech to the Magazine Publishers Association of America', 6 November, Bell Atlantic website: www.ba.com

Strong, M. 'Margot Williams: Teaching the Internet at *The Washington Post*', The Internet Newsroom (www.editors-service.com/articlearchive/wapost98.html).

Welch, M. (1999) ojr.org/stories_Kosovo_040999.htm

Index

....